Dirty Works

DIRTY WORKS

*Obscenity on Trial in
America's First Sexual Revolution*

Brett Gary

STANFORD UNIVERSITY PRESS
Stanford, California

STANFORD UNIVERSITY PRESS
Stanford, California

Printed in the United States of America on acid-free, archival-quality paper

Library of Congress Cataloging-in-Publication Data
Names: Gary, Brett, author.
Title: Dirty works : obscenity on trial in America's first sexual revolution / Brett Gary.
Description: Stanford, California : Stanford University Press, 2021. | Includes bibliographical references and index.
Identifiers: LCCN 2020052598 (print) | LCCN 2020052599 (ebook) | ISBN 9781503627598 (cloth) | ISBN 9781503628694 (ebook)
Subjects: LCSH: Ernst, Morris L. (Morris Leopold), 1888-1976. | Trials (Obscenity)—New York (State)—New York—History—20th century. | Trials (Obscenity)—United States—History—20th century. | Obscenity (Law)—United States—History—20th century. | Censorship—United States—History—20th century. | Sexual rights—United States—History—20th century.
Classification: LCC KF221.027 G37 2021 (print) | LCC KF221.027 (ebook) | DDC 345.747/0274—dc23
LC record available at https://lccn.loc.gov/2020052598
LC ebook record available at https://lccn.loc.gov/2020052599

Cover design: Kevin Barrett Kane
Text design: Kevin Barrett Kane
Typeset at Stanford University Press in 10/15 ITC Galliard Pro

TABLE OF CONTENTS

Dirty Works

CHAPTER I

MORAL GUARDIANS AND SEXUAL MODERNISTS

THE UNITED STATES IN THE 1920S was experiencing a grand cultural change. Historians have applied different labels to try to capture the essence of the dramatic cultural clashes and transformations that surged through American society in the 1920s. The Age of Intolerance describes the postwar Red Scare, Prohibition, new immigration restriction laws, the rise of the Ku Klux Klan, and the Scopes trial with its assault on science. Labels such as the Age of Ford or the Era of Prosperity convey the furious expansion of industrial production and consumption fueled by the automobile, resulting in a 40% increase in the nation's gross domestic product by decade's end. This economic vitality dovetails with the Roaring 20s, the Jazz Age, or the Flapper Era, all of which point to a culture increasingly marked by leisure and consumption, with an emphasis on speed, music, speakeasies, and an increasingly public presence of single women dressed in new styles. Cars, home radios, the advanced rotary press (with its celebrity magazines and inexpensive novels), and especially movie projectors produced new forms of leisure, amusement, and fantasy. And so the 1920s also witnessed an intense focus on the moral consequences of these new popular culture forms that might corrupt young audiences, unleash untrammeled female sexuality, and produce a dreaded "Revolution in Manners and Morals" (to use another label to describe the era). Moral critics especially feared that popular culture would uncouple sex from the idea of sin and that glamour and adventure would overwhelm the teachings of parents, religions, schools, and other institutions about modesty, self-control, and sexual restraint.[1]

In this book I explore this broader story about changes and conflicts around sex and morality in American culture in a booming, ever-expanding marketplace of information and entertainment. In particular, I focus on the tensions between a residual but still powerful Christian moral order on one side and, on the other side, the profusion of images, ideas, and desires distributed to an ever-more urban, secular, polyglot public in an increasingly commercial society. Those conflicts intensified as that marketplace became more unruly. Despite a vague ideological commitment to the free press and free speech ideals embodied in the First Amendment tradition, many thoughtful people disliked and worried about the varieties of tawdry, erotically alluring, or outright smutty materials that were circulating in the culture. This tension between free speech and free press ideals and the availability of unsavory goods resulted in legal and cultural conflicts over the enforcement of strict obscenity laws and other censorship practices. Whereas many found the sex-themed materials offensive, others believed that censorship threatened core principles of democratic life and starved a rational, capable public who ought to be trusted to make discerning choices.

The progressive sexualization of American culture, from French postcards in the mid-nineteenth century to the explosion of pornography by the 1970s, suggests that the fears of the nineteenth- and twentieth-century moral guardians were not entirely unwarranted. The emergent post–World War I civil libertarian commitment to free expression as a political and cultural ideal ran up hard against leaders who felt a strong need to control sexualized images and literary smut. Virtually no one expressed doubt about the overwhelming power of popular culture forms to deliver peoples' attention (and lusts) to the vulgar, the base, and the animal and, for those of a religious mind, to distract them from higher purposes. This perception of public susceptibilities—shared by religious, civil, legal, and economic elites—intensified broad agreement that obscenity laws were necessary tools for keeping dirt and sin at bay.[2]

Thus the anti-vice organizations in the nation's largest cities and smaller towns enlisted clergy from all denominations, found eager activists in women's civic groups, drew on the social authority and financial resources of leading male citizens, and could count on the police enforcing the laws and judges upholding them in the courts. They incurred virtually no opposition from politicians.[3] That lasted until a more robust anti-censorship argument took hold in the late 1920s and early 1930s, when the overarching fear of public vulnerability was countered by an equally powerful claim to the public's right of access to those goods. This book tells that story, using the actions of one particular law firm and one particular lawyer to trace its course. I illustrate how Morris Leopold Ernst and his colleagues, especially Alexander Lindey and Harriet Pilpel, won signature cases in their larger campaign against censorship and on behalf of free speech for sexual knowledge.[4] I tell the story of Ernst and his New York City law firm's fight against obscenity laws from the late 1920s to the mid-1950s, in defense of feminists, birth control activists and physicians, sexologists and sex educators, booksellers and publishers, novelists and journalists, burlesque theater owners, and sundry others.[5]

Instead of assuming harm caused by these so-called obscene materials, Ernst and his team tried to shift the courts' focus to questions of value—the public value of information and knowledge about human sexuality and its variations. Over time they worked to convince the courts that the average adult reader ought to be considered the main consumer in the literary and sexual modernist marketplace, rather than the most vulnerable youth, invoking a competent and rational adult public whose judgments and tastes ought to be trusted. They also repeatedly invoked the public value of an open marketplace of ideas as a founding faith enshrined in the First Amendment. Under Ernst and his colleagues' anti-censorship campaign, which shifted the query to the values of the targeted literary, aesthetic, scientific, or medical works, the courts became less willing to accept prosecutors' and anti-vice agents' arguments that literary works and other artifacts were presumptively harmful and thus obscene. The more the courts thought of literary and theatrical expressions or sexological information as also having protected value as speech, the less willing they were to condemn materials whose purposes were more significant than the mere arousal of prurient interests.[6]

Ernst and his colleagues pursued these arguments about harm and value because this clarified to the courts that censorship not only precluded the flow of valuable materials but also interfered with key democratic principles. They saw that the harmful impulse toward and the mechanisms of censorship were about more than determining whether reading certain kinds of materials aroused lust; they were also about depriving women (and couples) of control of their own reproductive capacities and of being able to engage in sex for pleasure. Ernst and his colleagues clearly understood the link between the obscenity law's coercive intent to constrain lust and its aim to restrict access to contraceptive information and sexual knowledge.[7] They also apprehended the positive connection—the value—of being stirred by written words and having the capacity to enjoy sex because one is educated about it and able to control its consequences. This benefit was, they understood, exceptionally important to modern adults.

Saving the Soul of New York City

Anthony Comstock was a nineteenth-century anti-vice crusader. He was the most effective propagandist warning about the dangers of obscene materials and the chief lobbyist behind congressional passage of the 1873 Act for the Suppression of Trade in, and Circulation of, Obscene Literature and Articles of Immoral Use.[8] The Comstock Act, as it has long been known, gave Comstock special authority as an agent of the Postal Service to search the mails, secure arrests and convictions, and destroy seized materials.[9] Virtually every study about obscenity law and censorship in American society features his looming presence.[10]

During the Civil War, the religiously devout Comstock pledged not to partake of alcohol, tobacco, or dirty pictures, and he began crusading against all sexually oriented materials. He was a notorious scold among his fellow Union soldiers, reportedly quite unpopular for pouring his whiskey rations on the ground rather than giving them to his brothers in arms. Aghast at the pornographic photographs passed around among his wartime mates, he eventually found his calling, hunting down and seeking the arrests of those engaged in the production and distribution of such materials. By 1872 he had so impressed the leaders of New York City's Young

Men's Christian Association (YMCA) with his zeal that they hired him to lead their anti-vice efforts and created the New York Society for the Suppression of Vice (NYSSV, or simply the Vice Society) as a separate entity to police the city for offensive materials.

Under the lobbying efforts of the YMCA's powerful leaders, the New York State legislature gave Comstock and the Vice Society official police powers to enforce the state's updated obscenity laws (which served as the model for the federal statute).[11] Comstock used his broad federal and New York state authority to seize and dispose of literally tons of materials. A highly controversial and frequently satirized figure, he maintained the support of his patrons in his forty-year reign as the nation's foremost censor and smut eradicator. He warned against the power of a sexualized popular culture to undermine the moral sensibilities and self-discipline on which the old social order depended, and he painted vivid tales of well-to-do youth falling prey to "traps for the young." A devout evangelical Christian, he pitted himself as an avenging hero against those forces of disruption and sin, calling himself a "Soldier of the Cross."[12]

These laws, widely known as the Comstock laws, took aim at materials that might stimulate sexual arousal and lust and would invariably lead, their proponents warned, to "corruption and depravity." Long before pornography became the object—and problem—most indelibly linked in the public imagination with "obscenity," federal and state authorities had used those laws to restrict literary expression, to constrain theatrical and film content, to proscribe virtually any discussion of homosexuality, and to keep a tight lid on information about sexual urges (especially masturbation and intercourse) from young eyes. The laws helped censorship authorities ensnare all matter of information and images that might disturb the moral order, especially including birth control devices and contraceptive information and anything related to abortion. The prohibitions were rooted in the assumption that among other things, sexually arousing materials would lead to temptation, lust, and sexual immorality. The nineteenth-century federal and state obscenity laws that Ernst and his colleagues battled well into the middle of the twentieth century aimed to contain minds and bodies, protect individual and collective morality, and ensure a sexual order organized around marriage, marital reproduction, and the repression of carnality.[13]

The Comstock laws sprang from nineteenth-century American Protestant morality colliding with dramatic changes taking place in post–Civil War American society. Fears of moral harm undergirded the obscenity laws, as did perceptions of public vulnerability, particularly of the nation's youth, who were perceived as being especially susceptible to moral trespass. Comstock had a particular anxiety about male masturbation. Although he worried about women's virtue, he especially feared that men and boys in the new media environment of inexpensive print and photography would fall prey to the "secret vice" of masturbation and would lose themselves (their souls, minds, and bodies) in it. He wrote floridly about the dangers of the secret vice. The direct line from sexual images to the arousal of animal lust, breakdown of self-discipline, habitual masturbation, crippling guilt and shame, and ultimately self-destruction recurred throughout his writings. He hated his own youthful shame resulting from such weakness, but he also thought that the shame was deserved and should be used as a deterrent. Comstock's view of masturbation was unforgiving: One should feel guilty because the "crime" of "self-abuse" was both a moral weakness and a path to personal failure. It should never be acceptable. As Ernst wrote about Comstock, "Original sin was burning reality to him, and he reposed no confidence in the deterrent powers of self-control, idealism or taste to save men from vice. He wanted everyone protected from moral evil, in all its forms."[14]

Middle-class cultural ideals elevated marriage and family as the central societal institutions, closely proscribed gender roles, assigned churches a ruling position in social life, and expected neighbors to keep tabs on one another. These ideals ran up against profound upheavals marked by massive immigration, urbanization, industrialization, and labor unrest alongside revolutionary developments in communications technologies and changes in media consumption, urban entertainment districts, and visual landscapes. Comstock gained and maintained his cultural clout by invoking upper-class white Victorian fears of declining social power and collective moral decay against these changes.

Immigration and emigration produced dramatic shifts in the size and the ethnic and religious makeup of American cities. Millions of American-born youth migrated from rural to urban locations to find their fortunes. They found themselves less supervised than at home, and the anonymity of city life produced anxieties about social class instability, racial mixing, wanton sexual behavior, and vulnerability to corruption. Youth might fall prey to the lures of "vice districts" with their saloons, gambling dens, dance halls, confidence men, painted women, smut peddlers, and homosexual subcultures. Thus, besides offering educational and economic mobility, artistic enrichment, and cosmopolitanism, cities also posed real (if exaggerated) threats of rape, forced prostitution, moral failure, penury, and disease. In this milieu, all kinds of new and provocative printed materials, from adventure-promoting dime-store novels to "French" postcards, were widely available and seemed to Anthony Comstock the first step toward dissolution.[15]

What Got Banned: Birth Control, Abortifacients, and Masturbatory Materials

The 1873 federal obscenity law barred importation and transportation of "any obscene, lewd, or lascivious book, pamphlet, picture, print, or other publication of vulgar and indecent character." The law collapsed categorical distinctions, expressly connecting erotic materials to all contraception-related items. It also specifically lumped together contraception with abortion and abortifacients—a linkage that remains fixed in much of the public imagination to this day. In so doing, the Comstock Act reinforced the idea that birth control was an "immoral purpose" and a crime against the natural order and just as troubling as abortion.[16]

Abortion had been outlawed in the 1850s, but a campaign to criminalize abortion took off in 1859 with the publication of the American Medical Association's "Report on Criminal Abortion." Anti-abortion agitation gained momentum in the post–Civil War period. Birthrates were rising among immigrants and declining among American-born white women, and notorious abortion providers carried out their trade in the public eye. Madame Restelle, New York City's most famous abortionist, lived in a mansion in a fashionable neighborhood in uptown Manhattan, making her an effective symbol of a bloody trade and a larger moral collapse. Madame

Restelle committed suicide after Comstock finally got her arrested, an event that he relished after her death.[17]

Birth control opponents also hoped to reverse behavioral changes already evident in the upper social tiers. Linda Gordon, Helen Lefkowitz Horowitz, Andrea Tone, Nicola Beisel, and other scholars have shown that by the latter third of the nineteenth century, middle- and upper-class white women were increasingly using a variety of birth control techniques to control their reproduction and alter their relationships to family and domestic duties and, for the most radical of them, to make sexual intercourse a greater source of pleasure for themselves and for their husbands.[18]

This turn toward greater reproductive autonomy elicited strong objections that intermingled medical, theological, demographic, and nationalistic concerns. Because women of means were not having nearly as many babies as the great masses of immigrants, Comstock and others warned that white upper-class married women were not carrying out their duties to their husbands and families, to their social class, and to the nation, accusing them of "race suicide." Birth control and abortion were not just selfish; they allowed women to hide their promiscuity and would thus lead to more sexual wantonness. They would also, critics averred, lead men to exploit their wives sexually. And birth control would diminish women's natural roles as mothers and as the primary moral force in society, depriving the nation of a future of strong young men and morally upright women.[19]

This cluster of concerns about the nation, marriage bonds, and sexual honor grew from foundational religious beliefs about marriage and gender roles. Marriage was a sacred institution with procreative purposes at its center. Marital intercourse should always potentially result in reproduction; any interference with the reproductive possibilities of sex interfered with God's purposes and women's physiology. Intercourse for carnal pleasure alone would separate the physical from the spiritual, and some even argued that it was analogous to prostituting one's wife (an argument, we shall see, still routinely used in the twentieth-century trials). In this late-nineteenth-century predominantly Protestant milieu, family honor was deeply bound with women's sexual decorum, so sexual purity was emphasized.

The 1873 Obscenity Law turned theological beliefs about contraception as sin into a federal crime. The second quarter of the nineteenth century had been an era of great progress, with a profusion of birth control books and pamphlets available in England and the United States.[20] The Obscenity Law stemmed that tide of progress and wreaked havoc on women's lives, according to birth control advocates.

In the early 1940s, Planned Parenthood's Gwendolyn Pickett and Ernst co-authored a major report titled "Birth Control in the Courts." The authors divided their history into two eras: a "golden age" lasting through the mid-nineteenth century and the age of Comstock. Pickett and Ernst argued that the Comstock laws thwarted a generative marketplace of ideas that might have solved many problems of contraception, including issues of safety, reliability, availability, and affordability. The result was that for seventy years the federal law "hampered the medical profession . . . and caused incalculable harm and suffering to thousands of American families."[21] Comstock and his allies did not "stop for nice distinctions in his headlong pursuit of vice," attacking "works of art and dirty postcards with impartial enthusiasm" and seeing "contraception, abortion, sexual perversion and obscenity all in the same dark light."[22]

Comstock was not alone in his anti-vice crusades, of course. By the time Ernst's law firm and their ACLU colleagues and other allies took up the battle against local and federal obscenity laws in the late 1920s, Vice Society agents, in conjunction with the New York City Police Department, had been badgering writers, publishers, bookstore clerks, actors and theater owners, and sexual rebels for nearly fifty years. Other cities and states had their own anti-vice organizations, among them, Boston, Cincinnati, New Orleans, Minneapolis, Philadelphia, and Baltimore. The federal and state obscenity laws were overlapping, mutually reinforcing, and well entrenched throughout the nation. Forty-five states passed "little" or "mini-Comstock" laws by the turn of the twentieth century.

Most important, the Comstock laws maintained support in the nation's courts. The U.S. Supreme Court's nineteenth-century rulings upholding the constitutionality of the federal obscenity statutes made the legal obstacles more durable. Getting judges to keep the forces of censorship in check and to provide greater legal protection for sexual expression and information that might disrupt the moral and social order would not be easy. Ernst and his colleagues would maintain that the courts lagged far behind evolving

ANTHONY COMSTOCK

SECRETARY

NEW YORK SOCIETY FOR THE SUPPRESSION OF VICE

FIGURE 1. Anthony Comstock, secretary of the New York Society for the Suppression of Vice, postal inspector, and chief enforcer of the 1873 federal obscenity law he authored.

SOURCE: New York Public Library digital collections.

public tastes and interest, and they would press this argument in a number of important obscenity trials they engineered.

The Hicklin Obscenity Standard in the Courts

The judges who presided over nineteenth- and early-twentieth century U.S. courts overwhelmingly ruled with Comstock, the Vice Society, and their supporters. (Indeed, the 1873 obscenity statute was drafted by a sitting Supreme Court justice, Justice Strong, who worked with Comstock to strengthen the statute before Comstock lobbied Congress on its behalf.) Judges never questioned their duty to maintain a decent media environment, protect vulnerable publics, and defend social and moral norms. Obscenity laws, whether state or federal, were valuable tools in this cause.

Judges routinely adopted the "Hicklin standard" or the "Hicklin test" as the guide for assessing whether or not a "libeled" book or object or artifact was indeed obscene.[23] Adopted directly from the 1868 English case *Regina v. Hicklin*, the Hicklin obscenity test held that an object was obscene if "the tendency of the matter [was] to deprave and corrupt those whose minds are open to such immoral influences, and into whose hands a publication of this sort may fall."[24] A book, pamphlet, play, photograph, engraving, or cervical cap was "libeled" when an official—a postal solicitor or a customs officer or a city police court magistrate—ruled it was obscene. Such a ruling would then set in motion the destruction of the seized materials and penalties against the distributor, or a court trial in which city, state, or federal prosecutors would pursue either a criminal or civil action against the seller, publisher, or recipient. A challenge to the charge of libel by plaintiff's lawyers would then bring the matter before a judge and/or a jury, which is what Ernst and his colleagues strategically aimed to do in their many test cases.

The Hicklin test proved a valuable tool for prosecutors, and the federal and state courts routinely embraced it as the best measure for determining whether materials were legally obscene.[25] U.S. courts routinely used it until the 1930s, when some federal courts began to question its all-purpose applicability. Under its long use, evidence that someone had been actually depraved or corrupted was not required, only the *possibility* of depravity or corruption. Depravity and corruption essentially referred to the likelihood of being sexually aroused by the artifact, but euphemisms for arousal and masturbation abounded in the law, so the phrase was ambiguously capacious.[26]

The matter of "into whose hands" an object might fall was key to the prosecutorial effectiveness of the test, because it meant that the courts should always have in mind some imagined reader or viewer into whose hands the object might fall and that they should routinely assume that they needed to protect the most vulnerable audiences. This essentially meant youth, but it could also be extended to young women and sometimes those described as "imbeciles." Indeed, prosecutors liked to invoke their own daughters as needing special protection from the materials (or from the mentally vulnerable who might, upon encountering suspect materials, ravage those same daughters). But anyone, really, could fall under that test. Prosecutors even worried that literary sophisticates might be particularly open to tales about homosexuality.

The entire work did not matter either—just an offending passage or image was enough for prosecutors to successfully assert that anyone in the vast audience of potential readers might be aroused or otherwise morally affected. Rather than assuming the public's capacity for mental or moral stability and continued adherence to powerful cultural and moral norms, the law and its standards assumed volatility and susceptibility.[27]

The Hicklin standard did not therefore distinguish between medical students and pimply youth. Nor did it distinguish between dirty postcards and literary classics. Lawyers would have to work out those distinctions over many decades. The Hicklin standard had considerable staying power as the operative "test" of obscenity used in federal courts for well over sixty years.

The First Amendment and the Comstock Laws

Before Ernst and his colleagues took up their challenges, an earlier generation of free love advocates, sex radicals, and their lawyers had done battle with Comstockery in the late nineteenth and early twentieth centuries and tried to argue against the laws' enforcement mechanisms and their unconstitutionality. Comstock's oft-prosecuted victims Moses Harmon, D. M. Bennett, Robert Dale Owen, and Victoria Woodhull challenged the laws and appealed their lower court convictions, but the U.S. courts were disinclined to defend the speech practices of those who flaunted the sexual order.[28]

In the early twentieth century a brilliant but eccentric lawyer named Theodore Schroeder developed a strong body of arguments against the laws in his work *"Obscene" Literature and Constitutional Law* (1911). But despite his astute critique of the obscenity laws, he had no success in the federal courts and produced no precedents that would help subsequent legal challenges. As David Rabban points out, Theodore Schroeder and the muckraking journalist Lincoln Steffens did lay out crucial intellectual groundwork for subsequent free speech advocates. But the Supreme Court would not budge on protecting sexual speech or accepting constitutional challenges to the Comstock laws on First Amendment grounds.[29]

The First Amendment offered (and still offers) no protection to obscene materials.[30] When the Comstock law was challenged on First Amendment grounds in the late nineteenth century in the *Bennett* and *Swearingen* cases, the Supreme Court upheld the law's constitutionality, saying Congress had legitimate authority to ban obscene materials in the public interest. Thus any challenges to the obscenity libel attached to any book or art object or other artifact would have to occur on a case-by-case basis, challenging that libel by demonstrating that the artifact was not obscene.

Ernst and colleagues thus had to selectively pick away at the laws. They had to choose cases carefully, where the materials on trial had either obvious scientific or artistic merit or obvious public value and where the claims of public harm seemed highly disputable. They were up against a body of laws, administrative mechanisms, a cultural tradition of reticence regarding sexual matters, and legal precedents that were not easily susceptible to reconsideration or reversal.

World War I Speech Catastrophes and an Emergent Free Speech Tradition

The more concerted challenges to the federal and state obscenity laws in the late 1920s and 1930s grew out of a broader civil libertarian movement that emerged in progressive U.S. legal circles following World War I and the postwar Red Scare. Historians have long understood World War I as a free speech catastrophe. The repression of dissident, antiwar voices and organizations during the war and its aftermath shook progressives and radicals and helped give birth to a more concerted free speech movement.

Civil liberties failures occurred at all levels—local, state, and federal. The failures at the federal level began with congressional passage of the 1917 Espionage Act and then the 1918 sedition amendment to the Espionage Act. Zealously enforced by the Justice Department and its U.S. attorneys to silence antiwar opinion, those laws resulted in more than 2,000 federal prosecutions during the war and several thousand deportations of alien residents following the war. It also resulted in a series of Supreme Court decisions following the Armistice in the *Debs, Frowerk, Schenck,* and *Abrams* cases, all of which upheld the constitutionality of espionage and sedition laws and their violations by the named defendants.[31]

During the war, progressive dissenters, embodied primarily by the Civil Liberties League, which became the American Civil Liberties Union (ACLU) following the war, loudly complained of civil liberties violations. Complaints fell on deaf ears in the federal judiciary, the Justice Department, and the wartime press. By war's end, though, the widespread violations of basic rights of due process, free speech, and free press shocked the conscience of legal progressives and gave rise to a broader free speech movement that included leading law school professors and even judges and government officials. The short-lived National Popular Government League—composed of law school deans, future U.S. Attorneys, and future federal court judges (including U.S. Supreme Court justice Felix Frankfurter)—extensively documented what it described as "the continued violation of the Constitution and the breaking of those Laws by the Department of Justice and the United States government" in its 1919 *Report upon the Illegal Practices of the United States Department of Justice.* This document and its authors' bona fides gave credibility to civil libertarians' concerns.[32]

Still, the federal courts continued to regard sex speech as a "lower" order of speech compared with religious or political speech. Even the judges most receptive to arguments about the problems with the Hicklin standard or the statutory vagueness of the obscenity laws continued to dismiss First Amendment–based arguments about sexual speech. This is crucial for understanding Ernst and his colleagues' work. Because First Amendment arguments for protecting sexually oriented materials failed in virtually every instance, the question was then focused on whether censorship authorities had been overzealous in labeling a particular work as obscene.

The ACLU, Anti-Censorship Activism, and the Banned in Boston Events

The ACLU emerged out of the war years as the preeminent organization dedicated to civil liberties. Composed of lawyers, law professors, economists, writers, social workers, philosophers, social scientists, women's rights activists, antiwar activists, anarchists, labor organizers, socialists, communists, and others, the ACLU was the vital force in the burgeoning free speech movement in the 1920s and beyond.[33]

The free speech movement gained force in the ACLU and independent of it. ACLU leaders slightly older than Ernst, including his co-general counsel Arthur Garfield Hays, Roger Baldwin, Forrest Bailey, Clarence Darrow, and Albert deSilver, began to challenge a broad array of laws that facilitated censorship across fields, from literary to scientific to sexual speech matters. As historian Leigh Ann Wheeler describes in rich detail, in Ernst's era the ACLU began a more sustained anti-censorship campaign and became more committed to engineering a longer term project of "making sex a civil liberty."[34] Likewise, the leading birth control activists and feminists Margaret Sanger and Mary Ware Dennett, and many others in their respective organizations, actively battled the administrative and censorship powers of the U.S. Postal Service and the U.S. Customs Service as well as local police forces and civic leaders for well over a decade before Ernst and his colleagues took up the cudgel.[35]

Virtually everyone who played a leading role in expanding free speech rights in the decades between World War I and World War II was affiliated with the ACLU. Indeed, the ACLU helped make a broader free speech ideology a core precept of modern U.S. intellectual life and progressive political organization. The ACLU focused on civil liberties broadly construed, primarily labor speech and organization. But, as Wheeler points out, the active role of women in the ACLU's leadership, along with political radicals who had unconventional sex lives, meant that the organization's leaders understood the need to define and protect sexual issues as civil liberties issues.[36]

Writers, publishers, and journalists moved in the inner circles of the ACLU, or close proximity, and actively took up direct confrontation with the culture of Comstockery in the post–World War I era, fighting "bad books" bills in the New York state legislature to contain the more sexualized commercial, theatrical, and literary culture that exploded in the 1920s. New York's art institutions and artists, radical journals, book publishers, booksellers, writers, and journalists also fought more aggressively against John Sumner, Anthony Comstock's heir at the helm of the Vice Society, and actually won some breakthrough skirmishes in the early to mid-1920s in the New York City magistrate courts, leading Sumner and his allies to redouble their efforts against bad books, birth control, burlesque theater, sex education, and risqué film. Sumner, like Comstock, was no easy foe.[37]

These collisions between the forces of 1920s cultural and sexual modernism and sexual censorship ran headlong into a major battle in Boston, galvanized by the notorious suppression of literary works carried out by the New England Watch and Ward Society and its civic and religious leaders. Boston had become the great symbolic center of enduring Comstockery with its harsh enforcement of Massachusetts's strict state obscenity laws. "Banned in Boston" became shorthand for that city's censorship practices. The Banned in Boston trials and the protests they provoked helped crystallize the anti-censorship ideology, making it a central tenet of progressive thought. Staged spectacles against "Puritan" prudery run amok in Boston gave form and language to the cause. In one key moment in 1929 Margaret Sanger stood on the stage of Faneuil Hall with her mouth taped shut while historian Arthur Schlesinger read her speech.[38] Morris Ernst was on the stage too, in his role as the ACLU's general counsel and an authority on obscenity law, as he had just published his first book about the follies of obscenity-law-based censorship, *To the Pure* (1928).

Although the Banned in Boston events garnered great attention, Massachusetts's censorship laws had strong backing in the courts, among police, and especially among Boston's increasingly assertive Roman Catholic Church leadership. Successful legal challenges to the Massachusetts obscenity laws took decades. New York City proved a far more propitious place for challenging John Sumner and his Vice Society as well as the Postal and Customs officials who teamed up with Sumner to enforce the federal obscenity statutes. The cases fought in New York by Ernst and his associates turned a cultural protest movement in Boston into a series of important victories in New York. They were not as high profile as the Boston battles, in part because Ernst won. But Ernst's battles received plenty of attention from and cooperation with New York City's journalists and the ACLU's national and New York City–based offices. Ernst and Lindey effectively channeled that anti-censorship energy from Boston into a strategic campaign to chip away at federal and state obscenity laws, skirmish by skirmish, in New York City, state, and federal courts.

New York was an ideal place to wage these battles, not least because John Saxton Sumner was a great foil. Ernst effectively turned Sumner into the symbol of The Censor by relentlessly tarring him with the Comstockery label, a smear first used by George Bernard Shaw to connote the censors' antimodern attitudes so at odds with New York's cosmopolitanism. New York City, with its burgeoning media industries and its heterogeneity, was also a prime battleground. Federal Postal and Custom officials, New York's police, Vice Society agents, and politically ambitious federal and state prosecutors buttressed the censorship arsenal with their various powers of raids, seizure, suppression, fines, indictment, and prosecution—and met plenty of resistance, too.

When Sumner took charge of the Vice Society in 1915 following Comstock's death, he continued using its preemptive power over the city's book and magazine publishing industry. He monitored publishers' lists and let them know he was waiting to pounce. Like Comstock, he knew where the smut peddlers were and which booksellers or magazine stands trafficked in banned books, and he liked to raid them. Ernst effectively painted him as Comstock's humorless, antidemocratic heir who held powers antithetical to the spirit and needs of New York City's cosmopolitan public. On his side, Ernst enlisted a great commercial city filled with writers and cultural producers, theaters (vaudeville, burlesque, and Broadway), bookstores, publishing houses, brimming newsstands, movie houses, and nightclubs. The city teemed with people interested in the new and the modern.

Ernst and Sumner shared a mutual animus. Ernst invoked the marketplace of ideas as expressive of the public's needs and interests. Sumner thought that marketplace undermined taste, respectability, and moral decency. It was filled with cheap sensationalism, catered to people's base instincts, and coarsened the culture. The moral economy he hoped to protect was not advanced by market motives or by the standards of a literati he thought "abnormal."

FIGURE 2. Official seal of the New York Society for the Suppression of Vice, led by Anthony Comstock and his successor, John S. Sumner.

SOURCE: Granger Images.

Morris Leopold Ernst: The "Smart Fixer"

In 1944 *Life* magazine, the twentieth century's most widely circulated periodical, published a multipage profile of New York City trial lawyer Morris Leopold Ernst (1888–1975).[39] The article illuminated the nation's arguably most prominent civil liberties attorney's accomplishments in the realm of sexual and literary free speech. *Life* journalist Fred Rodell observed Ernst's abundant physical energy, alert eyes, and athletic strength, describing him as "a smallish, darkish man whose birdlike eyes and manner belied his seeming physical solidity . . . and a general air of being about to take off."[40] An earlier 1938 profile in *Scribner's* magazine also noted Ernst's tendency for "exhibitionism," by which the writer, Marquis James, meant both Ernst's considerable skill at gaining publicity for his causes and cases and his self-promotion. Ernst regularly called himself an exhibitionist and would have agreed with both Rodell and James that he liked to light up his name in the city's newspapers. He also thoroughly enjoyed his near-celebrity status, which James characterized as "reaching for checks on the edge of New York's café society."[41] By the time these profiles were written, Ernst was already leading a packed social life spent at the Twenty One Club, the Algonquin, Sardi's, and his Greenwich Village brownstone. But he also had a reputation, according to James, for working "unflaggingly, inconspicuously, and well to further the public interest." Ernst performed two-thirds of his legal work either pro bono or well below what he could have charged, because "bearing the torch of public service" was vital to him.[42]

The son of a Jewish immigrant from Pilsen, Germany, on his father's side and a second-generation Jewish immigrant on his mother's side, Ernst grew up in New York City in homes filled with books, musical instruments, and immigrant aspirations for education and economic security. After arriving in America and settling in Alabama, Ernst's father took a business trip to New York and "went to where the immigrants were," as Ernst recalled later in life, where he met, courted, and married an "educated, literate, and cultured" New York City woman. His parents returned to Alabama after their marriage, but at his mother's insistence they moved to New York City when Morris was 2 years old, so that he and his siblings would have better educational opportunities. His father, whom Ernst described as "a peddler, like all immigrants," also valued education, "like all immigrants."[43]

Being a second-generation immigrant, Ernst did not feel rooted in either a sense of ancestry or place. This shaped his self-perception, including his penchant for publicity. He reflected in an interview late in his life that he had "no ancestors" and "had no past." Asked to explain, he said he had "no great grandfather, no rootedness," no sense of belonging to a longer stream, and, as a result, no sense of security. Comparing himself to his second wife, Margaret Samuels, who came from a well-established Jewish family in New Orleans, he said, "Margaret had security," adding that she was "one of the few secure people I've ever known. I'm not secure." He continued, "I'm a ham. I like publicity."[44]

Ernst's immigrant sensibility and the attendant insecurity come across potently. He did not discuss his Jewishness per se very often, perhaps because it made him feel vulnerable. Later in his life Ernst "recalled how he was mocked during his formative years for his appearance. 'I had been brought up to believe that I was ugly. . . . I had uncles who always kidded me about my big Jewish nose which did my ego no good.'" He also recalled being "told that I was Jewish, and for that reason, 'inferior.'"[45]

Ernst internalized the financial precariousness of immigrants too. His father made (and occasionally lost) money in the real estate business, so his family had difficult periods. But his father also had enough financial success that he could send Morris to the prestigious Horace Mann School for high school and then to Williams College. Upon graduation, Ernst returned to New York City, worked in the family shirt-making business (run by his uncle), and took up law school at night at the New York School of Law, where other immigrants and Jews took their legal education—both for financial reasons and because bigotry in the legal profession kept them out of the more prestigious schools (and law firms, when they graduated).

Ernst was also insecure and self-deprecating about his legal education and the fact that he went to law school at night while he worked in the family business by day. He often remarked that he was a "partially trained" lawyer. When Ernst was earning his law degree, just before World War I, there was intense disdain for and an active discussion in the elite legal community about the inferiority of immigrant and Jewish lawyers trained in night schools, as opposed to the WASPs trained at Harvard, Yale, Columbia, Wisconsin, and Pennsylvania (and also opposed to the Catholics trained at Fordham and Georgetown).[46]

Thus Ernst was acutely aware of the obstacles facing Jewish lawyers, and in 1939—perhaps at the height of his prestige—he "approached Supreme Court Justice Harlan Stone on behalf of other Jews in an attempt to counter such restrictions."[47] But the resistance to hiring Jewish associates in New York's most prestigious and successful corporate law firms continued for decades, until the post–World War II period, when Jewish lawyers had the opportunity to prove their talents in the New Deal and wartime agencies and when their knowledge of the administrative state made them useful to corporate firms trying to navigate federal agencies and their rules.[48]

These policies and attitudes of not hiring Jewish lawyers also meant that the "competition for a position in the top Jewish firms was fierce," and as a result the Greenbaum, Wolff & Ernst law firm that Ernst established with Eddie and Laurence Greenbaum and Herbert Wolff meant that they were able to secure first-rate talent, including the brilliant Jerome Frank (who became a legal star in FDR's New Deal and was a rising star as a federal court judge at the time of his early death in 1956), Harriet Pilpel (who argued dozens of cases before the Supreme Court on behalf of Planned Parenthood and under the auspices of the ACLU), and Benjamin Kaplan (who became chief justice of the Massachusetts Supreme Court).[49]

When Ernst formed his practice with the Greenbaum brothers and Wolff (who were also Jewish graduates of Williams College) in 1913, they began building a successful firm known for expertise in corporate law and real estate law. Their work in these fields provided considerable financial security for the partners and their many junior associates, allowing the firm's lawyers room to pursue other areas of interest and to offer their talents to their clients pro bono. Ernst and his junior associates Lindey and Pilpel did much of their obscenity law work pro bono.[50]

Ernst became the law firm's senior partner most directly involved in civil liberties work, and by the mid-1920s he had distinguished himself enough in New York City's progressive legal circles to become part of the

ACLU's national executive board (1927), working alongside the organization's founding generation.[51] Ernst became the ACLU's co-general counsel
with Arthur Garfield Hays in 1929 and served in that role until 1954. Ernst
cultivated an understanding of the relationship between sexual censorship
and free speech through this affiliation. The ACLU was *the* organization
that took on the longer-term project of "making sex a civil liberty."[52] Ernst
was instrumental in these efforts and forged his focus in the ACLU milieu.[53]

Ernst proved to be an enormously energetic, complicated figure that
one ACLU colleague described as "a smart fixer." His long-term legacy is
problematic, because he abandoned his liberalism later in life and lost his
credibility among many of his longtime allies in the ACLU for his ardent
anticommunism and his dubious alliance with the FBI's J. Edgar Hoover.[54]
But his early- to mid-career contributions to U.S. civil libertarianism were
profound, and at the height of his legal powers he transformed American
obscenity laws.

Ernst's focus on obscenity law issues was basically a parallel free speech
movement alongside the free speech battles on behalf of political radicals
and labor unions taken up by his ACLU colleagues. Those interests dove-
tailed with his inchoate First Amendment commitments to an unfettered
"marketplace of thought," a principle he adopted from the work of the
first Jewish Supreme Court justice, Louis Brandeis. The First Amendment,
Ernst believed, was premised on and should guarantee such a marketplace,
and he thought that this ought to extend to artistic expression to other
areas (such as sexuality), where the public needed scientifically dependable, up-to-date information that would make their lives better and less
filled with hazards.[55]

As the *Life* and *Scribner's* profiles explained, Ernst secured his reputation
as being "preeminent among lawyers crusading against censorship" with his
1933 defense of James Joyce's *Ulysses*.[56] This case certainly brought Ernst
his greatest fame (then and now), but it was just one victory in a series of
censorship cases that transformed obscenity jurisprudence, cases that were
fought because Ernst understood the crucial role that obscenity law played
in bolstering censorship—and interfering with the public's right to read
about and talk about sex, which was integral to having more intelligent

and gratifying sex lives, which in turn fundamentally required control over one's reproductive life.

Ernst was not squeamish about sex and was not afraid of the topic. Indeed, it is clear that he liked the topic of sex. He had, according to the 1944 *Life* profile, a "strong intellectual sex streak," which the writer also described as "an overpowering preoccupation with sex." "His conversation is full of it," and "he does not duck the short words. His office bookcases are crammed with sex literature, far beyond the number of books he has saved from suppression."[57] Ernst saw the value of knowing about sex. He thought the public was harmed by suppression of sexual materials, and no one of his era did more to protect public access to sexual information.

Ernst's use of publicity, for which the *Life* profile essentially ridiculed him, was not just self-aggrandizing. It was strategic, and he made it work for his anti-censorship cause. Indeed, the *Life* profile had to acknowledge that Ernst was "able to crow, with pardonable pride" that "no book published by a regular publisher, or reviewed by a regular critic, no book published honestly and without surreption, is in any danger of suppression."[58]

In this book I illustrate how Ernst and his colleagues, especially Lindey and Pilpel, won their publicity battles and legal cases as part of their larger campaign against censorship, a fight focused on the right to sexual knowledge, sexual ideas, and reproductive control. The story is about Ernst and his partners' targeted challenges to obscenity laws, running from the late 1920s to the mid-1950s, in defense of some of the most important and high-profile feminists, birth control activists, novelists, and sex educators of that era.[59]

This is crucial. Ernst and his colleagues were not the vanguard of the sexual revolution or the birth control movement or cultural modernism—but their clients were. Ernst and his allies worked diligently to break the hold of Comstockery as a legal and cultural force. But as Ernst and his colleagues pointed out, the law was far behind the public, and they helped it catch up with the culture.

Although contemporary journalists and others reporting on these battles gave Ernst the public credit for the firm's work, it is abundantly clear that he (and their clients) benefited profoundly from the intellectual labor and

FIGURE 3. Morris Ernst sitting in his office, with photograph of Justice Louis Brandeis on wall.

SOURCE: *Life* Picture Collection, Getty Images.

legal talents of his associates, especially Alexander Lindey in the late 1920s through the mid-1940s, and Harriet Pilpel beginning in the late 1930s. Ernst was the impresario and managed the firm's stagecraft, and others managed the many moving parts behind the scenes. Theatrical analogies seem appropriate, because the trials involved theatrics and Ernst certainly understood the value of promotion, showmanship, and courtroom performance.

Part of the stagecraft of their cases was choosing clients wisely with strategic aims of both advancing a larger anti-censorship argument and seeking particular outcomes against obscenity law administration by different agencies using different statutory rules. Lindey was the architect who developed their strategic map or blueprint. Ernst and colleagues sought reputable (as distinct from seedy) clients. They focused on works, figures, and bodies of information whose value to the public they could defend, so that they could spend their energy and resources on winnable cases. And they looked for weaknesses in those federal and state statutes and in the agencies that administered the web of obscenity laws, searching for openings where they might achieve piecemeal victories, one case at a time. They were also strategic in working to bring their cases before sympathetic judges whenever possible and figured out how to cooperate with prosecutors to do this. But perhaps most important of all to their successes, Ernst and his colleagues represented clients who were among the most transformative figures in the early decades of the twentieth century, across the fields of literature, birth control advocacy, and the scientific study of sexuality.

The focus of this book is the legal arguments, defense strategies, and trial work that the Ernst team used to defend their clients as well as those arguments made by the prosecutors and their allies. The chapters proceed chronologically through the twenty-year period that Ernst and his team worked on these cases. Each chapter is organized around a trial (or two) and the judicial opinions that (mostly) resolved the legal questions at hand.

Beginning with scandals surrounding education about sexual pleasure, in the first two chapters we explore the legal travails of two birth control activists who also became sex educators, Mary Ware Dennett and Marie Stopes. In Chapter 3 we examine the taboo of lesbianism and Radclyffe Hall's novel, *The Well of Loneliness*. The larger concerns around censoring works of literature are taken up in Chapter 4, which focuses on a series of orchestrated showdowns with John Sumner and his Vice Society in New York City. Ernst's work on literature culminates in Chapter 5 with his famous defense of James Joyce's *Ulysses*, securing a landmark decision on behalf of literary modernism. In Chapter 6 we return to the subject of birth control and women's need for contraceptive devices and instruction under medical supervision. I show how the long-term relationship between the Ernst firm and Margaret Sanger and Dr. Hannah Stone began in 1929 following a New York City police raid of their Manhattan birth control clinic, the Clinical Research Bureau. That raid began Greenbaum, Wolff & Ernst's long involvement with Sanger and her leadership in the birth control movement, leading eventually to a series of federal court cases contesting Customs' prohibitions on physicians' and medical researchers' efforts to import birth control devices and information.

Following a hiatus resulting from the prolonged chaos of World War II, Ernst returned to obscenity law, this time with the defense of Indiana University's Dr. Alfred Kinsey and his Institute for Sex Research. This case is the focus of Chapter 7. Ernst and Pilpel defended the Kinsey Institute's right to receive research materials, no matter how obviously pornographic those materials were. This trial offers an interesting capstone to the harm versus value framework that Ernst and associates used throughout their trials, from which we can reflect on the long-term legacy of their work.

Ernst's commitment to an open information marketplace buttressed his broad anti-censorship principles and also informed and justified the vigorous anti-communism that shaped his thinking and focused much of his extralegal work from the late 1930s on. On the progressive side, he used that open marketplace framework to oppose monopolistic or oligopolistic concentrations in the communications industries, to argue for the right of labor organizers to hold mass gatherings, and to defend burlesque theaters against obscenity ordinances, in addition to the work detailed in this book. As part of that same set of beliefs about what the public ought to know, Ernst took a more speech-restrictive position in the face of the international political upheavals of the mid- to late 1930s and argued that those individuals and groups affiliated with American fascist and communist movements ought to be forced to "disclose" their bases of financial and organizational support.[60]

Within the ACLU's executive leadership, Ernst was the foremost advocate of disclosure as a policy, and this became one of the many issues that fragmented the ACLU's leadership at the end of the Popular Front era (1935–1939). Ernst and others had already been alarmed about how Communists' membership in the ACLU was being used by anti-Communist journalists and congressman to tar the ACLU, and he used this same marketplace of ideas framework to insist that American Communists ought to be transparent about who was bankrolling them and whose bidding they were doing. Following the Nazi-Soviet pact of August 1939, Ernst essentially shelved his anti-censorship program for the duration of the long World War II years, focused his attention on national security generally, and aligned himself with the president and vigorously defended him and his policies within the ACLU.[61]

More surprising (and damning for Ernst's longer-term reputation), this shift of attention to national security issues (and fear of domestic subversion) led Ernst to pursue a relationship with the FBI's J. Edgar Hoover. In what clearly appears to be a near abrogation of commitment to his core civil libertarian values, by the postwar years Ernst had become an informant to and the highest profile liberal defender of Hoover. I do not attempt to burnish the Morris Ernst who made anticommunism the framework through which he filtered virtually all issues from the end of World War II through the late 1950s. Instead I hold the two sides of Ernst up together, arguing for the real value of his, and his firm's, legacy in paving the way for much broader sexual freedom, which exists alongside the civil liberties costs of his other ideas.

This legacy helped pave the way in the courts for the sexual revolution of the 1960s and 1970s and beyond into our own era. Sexual materials are ubiquitous in ways that Ernst and his colleagues could not have imagined. Sexual identity is widely recognized as a fundamental starting point for understanding an individual's personhood, an outcome that would astonish Ernst and his colleagues. So would legalized gay marriage. The fact that men won extensive rights to access pornography and to visually possess and exploit (mostly) women's bodies for pleasure would be a logical outcome of Ernst and associates' arguments about the state's inability to prove harm to readers (although they never intended to defend pornography per se). The fact that women still struggle to obtain rights and agency over the physical autonomy of their own bodies would rile them, and it is certainly not the logical outcome of their arguments about women's reproductive needs, health, and well-being, the needs of their offspring, and the necessity that scientific and medical criteria be determinative in birth control law, not moral categories. They might have anticipated that masculine interests in sexual freedom would prevail over feminine or feminist ones, but that was certainly not part of their agenda or desire in transforming obscenity laws. For Ernst and his colleagues, the need to significantly shrink the reach of the obscenity laws so that the public could have access to a dependable, well-sourced marketplace of sexual knowledge was fundamentally premised on the understanding that guaranteeing women reproductive autonomy and knowledge was the starting point for everyone's sexual enlightenment. They would apprehend that the battle is far from over.

CHAPTER 2

FIGHTING FOR SEXUAL EDUCATION

Mary Ware Dennett Versus Postal Power

IN 1915 FEMINIST ACTIVIST Mary Ware Dennett set out to give her two sons, ages 10 and 14, some straightforward guidance about sex. She read more than sixty publications about adolescent sexual development. Almost all evaded what she called the emotional and spiritual side of sex, and they were euphemistic at best about the physiology of puberty, arousal, and intercourse. After consulting physicians and medical manuals to find the most current, scientifically accurate information, she wrote her own pamphlet, eventually published as *The Sex Side of Life* (1918). Her experience as a women's suffrage activist and birth control pamphleteer, combined with her idealism about the power of knowledge and her belief in direct talk about sexuality, resulted in a short work that stood out for its clarity and frankness. It quickly gained a large audience and eventually drew opponents.

Dennett addressed the taboo subject of masturbation, vividly described the physical pleasures of intercourse, and endorsed the role that birth control could play in enhancing married couples' sex lives. In so doing, she shattered the usual silences about sexual gratification in sex education materials. She refused to bludgeon her young readers with the standard warnings about sex as animalistic, base, and surrounded by moral shamefulness. She thus left herself open to charges of violating the 1873 Comstock obscenity laws. When federal officials indicted her in January 1929, Dennett became something of a cause célèbre. Her plight helped focus the ACLU's attention on sexual censorship issues, and it gave Morris Ernst and his law firm a high-profile platform to launch their offensive against federal obscenity statutes. The *Dennett* case also exposed the deep cultural agitation over the difficulties of containing sex in a period marked by dramatic changes in acknowledging the centrality of sexuality in people's lives. Rapid urbanization and the commercialization of leisure, along with burgeoning entertainment industries that were marketing sex to consumers young and old, alarmed those who advocated for more traditional social and religious strictures around sexuality.

Dennett's critics warned that her work threatened standards of personal virtue, undermined self-discipline, eroded the principles of chastity, promoted out-of-wedlock sex, and would even result in "race suicide" and national military weakness. Extravagant claims suffused the oral arguments and documents proffered by the prosecution and its experts. The overall tone is merely hinted at in the statement by the prosecutor, U.S. Attorney James A. Wilkinson: "In this pamphlet there is not one word about chastity; not one word about self control; nothing about that which distinguishes sinful lust from lawful passion. There is nothing that attracts the child's attention to other things outside sex enjoyment."[1] For Wilkinson, these absences portended cultural doom, and he warned that he would use all his powers for God, country, and his own four daughters to keep Dennett's writings out of the hands of young people.

Dennett's supporters guffawed at Wilkinson and the idea that the pamphlet was obscene. There was nothing prurient or indecent about it. They asserted that Dennett's language was clinical in its accuracy and honest in its treatment of her subject and that those features explained the pamphlet's durable popularity among parents, sex educators, and youth ministry leaders in such respectable institutions as the YMCA and the Union Theological Seminary in New York City. Dennett's own respectability was established by the fact that she was regularly described by supporters and the press as an earnest gray-haired grandmother, intent on keeping young people from getting their information about sex from the gutter. She was, they averred, wrongly under attack by forces of anti-intellectualism and puritanical Comstockery. Their preoccupations with Dennett could best be explained by their "primitive sex fears" and desire to keep young people "in the terrible darkness," as *The Nation*'s Dudley Nichols wrote. Dennett's prosecutors and critics were "medieval" in their outlook, "moralists" who wanted to build high fences around the truth. The gulf "between Mrs. Dennett and her persecutors is," Nichols wrote, "simply the eternal gulf between those who love and those who fear."[2]

What was it about *The Sex Side of Life* that pulled Dennett before a federal district court judge in Brooklyn in January 1929 with possible imprisonment in her future? Why did Ernst conceive of Dennett's pamphlet as a perfect test case to challenge the federal obscenity laws, months before either had an inkling she would actually be indicted? Why did her trial galvanize the ACLU and its growing membership to pay attention to sexual censorship issues? And what was it about the threat of censorship and the ongoing legal power of Comstockery that found the local and national journalists who covered the case portraying Dennett as a matronly figure rather than the leading feminist activist she was?

Mary Ware Dennett

Born in 1874 and raised in a world of social reformers in Boston, Mary Ware studied at the School of Art and Design at the Boston Museum of Fine Arts. She took a job at the Drexel Institute of Art in Philadelphia and there, and later in Boston, became instrumental in organizing the first arts and crafts society in the United States. She grew more interested in political issues, first with the women's suffrage movement starting in 1910; she served as field secretary of the Massachusetts Suffrage Association and then as secretary of the National Suffrage Association. In 1914 Dennett shifted her attention to birth control issues and peace activism. She was the field secretary for the American Union Against Militarism, helped found the People's Council for Peace and Democracy, and joined the New York City branch of the Woman's Peace Party. But as historian John Craig points out, even during the war years she gave most of her attention to birth control issues, founding the National Birth Control League (NBCL) along with fellow birth control activists Jesse Ashley and Clara Greuning Stillman in 1915 and leading it until 1918.[3]

Directly germane to her interest in birth control issues, Dennett had suffered through difficult pregnancies, and her marriage to the MIT architect

Hartley Dennett endured long periods of sexual abstinence because of the absence of information about contraception. Eventually she suffered through a painful, quite public divorce, making her hesitant to take up a test case at Ernst's urging years later. She told him she had "a deep aversion to being spotlighted."[4] That aversion never interfered with her commitment to promote women's issues, though. Dennett gained experience and confidence as a strategist, an institution builder, a pamphlet writer, a lobbyist, and a vigorous promoter of women's issues. Through the NBCL she worked closely with the nation's most forceful and well-known birth control pioneer, Margaret Sanger. However, because of the NBCL's chronic shortage of funds, many differences over goals and tactics, and Sanger's insistence on being the movement's recognized leader, they parted ways.[5] Dennett started a new organization, the Voluntary Parenthood League (VPL) in 1919, and it became the principal rival to Sanger's American Birth Control League (ABCL) when Sanger formed that organization.[6] (They would remain rivals throughout the 1920s and into the early 1930s, and Ernst would occasionally have to mediate between them, as he was counsel to both.)

Dennett later reckoned that her birth control activism led to the 1922 ban of *The Sex Side of Life* by the postmaster general and the postal solicitor. Through the VPL she had worked tirelessly to eliminate the ban on contraceptive devices and information from the federal obscenity statute, as nothing posed a greater obstacle to the distribution of information about contraception than the Comstock Act of 1873 and the mini-Comstock laws passed by the states.[7] She argued, "Striking down the features of the state and federal laws governing the mailing of birth control information should be the [birth control] movement's main concern."[8] In 1922, however, Congress tightened the tariff laws, expanding Customs' restrictions on contraceptive information and devices and making Postal and Customs authorities twin bureaucratic obstacles to women and their reproductive needs.[9] Dennett fought those laws and their administrators, particularly Postmaster General Hubert Work. This explained why, she later argued, Postal officials went after her pamphlet in 1928 and 1929 for continually violating the ban on it they had imposed in 1922. Throughout the 1920s Dennett insistently lobbied Congress and Postal officials, trying to lift the federal prohibition on information about birth control.[10] Her lobbying efforts and her book on birth control laws in 1926 made her well known to congressmen and top Postal officials as a so-called sex radical—and she was a vociferous, unstinting critic.

Dennett routinely described the Postal Service and its administrators as having an "un-American power" to control the mails. Plus, in failing to distinguish contraceptive information from abortion materials, or sex hygiene issues from expressly pornographic photographs, the laws blurred all distinctions between materials with quite different purposes. The Postal administrators seemed unwilling to see distinctions and hewed to the letter of the 1873 law. Dennett railed against their power in her VPL newsletter, describing how they operated by executive fiat to enforce an obscenity law that she described as being defined by its "revolting undefinitive adjectives." Her extensive lobbying efforts and firsthand encounters with Postal authorities taught her that individual Postal officials had far too much power, were not answerable to anyone, and were openly antagonistic to women's issues.

The Pamphlet

Dennett wrote *The Sex Side of Life: An Explanation for Young People* in 1915 as a side project. Her sons found her pamphlet useful, as did her friends who were also looking for instructional materials for their children. Dennett distributed the pamphlet for the next four years, unadvertised.[11] Despite the lack of promotion, "The circulation grew steadily and soundly" and it achieved a glowing reputation.[12] In 1918 the owner and publisher of the *Medical Review of Reviews* asked Dennett to send the pamphlet to the journal's editor, Dr. Victor Robinson. He published it straight away. In his Editor's Foreword, Robinson wrote, "After reading a few pages of the essay itself, we realized we were listening to the music of a different drummer. Instead of the familiar notes of fear and pretense, we were surprised to hear the clarion call of truth." Calling it a "rational sex primer," he added that he and the other editors "sincerely hope that this splendid contribution will be reprinted in pamphlet form and distributed by thousands to the general public."[13] It was. Within the year, the *Medical Review of Reviews* issued the essay in pamphlet form, and it was soon used by a variety of educational and religious organizations, including the YMCA.[14] When Dennett's case came to trial in 1929, the pamphlet was still regarded as among the best, if not *the* best publication available for sex education instruction.[15]

Postal officials banned the pamphlet as obscene in 1922, after four years of circulation. In the four years after the *Medical Review of Reviews* reprinted the pamphlet, Dennett sold thousands of inexpensive copies (usually in bulk) to educators, organizations committed to young adults, church groups, and individual parents. Despite the 1922 ban, Dennett kept mailing the pamphlet (paying second-class postal rates) to those who requested it.[16] She chafed at having the pamphlet labeled obscene. So in 1925 she mounted a small campaign, recruiting sex education teachers and others who had used the pamphlet to sign a letter to the postmaster general explaining that *The Sex Side of Life* was widely used by "schools and colleges and all manner of public welfare organizations, and by many thousands of responsible parents, as well as by the young people for whom it was written." The postal solicitor nevertheless upheld the ban. Characteristically, Dennett insisted on a meeting but got no explanation from the nation's top Postal officials about what made the pamphlet obscene.[17] She kept mailing the pamphlet and kept criticizing Postal officials in her VPL publications for their "unrestricted power."[18]

The seventeen-page pamphlet she mailed from 1918 to her trial in 1929 began with a brief, frank "Introduction for Elders." Dennett explained her purposes to the adults who might provide it to their children or students. She told them that she did not want to use euphemisms and evasions about reproduction and sexual pleasure. She took young people's information needs seriously and stated that these issues, so compelling to youth, should be explained using suitable terminology. She also refused to use the "fear of venereal disease as an appeal for strictly limited sex relations" and instead reported that it was "becoming curable." And, most damningly, she told her adult readers that she did not want her own children to have to contend with the "misleading and harmful impressions" about masturbation circulating in the larger culture and in the typical sexology literature.[19]

The bulk of the pamphlet directly addressed adolescent readers. Dennett told her young readers that the "emotional side" of sex was "the key to the whole situation."[20] Describing the passionate abandon between mates and the union of their souls as great spiritual pleasures, she averred that they were made even more delightful by the pleasures of intercourse and orgasm: "The climax of sex emotion is an unsurpassed joy, something which rightly belongs to every normal human being, a joy to be proudly and serenely experienced."[21]

Dennett also warned her readers about sex: It could become a source of trouble when separated from love. Those who did so risked disease, shame, and self-loathing, "usually . . . despis[ing] themselves for their weakness and their bad taste."[22] Sex should not be coarsened by smutty talk, she said, because "it can be easily perverted and ruined and made the cause of horrible suffering of both mind and body."[23] But even while offering these strong warnings, she advised her readers to take care of their bodies and their minds so that they might enjoy the emotional and sensual joys of their eventual married unions.

Although Dennett celebrated the emotional union of husband and wife, she also frankly discussed genitalia and their physiological responses to stimulation. Explaining how those "wonderful sex organs" work, she graphically described the physiology of foreplay, intercourse, orgasm, and the euphoria that follows. More directly, she described the physiology of intercourse: "By a rhythmic movement of the penis in and out, the sex act reaches an exciting climax or orgasm, when there is for the woman a peculiarly satisfying contraction of the muscles of the passage and for the man, the expulsion of the semen, the liquid which contains the germs of life. This is followed by a sensation of peaceful happiness and sleepy relaxation. It is the very greatest physical pleasure to be had in all human experience, and it helps very much to increase all other kinds of pleasure also."[24]

Dennett also addressed more controversial topics: birth control, masturbation, venereal disease, and prostitution. She unequivocally advocated access to and use of birth control technologies, finding it impossible to separate her discussion of contraception from her criticism of obscenity laws. Her critics seized on her discussion of all these issues as evidence of the pamphlet's dangers to youth.

Dennett's attitude toward masturbation received the widest discussion outside the courtroom. Acknowledging the strong masturbatory impulse among boys, she counseled that this was not something to worry or be embarrassed about, unless it became an obsession: "For generations [masturbation] has been considered wrong and dangerous, but recently many of the best scientists have concluded that the chief harm has come from the worry caused by doing it. . . . There is no occasion for worry unless the habit is carried to excess."[25] Clearly aware that she was taking an unorthodox position, Dennett cautioned that excessive masturbation could be a problem, because it depletes the body of the "sex secretions" needed to keep the "delicate machinery" in top shape—not because of the so-called crime of self-abuse. She warned her readers, "Do not stimulate your sex organs into action intentionally," but then gave them permission, adding "unless you find that nature does not bring you relief during sleep."[26] She dangled psychological relief for the act of self-relief. Her critics thought she was licensing the loss of self-control.

The Indictment

When the Justice Department brought a grand jury indictment against Dennett for distributing obscene literature in the early days of 1929, U.S. Attorneys were enforcing an obscenity "libel" imposed years before. Dennett was not surprised. She was no stranger to conflict over the pamphlet, had been confronting Postal officials for years, and was, by the standards of her era, a radical on sexuality issues. But virtually none of this history made its way into the coverage of the *Dennett* case. As Weinrib writes:

> Newspaper accounts, in order to make her a more sympathetic defendant, would later portray Dennett as a matronly grandmother who had been dragged into a humiliating judicial entanglement against her will. Many journalists quite consciously constructed Dennett as an unassuming figure. . . . According to most reports, Dennett's only ambitions were to educate her children and to help other mothers

FIGURE 4. Mary Ware Dennett, in suffragist garb (1913), leader of the Voluntary Parenthood League and author of *The Sex Side of Life*.

do the same; they painted the outspoken feminist as an appropriately modest woman, the unwitting victim of a ruthless legal assault.[27]

Dennett was anything but an unwitting victim and had long before thought about a legal challenge to the ban. In 1926 she reached out to a leading ACLU lawyer, Arthur Garfield Hays, about challenging the ban in court. According to Weinrib, Hays thought that the 1922 Postal ruling would be "a decidedly difficult hurdle. Dennett's pamphlet was explicit in its description of sex," and a court might well "uphold the ban."[28]

In 1928, however, Ernst thought Dennett had a potentially winnable case that was worth the risk. Mere months before the U.S. Attorneys handed down the grand jury indictment, Ernst and Dennett discussed a possible test case. According to Craig, Dennett had sent a copy of her pamphlet to Ernst after reading an article he wrote condemning censorship. He wrote back, telling her that he had followed her work for years, and he asked whether she "ever considered testing out the legality of the pamphlet in the courts?"[29] Ernst wanted to aim high, thinking *The Sex Side of Life* was ideal for challenging the constitutionality of the Comstock laws, given its credibility, long history of use, and serious educational intentions. This made it a good vehicle for trying to rein in the "unchecked postal power" they both railed against. In October 1928 Dennett told Ernst she had "decided to take the gamble and be game."[30]

However, in April 1928 Postal officials in Washington, D.C., had already decided to lure Dennett into illegally mailing her pamphlet so that they could prosecute her. In purported response to a complaint by members of the Daughters of the American Revolution, Postal officials worked with an Office of Naval Intelligence investigator named T. DeLeon Sullivan to work up a plan. (Sullivan would later volunteer as an "expert" witness against Dennett and years later as a researcher for Senator Joe McCarthy.) They forged stationery and a letter from a fictitious person—Mrs. Carl A. Miles of Grottoes, Virginia—requesting that Dennett mail her a copy of the pamphlet. When Dennett received Mrs. Miles's request, she did what she had been doing for years: She sent the pamphlet in a sealed package as second-class mail, accompanied by the small booklet *Representative*

Opinions testifying to the pamphlet's value. (Incredibly, Ernst and Dennett had no idea that Mrs. Miles and her stationery were a fabrication until after the jury trial.)[31] Armed with the evidence of the mailed pamphlet, Justice Department officials took Dennett's pamphlet before a grand jury, which authorized an indictment on the grounds that the pamphlet could reasonably be found obscene. In early January 1929, U.S. Attorney James Wilkinson of the Southern District of New York mailed Dennett a letter telling her she had been indicted. When she showed up at Ernst's office with the indictment in hand, Ernst was primed for the moment.

Ernst's Motion to Quash

Wilkinson's letter informed Dennett that she needed to appear in the U.S. District Court in Brooklyn on January 7, 1929. She faced a maximum of five years in prison and a $5,000 fine. Wilkinson claimed that the original document was so offensive that he would not make the contents part of the official record, employing a tactic he would use throughout the subsequent trial. A graduate of the Jesuit-run Fordham Law School, he told Ernst and Dennett that the pamphlet was "lascivious, vile and indecent" and "unfit to be set forth in this instrument and to be spread before this Honorable Court."[32]

At the January 7 hearing, Ernst filed a motion to quash the indictment, asking the presiding district court judge, Grover M. Moscowitz, to rule that *The Sex Side of Life* was not obscene as a matter of law. Like Wilkinson, Ernst introduced a line he would routinely make in subsequent cases, suggesting that the pamphlet itself was not dirty and that those who found it so were the ones with dirty minds. "This pamphlet is not obscene. . . . Its motive is clean and healthy. It is pure, if you use the word in that way. Obscenity is a subjective thing. It exists in the minds of dirty vice-hunters who are always looking for dirt. They can always find dirt because it is a subjective thing. And I say not Mrs. Dennett but the grand jurors were obscene."[33] As he did throughout this trial, Ernst suggested that the choice was between Dennett's pamphlet—"the truth, unadorned and respectful"—or the trashy materials from which young people otherwise learn about sex—the "filthy misinformation of the streets, the dirty words chalked upon signboards and the obscene gossip of other children."[34]

Ernst explained Dennett's motives and the circumstances of the pamphlet's publication. Her intentions were educational, not financial. She had found the existing literature inadequate and produced a document entirely in accord with modern scientific thought. She did not publish it to make money. Ernst then pursued a strategy he would use in other cases, limiting the definition of obscenity to the more familiar or vernacular understanding of what was meant by the word, not the statutory meaning, explaining that an artifact had to be purposefully filthy and pornographic to be considered obscene. Dennett's pamphlet did not fit this definition. The pamphlet, he insisted, "is neither smut nor pornography. There is not a dirty word or a dirty thought in it." Moreover, he argued that it was well in line with contemporary thinking about these issues and fit right in with what public health officials thought was needed, proving this by quoting extensively from a document produced by the New York State Department of Health that called for the kinds of materials that Dennett had written.[35]

However persuasive Ernst's arguments might have been, Judge Moscowitz had enough doubts about whether the pamphlet was obscene that he denied Ernst's motion to quash the indictment. After all, the grand jury had found it questionable, and in view of what he described as the tremendous social consequences of the case, he wanted to know more about it and needed more expert opinion. The issues of adolescent sexuality were so inextricably framed by religious sensibilities and were of such import that the judge thought he should have direct access to the opinion of clergy. He impaneled a Catholic priest, a Jewish rabbi, and a Protestant minister to sit with him for this initial hearing.[36] Tellingly, his request that clergy aid the court generated virtually no media commentary and not a single objection from Dennett's defense team, suggesting that virtually everyone involved understood that Dennett's trial was really about whether her pamphlet had offended religiously defined moral norms and that the operative definition of obscenity was based in moral offense.

Moscowitz wanted the clergy "to aid the conscience of the court" during this hearing, but he also told both counsel that before the next hearing he wanted to hear from additional clergy, physicians, educators, and those accustomed to dealing with the problems of adolescents. He instructed the lawyers to line up potential expert witnesses and proposed an open hearing at which representatives from both sides would express their opinions on the pamphlet. According to Weinrib, Judge Moscowitz felt vulnerable because there were charges of judicial misconduct swirling about him in an unrelated matter and "he feared the publicity that might attend a decision either way in the highly publicized *Dennett* case."[37]

Dennett's trial met with many delays. She reported fourteen separate trips to the federal courthouse in Brooklyn by the time of her next hearing at the end of January. Judge Moscowitz's request for expert testimony set in motion a storm of activity by Dennett's defense team, lining up experts and also generating publicity for the upcoming trial. When the court reconvened in late January for a two-day hearing on the motion to quash, the Brooklyn federal courtroom was filled with Dennett's supporters and the press.[38]

Both counsels made clear by their performances that this case would be fought in the press and the courtroom. Each side conveyed that they were protecting the future of civilization, whereas the other side would lead to ruin. From Ernst's perspective, the case exemplified the collision of science, education, and rationality with willful ignorance.[39] From Wilkinson's point of view, the stakes were also clear: moral restraint giving way to moral slippage, girls made vulnerable to wanton youth, and national decline. The case embodied a generational clash, between those embracing claims of being modern and scientific and those defending timeless moral norms and codes of sexual reticence they felt were under siege in the larger culture.

Wilkinson's closing statement to Judge Moscowitz asserted that the state saw in Dennett's pamphlet not just a threat to "ethical self-determination of the will" but grand historical failures. He invoked the fall of nations, the decline of the Roman Empire, and the potential incapacity of the United States to defend itself, warning that because of works like Dennett's, "When the clarion bugle call of war resound . . . God help America if we haven't the men to defend her at that hour of need."[40] How would this happen? The obscenity laws were aimed at preventing lust in vulnerable audiences, he told his listeners, but this pamphlet must "of necessity excite a morbid spirit of curiosity and experimentation" by describing marital intercourse as "an unsurpassed joy." This would undermine marriage, "the institution of our home, the foundation of our society, the safeguard of our Nation," and it would lead to sexual depravity in the streets. If "this pamphlet fell into the hands of one who is abnormally minded . . . it is not hard to realize that with his thoughts inflamed with its lurid descriptions he would waylay some decent girl in a dark alley and attack her."[41] He went on to explain that it was not just the "abnormal" who were at risk, adding, "I say it would excite any child abnormally and make it curious to find out and enjoy this 'Supreme pleasure' [intercourse]."[42] He told the court he would not even trust his own 22-year-old schoolteacher daughter with it, let alone his younger children.[43]

Moving back and forth from the failure of individual self-discipline to collective decline, Wilkinson cautioned that the court had an obligation to protect "the youth of the Nation from this overwhelming idea of sex that in the modern mind pervades the world today." Detouring into a stunning historical analogy, he invoked ancient Roman practices as a useful model for thinking about a daughter's maiden chastity. "Why, let a daughter of a senator offend against the moral law and her father condemned her to death." This was time honored, he said, "something man has held through the ages as something to be aspired to and respected."[44] He also asserted a direct line between birth control, race suicide in the United States—especially among "the great families"—and national weakness.[45]

Wilkinson's statement produced plenty of smirks among Dennett's supporters, and he was all but mocked in the press. But he also reminded the court that the Comstock law's goal, as reinforced by the Hicklin test, was to protect "those into whose hands the object may fall" from "depravity and corruption."

Ernst needed to persuade Judge Moscowitz to quash the obscenity indictment and clear the pamphlet of the obscenity libel. He described the pamphlet's history, its popularity, its seriousness, and the public's largely unmet need for such a work. He also elaborated the problems of using an obscenity law from the 1870s to police sex education literature in the late 1920s. He explained the great respect for the pamphlet in youth sex education circles, with nearly 30,000 copies purchased and distributed over a ten-year period. He also reiterated that his client was merely doing what the federal government's public health officials were doing with similar documents: meeting vital public health needs by publishing sex education materials offering accurate, up-to-date information.[46] It fit well within the moral norms of the moment.

Responding to Wilkinson's line about how some "abnormally minded" people might be corrupted, Ernst argued that "obviously the statute did not mean to imply that all literature dealing with sex would be banned just because some filthy-minded person comes to the conclusion that he procures an impure stimulation from the material."[47] Assessing the value of a widely used document based on the possible effects on a mentally disturbed person was, he argued, not a rational solution to a well-recognized public health need for good sex education.

The nineteenth-century obscenity statute created serious obstacles for contemporary sex education, Ernst argued, but the need for that education was clear. Rehearsing a point he would repeat many times in his obscenity cases, Ernst explained that society's standards change over time and that any artifact should be measured by contemporary moral standards, not by the attitudes about sex that were prevalent when the Comstock Act was written. "The test of obscenity is a constantly changing test," he said, and the public needed—demanded, even—serious, high-quality information. The sources for such information mattered. Young people should learn about sexual matters from parents and educators rather than from their ill-informed friends, or worse, from lewd ideas picked up on the streets. Responding to a question that Judge Moscowitz posed to him about whether he would want his own young daughter to come upon this pamphlet, Ernst said he would have no difficulty having it in his home, because it was best to satisfy young people's curiosity through high-quality information. Ernst closed his motion to dismiss the indictment with his own rhetorical flourish, saying, "If this pamphlet is obscene, then life itself is obscene."[48]

Wilkinson's performance may have drawn guffaws, but it persuaded Judge Moscowitz that the pamphlet might in fact be obscene and that youth might be harmed by it. Following the two-day hearing in late January, Judge Moscowitz decided that a jury should consider the matter, and so Ernst's motion to dismiss the indictment failed. The matter would go to trial.[49]

Judge Moscowitz asked that each side provide him with twelve letters from experts in the fields of sex education, religious instruction, and adolescent development. Ernst's team decided that, beyond the twelve they directly solicited, anyone else of high reputation and with the appropriate kind of educational or theological association who wanted to write should send their letters directly to the judge. Letters poured in. Moscowitz received at least three dozen from Dennett's supporters, perhaps more.[50] Unfortunately, these letters did not inform the proceedings or become part of the official record of the subsequent trial. Judge Moscowitz recused himself from the trial. (He would be exonerated by the investigation into a possible conflict of interest but withdrew in part because he feared that the investigation would taint whatever decision he made in the *Dennett* case.) Judge Marcus B. Campbell, the next judge involved in the matter, said he would accept the expert testimony, but he too withdrew from the case. The eventual trial judge, Warren Burrows, refused to admit the letters into evidence or allow them in the official record.

These letters nevertheless provide rich evidence about how Dennett's contemporaries thought about either the dangers or the virtues of her pamphlet. They also illustrate that Ernst and Wilkinson's rhetorical framings were not exceptional but were in fact exemplary of the gulf dividing Dennett's supporters and opponents. Although Wilkinson may have shocked journalists and Dennett's allies with his warnings of lustful youth running loose and the women of the "great families" making the nation vulnerable, he was not the only one who saw the threat of a more sexually open society in such dire terms.

Wilkinson invited letters from clergy, doctors, police, and mental health experts. In general, they agreed that the pamphlet failed to teach (and was not adequately grounded in) Christian principles. Dennett's materialist approach to sex despiritualized humans, they argued, and Dennett was not attentive enough to the divine purposes of sexual intercourse in marriage. She offered no fundamental encouragement of chastity. She was too graphic about sexual pleasures. She failed to emphasize self-control, especially about masturbation, and also seemed to give license to sexual relations outside marriage. Collectively, those critics feared that the pamphlet was both a product of and contributed to an interrelated body of ideologies threatening society, including materialism, modernism, relativism, and secularism. Her permissiveness portended decline across many fronts.

Two prominent New York City Protestant clergy who regularly spoke about the necessity of censorship, Canon William Sheafe Chase, rector of Christ Church in Brooklyn, and Reverend John Roach Straton, pastor of the Calvary Baptist Church, sent Judge Moscowitz the most ardent critiques.[51] They also helped to get him letters from others, including Dr. G. A. Smith and Dr. R. G. Wearne, both administrators at Central Islip State Hospital for the Insane, who described Dennett's work as "evil" and "blighting."[52] Dr. Howard Kelly, a professor of gynecology at Johns Hopkins, warned, "The booklet is with one exception the most prurient statement that has come to my notice."[53] Dennett's birth control advocacy was both evidence of a subversive threat and a sign of the patriarchal family order under attack. Reverend Chase warned that birth control contributed to the breakdown of women's "natural sex virtue" by allowing women with "empty wombs" to be ruled by "sexual lawlessness," leading to the abandonment of marriage, the foundation of civilized society.[54] Dennett's critics, including Sumner, also complained that Dennett was too enthusiastic about the pleasures of intercourse and too graphic in describing the act itself.[55] And all agreed that her greatest sin against youth was her attitude toward masturbation, which they thought undermined the principles of "heroic self-sacrifice" and chastity.[56] Her pamphlet, Reverend Chase warned, advocated "free sex indulgence and a return to the morals of paganism."[57]

In stark contrast, the authors of the thirty-three letters supporting *The Sex Side of Life* could not fathom the idea that Dennett's sober pamphlet had been labeled obscene. Arguing that she penned one of the most useful and straightforward works available for the education of young people, they warned that it would be a great loss to educators and children if the pamphlet were held obscene. Most writers told Judge Moscowitz that Dennett wrote in a spirit of high-minded idealism, and many emphasized how helpful Dennett's pamphlet had been for them in advising their own offspring, making it easier to convey healthy attitudes about the body and sexuality.[58]

Ernst's team directly solicited their twelve "official" letters from theologians, physicians, professors, and youth educators and counselors. The unsolicited ones came from these professional ranks as well but also from citizens who wanted to weigh in on Dennett's behalf, including self-described housewives, grandmothers, mothers, and fathers, all mentioning the difficulties of trying to discuss "the sex side of life" with young people and their gratitude for Dennett's work.[59] (The Ernst firm also promoted Dennett's pamphlet by offering to mail it to those who ordered it from the Greenbaum, Wolff & Ernst offices, making sure that the pamphlet would get a wider readership at the moment it was on trial.)[60]

The richest unsolicited letter came from Mrs. Anne Bronson, a mother of seven from Woodstock, New York, who reported that she always answered her children's questions matter-of-factly. Although her children had learned physiological facts about mating from their many pets, she wrote, "I wanted to give them some book that would treat of love and marriage from the standpoint of human beings. I read book after book *ad nauseam*. . . . There was no hint of the joy of falling in love, of the pleasure in the marriage relation, nor of the ecstasy that so far transcends pleasure in a really noble love. And when I came to the chapter on what they all designated as 'the sin against one's self,' I found what seemed to me like criminal lies. I gave it up, I didn't lie to my children, nor they to me." She said Dennett's approach to masturbation was the "true view." Isn't "it better that young people . . . in the confusion and turbulence of adolescence . . . should know that their experience is a common one and that they can still hold up their heads and be happy, than that they should believe themselves vile and go in secret terror, watching for signs that they are becoming physical wrecks or headed for the mad-house?" She asked the judge the same question Ernst would ask in virtually all his obscenity trials: "How can a plain statement of facts about sex be obscene unless sex is a nasty subject? If it is a nasty subject then life itself is unclean and it would be well if the earth would open and swallow us all."[61]

In preparation for the trial, with the anticipation of being able to call on expert testimony, Ernst's team worked closely with leaders in the birth control and sex education communities to get them ready.[62] They asked their twelve letter writers to address the four most damning charges against

Dennett and to specifically state whether Dennett had been scientifically accurate (or obscene) in discussing masturbation, venereal disease, and birth control and whether her description of sexual intercourse was "in your opinion obscene and would it have a tendency to cause young men and women to indulge in immoral practices?"[63] Faculty members from New York's Union Theological Seminary, YMCA executives, social hygiene specialists, and other educators lined up as key expert witnesses—all expressing some variation on the theme that "sex adjustment" was absolutely necessary to healthy manhood.[64] YMCA officials were especially vital to the defense, as the YMCA had ordered as many as 25,000 copies of the pamphlet since its publication, making it the organization with far and away the greatest experience using *The Sex Side of Life*.[65] Ironically, fifty years earlier the YMCA had been Anthony Comstock's employer and his most powerful ally. Cultural standards about sexuality were changing.

The Trial Court

When the case finally went to a jury trial in April 1929, it immediately became clear to Ernst's team that Judge Burrows had not reviewed the record established by Moscowitz or by Judge Campbell, who briefly succeeded him. Both men had stipulated that the letters would be admitted as evidence, but Judge Burrows had read none of them and knew nothing about the pamphlet, its legal history, or its widespread use. As Dennett wrote after the trial, Burrows "had evidently not even scanned the indictment with care."[66]

Once the jury trial began, Burrows essentially agreed to all of Wilkinson's motions and objections. He refused to admit any evidence about the pamphlet's considerable history of institutional uses over the previous decade. More critically, he would not admit the physical pamphlet into evidence so that the jury could study it. The all-male jury's only knowledge of its contents came from the prosecutor's theatrical reading of it aloud to them. As Dennett described Wilkinson's performance, he read "as fast and as monotonously as possible" in a "droning low tone, except in those portions which he considered most 'filthy.' These he delivered in a louder emotional tone, pausing to let the matter sink into the minds of the jury."[67]

Judge Burrows rejected the letters that Judge Moscowitz had requested to aid the court as mere "opinion" evidence. He did not want the jury to know of their existence. When Ernst tried to enter them into evidence at trial, he told the jury that they came from "leaders in practically every field of social contact in the community—medical men, teachers of theology, a Rabbi, public health officials, educators, doctors," and contained extensive firsthand evidence of "actual experience with the pamphlet."[68] Judge Burrows told the jury to disregard this, as it was merely opinion and might confuse them. Ernst told the judge and jury that he would call fourteen witnesses to the stand, including four women, all of whom could testify to the pamphlet's widespread use by churches and educational and charitable organizations over ten years. None were allowed to testify.[69]

Wilkinson succeeded in reducing the April jury trial to two simple issues of fact: Did Dennett mail the pamphlet to the fictitious Mrs. Miles? And was the pamphlet obscene?

Ernst persisted. He could get his witnesses on the stand but could not get his questions answered. The court's treatment of the first witness, Abel Gregg, executive director of the YMCA, reveals the pattern.

MR. ERNST [TO GREGG]: Did you use this pamphlet by Mary Ware Dennett, in connection with classes conducted by the Y.M.CA.?

MR. WILKINSON: That is objected to as being incompetent, irrelevant and immaterial and not within the issues joined in the indictment.

THE COURT: The objection is sustained.

MR. ERNST: Exception.

MR. ERNST: Did you recommend this pamphlet at various meetings of parents?

MR. WILKINSON: That is objected to as being incompetent, irrelevant and immaterial.

THE COURT: Objection sustained.

MR. ERNST: Exception.

Ernst wound up accumulating more than 150 of these "exceptions" with each of his witnesses, including Dennett herself.

When Dennett was sworn in, she was not allowed to testify about her purposes, the number of pamphlets she had sold or mailed, the pamphlet's low price (to show she was not motivated by crass commercial interests), or anything else—except whether she mailed the particular pamphlet to the fictitious Mrs. Miles. Ernst and Dennett tried to do an end run around Burrows's sustaining every objection by having Dennett immediately answer Ernst's questions before Wilkinson could object. They used a rapid-fire yes-no question-and-answer technique: "Did you send at the request of the Union Theological Seminary one or more copies of this pamphlet to them?" "Yes." "Did you receive orders from the Young Women's Christian Association?" "Yes." "Did you receive orders from the Public Health Departments of various states?" "Yes." "Did you receive orders from no less than 400 welfare or religious organizations?" "Yes." "Have you received over a period of the last ten years orders for this pamphlet from members of the clergy?" "Yes." "Have you received orders from great numbers of doctors all over the United States?" "Yes." "And, have you received orders from Judges and Congressmen?" "Yes."[70]

Besides refusing this testimony, Judge Burrows also refused to admit the *Representative Opinions* booklet into evidence, even though it was originally mailed to Mrs. Miles along with *The Sex Side of Life*. It contained a compilation of testimonials from public health experts, clergy, and educators endorsing the pamphlet. Wilkinson objected to its introduction as mere opinion because the authors could not be cross-examined. The court agreed. At trial's end Judge Burrows instructed the jury to disregard the matter of the *Representative Opinions*, describing them as "simply some things which purport to be the statements of certain persons."[71]

Ernst also tried to introduce other government sex education and sex hygiene publications used by the same federal government prosecuting Dennett, including *Today's World Problem in Disease Prevention* and *Sex Education: Symposium for Educators*, both issued by the U.S. Public Health Service. Judge Burrows blocked these and two publications issued by the New York State Department of Health, *The Problem of Sex Education in the Schools* and *Healthy Manhood*. So the jury heard no discussion of and was not permitted to study comparable publications in the fields of sexual health, hygiene, and education, essentially making it impossible to create any understanding of what was taking place in the fields of sex education or sex hygiene.

Wilkinson succeeded entirely in keeping all contextual evidence out of the courtroom and the legal record, including Dennett's own explanation of her motives. Then, when he gave his closing arguments to the jury, he used the same outraged rhetoric about Dennett's pamphlet and national decline he had used in January in the pretrial hearing. As Dennett described it, he assured the jury that "if he could 'stand between the children of the country and this woman who was trying to lead them not only into the gutter but below the gutter into the sewer' he would feel that he had accomplished something."[72]

Judge Burrows used more sober language, but his jury instructions validated Wilkinson's framing of all the issues. Although the jury would determine whether the pamphlet was obscene, based entirely on the prosecutor's dramatic reading of it and without further study, Burrows's instructions to the jury made it clear that he had no doubts about the pamphlet's obscenity, referring to it throughout as the "non-mailable matter." These instructions became part of the grounds for appeal, along with the evidence and testimony Burrows denied during the trial.[73] Not surprisingly, the twelve male members of the jury returned a verdict of guilty, although it took multiple votes for them to do so.[74] *The Nation's* Dudley Nichols quoted one of the jurors as saying, "Judge Burrows didn't leave us much of anything to do but convict Mrs. Dennett." Nichols added, "The judge himself said during subsequent argument that the jury had done the right thing."[75]

Media Response

New York City and national journalists watched closely and reported on Burrows's trial management, his jury instructions, and the verdict. Audience members were not surprised at the outcome but were outraged that Dennett had been found guilty of a criminal act and was subject to federal criminal penalties.[76] The progressive lawyer Amos Pinchot captured their frustration in a letter to Ernst following the trial: "It is no new thing for society to fail to distinguish between its vanguard and its rear guard and to accord to its wisest, most useful citizens the same treatment it gives to criminals. For a federal judge and district attorney to prove themselves unable to distinguish such a pamphlet from what is obscene and vulgar, is a sad commentary on the discretion with which federal officers are selected."[77] Journalists and others with access to print fueled the anger.

Stella Hanau, editor of *Birth Control Review*, asked Ernst to write an article for her journal. Ernst turned it over to his colleague Alexander Lindey, who evinced the anger felt by Dennett's legal team and said things in Hanau's journal that he could not say in court or in the official leading documents they produced.

> Technically, Mrs. Dennett was convicted of sending obscene matter through the mails. In effect, however, she was adjudged guilty of being a sex-heretic. She had dared to advocate the dissemination of basic biologic facts. . . . She had dared to admit that the sex union might be pleasurable; a fact universally known, but apparently unmentionable. She had dared to hope for the day when birth control would be legally recognized. She had dared to present the modern medical and psychiatric viewpoint on masturbation that does not consign the practitioner to eternal damnation.[78]

Lindey continued, explaining that the current skirmishes over censorship were rearguard actions inspired and led by "bigoted and reactionary elements in the community" who were trying to turn back "signal progress in the last decade." These "insurers of purity" had restored "all of the old deterrents," including "threats of disease, public scorn, promises of eternal damnation."[79]

New York newspapers were particularly unkind to the prosecution. The *New York Telegram* labeled the proceedings "inquisitional injustice," and the *New York World* assessed the results as "deeply disturbing." In a framing that Ernst himself used, a journalist in Indianapolis "praised *The Sex Side of Life* as 'a prophylactic and disinfectant against common gutter smut,' calling the suppression of Dennett's work a 'miscarriage of justice.'" John Craig noted that other editorials suggested that a "positive side effect" of the trial was that it would draw greater critical attention to the laws.[80]

Journalism historian Dolores Flamiano studied coverage in the *New York Times* and the *New York Herald Tribune*, which published dozens of articles about Dennett's case, along with reportage in *Literary Digest*, *Time* magazine, *The Nation*, the *New Republic*, the *Woman's Journal*, and the *Outlook and Independent*.[81] She explains that because of the obscenity laws, the newspapers were reticent to describe much of what the pamphlet actually said, whereas the journals tended to be a bit bolder about this but also tended to avoid quoting the pamphlet's sections on masturbation and intercourse. They focused instead on the prosecution, the usefulness and value of the pamphlet, and the problems with the obscenity law. Even when the *New Republic* reprinted the pamphlet in May 1930, "to demonstrate to its readers that Dennett's obscenity conviction was 'false and unfair,'" it "still excluded the most controversial sections," including the "passages which describe the physiology of the reproductive organs and of sexual intercourse" and the passages that mentioned birth control and masturbation. Reprinting those passages would have pulled the publications into violation of the laws, so editors were careful.[82]

In other words, the obscenity law had a chilling effect on journalism. As a result, journalists became more aware of the relevance of obscenity laws to their trade and saw the need for reform. They also became more willing to write about sexuality as an issue of public interest.

The ACLU

The *Dennett* trial inaugurated an important shift in the official position toward and attitude about sex for the ACLU as well, as it was that organization's first major foray into the field of sex censorship.[83] Scholars have noted the long relationship between political radicalism and "free love," in particular, the unconventional sex lives of the ACLU's founding generation.[84] However, the ACLU's leadership had "resolutely excluded the regulation of sexual relations from its purview." But increasingly they came to understand that sex was an important form of personal liberty and social change, both of which needed protection from state encroachment.[85]

The *Dennett* case was at the center of the ACLU's shift from protecting political and economic speech to a broader conception of free speech, extending to issues surrounding the body, including matters of sexual autonomy. Wheeler's *How Sex Became a Civil Liberty* is a sweeping, deeply researched history of the ACLU's attention to the legal defense of sexuality across a range of issues. Both Wheeler and Samuel Walker note that the *Dennett* case was a turning point for the ACLU, in that it galvanized an inchoate recognition that sex censorship was an important arena for ACLU intervention and organization. Weinrib adds that the case made the ACLU "the undisputed leader of the anticensorship campaign and an aggressive advocate of artistic freedom and birth control."[86]

Ernst emphasized the shifting public sensibilities and moral standards around sexuality issues to promote greater focus on sexual censorship to others in the ACLU's leadership. Ernst understood that legislation was unlikely to succeed and used the case to "convince colleagues in the ACLU that 'ordinary citizens were more tolerant than government bureaucrats' and that the organization should try to 'transfer the power to determine what was indecent from public officials to juries.'"[87] In short, Ernst proposed litigation instead of legislation. Arthur Garfield Hays, Ernst's co-general counsel in the ACLU, also recognized that litigation had promise as a strategy for moving these sexual censorship cases forward and reforming the laws.[88]

A first manifestation of this greater attention within the ACLU was the formation of the Mary Ware Dennett Defense Committee to support Dennett's appeal. In the months between the trial before Judge Burrows and the appeal in the circuit court of appeals, the Mary Ware Dennett Defense Committee was busy promoting the cause, raising money, drawing public attention to Dennett's case, and trying to shape public opinion on the matter. Within a month it raised more than $1,000 for her defense, ultimately raising over $3,000, including organizing a gathering on May 21 at New York's Town Hall with over 1,500 people in attendance. Ernst and Dennett were the main attractions.

Preparing the Appeal

Part of Ernst's overarching argument, and thus his appeal to his ACLU colleagues, was that serious sexual speech ought to have First Amendment protections. The general free speech arguments were part of his promotional appeal to a sympathetic press, and the detailed appellate brief written to the three-judge panel of the U.S. Court of Appeals for the Second Circuit made formal First Amendment claims. These were not the core arguments in the appellate brief, however. The gravamen of their case was convincing the circuit court judges that the pamphlet was not harmful and certainly not obscene by conventional understanding and that it was in fact utterly respectable, widely used, and of demonstrable public value. To do this, they had to finesse those frank parts of Dennett's pamphlet on masturbation, intercourse, birth control, and sexual instruction that resulted in the trial jury's guilty verdict and her $300 fine (which she refused to pay).

They had to persuade the court that Dennett's controversial treatment of those four issues of masturbation, intercourse, birth control, and frank sexual instruction generally were not obscene according to the letter of the law. This was not altogether clear. Even Ernst's ACLU colleague Arthur Garfield Hays had been hesitant to take up its defense. Judge Moscowitz had had enough doubts about it that he impaneled clergy and asked for experts to help him sort things out. The trial jury had held that the pamphlet was obscene. The broad language of the obscenity statute, combined with the widely used Hicklin test, made the obscenity laws tough to escape if one was dealing with sexually frank materials, even "scientific" ones. Plus, the federal courts had not really admitted to any fundamental problem with the federal obscenity statute in fifty years, and Congress had enhanced Customs' censorship authority in 1922, so there were not good precedents to draw on and expand.

Treating Dennett's most legally vulnerable passages would require some delicacy. Newman Levy, another Greenbaum, Wolff & Ernst associate who was regularly involved in their obscenity cases, pushed Lindey to think through these issues for their appeal brief.[89] They agreed that the main grounds for appeal would be the extensive expert testimony that Judge Burrows had refused to hear, along with his refusal to even consider comparable sex education manuals printed by New York State and the federal government as potentially exculpatory evidence.[90] But Levy and Lindey puzzled over the question of whether or not their brief could or should aggressively defend Dennett's stance toward masturbation and the pleasures of intercourse. Should they dance around these topics? Not addressing the issue head on would be disingenuous and evasive, Levy warned, whereas Lindey thought calling the court's attention to those particular sections of the pamphlet could be dangerous, especially when the strength of their appeal lay in the trial judge's errors in denying direct testimony about the pamphlet's long use by reputable organizations. Lindey told Ernst that he found Levy's suggestion risky: "We will find it very difficult to justify Mrs. Dennett's attitude [and] our decision to do so will be suicidal." Yet he agreed with Levy that they should not "completely dodge the two points" by maintaining "this smoke screen to the end."[91]

Lindey and Ernst ultimately opted for caution in their appellate brief. They did not address the offending passages head on, essentially diverting attention from them by focusing instead on the overall respectability of Dennett's pamphlet. They kept their eyes on their larger goal: combating the enforcement of the overly broad and definitionally capacious obscenity statute that gave federal Postal authorities such wide latitude. Treading carefully, Ernst and Lindey barely treated the troublesome elements of Dennett's pamphlet.

Ernst and Lindey's appellate brief repudiated the jury's verdict, complained of the lower court's treatment of evidence, and offered a forceful critique of the U.S. obscenity statute. The law was the problem, they argued, as it lacked the specific "bright line" tests that ought to make it utterly clear to writers, publishers, artists, and others, as well as judges and juries, what was and was not conclusively obscene. This problem of vagueness as a basis for censorship and especially for criminal laws resulting in steep fines, loss of livelihood, or incarceration had clear implications for due process, free speech, and democratic life. Lindey, who wrote the appellate brief, reiterated the problem of vagueness that plagued obscenity law in an in-house memo, titled "Guessing Oneself into Jail," explaining how the law's imprecision violated basic due process standards. In criminal law (especially), there must be a standard of conduct that is possible to know as crossing the line into criminality. "If definiteness is essential to law in general, it is doubly so to criminal law; it should be made impossible for a man to guess

himself into jail."[92] This "guessing oneself into jail" as a due process problem emerged as a core argument in Ernst and Lindey's developing critique
of U.S. obscenity laws.[93]

The appellate brief, submitted in September 1929, had three core arguments. First, Ernst and Lindey's central claim was that the pamphlet was
not obscene as a matter of law. They reinforced this argument by raising
a series of points about the changing standards of morality and how community standards are the best measure of social mores and by giving evidence of their client's intention to meet community needs. Second, they
asserted that the district court improperly excluded evidence of Dennett's
motivations and of the pamphlet's positive reception. Evidence about the
actual use and distribution of the pamphlet would have proved the work's
value. They devoted the bulk of the brief to this second part, enumerat-
ing the appealable errors committed by the lower court. Third, they introduced a new constitutional argument, asserting that the federal obscenity
statute violated the First Amendment and was thus unconstitutional. The
First Amendment overrode the obscenity law, and by forcing defendants
to guess themselves into jail, the statute also violated constitutional guarantees of due process under the law.

As in the trial court, Ernst and Lindey tried to narrow considerably what
was meant or commonly understood by the word *obscenity* and argued that
The Sex Side of Life did not fall within those commonly understood meanings.
They argued in their brief that the "essence of the crime [of obscenity] is
sexual impurity, not sex itself." Dennett's text was not impure, did not lead
to impurity, and did not "pander to the prurient taste," so it did not fall
within the meaning of the statute. In addition, they rebutted the government's claims about the cultural and moral chaos the pamphlet would let
loose, reassuring the appeals court judges that Dennett was highly respectful of marriage, idealistic about married love, cautious about sex instruction, and diligent about offering appropriate warnings about the dangers
of promiscuity, venereal disease, and prostitution.[94] Dennett's work neither
ignored nor minimized the perils of sex, Lindey wrote, and she dutifully
warned her readers that the "sex machinery is delicate," giving her readers
"earnest counsel against permitting filth of speech or mind."[95]

Ernst and Lindey made a strong community standards argument for defining what is, or is not, obscene in a given moment. Community standards were the best evidence for determining the respectability or obscenity of materials, and those standards were best measured by the attitudes and values of the serious adult members of that community. Dennett's work was highly valued among doctors, educators, and public health officials as an educational resource. Its value could be easily ascertained. It was implausible to think that "all of the distinguished champions of the defendant, representing every element of the community, could have been wrong."[96]

Their community standards argument took direct aim at the Hicklin obscenity test and its operative assumptions about protecting the most vulnerable members of the community from corruption. The prosecutor and judge had relied "repeatedly—and erroneously" on the Hicklin standard, Ernst and Lindey asserted, arguing that recent progress in obscenity law cases had revealed a steady narrowing of the Hicklin test's reach. They referred to Judge Learned Hand's dicta in the 1913 *Kennerley* case, which articulated the idea that there was no fixed, timeless definition of what constituted obscenity or decency and that the law did not intend to keep all manner of sexually related matters from all audiences. Ernst and Lindey's brief similarly averred that the "test of obscenity is a living standard. Any publication must be judged by the mores of the day."[97]

What constituted the obscene, the lewd, and the lascivious had changed considerably in the five decades after the Comstock law.[98] Ernst and his colleagues had tried to provide extensive testimonial evidence to the trial court to show that Dennett's pamphlet fell well within the mores of its time and met important community needs. The trial court had clearly erred in excluding this evidence. "If allowed, the testimony would have enabled the jury to estimate with reasonable certainty—not to speculate at random" as to "the persons into whose hands the book was likely to fall."[99] It certainly would have showed that those agencies that purchased it did not worry that it would "deprave and corrupt" those young people they gave it to for instruction.

The issue of distribution was inherent in every definition of obscenity, Ernst and Lindey argued, and they could have easily demonstrated the "mode of circulation" of this pamphlet.[100] YMCA leaders, parents, Union Theological Seminary faculty members, instructors affiliated with Columbia University's Seth Low Junior College, and other respectable organizations that disseminated the pamphlet showed the moral standards of the community of its primary users. Distilling Judge Hand's framework, Ernst and Lindey argued that "community morality . . . may be summed up as follows: *That which society accepts is moral: that which it rejects is immoral.*"[101]

The obverse was true is well—"that which society condemns is driven to cover, and compelled to flow through devious subterranean channels. Witness the customary course of pornography. Salacious pictures and literature travel the paths of secrecy and stealth. They are purveyed surreptitiously, under counters, in back alleys, behind closed doors, by ratty individuals."[102] Dennett's pamphlet did not fall into that category of subterranean, surreptitious, or stealth. It offered an "honest presentation of sex facts," was firmly planted in an educational mission, and was entirely distinct from the pornography that circulated in black market channels.[103] Distinguished educators and attentive parents had widely and publicly used the pamphlet for fourteen years. There was nothing surreptitious about it.

Pursuing another line, Ernst and Lindey argued that the U.S. Supreme Court had narrowed the definition to those materials that expressly intended to produce sexual arousal and immorality, claiming that in the *Swearingen* decision (1896) the Court had held that something was not obscene (or lewd or lascivious) unless it intended to produce sexual immorality or impurity.[104] To be obscene, a work *had to be calculated* to produce such outcomes as impurity, immorality, or lust. Intention mattered, and so did the nature of the content: "The essence of the crime is sexual impurity, not sex itself," they wrote, "and the matter charged must be naturally calculated to create sexually impure thoughts."[105]

The lower court also erred, Ernst and Lindey argued in their appellate brief, in excluding evidence about comparable publications issued by the U.S. Public Health Service and the New York State Health Department. The defense could have shown that Dennett's work was very much in concert with government agencies (federal and state) working on the same important topic.[106] Their point was tough to repudiate: "It is utterly inconceivable that any sane government would, on the one hand, prohibit the publication of certain materials, and on the other hand, become an active disseminator thereof on its own account."[107]

In the brief's final section, Ernst and Lindey tried to push a constitutional argument. This argument seems more experimental and not fully developed, but it pushed free speech claims they had not made in the trial court. As Weinrib explains, their brief argued that obscenity law gave more power to Postal officials than the Postal powers that had been defined in the Constitution, and so it violated the First Amendment.[108] They "did not merely suggest that the statute fell outside the federal power to control the post roads under Article I, Section 8 of the Constitution" but that "it flatly contravened the First Amendment to the Constitution of the United States."[109] Their claim that the obscenity statute violated the First Amendment to the U.S. Constitution would recur in their future obscenity cases, but the federal courts, still at least two decades away from being willing to hear this line of argument, kept batting those First Amendment arguments away. This final point about the statute's unconstitutionality because of First Amendment protections was linked with Ernst and Lindey's due process argument about standards of proof and statutory vagueness and the need for defendants (or potential defendants) to have a clear understanding (an "unequivocal warning") of what was or was not legal in criminal law.[110]

In bringing their brief to a close, Lindey and Ernst argued that the case had two hugely significant issues. The first had to do with the obscenity statute—its vagueness—which, combined with enormous Postal and Customs authority, threatened freedom of the press. "By reason of its vagueness," they wrote, obscenity law could be abused and "perverted to uses for which it was never intended."[111] The other overarching issue had to do with young people and the larger social interest in their sex education. If the Mary Ware Dennett conviction stood, they argued, "incalculable harm will result. The outcome will mark a further invasion of constitutional liberties. It will run counter to all the previous rational interpretations of the obscenity statute. . . . It will deal a disastrous blow to the cause of sex education."[112] Those harms would be far more grievous than the putative harms asserted by the prosecution, because the value of Dennett's work was fully evident, its value reinforced by the fact that U.S. government agencies were also addressing these same public needs for rational sex education. If the government defeated its own public health initiatives and succeeded in its prosecution, the nation's youth would be left to learn about the facts of life from a far more invidious gutter than the one Wilkinson imagined: "Children seeking information will once more be forced to turn to the streets and the walls of latrines, to fragments of conversation not intended for their ears, to eavesdropping and guessing, to corrupt companions."[113]

The Justice Department, meanwhile, did not doubt the constitutionality of the obscenity statute, and "clear precedent seemed to be on their side," as Craig writes. The extensive power exercised by Postal authorities to censor the mails rested on two landmark cases, *Ex parte Jackson* (1878) and *United States v. Bennett* (1879). In the former, which was not an obscenity case, the U.S. Supreme Court ruled that the First Amendment did not apply to the mails. In *Bennett*, decided fifty years before the *Dennett* case, the court of appeals upheld the Comstock Act and expressly embraced the Hicklin standard as the test for obscenity, "something the Comstock statute of 1873 had failed to do," Craig continues. So with the *Bennett* decision, the Hicklin rule became the recognized test of obscenity used in American courts. In the Dennett appeal, Assistant U.S. Attorney Herbert Kellogg "relied on the Hicklin rule, noting simply that the pamphlet in question was, indeed, 'lewd and lascivious'" and that "*The Sex Side of Life* had failed the long-recognized test of obscenity."[114]

Victory in the U.S. Court of Appeals

In March 1930 the U.S. Court of Appeals for the Second Circuit handed down a unanimous decision, written by Judge Augustus Hand (cousin of Learned Hand) and signed by Judges Thomas W. Swan and Harrie B. Chase. The brief decision accepted Ernst and Lindey's arguments that Dennett's pamphlet was not obscene and reversed her conviction. The court did not accept Ernst and Lindey's two claims of unconstitutionality—that the Comstock Act violated First Amendment protections and that it gave excessive power to Postal authorities. It did not accept challenges raised by Ernst about Dennett's personal motives and also held it was "perhaps proper to exclude the evidence . . . as to the persons to whom the pamphlet was sold."[115] But it did modify the usual application of the Hicklin standard in which even sober, factual materials were held obscene because of fears that the most vulnerable readers would be corrupted. The court accepted Ernst and Lindey's argument that those key words in the Comstock Act—"obscene, lewd, or lascivious"—could not be applied to Dennett's serious pamphlet and that the pamphlet did not cause "sexual impurity." Judge Hand wrote, "Any incidental tendency to arouse sex impulses which such a pamphlet may perhaps have, is apart from and subordinate to its main effect. The tendency can only exist in so far as it is inherent in any sex instruction and it would seem to be outweighed by the elimination of ignorance, curiosity, and morbid fear. The direct aim and the net result is to promote understanding and self-control."[116] So, although Ernst and colleagues did not persuade the court on all their claims, the court recognized that Dennett's pamphlet was not obscene and reversed her conviction.

This was a landmark decision in obscenity law jurisprudence. *United States v. Dennett* (39 F.2d 564 (1930)) reverberated in the courts for decades because of its rich language about society's interest in sober, dignified information about sexuality as a matter of abiding interest to all humans. The decision would prove of immense value to Ernst, Lindey, and their firm in subsequent federal court cases as they continued their battles over the importation, publication, and distribution of serious, respectable materials that dealt with peoples' interests in sexuality, marital sex, contraception, maternal health, and artistic expression. The court held that "an accurate exposition of the relevant facts of the sex side of life in decent language and in manifestly serious and disinterested spirit cannot ordinarily be regarded as obscene."[117] Decent sex education was, the appellate judges asserted, a matter of both common sense and social importance and should not be a discussion barred or banned simply because some people might be aroused by discussions of sex. It effectively diminished the reach of the Hicklin standard, even if it upheld the constitutionality of the Comstock Act.

By embracing the Hicklin obscenity test in *United States v. Bennett*, the courts had held for fifty years that a work could be judged obscene on the basis of a single passage that would corrupt the youth, the most susceptible of audiences. But in the case of Mary Ware Dennett the opinion was "more permissive," Weinrib writes, with the court holding that "a work must be judged in its entirety; an explicit passage in a truthful and socially constructive sex education pamphlet would not render the whole work obscene."[118] This notion that a work should not be found obscene based on isolated passages and should be judged in its entirety would be especially influential in subsequent cases with respect to literary works and would also be used to argue for the protection of adult interests in sexual materials.

According to Laura Weinrib, because the decision was "a matter of statutory authority" and was "modest in its reasoning," it "left the Comstock Act more or less intact."[119] But still, the decision was a victory for Dennett and Ernst beyond reversing her conviction and limiting the sweeping application of the Hicklin test. It also achieved an outcome Dennett had been aiming at for nearly a decade: It meant that judges would not automatically defer to decisions made by Postal officials and that those texts or artifacts libeled as obscene would receive closer examination by judges. This served as a useful precedent not just for challenging Postal officials' decisions but Customs officials' decisions as well.

Another significant feature of the decision was that it challenged the operative assumption that sexual information was necessarily "destructive of social values."[120] Indeed, such materials could be quite valuable in serving the public good. These ideas—that the public could be served by sober, dignified materials and that the public had a legitimate interest in matters related to sex and sexuality—would also give Ernst and Lindey key phrases in their subsequent defenses of other kinds of serious, high-minded sexual materials. Judge Hand's language and the court's unanimous decision provided considerable leverage as a landmark ruling from the nation's most influential appellate court.[121]

The court essentially adopted Ernst and Lindey's threat-of-the-gutter argument, holding that it would hardly be reasonable to think "that the risk of imparting instruction outweighs the disadvantages of leaving [the young] to grope about in mystery and morbid curiosity." The court's key words were *reasonable, clearly indecent,* and *accuracy.* "Like everything else," the court held, "this law must be construed reasonably with a view to the general objects aimed at. While there can be no doubt about its constitutionality, it must not be assumed to have been designed to interfere with serious instruction regarding sex matters unless the terms in which the information is conveyed *are clearly indecent*."[122] This test of whether an object was "clearly indecent" was a significant modulation in obscenity law jurisprudence that would resound in the next decades as the nation's courts sought to find language that could both accommodate *high-minded*, legitimate interests in sexual matters and fend off the vulgar, course, and prurient materials whose primary aim was arousal and purposes (or outcomes) that were *clearly indecent*.

Turning to the specifics of Dennett's pamphlet, the court showed a judicious willingness to parse those differences, between highbrow and lowbrow materials and between demonstrable values and putative harms. The court wrote that the pamphlet tended to "rationalize and dignify" sexuality rather than to "arouse lust," and even though "it may be thought by some that portions of the tract go into unnecessary details that would better have been omitted, it may be fairly answered that the curiosity of many adolescents would not be satisfied without full explanation, and that no more than that is really given." It also asserted that "accurate information" "is better in the long run and is less likely to occasion lascivious thoughts than ignorance and anxiety."[123] In short, society ought to accept the risk of a little arousal in the interest of greater factual knowledge. This framework came to be labeled the "dominant theme" requirement.

Inspired by Victory

Dennett's case galvanized Ernst and his firm's commitment to anti-censorship aims. This was their first significant opportunity to begin their attack on federal obscenity law and its administration by Postal authorities. It also gave them considerable publicity that helped mobilize public opinion against obscenity-law-based censorship practices more generally.

It has been noted that as a result of the case U.S. journalists became more attentive to the problem of the obscenity laws as instruments of censorship and better understood how those laws contradicted free speech ideals. Coverage of Dennett's trial became "intimately linked to changes in journalism, especially greater public acceptance of sex in popular culture and a growing belief in the value of public opinion."[124] Relatedly, Dennett was certainly aware of the role of the press in reflecting and arousing public opinion during her trial. Ernst's allies in this and future cases, especially Roy Howard of the Scripps-Howard chain and Lewis Gannett of the *New York Herald Tribune*, railed against prosecution and understood that obscenity-law-based censorship was their battle too, especially given growing public interest in sexual expression and information. An editorial from the *New York World* hailed the circuit court's decision as "manifestly of the first importance" and celebrated the reversal of Dennett's conviction as "a denial of the archaic idea on which this prosecution rested and which threatened free thought so seriously."[125]

Scholars suggest that the public pressure manufactured by the ACLU, particularly by its Mary Ware Dennett Defense Committee, helped shape public opinion surrounding this case and transformed public understanding over time that sexual censorship had civil liberties implications.[126] The ACLU described the decision as "an outstanding victory for free speech," using the same implicit First Amendment framing that Ernst employed during and subsequent to the decision.[127] Even if the court did not render its decision on First Amendment grounds, Ernst and his allies still argued that obscenity laws violated free speech principles, and the *Dennett* decision advanced the free speech cause.

Other leading civil libertarians came to agree with Ernst and Lindey that challenging obscenity laws through litigation was a winning approach and might result in other "test cases of vital importance," as Ernst described the *Dennett* case. When Ernst and Lindey took their challenges against obscenity laws into New York City, state, and federal courts, they had the backing of the ACLU's leadership and its promotional apparatus.

Ernst and Lindey were leaders in helping direct the ACLU's internal efforts to focus on censorship policies and to produce a more coordinated anti-censorship agenda. Almost immediately after the case the ACLU transformed the Mary Ware Dennett Defense Committee into a more "permanent" entity, the National Committee on Freedom from Censorship (NCFC).[128] Over the next decade the NCFC would play a key role in managing the ACLU's policies and publicity on a whole host of censor-ship issues—from film, theater, books, schools, and radio to policies around Nazi and communist speech.

The *Dennett* case had other implications too. Ernst proved a deft court-room performer and publicist, and the *Dennett* case helped him earn his reputation as a leading free speech champion and a savvy battler against nineteenth-century Comstockery and its twentieth-century avatars. From U.S. Attorney Wilkinson to Postal and Customs officials, to New York City's Vice Society officials, Ernst knew how to play them in the press as antimodern or antidemocratic foils and himself as the guardian of "sex enlightenment." But he was successful in the courtroom too, and this earned him and his firm a roster of influential clients who were dogged by the censorship laws.

Because the courts, prosecutors, theologians, and other public-minded people did have legitimate concerns about the profusion of indecent ma-terials circulating in the streets, on stages, and in the mails, Ernst and his team would have plenty of fights on their hands. The cultural guardians' refusal to cede public morality to marketers of sexuality meant that there would be many legal battles over obscenity laws to come. Legal challenges to the nation's obscenity laws would be slow and complicated, with plenty of setbacks along the way. Ernst, Lindey, and others would have to play it slowly, carefully pushing the courts to find language that could effectively balance the need for social decency with growing recognition of legitimate public interests in sexual materials.

The late 1920s and early 1930s would prove to be a moment of con-siderable social and legal conflict over these competing needs for moral norms and public interest in sex. Ernst and his firm would be at the center of those conflicts, including a series of cases that were nearly simultaneous with their defense of Dennett, including the defense of Margaret Sanger's birth control clinic, of British novelist Radclyffe Hall's *The Well of Loneli-ness*, and of the famous British birth control activist and sexologist Marie Stopes, whom Mary Ware Dennett sent their way.

CHAPTER 3

WOMEN'S RIGHT TO SEXUAL PLEASURE

Marie Stopes Versus Customs Authority

FOLLOWING THEIR 1930 VICTORY against Postal officials in the *Dennett* case, Morris Ernst and Alexander Lindey wanted to challenge the vast authority that Congress gave to U.S. Customs officials in the 1873 Obscenity Act. Customs enjoyed an administrative censorship reach akin to what Dennett described as the "unchecked postal power" they had just battled. The attorneys also hoped to keep their momentum. As Lindey wrote to Ernst shortly after the *Dennett* decision, "I am feeling fine and ready for work. I look forward with a great deal of gusto to a whole raft of obscenity cases."[1] Recent congressional reform to the Tariff Act of 1930 potentially gave Ernst an angle, as new provisions in the tariff law finally gave libellants (those whose works had been libeled obscene by Customs) the right to challenge a Customs decision in the federal courts.

Ernst's firm's interests coincided with those of Marie Stopes, a well-known British sexologist and birth control activist whose works had been denied entry into the United States by Customs bans since 1922. Dennett and Stopes knew each other from their mutual work in birth control, and Dennett knew that Stopes was having problems with a pirated edition of her most popular and famous book, *Married Love* (1918), so she encouraged Stopes to contact Ernst.[2] Unlike Dennett, who was not motivated by profit, Stopes had much to gain financially by stopping the piracy of *Married Love* in the United States; by 1930 the book was in its eighteenth edition and had sold over 750,000 copies in the United Kingdom. Ernst and Lindey were only minimally interested in the piracy problem. It was complicated and distracted from their main goal of dismantling federal censorship laws. They were far more interested in challenging the Customs ban on *Married Love* so that Stopes could compete in the U.S. market with a legal and authorized edition. Ernst and Lindey convinced Stopes and her British publisher, G. P. Putnam's, that she could tap the rich market opportunities in the United States only if they could get the 1922 Customs ban lifted.[3] They were confident that the *Dennett* decision gave them a potentially expansive precedent, especially in concert with the newly amended Section 305 of the Tariff Act, which permitted challenges to Customs Court rulings. Ernst believed that Stopes's case could advance the cause of what he called sex rationality and would augment the premises of the free speech ideal by protecting sexually oriented materials. As Ernst told Stopes, "In my opinion, the entire cause of freedom of thought and the spread of decent sex education will be helped by contesting the ban at Customs."[4]

The law firm's representation of Marie Stopes simultaneously deepened their commitment to feminist causes and an expanded marketplace of ideas about sexuality and its complexities. In promoting Stopes's work against censorship, Ernst and Lindey expressly defended women's needs for and right to sexual pleasure in marriage as a matter of marital health and human happiness.

Marie Stopes, the "Virgin Wife"

Born in 1880 to well-educated and intellectual parents, Marie Carmichael Stopes often remarked that she was "a child of the British Association for the Advancement of Science," because her mother, Charlotte Carmichael, and father, Henry Stopes, met at a BAAS meeting in Glasgow, Scotland. Stopes's parents introduced her to serious intellectual conversation about Darwinian evolution and the natural sciences, nurtured by fossil-hunting expeditions with her father and also by their associations with leading scientists of the era. From early on in her life, she moved in a world where scientific inquiry and evidence were the route to truth.[5]

Stopes came by her feminist credentials naturally. Her mother set a strong example of intellectual inquiry as an activist on behalf of women's political equality. June Rose writes that Stopes gained "the confidence and freedom to take women's emancipation for granted" from her mother's example, describing her as a "second generation emancipated woman" who developed the determination "to prove herself as a woman and to change women's lives too."[6] At her all-girl boarding school Stopes came under the tutelage of Dr. Sophie Bryant, who had taken a science degree (in chemistry) at London University and encouraged Stopes's interests in the sciences. When Stopes matriculated to University College, London, she studied botany, geology, and zoology (at Birbeck College). She became president of the Debating Society and completed her degree early with first-class honors in botany and third-class honors in geology. This record earned her a scholarship at the Botanical Institute in Munich, where she completed the first of her two doctorates and was the only woman among 500 men.[7]

A talented, prolific young paleontologist, Stopes quickly gained an international reputation, traveling widely to deliver lectures and to conduct research.[8] Not only was she the first woman at Munich University to take a doctorate in botany with honors, but she also completed her doctorate with distinction, in German. She also became the first woman appointed to the botany faculty at Manchester University in England. She taught there and also earned a doctorate from Manchester in 1905, in the new field of paleobotany, becoming the youngest person in the country at the time with a doctorate in science.

In 1911, at the age of 31, Stopes met and quickly married a Canadian scientist, Reginald Ruggles Gates. Stopes and Gates married after a whirlwind romance, barely getting to know one another, and they proved a mismatch. Stopes worked and wrote all the time—and not just scientific works but also plays and novels—and soon began digging into the available literature on sexology, physiology, and the legal issues surrounding marriage. She hated housework, expected Gates to help out on the domestic front, and, against convention, kept her own name because she had already made a professional reputation and was more successful professionally than her husband. A modern woman in every way, she also became increasingly involved in the woman's suffrage movement in England.

More important for Stopes—for this story and for the history of sex education and the birth control movement in Britain—their sex life was a "complete flop." According to Rose's biography of Stopes, "Despite the kisses and embraces and the great hopes and excitement of both of them when they first married . . . Ruggles could not satisfy Marie as a lover."[9] They fought bitterly. She grew bored with him and fifteen months into their marriage began giving her emotional attention to Aylmer Maude, a married man twenty-two years older who was distinguished, masculine, literary, and well connected. They enjoyed not just an innuendo-filled flirtation in their letters but physical proximity as well. Because he was short on money and estranged from his wife, who wanted a platonic marriage, Maude wound up renting a room in the already unhappy Gates-Stopes household.

"The basic trouble," Marie told her lawyers when she consulted them about getting her marriage nullified, "was that Gates indulged in foreplay for hours but could not get a real erection, leaving Marie feeling drained and unsatisfied."[10] The lawyers advised her that an annulment would be difficult to obtain and that grounds for divorce would be difficult to obtain too, essentially requiring an admission of adultery. Gates would make no such admission, nor would Stopes. Ever the scholar, she turned to the restricted access section of the British Museum, known as "the cupboard," where she read "voraciously almost every learned treatise and medical account of sexual theory and practice in English, French, and German."[11] She also learned from poring over innumerable legal tomes that the "non-consummation of marriage" would give her grounds for seeking divorce. Stopes thus used the complaint of her husband's impotence to get out of her marriage. Her claim, that after three years of marriage she remained a "virgin wife," was enough to end the marriage legally. It was also eventually part of the publicity she used to promote *Married Love*.

This began a pattern that would recur at other points in Stopes's life: "She used her own life as the raw material to wreak change in social attitudes with startling courage and with equally startling indifference to other people's feelings."[12] Gates was humiliated by Stopes's claims of his impotence, and after the annulment he even went to a physician who examined him and gave him a certificate of "perfect normality." He also described Stopes as being "super-sexed to a degree which was almost pathological."[13] Stopes, on the other hand, came away from their battles somewhat antagonistic to the confines and restrictions of marriage and certainly to the traditional understanding that women's sexual satisfaction in marriage did not matter and that women's "duty" to their husbands was expected. Out of the marriage to Gates, she channeled her energies into women's issues, including becoming more involved in the women's suffrage movement, advocating for women's tax resistance, and taking part in protest marches, where she had garbage and horse dung flung at her.

Stopes also dug further into the literature on sexology and began discussing with other women (mostly suffragists) the nature of their sexual drives, their frustrations, cycles of arousal, and other data that would make its way into her eventual book. She likewise began taking notes on her own sensations of arousal, desire, and sensitivity, titled "Tabulation of Symptom of Sexual Excitement in Solitude." She discussed her ideas with Aylmer Maude and seems to have learned from him techniques men could use to delay ejaculation; in a long section in *Married Love* she described a male sexual "continence" technique (called Karezza) particularly useful for older men.

Stopes began this project on women's drives and pleasures in 1915. She sent an early manuscript to many readers, including the well-known English sexologist Edward Carpenter, author most famously of *The Intermediate Sex*, who sat down with her and went through the manuscript page by page. "His mystical glorifications of sex appealed to Marie's romantic instincts," Rose writes.[14] Stopes accumulated more data and began giving lectures on the subject of women's sex drives. She was appalled by what she saw as the medical profession's ignorance on the subject, reporting that a London gynecologist had blandly assured her "that normal women do not have orgasms, even in coitus."[15] Stopes told her audiences that it was not women's inability to have orgasms but their socialization. They had been long trained "to be reticent and guilty about their sexual instincts." She asserted that women's sexuality was as powerful and important as men's.[16]

When Stopes began looking for a publisher for her evolving manuscript, one firm, Blackie and Son, rejected it as too prurient. Others found the manuscript similarly shocking and were fearful that it would be charged as obscene, and under British law the publishers themselves would be subject to criminal penalties. Fortunately for Stopes, several members of the Malthusian League, a birth-control-focused organization, thought the manuscript was promising. One member sent the manuscript to a wealthy young Manchester industrialist, Humphrey Roe, who was interested in promoting women's issues, especially birth control for poor women. When he read the book, he agreed to finance its publication with a small publishing house, Fifield. When Roe and Stopes met face to face to discuss the details of his support, something else happened: They began a courtship.

Initially published in 1918 under the title *Married Love*, the book was immediately a runaway success, and so was Stopes and Roe's courtship. The small publisher was overwhelmed by the sales and was shortly thereafter even more swamped by public interest in the birth control tracts Stopes was also writing. By 1920 the much larger firm G. P. Putnam's had taken over Stopes's publishing interests, and birth control matters became her primary focus.

Residual Victorian Assumptions

Married Love sharply challenged residual Victorian values about sexuality as something to be ashamed of or silent about, assumptions about married women's presumed asexuality, and expectations that they fulfill their "marital duties" without consideration of their own sexual desires or pleasures. To a large extent Stopes was arguing against the constructions of womanhood with which she came of age and which still shaped the values and expectations of her social class, in which proper young women did not think much about sex and were raised to endure it more than enjoy it. From the mid- to the late nineteenth century, in response to industrialization, urbanization, and suffrage activities, a powerful cluster of ideas rearticulated and heightened the emphasis on women's family duties, the importance of their religious and sexual purity, and the centrality of marriage as the most important institution in Anglo-American middle-class societies. Known as the true womanhood ideology, its precepts were re-inforced by the influential institutions in the lives of middle-class families, including churches (especially Protestant ones), schools, medicine, and a burgeoning popular literature of manuals, magazines, and "domestic" novels written for women that provided instruction about women's duties in their private spheres of influence.

The ideal of sexual purity functioned as a form of self-discipline and was reinforced by the internalized fears of sin and public shame and dishonor. The assumption that women were asexual undergirded the purity discourse, and the fear of sexual weakness as sinful served as a prophylactic against premarital and extramarital affairs. The vast silences around female sexual desire contained women as sexual beings and also buttressed enforcement of the obscenity statutes in the United States. When materials that might unleash women's "unnatural" sexual desires circulated, the purity discourse was ever at the ready to remind women and men about what was natural and unnatural, sinful, and threatening to the family. These ideological un-derpinnings also had scientific and medical reinforcement, rooted in deeply held assumptions that reproduction was essential to fulfilling a woman's biological destiny. Within this framework anything that interfered with re-production was unnatural, and a woman's failure to reproduce was a sign of her shortcomings, biological and moral. In the mid-nineteenth century these arguments were particularly powerful to the all-male legislators in Congress who overwhelmingly passed the Comstock Act.[17]

Married Love: Sex as Mutual Pleasure and Desire

Marie Stopes built *Married Love* around two central ideas: that both men and women want and need sexual pleasure and that married happiness is built on the satisfaction of those mutual interests. She wanted married sex to be good sex for her readers, male and female, and in fact dedicated her book to young husbands. Stopes, who tells readers that she did not have any satisfying experience with marital sex, begins the book with what was apparently a common experience among couples: high hopes before the wedding and quickly dashed promises after the honeymoon.

Stopes idealized the power of sex as a force for deep marital happiness and the union of souls. Beginning with the chapter "The Heart's Desire," she asserts that all of us share the instinct to find a lifetime mate and union with another soul and have hopes for "the perfecting of oneself which such union brings" (*Married Love*, 4). Although driven by these deep spiritual needs, humans cannot escape their fundamental physicality and thus the desire for physical union. To explain both the physical and the spiritual desire for connection and sexual release, Stopes used physical chemistry metaphors: "One might compare two human beings to two bodies charged with electricity of different potentials. Isolated from each other the electric forces within them are invisible, but if they come into the right juxtaposition the force is transmuted, and a spark, a glow of burning light arises between them" (9).

From this ideal of the union of hearts, souls, and bodies, Stopes turns to "The Broken Joy," the inexorable disappointments that descend so quickly in many marriages. The sexual honeymoon is short, she argues, largely because the newly married know so little about one another as sexual beings and because the sexual differences that were the source of attraction become their undoing. Prohibitions on premarital sex and ignorance of basic physical and emotional differences between men and women made most couples unprepared for the "fundamental and vital problems of Sex" that emerge in a marriage (*Married Love*, 11). These problems are a result of cultural patterns and habits that lead to individual reticence and fear, of people not having a language to discuss these matters, and of an absence of cultural traditions for imparting this knowledge. Women especially enter marriage not knowing much about their own sexuality, or about men's. And men somewhat brutishly assume that their marital "rights" are to be consummated whether or not their wife is interested. This is the fundamental difference around which the gap begins to grow. Of the two, the woman is eventually "more profoundly wounded, with a slow corrosive wound that eats into her very being and warps all her life" (13).

Individuals and couples must therefore study the "Art of Love," especially because the sped-up conditions of modern life magnify the problem of couples not having enough time for "peaceful, romantic dalliances," for

leisure in the "woods and gardens where the pulling of rosemary or laven-
der may be the sweet excuse for the slow and profound mutual rousing of
passion" (*Married Love*, 17). A research scientist and naturalist by training, Dr. Stopes offered her readers evidence about women's physiology to
show a way out of these marital sexual woes. Women, like men, also have
periods of peak sexual desire, and they too are subject to the ineluctable
laws of nature that shape all species' patterns of behavior. Her data helped
her explain that the ebbs and flows of women's sexual desire are not a result of female whimsy, as cultural explanations suggested, but are "set to
rhythms" over which humans have "no more control than [they have] over
the tides of the sea" (25). The problem is that men and women themselves
are only "dimly half-consciously" aware of the natural laws of female desire
(26). The legal and cultural traditions of protecting men's "conjugal rights"
are based entirely on his more self-evident desires and strengthen the belief "that he has the right to approach his wife whenever he wishes, and
that she has no wishes and no fundamental needs in the matter at all" (33).
These cultural norms sanctioned imbalance in marriages, and ignorance of
the "natural laws" of female desire kept marital sex fraught and marriages
unhappy. Attentiveness offered the remedy, Stopes argued. Attentive men
could find those subtle expressions of desire lurking behind the elaborate
cultural performance of female virtue, especially if they notice what she
called women's "Periodicity of Recurrence of desire."

As in men, female desire is also a powerful "*creative* impulse" and an
"expression of a high power of vitality." All the taboos, however, proscribe
broader understanding of how deep these desires can be: "So widespread
in our country is the view that it is only depraved women who have such
feelings (especially before marriage) that most women would rather die
than own that they do at times feel a physical yearning indescribable, but
as profound as hunger for food" (*Married Love*, 34). Given these facts of
nature, Stopes counseled her male readers to adapt their behavior and to
pay closer attention, and she advised women to reveal a certain coy sen-
suality and openness to being seduced: "A husband who thus feels himself
successful is far more likely to be willing to modify and adapt his demands"
(47). Arguing thus for a "Mutual Adjustment" that required men to slow

down and women to be more forthright, Stopes exhorted both men and women to eliminate the imbalance in the marital sex patterns.

The "Art of Love" also required greater knowledge of women's bodies. Stopes was quite clinical about sexual organs and their responses. This particular passage almost always caught her critics' attention and no doubt the attention of U.S. censors in 1922 as well:

> After the preliminaries have mutually roused the pair, the stimulated penis, enlarged and stiffened, is pressed into the woman's vagina. But when the woman is what is physiologically called tumescent (that is, when she is ready for union and has been profoundly stirred) local parts are flushed by the internal blood-supply and to some extent are turgid like those of the man, while a secretion of mucus lubricates the opening of the vagina. The walls of the vaginal canal, being ridged with very extensible muscles, readily stretch to receive, and fit the enlarged organ of the man. In an ardent woman the vaginal orifice may even spontaneously contract and relax. (*Married Love*, 59)

Men should know the signs of desire. Rousing women takes time, and most "uninstructed" husbands simply do not give it the time needed or know what to do along the way. Stopes recommended trying various positions to enhance pleasure and induce abandon, especially positions that might result in mutual orgasms. Stopes was particularly frank about the clitoris: "This little crest, which lies anteriorly between the inner lips round the vagina, enlarges when the woman is really tumescent, and by the stimulation of movement it is intensely roused and transmits this stimulus to every nerve in her body" (65). Not only would clitoral stimulation help women achieve the orgasms they deserve, but women, like men, would be much healthier because they would sleep better following their orgasms.

For Stopes, the female orgasm was crucial to women's good health, a fact overlooked by their physicians and cultural assumptions, and its absence explained bad health and bad marriages too. For a married woman "who is thwarted in the natural completion of her sex-functions after they have been directly stimulated," the result would lead not just to sleeplessness but

FIGURE 5. Marie Stopes (1904), scientist, birth control pioneer, and author of *Married Love*.

SOURCE: Wikimedia.

to "embittered sleeplessness," as she called it, along with neurasthenia and resentment (*Married Love*, 73). The remedy was simple: mutual adjustment, mutuality of orgasms, and male knowledge of and attention to female sexual needs. No wonder the book went through so many printings. Stopes's *Married Love* found a vast audience of British women and men who were eager for new instructions about sexuality and marriage. Change was afoot.

The British Public's Response

Married Love came out in March 1918, eight months before the end of World War I, which doubtless explains part of its success. Stopes gave voice to new attitudes toward sex, courtship, and marriage that had been accelerated by the war and its upheavals.[18] Not only had the women's suffrage movement finally won political enfranchisement for women (although limited to property owners, or "householders," the wives of householders, and women over 30), but World War I had transformed women's roles in many other ways. "Because of labour shortages, women had been given a chance to prove their ability to take on 'men's jobs,' working not only as doctors, nurses, landgirls [farm workers] and civil servants, but also as plumbers, bus conductors, van drivers and factory hands and, latterly in the newly-formed Women's Corps of the armed services." The war had transformed dating and courtship practices too. The wartime upheavals created more opportunities for and acceptability of premarital (and casual) sex. As Rose explains, "Sex between a girl-friend and a soldier on leave from the Front became, if not acceptable, widespread." Moreover, the fear of venereal disease, a product of the wartime publicity about the problem, heightened the expectations for better sexual relations within marriage when those soldiers returned home.[19]

Written from a woman's point of view, about women's sexuality, by a scientist with two doctorates, *Married Love* had immediate credibility. In addition, Stopes's tone, her idealization of romantic love, and her hopes for the union of souls in marriage reassured readers. "Marie was so abundantly feminine, so confident in her own womanhood, so conscious of her feminist pedigree that her tone was exactly right for her time."[20]

Ideas about sex were circulating in the intellectual atmosphere and in the larger culture. Freud was popular, and so were Edward Carpenter and Havelock Ellis, who have been described as "the most important sexologists in the late nineteenth and early twentieth century."[21] All helped open up the subject of sex and made it more acceptable to think about and discuss. Here Stopes had a great advantage, because compared to Ellis, Carpenter, and Freud, all of whom dealt with homosexuality, pathologies, and repression, Stopes wrote for "healthy young men and women and was a celebration of sex."[22] She also took somewhat familiar ideas from the late Victorian and Edwardian eras and updated them for her readers. As Alexander Geppert writes, "*Married Love* synthesized a poetical-romantic attitude toward love with a new scientific view of sex, and successfully popularized this flowery amalgam of 'poetry' and 'science'—precisely what a reviewer expressed by praising it as a 'thrilling combination of very explicit information and sentient idealism.'"[23]

Naturally, Stopes's book met with criticism for raising such topics. Reviewers warned that it would potentially lead to masturbation and other lustful behaviors. One complained that Stopes was "encouraging stimulants to passion which 'ordinarily do not enter the head of a normal married woman.'"[24] Another reported that copies of her book are read "extensively and secretly in girls' schools and by boys in the same spirit that indecent literature in general is enjoyed" and should be "considered as practical handbooks of prostitution!"[25] Stopes had a built-in legal defense: She could insist "emphatically that the sexual knowledge she had made available was intended only for married couples"; the book's "aura of ultra respectability" gave it credibility as well.[26]

Stopes met with far more favorable responses than critical ones and from across the social ranks. Her "book was read in men's clubs and . . . in women's drawing-rooms"; "grocers in Wales, deckhands on the high seas and women waiting outside pawnshops whispered and gossiped over a shared copy of The Book, wrapped in brown paper."[27] Her readers let her know that *Married Love* had been important to them. Her publisher received hundreds of letters, and Stopes received thousands directly from people who told her that she had helped to remove the shame they had always felt about sex or had given them hope that their married sex lives could improve. Men relied on her expert advice about impotence or premature ejaculation. Women were grateful to learn that they could have orgasms, indeed that it was normal for them to have them, and she offered readers dreams of "ecstatic sexual union safe within the romantic bonds of marriage."[28]

Because Stopes had written two pages about contraception in *Married Love*, she had begun to develop a reputation as a birth control expert. Even though the book was primarily about the art of sex, "the majority of letters asked for advice and help on birth control." Stopes opposed abortion, however, and "almost invariably refused" to provide abortion advice to the "many desperate women who asked for help."[29] Through the thousands of letters she received, Stopes became deeply aware of people's suffering around sex and especially around unwanted pregnancies and women's fear of them. She took up these issues in her next work, *Wise Parenthood* (1919), offering readers a more extended guide to birth control methods and establishing Stopes as Britain's best known birth control advocate and expert.

A Flourishing Marriage Manuals Market in the United States

Although battles around Stopes's birth control advocacy raged in Britain, they simply did not make their way into either the formal legal materials or the discussion about her work in the U.S. case of *Married Love*, suggesting that Ernst and Lindey were wise in strategically stripping the contraceptives issues out of *Married Love* before its adjudication in the United States. Another reason that so little of the controversy from Stopes's life in England followed *Married Love* into the United States owes no doubt to the cooperative, productive relationship between Ernst and Lindey and the U.S. Attorneys who handled the government's eventual prosecution of the book.

But the post–World War I cultural transformations concerning women's public and private sexual lives had also reshaped women's and couples' lives in the United States. By the time her famous marriage manual was adjudicated in the United States—a full twelve years after its original publication—cultural attitudes about women had shifted, and the controversies around gender roles and female sexuality that swirled around the book in England in the late 1910s and early 1920s were not so germane in the United States. There was already a burgeoning marketplace of marriage manuals that essentially reinforced the very ideas Stopes had achieved fame for promoting: that women were sexual beings, that their orgasms mattered too, and that their husbands ought to be attentive to their sexual needs.

As in Britain, World War I had a significant impact on American discussions about sex. The problem of venereal disease was at the forefront of these issues and made it not just feasible but necessary for the government (especially the military) to campaign against venereal disease. But other cultural factors facilitated discussion about and increased public attention to sexuality. Postwar consumerism put sex at the forefront of consciousness. Hollywood movies, popular music, magazines, pulp fiction, and a revved-up advertising industry all sold sex. In addition, greater access to college (and thus more time before marriage), new courtship patterns, the automobile, and an ever-expanding leisure culture put such phrases as "petting" and "inhibitions" into the popular lexicon.[30] All these forces contributed to more widely held ideas that women's roles were changing, that they had a larger role in public life, and that modern marriage should provide for women's pleasure.[31]

As with Stopes's *Married Love*, these marriage manuals also pushed back against older notions that sex was shameful and that the silences around it were a sign of one's respectability. Instead, the manuals suggested that cultural silences had "created barriers to a woman's sexual pleasures."[32] This was very much the sex rationality position that Ernst and Lindey promoted in the courts. The manuals' "overriding concern with the importance of female sexual pleasure and the husband's central role in that pleasure" provides evidence, Jessamyn Neuhas writes, that a new "middle-class view of sexuality" was being constructed in the post–World War I era. It was "middle- and upper-class readers who snapped up published marital sex and contraceptive advice."[33] The most popular of these manuals, Joseph Collins's *A Doctor Looks at Love and Life*, put the onus on husbands to attend to their wives' sexual needs to produce her happiness, which in turn would produce happy marriages; another popular manual, also published in 1926, by Bernard Bernard, *Sex Conduct in Marriage: The Art of Maintaining Love and Happiness in Marriage* (1926), stressed the same thing. By the time Stopes's book came before the U.S. federal courts in 1931, the marriage manual had become a familiar artifact and the idea of a sexually satisfied bride was part of the marriage discourse.

Determining Ownership and Legal Strategy

Because *Married Love* had been banned in the United States in 1922, it had not produced much noise among the public or in the press by 1930. But as Stopes knew and as Ernst and Lindey would learn, there was a substantial underground traffic in the book and it had an excellent reputation among sexologists. When she first contacted Ernst by letter in January 1930, at Mary Ware Dennett's suggestion, Stopes was mostly interested in stopping the traffic in pirated editions of her work in the United States. She said nothing of the Customs ban on her book, writing instead about the fact that she was suffering financially from bookleggers, a name for the literary pirates who violated copyrights by printing and selling bootleg versions of books. She wrote, "Although thousands of my books circulate in America, I get no royalties from them owing to the swindling pirating which is going on. Mrs. Dennett sent me an advertisement of the Pioneer Press announcing an edition of 'Married Love' and wonder whether you could do anything, without running me into too much expense, to put a stop to it?"[34]

Ernst and Lindey did not know much about Stopes or her works. They learned from Dennett that *Married Love* had been declared nonmailable by the U.S. Postal Service in 1921 and banned as nonimportable by the Customs Service in 1922 and also that a Dr. William J. Robinson (one of the bookleggers of the era) had taken "various liberties with the book" without ever consulting Stopes, including editing out the section on birth control for the American edition.[35] They also learned that copies of Stopes's version published by Putnam's continued to be smuggled into the United States and that those editions were also surreptitiously circulated in the underground market for sex-related books.[36]

Tracking down the pirated editions and those responsible was not a priority for Ernst and Lindey. (That was the job of John Sumner and the Vice Society.) They had other ideas, however, and Stopes's inquiry could not have been more serendipitous. They were keen to test the recent *Dennett* decision's applicability to a Customs case and leapt at the prospect of using one of Stopes's widely read, respectable, scientifically credible books for such a test. After several weeks they reported back that they had tried to use their contacts in the publishing world to track down the booklegging Pioneer Press, had not succeeded, but were enthusiastic about challenging the Customs bans on her books.

As the Greenbaum, Wolff & Ernst legal researchers dug into *Married Love*'s publishing and legal history, they learned not only that it was banned from the mails by Postal officials and from importation by Customs but also that it had a complicated and unresolved copyright history. The British publisher, Putnam's, had publishing rights and sold thousands of copies in the United Kingdom, but they had never published an American edition, so all copies circulating in the United States were either illegal imports or pirated editions (of which there were several versions, including one from Eugenics Press, and the Pioneer Press version). Customs had also banned at least two other books by Stopes, including *Enduring Passion* (G. P. Putnam's, London, 1928) and *Contraception: Its Theory, History, and Practice* (Bales Sons & Danielson, London, 1923). The U.S. Customs Court's Judge Israel F. Fischer harshly denounced *Enduring Passion* in 1929 and also banned *Contraception* in 1930.[37]

Lindey and Ernst learned that Stopes had no end of legal controversies swirling about and was engaged in yet another major libel suit with her Catholic Church critics in England.[38] All these legal wrangles generated enormous press attention in England, making Stopes more famous but also making her something of an exhausting lightning rod for allies. As Ernst and Lindey discovered, she had employed numerous lawyers for her various entanglements, so her legal records were scattered among different law firms, and her own copies of her records were incomplete, making it more difficult for Ernst and Lindey to get a clearer understanding of her various contractual arrangements.[39]

Despite all these unpromising details, the more Ernst and Lindey knew about *Married Love* and its reputation among sexologists and sex education experts, the more confident they felt about *Married Love* as a test case for challenging the Customs Service's authority to block serious, credible sexology books sent from abroad. In short, they wanted to see whether they could extend Judge Hand's language from *United States v. Dennett* "that an accurate exposition of the relevant facts of the sex side of life in decent language and in manifestly serious and disinterested spirit cannot ordinarily be regarded as obscene."[40] The timing was perfect, given the recent *Dennett* decision and the fact that Congress had recently revised Section 305(a) of the Tariff Act of 1930, which now allowed legal challenges to Customs decisions in the federal district courts.[41] Challenging the Customs ban in the federal courts would minimize the author's and the publisher's longer term legal problems.[42] In addition, under the new tariff law, they would have recourse to the federal courts, all the way to the U.S. Court of Appeals or the U.S. Supreme Court, so they could potentially get a precedent with significant binding authority.

In March 1930 a confident Ernst wrote Stopes, telling her that he thought they had the censors on the run, "and if you are interested in having me take up the matter along these lines, I would like to hear from you further."[43] Stopes responded enthusiastically, promptly shipping him two copies of *Married Love*. She also sent her agent, Mr. George Bedborough, to New York City, who also brought a copy with him.[44] Bedborough began working with the Greenbaum, Wolff & Ernst firm to straighten out what Ernst described to Stopes as "the terrible mess in which your books have existed for some years."[45]

Ernst and Lindey had a number of issues to consider as they prepared to take up the defense of *Married Love*, including clarifying its ownership and copyright history, determining who would publish a U.S. edition, and working out the financial arrangements for their defense. Not least, they had to figure out what to do about Stopes's treatment of contraceptive matters in the book, which would be an obvious violation of the Comstock law and might stop their efforts altogether.[46] They came up with a plan to edit out all discussion of contraceptive matters in *Married Love*. This would eliminate those grounds for an obscenity holding and would make it easier for a test case to proceed on the legitimacy of Stopes's advice to married couples.

Ernst proposed this to Stopes and her agent and to the London branch of Putnam's, reiterating that the case would likely have considerable legal importance in the United States. He also proposed that he write a foreword testifying to the work's legal importance. The foreword, he explained, would stave off additional censorship attempts against the book by U.S. Postal officials and would place Stopes's book at the center of the battles with censorship "in the United States and elsewhere." He would also use the foreword to educate a larger audience about the core legal arguments that had loosened the grip of censorship on important works such as Stopes's.[47] Stopes and Putnam's accepted the proposed plan of action and agreed on a compensation plan, including contingencies for appeals up to the Supreme Court. Stopes wrote enthusiastically in support of this, wishing Ernst "all success in your gallant venture to secure liberty in free America."[48]

The ownership matters (and hence copyright claims to the U.S. edition) proved to be a tangled mess that would bedevil Ernst and colleagues for months and months. Customs' inefficiency—or conscious obstructionism on the part of Customs officials—would also bog them down, leading to long and exasperating delays in setting in motion the official challenge to the book's banned status. Stopes wanted to limit her out-of-pocket liabilities and was especially concerned about the labyrinthine American legal system.[49] She was mollified somewhat by the fact that Putnam's had agreed to pay half the legal fees, but she feared the "foreignness" of the U.S. legal process and the difficulties inherent in challenging Customs offices in general.[50]

For Ernst and Lindey, however, the copyright issues and U.S. publishing rights were incidental to their larger project of fighting against administrative censorship and expanding the *Dennett* decision's logic to Customs. Indeed, they just wanted to pursue the matter with Customs rather than worrying about publishing a U.S. version and then seeing what would happen with Postal officials or local vice societies, as Putnam's had suggested. As Ernst told George Putnam, one of the principals of the publishing house, challenging Customs would be best because then they would avoid "the possible influence of Sumner and his New York Society for the Suppression of Vice" and keep the matter out of the New York magistrate and state courts, where Sumner could possibly hang it up.

Administrative Obstacles in Creating a Test Case with Customs

Although the market in marriage manuals flourished, Stopes and her publishers were stymied by Customs officials' inability (or unwillingness) to actually seize the specially edited volumes that Stopes and her team had shipped from England to Ernst in the United States. The book needed to be seized by Customs to put the legal challenge in motion, but that took months. In addition, Customs officials seemed stubbornly unwilling to acknowledge modifications in the 1930 Tariff Act, refused to recognize distinctions among Stopes's different books, and were consistently blundering in their handling of the edited volumes sent from England to the United States. (Even after two judicial opinions in Stopes's favor, Customs continued to mismanage the importation of her books.)

When Ernst first wrote Customs officials in April 1930 announcing the book's imminent departure from England aboard the SS *Homeric*, he argued that *Married Love* should be permitted entrance based on the *Dennett* decision and asserted that Judge Fischer's recent (1929) Customs

Court decision on Stopes's *Enduring Passion* should have no bearing on *Married Love*.[51] Walter Eaton, the acting solicitor to the collector, warned Ernst that the spirit of Judge Fischer's earlier decision against *Enduring Passion* might well prejudice him against *Married Love*.[52] Ernst objected that these were two different books and "obviously a condemnation of one book by an author cannot act as a blanket condemnation of all of that author's works. If such were the case, our good friend Mark Twain would be barred in toto from all of the civilized world." More to their legal point, Ernst argued that the *Dennett* ruling should shape Customs' interpretation of the book's status: "Whether we like it or not, the decision in the *Dennett* case does lay down new law in the Federal jurisdictions."[53] Eaton was not convinced, and he and other Customs officers proved either woefully bungling or outright obstructive in moving this case forward to the U.S. Attorneys and into the federal courts.

Despite the notice from Ernst to Customs officials in April that two copies of the book addressed to him would be arriving on the SS *Homeric*, they were not seized. Customs instead sent them directly on to the post office, which delivered them to Ernst's office. Ernst asked whether this meant he had persuaded Eaton in their earlier exchange and that Customs had knowingly admitted the books, or whether Customs had simply failed to apprehend them. Eaton replied that the Treasury Department still deemed the book prohibited under provisions of the Tariff Act of 1922 but that the particular copy of the book sent from London had "inadvertently" slipped through.[54]

This delayed matters by months. In August 1930 Putnam's tried again, shipping another two copies to Ernst. He once again notified Customs of the book's pending arrival, explaining that it had been "completely expurgated" of contraceptive information. He reiterated his argument that "the copy in its present form is well within the law as interpreted and crystallized in the recent decision handed down by the Court of Appeals for the Second Circuit in the case of *United States v. Mary Ware Dennett*."[55] Ten days later, Customs informed the lawyers that they had detained the book, again under the authority of the Tariff Act of 1922 (instead of the Tariff Act of 1930). Ernst duly reminded Customs that the Tariff Act of

1930 had revised the 1922 law, modifying both the categories of censorable materials and the procedures for challenging Customs seizures. This meant, for instance, that the seized copies should immediately be turned over to the U.S. district attorney in New York, who would make the decision whether or not to libel the book as obscene. It should not be held by Customs officials. Moreover, any determination of obscenity should not be made by Customs officials or adjudicated in the Customs Court. Rather, these decisions would be made by U.S. Attorneys and if necessary tried in the federal district courts.

For whatever reason—their investment in censorship practices, bureaucratic ineptitude, sloth, or antagonism to sexual modernism—Eaton's office sat on all the case materials. Nearly two months after actually seizing the two "official" expurgated books, Customs had still not passed them on to the U.S. Attorney's office for a libel decision.[56] Immensely frustrated, Ernst finally went to Washington, D.C., to meet with Customs officials. With the *Dennett* ruling, the new Tariff Act, and a volume purged of anything having to do with contraception, Ernst thought the matter could be quickly resolved. But he met resistance in Washington too. The two staff lawyers, Nevius and Stevens, in the Office of the Counsel of the Customs Service reported that they found the book obscene, although this was not their decision to make.[57] Reiterating the presumptive authority of the *Dennett* ruling, Alexander Lindey sent Nevius and Stevens a copy of Dennett's *Sex Side of Life* pamphlet and a copy of Judge Hand's decision in that case, urging them that Customs "will be not only legally in error, but will be holding itself out for ridicule from the entire civilized world by declaring *Married Love* obscene."[58]

During the error-filled seven months' wait following the initial shipment of the books, Ernst and Lindey learned about a favorable development in a Philadelphia federal court case involving three of Stopes's books: *Married Love*, *Wise Parenthood*, and *The First Five Thousand*. Customs officers in Philadelphia seized them and passed them on to the U.S. Attorney in Philadelphia, and U.S. District Court judge William H. Kilpatrick subsequently cleared all three of obscenity, even though the *Married Love* version he read was the unexpurgated version and *Wise Parenthood* also contained extensive discussion of contraception. Once Ernst learned of Judge Kilpatrick's ruling, he immediately wrote Nevius, the Customs lawyer in the Washington office, with this information, arguing that Judge Kilpatrick's decision should be authoritative and applicable to the present action. He called for a "prompt determination," repeating his complaint that "our clients have been seriously prejudiced by the red tape of the United States government in this matter," as the legal uncertainties enabled bookleggers to continue to circulate pirated editions.[59]

Judge Kirkpatrick had found that Stopes's work was not obscene and also ruled that the books did not violate provisions of Section 305 of the Tariff Act of 1930 as containing contraceptive information because "he construed that provision to apply only to contraceptive mechanical apparatus and not to mere information in book form."[60] The judge had ruled from the bench and did not hand down a written decision, but Ernst and Lindey learned that he had been very much influenced by the decision of the court of appeals in the *Dennett* case, which was exactly the result they hoped that decision would produce.[61]

Despite the Eastern District of Pennsylvania federal court decision and many months of inaction by the New York Customs office, in November 1930 the commissioner of customs, F. X. A. Eberle, finally informed Ernst and his colleagues that Customs' legal counsel in New York had determined that the *Dennett* case was "not decisive of the matter under consideration" and that he had been "instructed to seize importation of this publication under Section 305 of the Tariff Act of 1930" and to transmit this information to the U.S. Attorney "with a view to securing condemnation of the same."[62] Customs solicitors argued that because *Dennett* was a Postal case tried under a criminal statute and not a Customs case tried under a civil statute, it had no authority pertaining to Customs. When Ernst wrote Eberle asking why the Eastern District of Pennsylvania decision was not decisive, Eberle hardly clarified matters, stating, "It is the opinion of the Bureau that the Treasury Department is not bound by the decision above referred." He pointed only to the jurisdictional issue—that *Married Love* "was received in New York."[63]

For Ernst and his colleagues, the Treasury Department's decision raised quite a few questions to be addressed at trial: Why wasn't the U.S. District Court in New York bound by the parallel U.S. District Court in

Pennsylvania decision? Judge Fitzpatrick's decision should have been res judicata on the admissibility of the book into the United States, so why was it not? (That is, because the U.S. Court for the Eastern District of Philadelphia was a parallel court to the U.S. Court for the Southern District of New York, why should the question of *Married Love*'s obscenity have to be retried in a parallel court?)

The apparent administrative caprice of Eberle and the Customs solicitors and the extraordinary (or ordinary) delays by Customs and then by the U.S. Attorney's office illustrate how onerous and punitive Customs and other forms of state-based administrative censorship could be. These delays added significant aggravation and expenses for authors and publishers, including legal costs, months (or sometimes years) when works were not available to compete in a burgeoning marketplace of similar works, and opportunities for bootleggers to make profits with no recourse by authors or publishers to halt the piracy—not to mention the hundreds of hours spent recovering from bureaucratic miscues and the hundreds of pages of documents that legal counsel were forced to produce.[64]

All of this took place well before the process of writing formal legal briefs had even begun or before judges had heard from lawyers or witnesses. Whether this was an express form of administrative stonewalling based in strategic opposition to sexual modernism or out-and-out ineptitude is not clear. But several things are conclusive: Ernst and his clients routinely encountered administrative delays and stonewalling in their many censorship cases, not just from U.S. Customs but also from the Postal Service, the New York Society for the Suppression of Vice, and the New York City Police Department. This particularly egregious encounter made Ernst an unstinting vocal critic of the Customs Service's bureaucratic powers. It also made him even more determined to defang federal censorship authority wherever it interfered with the flow of information and ideas.

Securing Expert Testimony and Opinion

Because of the Customs delays, Ernst and Lindey had troubles distributing copies of *Married Love* to potential expert witnesses who might be able to testify to the book's seriousness and high purposes. Ironically, they needed to rely on the underground traffic in illegal books and on the networks of people who would know how to secure copies of bootlegged books and might also offer expert testimony about sexology as a field.[65] Dennett proved an excellent route into these networks. She was deeply invested in the case and Ernst and Lindey's overall project. As she told Lindey, "I will do anything I can to help on the Stopes case. . . . Dr. Stopes is a dear friend of many years back, so I have every kind of reason for trying to help." Through Dennett, Ernst and Lindey were able to solicit the assistance of a New York City book merchant who had sold more than 200 copies of an original version of *Married Love*. "He is much interested to know that the case is pending," Dennett reported, "and was glad to fill in with my suggestion that he send to you a list of worthwhile people." She added that she could put them in touch with others in this network, including Stopes's devotees in Chicago and Minneapolis.[66]

Using Dennett's network, along with the sexologists, theologians, educators, and public intellectuals they had been cultivating in their opposition to censorship and defense of sex rationality and cultural modernism, the Ernst team set about building a raft of favorable opinions on the book. They wrote to solicit written and courtroom testimony and, by way of informing their experts, gave a quick background to the case, described Stopes's bona fides, and offered a tutorial on the current state of obscenity law. They hoped to generate support similar to the *Dennett* case, where the "pressure of public opinion" had proved consequential. They also told their potential expert witnesses, "We are not so much desirous of a literary estimate as of an appraisal from a scientific or sociological point of view." Scientific credibility mattered more than felicitous expression.[67]

The Ernst team garnered strong support, with the most forceful coming from Dr. Smith Ely Jellife, managing editor of the *Journal of Nervous and Mental Disease*, who railed against anyone who would ban a book this worthy: "It is one of the ridiculous outrages of a 'democracy' that pimply minded, petty tyrants can be placed in high places and impede the advance of enlightenment that would lead to healthier men and women in such a democracy." Jellife's was not the kind of testimonial Ernst and Lindey could afford to quote at length in their brief, but his professional authority and intense response to the censorship of Stopes's work staked out one pole of the debate over sexual materials. Although he was the only respondent who addressed Stopes's radical critique of marital imbalance, women's economic dependence on men, and men's sexual exploitation of women within and outside marriage, his larger concern echoed others who were hugely frustrated by the suppression of materials that had clear educational purposes.[68]

Other testimonials were less angry than Jellife's, sounding more like the YMCA official who complained that "if we are to raise the level of thinking about and participation in wholesome marriage relationships," then more information is always better.[69] Another YMCA official, A. J. Gregg, who would have been the lead witness in the *Dennett* case had he been allowed to testify, reported that he and his wife read the book and could endorse it both professionally and personally: "Our own study and experience in the field of marriage relationships and marriage adjustments have strengthened the belief that the information carried in the book *Married Love* is scientifically sound and socially necessary."[70] Their testimony as leaders of the YMCA was symbolically resonant, because that organization had been Anthony Comstock's primary benefactor and employer.

The only somewhat critical letter Lindey and Ernst received came from Dr. E. L. Keyes, president of the American Social Hygiene Foundation, who had also thought Dennett had been too permissive about masturbation. He feared that Stopes's work might produce too much masturbation among the laypersons who might be aroused by the book, though he allowed that "most medical men and perhaps clergymen, sociologists," and other experts "might read it with profit." He also wondered whether Stopes had really been as scientifically rigorous as she contended.[71] Keyes's critique echoed Stopes's critics in the British medical community who regularly admonished her for her lack of medical training in her birth control work.

Married Love on Trial: The Defense's Memorandum

As in their other obscenity law cases, Lindey and Ernst's formal legal memorandum was a persuasive masterpiece. Elegantly written by Lindey (he wrote and Ernst argued), their memorandum opened by explaining that *Married Love*, written more than a decade earlier, had "met with

instantaneous recognition as a work of far-reaching importance in rational sex education."[72] The book's good reputation, evidenced by endorse-
ments in leading medical, scientific, and cultural publications, primarily
in England, spoke to its scientific authority. The reception "on the part of
laymen and physicians alike has been vividly enthusiastic," Lindey wrote,
citing the *British Medical Journal*, the *London Lancet*, *British Medical
Times*, the *Times Literary Supplement*, *Cambridge Magazine*, and other
reviews. A quote from *The Atheneum* described the book as "one of the
most sensible we have met on the subject."[73] He quoted Havelock Ellis,
the "leading world authority on sexology," who said that Stopes's book
"seems to represent the most notable advance made during recent years in
the knowledge of women's psycho-physiological life." Dr. E. H. Starling,
considered "by many . . . the greatest British authority in medicine," had
written Stopes directly, telling her, "The need of such guidance as you
give is very evident." In addition, Lindey and Ernst included a statement
signed by "fifteen leading figures in the contemporary literary, religious,
medical and sociological life of England," including Stopes's strong supporters Arnold Bennett, George Bernard Shaw, and H. G. Wells. Dean
Inge of St. Paul's Cathedral also endorsed the book as "a valuable contribution to the Sex Education Movement now being conducted in all civilized countries of the world."[74]

Ernst and Lindey contended that *Married Love* had "been no less enthusiastically received in the United States," quoting an April 1920 review
(predating the 1922 Customs ban) in the *Journal of Social Hygiene* that
extolled "the normal, refreshing point of view and the frank presentation
of the need for a well-adjusted physical life as an essential of marriage."
American educators, theologians, and social hygienists endorsed the book,
including Clara Savage Littledale, editor of *Parent's Magazine*,[75] and the
leaders of the YMCA who had used the book in their educational and
pastoral work.[76] Perhaps the most symbolically valuable testimonial came
from the ranks of the vice hunters. William J. Schieffelin, vice-president
and director of the New York Society for the Suppression of Vice, said,
"In my opinion this book should not be banned from the United States
under the tariff law."[77]

Lindey's brief organized their claims around three arguments. First, following the *Dennett* ruling on rational sex education, a book such as Stopes's could not be found obscene, as that decision had "clearly defined the extent to which sex information could be legally disseminated in this country." Second, Judge Kirkpatrick's decision of October 30, 1930, in the U.S. District Court for the Eastern District of Pennsylvania should be "conclusive" of the book's status in New York. And third, *Married Love* was not obscene by definition.

Ernst and Lindey drew on Judge Learned Hand's appeals court decision in the *Dennett* case to make a series of points central to a whole raft of cases they would argue through the decade. They distilled his core arguments: that although any discussion of sexual matters may arouse lust in someone, such arousal does not necessarily mean that a work is obscene; that sex itself is not ipso facto obscene; and that accurate discussion of sexual matters usually is not obscene either. Curious people will seek information about sexuality, and ignorance about such matters is not an acceptable option, either for individuals or society. In balancing the risks of too much information versus too little, more is better, especially when that information is sincere, high-minded, and scientifically credible. In addition, public officials believe that the public needs sex education materials, evidenced by the fact that federal and New York State public health officials had taken active roles in distributing pamphlets. (Interestingly, they did not refer to any of the marriage manuals, presumably to locate Stopes's work within a field of "scientifically" grounded sex education.) Ernst and Lindey quoted directly from Judge Hand's eloquent *Dennett* decision.

> Any incidental tendency to arouse sex impulses which such a pamphlet may perhaps have, is apart from and subordinate to its main effect. The tendency can only exist in so far as it is inherent in any sex instruction, and it would seem to be outweighed by the elimination of ignorance, curiosity, and morbid fear. *The direct aim and the net result is to promote understanding and self-control.*[78]

Hand's characterization of Dennett's work applied directly to Stopes's, Ernst argued. *Married Love*, they wrote, was "precisely the kind of book which the Circuit Court of Appeals for this Circuit wished to exempt from the application of our obscenity statutes."[79]

Turning to Judge Kirkpatrick's recent decision from the U.S. District Court for the Eastern District of Pennsylvania (which Customs Commissioner Eberle had refused to accept as res judicata), Ernst and Lindey averred that this parallel federal court ruling was "conclusive of its legality in the present proceeding." The circumstances were identical. In both cases the book was seized by a collector of customs, who then transmitted the book to the U.S. Attorney for libel proceedings under the Tariff Act. Judge Kirkpatrick held that "as a matter of law the book, *Married Love*, was not obscene or in contravention of the provisions of the Tariff Act," and his analysis of Stopes's books had directly and positively assessed *Married Love*'s effects in relation to the Hicklin test. Her works did not fall within any definition of obscenity.

The State's Halfhearted Prosecution

The state's brief, the Memorandum for the Libellant, by U.S. Attorney George Z. Medalie and Assistant U.S. Attorney Morton Baum, was an exercise in brevity. It did not convey either the concerns of experts or the outrage of moral guardians and hardly intimated any of the ill effects of lust and prurience warned against by the Comstock laws or implicitly accepted by the Customs officials, particularly Eberle. Its minimalism suggests that the U.S. Attorney's office had limited actual concern about the book's obscenity and no actual "evidence" of its ill effects. Pretrial communications between Baum and Ernst's office reveal that the federal prosecutors were not bent on finding the book obscene and that Customs officials were the ones intent on holding it obscene. Medalie and Baum did not do much more than argue that there was "reasonable doubt" about the book's legality.

The state's legal memorandum was workmanlike and dutiful, but it evoked little of the cultural agon surrounding the *Dennett* case. Its primary concern was less about the book per se and more about the legal question of whether the *Dennett* decision would be authoritative as a precedent in the federal courts in all future sexology cases and would extend to U.S.

Customs. They asked a rhetorical question: Did "the decision of the Circuit Court of Appeals . . . that the adolescent may properly be instructed in the simple biological functions connected with sex" in any way addressed approve of "'refinements in the art of Love' for all adults as such?" They went no further in developing the rationale behind their question or in probing its implications and shifted to a comparison of Dennett's and Stopes's treatment of sexual pleasure. Although both "describe the sex organs in great detail," *Married Love* was more explicit about sexual pleasure because it included "a discussion of positions during sex relations" and a discussion of "methods of stimulation for greater pleasure." The result was that *Married Love* did not have "the restraint and simplicity present in the work of Mary Ware Dennett, and by its subtle innuendos unduly stimulate the unsatisfied imagination."[80] In short, it might lead to masturbation.

As for the book's lewdness, its incitement to lust, its production of impure thoughts, and other implicit qualities of obscene works, Medalie and Baum essentially only speculated that its "suggestive title" might "cause the book to fall into the hands of adolescents." They also offered a not very serious argument about comparative readerships, suggesting that "there is a clear distinction between the mental attitude of one who reads a small pamphlet written in simple and direct style and one who reads a book in the nature of a novel, whose discussion is so much the more extensive," implying in this reversal of the usual hierarchies about readers and texts that somehow those adults with greater reading stamina would be more vulnerable than curious youth.[81] This was not a point carefully developed to persuade a federal jurist, as Medalie and Baum offered neither evidence nor case law to expand on this speculative line.

In addition, Medalie and Baum offered no expert opinion about the book and its possible effects. As to Judge Kilpatrick's decision, Medalie and Baum simply asserted that it was "not conclusive of the present proceedings,"[82] primarily because the two other books at trial in that court, *Wise Parenthood* and *The First Five Thousand*, dealt with contraception and should have been barred from admission into the United States. It was a perfunctory memorandum at best, revealing a significant difference in opinion and disposition between the U.S. Attorneys for the Southern District of New

York and New York's Customs officials over what constituted obscene materials, a gap that would recur in other cases.

More important—for this and subsequent obscenity cases that Ernst and Lindey tried in the federal courts—the correspondence between Ernst's office and the U.S. Attorneys in New York shows that Assistant U.S. Attorney Morton Baum was not interested in achieving a verdict of obscene libel. Lindey, Ernst, and Baum had a series of conversations and meetings about the case before submitting their formal legal memorandum, and all agreed on the goal of getting the case on the docket of a liberal judge. They all met with the different federal judges who might sit on the case, including Judges Knox, Coxe, Patterson, and Woolsey. Lindey's notes indicate that Ernst had a conference with Judge Coxe and was sure he would rule against them ("I have 2 sons" it says in handwritten notes Ernst took at the meeting). Baum did not want to take it before either Judge Knox or Judge Coxe, both of whom were antagonistic in other obscenity cases, and he thought that Judge Patterson would be best.[83] However, Judge Patterson was too busy, and they learned along the way that he apparently did not like "these kinds of books."[84]

This is a fascinating instance of a prosecutor working with the opposing counsel, trying to facilitate a ruling for the defendants by finding a sympathetic jurist under the guise of trying to move the case toward a speedy disposition. Both sides wanted a formal opinion from the courts to resolve the matter and thought that the Customs solicitor was wrong. (Other cases would show the same inclination by the U.S. Attorneys in New York to get a judicial resolution of a controversial matter, rather than making an in-house decision on a work's obscenity.)

Fortuitously for Lindey and Ernst, Judge John M. Woolsey was on the docket for April 1931 and agreed to take case. Not only was Woolsey open to sexual modernism, but he had also come into the case "having read Dr. Stopes."[85] Judge Woolsey was especially attentive to the specific question of whether the *Dennett* Postal decision would apply to the Customs Service. In preparation for the hearing, he asked for a full record of the *Dennett* trial, including the lawyers' briefs and Dennett's book.[86] Lindey dutifully sent the materials and added a quick note drawing attention to the irony of the case's title—"I cannot help adding my constant amusement at the abbreviated title of this action"—*United States v. "Married Love."*[87]

When Judge Woolsey finally heard Ernst and Lindey's motion to dismiss the libel—that is, to rule on the book's obscenity—on April 6, 1931, a full sixteen months after the book had set sail to the United States, he did not hesitate in granting the motion. He offered a forceful endorsement of Lindey and Ernst's positions, writing a characteristically thoughtful and quotable opinion, arguing not just that the book was not obscene but also that its sensitive, sound advice made it a desirable resource for modern marriages.[88]

Woolsey's Decision

Although Lindey and Ernst tried once again to make the argument that they had made in *Dennett*—that the Tariff Act was unconstitutional because it impinged on the First Amendment right of freedom of the press—Judge Woolsey quickly dismissed it. (They would try to make this First Amendment argument in other cases before Woolsey, and he would dismiss it in those cases as well.) The Tariff Act did not involve prior restraint; rather, it dealt with "the exclusion of an already published book which is sought to be brought into the United States." Explaining, Woolsey offered a quick reprisal of the standard First Amendment jurisprudence distinction between prior restraint and post-publication suppression: "After a book is published, its lot in the world is like that of anything else. It must conform to the law and, if it does not, must be subject to the penalties involved in its failure to do so. Laws which are thus disciplinary of publications . . . whether involving exclusion from the mails or from this country, do not interfere with freedom of the press."[89]

Having asserted that the government and its Customs officers had a legitimate interest in banning the importation and distribution of obscene materials, Woolsey then turned to the particular question of whether or not this particular book was obscene. It was not, Woolsey ruled. Because the contraceptive matters had been excised from the particular book sent by Stopes and Putnam's in London, it did not violate that particular component of the Tariff Act.

Thus the sole question was whether other parts of the book were obscene. To this question Judge Woolsey deferred to the previous judgment of Judge Kirkpatrick. Because the government had not appealed Kirkpatrick's decision, the Philadelphia case therefore "stands as a final decision of a coordinate court in a proceeding *in rem* involving the same book that we have here."[90] He made it clear that this ruling on the book's status should apply to all Customs ports of entry.[91] Anticipating, however, that the government might appeal his decision, Woolsey addressed the question of the book's obscenity at law. He began by referring to the standard definitions of *obscene* and *immoral* in the *Oxford English Dictionary.*[92] Judge Woolsey then stated, "I do not find anything exceptionable anywhere in the book, and I cannot imagine a normal mind to which this book would seem to be obscene or immoral within the proper definition of these words or whose sex impulses would be stirred by reading it. Whether or not the book is scientific in some of its theses is unimportant. It is informative and instructive."[93]

The remainder of Woolsey's decision was music to Ernst and Lindey's ears, for Woolsey accepted their entire framework comparing *Married Love* to Dennett's *The Sex Side of Life* and, by extension, embraced the logic of and applicability of the *Dennett* Postal decision to the Customs Service. "Dr. Stopes," he wrote, "treats quite as decently and with as much restraint of the sex relations as did Mrs. Mary Ware Dennett." Then, in a key rephrasing of Lindey and Ernst's claims for Stopes, he added, "The present book may fairly be said to do for adults what Mrs. Dennett's book does for adolescents."[94]

Following the verdict, G. P. Putnam's Sons quickly published an American edition of *Married Love* in 1931. The foreword, written by Ernst and Lindey, framed the case and its significance as part of their campaign for free speech for sexual materials, for sex rationality, and against enforced silences imposed by government censorship. It is worth quoting at length.

The appearance, at this time, of an authorized American edition of *Married Love* is of many-faceted significance. It comes at a moment when its extrinsic importance almost rivals its intrinsic worth. It marks a further advance in the struggles for sex enlightenment that, in 1930, received such salutary impetus from the disposition of the *Dennett* case in the United States Circuit Court of Appeals. It demonstrates once more, and with shocking conclusiveness, that the governmental agencies vested with the power of initiating suppression are grossly unfit for the task. It emphasizes once more the truth that changing times mean changing morals; . . . we have come to regard sex not as something vile and unmentionable, not as something to be thrust into the background and to be smirkingly whispered about, but as a human function of momentous importance both to the individual and to society. And so the advent of *Married Love* fits into the orderly mosaic of the new scheme of things. We are beginning to realize that sex ethics are something more than blushes and stony silence on intimate matters and a revulsion from nudity; . . . that intelligently directed information is better than blundering innocence. "Married Love" crystallizes all that is sane and beautiful about our new attitude.[95]

The successful challenge buoyed Ernst and Lindey's confidence in their own project and in the ability of the federal judiciary to offer remedies to the censorship obstacles posed by those two great administrative powers, the Postal Service and the Customs Service. They would keep pushing.

Building on Victory with a Defense of *Contraception*

A month after Judge Woolsey's decision, Ernst proposed the pursuit of yet another milestone, this time taking action on behalf of Stopes's 1923 book, *Contraception: Its Theory, History, and Practice*, challenging a recent Customs seizure of the book. Whereas the Postal statute expressly prohibited the distribution of any information about contraception, the Customs statute only expressly prohibited contraceptive *devices*, not contraceptive information. Ernst and Lindey wanted to challenge *Contraception*'s recent seizure by Customs officials so that they could test and extend the logic of Judge Woolsey's *Married Love* decision to a book dealing with contraceptive matters.

Moreover, Ernst and Lindey wanted to extend Judge Kirkpatrick's recent decision holding Stopes's works *Enduring Passion, The First Five Thousand*,

and *Married Love* importable, under the reading that the Customs statute did not interfere with serious, nonobscene materials that provided information about contraceptives, only with contraceptive drugs, devices, or abortifacients. To this end, they wanted to clarify those distinctions between the Postal laws and the Tariff Act, which would, at the least, make their future challenges on Customs seizures easier with a larger body of law to supply to Customs officials. But they also wanted a ruling on whether the content of Stopes's book on contraception was obscene in and of itself.

Using the same language that he had used in convincing Stopes to take a risk with *Married Love*, Ernst wrote, "In my opinion, the entire cause of freedom of thought and the spread of decent sex education will be helped by contesting the ban at Customs. . . . It is our judgment that a victory in the pending case—limited, to be sure—though important, would nevertheless act as a substantial drawback to public officials who might otherwise attempt to interfere with the distribution of the revised edition to doctors and other professional men."[96] Ernst signaled their strategy here—they weren't going to defend the importation of *Contraception* by just anyone but rather by physicians.

Stopes's Birth Control Advocacy

Stopes's interest in birth control matters began to crystallize when she was writing *Married Love*, and she was well positioned to quickly follow that book with a series of tracts on birth control. She came to her interests in the topic primarily because of eugenics-based concerns about the future of the British "race" during World War I, fueled by the massive wartime casualties of well-educated and healthy young British men. Some of the most forceful scholarship on Stopes, especially the work of Richard Soloway and Jane Carey, remind readers of the necessity of paying attention to the eugenicist roots of the birth control movement in the British Empire, as well as in the United States.[97] But it is important to recognize that Stopes's birth control analysis and arguments did not always have a eugenicist framing.

In 1915 Stopes met Margaret Sanger, the charismatic and revolutionary American birth control activist, who came to speak at Fabian Hall in London. Upon hearing Sanger speak and subsequently dining with her,

Stopes became more committed to the idea of providing birth control for poor women, who might find relief from poverty with contraceptives. Sanger and Stopes bonded over their shared interests in birth control and women's sexual pleasure, and Sanger made sure Stopes received a copy of her *Family Limitation* pamphlet. Stopes, meanwhile, got Aylmer Maude's help soliciting Arnold Bennett, H. G. Wells, Gilbert Murray, and others to sign a plea to President Woodrow Wilson to drop obscenity charges against Sanger for *Family Limitation*.[98]

Stopes dove into publishing about birth control issues as soon as she had published *Married Love*. Her first short book on the subject, *Wise Parenthood*, came out in November 1918, a week after the armistice. In it she explicitly endorsed the idea of "planned childbirth," aimed at helping British families produce happy, healthy children. She antagonized religious leaders when, extending an argument from *Married Love*, she described sexual intercourse as "an 'act of supreme value in itself' in married life," something that could and ought to be separated from procreation.[99] And Stopes incurred criticism from some medical authorities because her instruction to keep cervical caps, her recommended form of birth control, in for as long as two weeks was not good advice.

Married Love, followed by *Wise Parenthood*, made Stopes an important public voice on these issues. Her stature as a birth control expert grew when she was appointed a member of the National Birth-Rate Commission and used that platform to report that "the simplest way of dealing with chronic cases of inherent disease, drunkenness or bad character would be to sterilize the parents."[100] Stopes never really backed away from such pronouncements, and her critics then and more recently note an insistent eugenicist preoccupation.[101] Her eugenicist concerns and educated class elitism were abundantly evident in *Wise Parenthood*, where she complained about the demographic problems for the nation due to the "less thrifty and conscientious," who reproduced too frequently, resulting in children "weakened and handicapped by physical as well as mental warping and weakness," an effect that would ultimately harm the nation and "the Race."[102]

June Rose, who is overall sympathetic to Stopes's trajectory as a thinker, argues that, under the influence of her husband and other birth control campaigners and the power of her own experience trying to get contraception to poorer women who were often overwhelmed with too many children, Stopes did come to see "birth control as a crusade against poverty." Stopes quickly followed *Wise Parenthood* with a 16-page pamphlet written in simple language for less educated women, titled *A Letter to Working Mothers on How to Have Healthy Children and Avoid Weakening Pregnancies.* As Rose explains, Stopes had been moved by the plight of poor women who feared pregnancy and knew too little about how to prevent it, and the impetus to help them gave new focus to her work: "Once she realized that helping poor women to limit their families lay at the heart of the birth control campaign, Marie set about working for that aim with her usual energy."[103]

Rose acknowledges, however, that Stopes maintained an insistently eugenicist position, never escaping her concerns that people from the "better" social classes were not having enough babies and that the poor were having too many. As Rose writes, "Brought up on the ideas of Darwin, she responded enthusiastically to the view that his theory of natural selection argued for the need to create a super breed of humans." In *Radiant Motherhood* (Putnam's, 1920), Stopes revealed her attitudes about the lowest social classes and the tax burdens they imposed on the "hard working" middle and artisan classes who had to pay for the "the diseased, the racially negligent, the careless, the feeble-minded, the very lowest and worst members of the community to produce innumerable tens of thousands of warped and inferior infants."[104]

Undaunted, Stopes and her husband, Humphrey Roe, opened the first of their public birth control clinics in March 1921, called the Mother's Clinic, established in a poor neighborhood in North London. The Mother's Clinic was aimed at helping the poor and offered free examinations, consultation, and advice. The clinic was staffed entirely by women, with a certified midwife to conduct examinations and a female doctor attached to the clinic and available for unusual cases. The only cost to the patient was for the contraceptive device itself. Stopes's clinic used pessaries, in particular a high-domed rubber cervical cap that she designed, based on French models, which she called the "Pro-Race" cap.

Scholars Deborah Cohen and Lesley Hall have studied the letters written by the patrons of Stopes's clinics and find an overwhelming consistency that the women expressed gratitude for being warmly received and treated respectfully, for being shown how to use a cervical cap, and for having their lives improved considerably by getting contraceptives through Stopes's Mother's Clinics.[105] Although Stopes's opponents attacked her in the press, that same press gave Stopes and her work publicity, and thousands of British women took advantage of the information and instruction she made available. According to Alexander Geppert, Stopes reported that by 1929 her two clinics' midwives and nurses had taught 10,000 female patients the use of birth control appliances; by 1937 this number had increased to 26,000 "individual poor women."[106] Stopes also formed a birth control organization in 1921 called the Society for Constructive Birth Control to build support for the movement and to publicize the cause.[107]

These efforts especially raised the ire of two Roman Catholic physicians, Dr. Anne Louise McIlroy, a professor of obstetrics and gynecology at the Royal Free Hospital, and Dr. Halliday Gibson Sutherland, a national expert on tuberculosis and an opponent of eugenicists. They sought to discredit Stopes for not being trained as a physician, criticized the pessary she recommended, and opposed her birth control campaign in general. Sutherland wrote a book against birth control, called *Birth Control: A Statement of Christian Doctrine Against the Neo-Malthusians* (1922), in which he especially targeted Stopes, describing her as a "Doctor of German Philosophy" (just following a brutal war with Germany) and accusing her of "experimenting with the poor" in her clinics with her use of the cervical cap. She responded by accusing Sutherland of libeling her, beginning a lengthy legal ordeal against him and McIlroy in which every argument and detail from the testimony was reported in the British press.

Catholic doctors were not Stopes's only critics in the medical community. As Geppert explains, "While leading physicians had only begun in the last third of the nineteenth century to declare the control of fertility to be an essentially medical matter, the medical profession as a whole had never adopted the public provision of effective forms of contraception as its task." It focused more on biology, less on sexuality, and did not really

High domed occlusive pessary with soft rim.

FIGURE 6. High-domed pessaries, the type of contraceptive Marie Stopes recommended for use in her birth control clinics.

SOURCE: Marie Stopes Birth Control Collection, University of Santa Barbara Library, Special Collections.

consider birth control a preventive strategy. Geppert suggests that the "field of individual birth control was, if not completely ignored in practical terms, reluctantly condemned either on moral grounds or for fear of the loss of respectability."[108]

Stopes's *Contraception* was an attempt to fill this gap in medical knowledge and to attract the legitimating support of scientists and medical doctors. She produced a massive textbook, a compendium of sorts that was the best available source, and was simultaneously attacked by some and praised by others in the medical community. To give the book more authority, she changed publishing houses from G. P. Putnam's to John Bale, Sons & Danielson, a medical publisher in London. *Contraception* appeared in 1923, at 441 pages in length.[109] According to Geppert, the book sold 40,000 copies in its first four years. It had all the features of a "scientific" textbook, he writes, with an "extended scholarly apparatus" and fourteen chapters that tried to treat the topic "as comprehensively as possible." Stopes had several audiences in mind, hoping it would be useful to laypersons and to experts. Along with compiling "all that is valuable of available human knowledge" for her medical readers, she also provided the lay public "extensive descriptions" of various contraceptive methods and gave them preformulated answers to "possible objections to birth control."[110]

The response was mixed among medical authorities and newspaper publishers. Some journals refused to run advertisements for the book, including the *Practitioner*, the *British Medical Journal*, the *Guardian*, and the *Times Literary Supplement*.[111] But others did. The book's value, testified to by experts, gave it authority. This mattered significantly when the book came before Judge Woolsey in 1931, months after he had rendered his decision in the *Married Love* case.

The *Contraception* Case

In December 1930 the collector of customs at the Port of New York seized a copy of *Contraception* intended for Dr. R. L. Taylor. Two months later, in February 1931, the collector of customs informed George Z. Medalie, U.S. District Attorney for the Southern District of New York, that Customs was holding the book for violating Section 305 of the Tariff Act of 1930. In June 1931 Medalie (with whom Ernst and Lindey had worked in the *Married Love* case) reluctantly filed a libel against the book. Ernst and Lindey took up the representation of Dr. Taylor's interests in the book, and Ernst's ACLU colleagues Forrest Bailey and Ida Epstein agreed to pay all costs and expenses. U.S. Attorneys Medalie and Morton Baum, intent on getting this resolved by bench trial, and in front of Judge Woolsey, agreed to waive trial by jury in order to have Judge Woolsey sit on the matter.

Interestingly, in the *Contraception* case, Medalie and Baum developed no substantive argument against the book itself and its putative obscenity, only that the intention of the federal obscenity law was to prohibit the distribution of contraceptive devices and information. They made an argument based strictly on a literal reading of the statute and made no claims whatsoever about the book's obscenity.

Ernst and Lindey essentially evaded those parts written for the general public and addressed the book's professional uses, giving Judge Woolsey an overview of the book's design and explaining that there were two salient facts: first, that the work was not a lay discussion intended for the perusal of the general public but a highly technical, wholly scientific manual designed for professional use; and, second, that Dr. Stopes was concerned with contraception "not for the purpose of encouraging illicit intercourse" but for legitimate medical and public health purposes. Here they tiptoed around the eugenics elements endemic to Stopes's work, describing those purposes as including limiting the "increase in stocks known to be bad, such as those with hereditary disease of heart and mind," bringing relief to mothers "whose health is seriously jeopardized by repeated pregnancies," ensuring that scientific knowledge should be available and people should not be left in the dark about such significant matters," and "extirpat[ing] venereal disease." Treading somewhat more clumsily on the language of eugenics, they also explained that the book's purpose was "to make a better, finer race of wanted offspring" and that the use of contraception was a "great preventive measure to arrest the spread of disease and degeneracy."[112] The brief also reminded the judge that quite recently this very court had "sanctioned her dignified and idealistic work entitled *Married Love*."

Ernst and Lindey then straightforwardly argued that the Tariff Act of 1930 banned obscene books and "any drug or medicine or any article whatever for the prevention of conception or for causing unlawful abortion," but it did not ban contraceptive information. "The wording is so explicit and unambiguous," they wrote, "that it does not call for any construction or interpretation or explanation." They explained that, although the prosecution argued that the book fell "within the . . . prohibited class of Section 305, i.e., the class embracing drugs, medicines or articles for the prevention of contraception," "a book is not an article of contraception." "Had Congress intended to exclude contraceptive information as well as contraceptive materials, Congress would have doubtless done so in explicit language." Congress had done so with the Postal statute, they argued, using such explicit language, but "since similar words were omitted from the Tariff Act, the conclusion is inescapable that the omission is intentional, not accidental."[113]

The recent Eastern District of Pennsylvania case provided a clear ruling and precedent, as it too dealt with books by Marie Stopes that discussed contraception, and that decision had "established that a book is not a drug, medicine, or article." Judge Kirkpatrick had expressly stated, "I do not think the question of whether they contain birth control information is material under this act." The brief also reminded Judge Woolsey that in his *Married Love* decision, he had written that "a book dealing with such matters [as contraception] [probably does not] fall within the provisions of this Section." Their second point, elaborated in descriptions of Stopes's expert bona fides, was that the book clearly passed the Hicklin test and was not obscene: "The book is transparently not one which would tend to deprave the morals of persons into whose hands it might fall, by suggesting lewd thoughts or exciting sensual desires."[114]

On July 16, 1931, Judge Woolsey ruled on behalf of Stopes's *Contraception*, in the case formally titled *United States v. One Book, Entitled "Contraception," by Marie Stopes*.[115] He began his decision by noting that there was not "any possible question of res adjudicata, for the book 'Contraception,' so far as I am aware, is now for the first time libeled in a federal court to test the question of its admissibility under the section of the statutes above quoted." He noted that it was true that Judge Kirkpatrick, in the Eastern District of Pennsylvania, "had before him three books by this same author, which contained contraceptive information, namely, 'Wise Parenthood,' 'The First Five Thousand,' and an edition of 'Married Love'" that had not been expurgated as the previous edition before him had, and he directed the jury to return a verdict for the defendant on the ground that the said three books were not obscene and that they did not fall within the Tariff Act's prohibition on contraceptives. Considering then the only germane question of whether the book was obscene, he explained that *Contraception* was written primarily for the medical profession and "certainly does not fall within the test of obscenity or immorality laid down by me in the case of *United States v. One Obscene Book, Entitled Married Love*."[116]

Then, in language that expressed a sentiment and understanding not dissimilar to his *Ulysses* decision (issued three years later), he explained the effect the book had on him.

Actually the emotions aroused by the book are merely feelings of sympathy and pity, evoked by the many cases instanced in it of the sufferings of married women due to ignorance of its teachings. This, I believe, will be the inevitable effect of reading it on all persons of sensibility unless by their prejudices the information it contains is tabooed.[117]

As with his *Married Love* decision, Judge Woolsey steered clear of all the controversies circling around Stopes in the United Kingdom. He focused entirely on the language of the Tariff Act and on Stopes's text, regarded it as a serious work of considerable value to scientific and medical personnel, one that would not corrupt its readers, and held that it neither met the definition of obscenity nor was prohibited by the Tariff Act of 1930.[118]

One Strategic Step at a Time

Married Love and *Contraception* were among the first cases seeking to test the 1930 Tariff Act revisions. Those revisions included key provisions that Ernst and Lindey would effectively use in other cases (including in defense of James Joyce's *Ulysses* and on behalf of Indiana University's Institute for Sex Research), primarily that seizures by Customs officials could be challenged and appealed in the federal courts. This amended the virtually unchallengeable censorship authority that Customs had enjoyed before 1930, and libellants and their lawyers gained access to federal judges who were not expressly affiliated with the Customs Service and who could be more neutral referees.

Roughly sixteen months after Stopes and Ernst first discussed her legal problems, Judge Woolsey paved the way for her book to enter the marriage manuals marketplace in the United States, with a new version published in New York by Putnam's Sons, replete with a foreword written by Ernst and Lindey. Three months later, on July 16, 1931, Judge Woolsey held that *Contraception* was not obscene and was importable.[119] This decision helped limit Customs restrictions on the importation of information about birth control and its history (but not on birth control devices per se). It also clarified differences between Postal and Customs statutes. As the Ernst firm would note in their records of the *Contraception* case, "This was the first important decision on liberalizing the customs laws with reference to the importation of contraceptive literature."[120]

As Ernst had hoped, Judge Woolsey expanded the reach of the *Dennett* decision in *United States v. "Married Love,"* enhancing its value as a landmark ruling for future sexual information cases generally and also applying it to Customs authority. In addition, Judge Woolsey's decision quietly advanced the argument—available from Learned Hand's earlier *Kennerley* dicta language—that the courts could assume that audiences for these materials were reasonable and mature adults with justifiable, not salacious, interests in the profoundly complicated and sometimes unsettling issues of human sexuality. He noted that people suffered from an absence of adequate information.

Although Woolsey focused on the literal wording of the statutes, he was also clearly sympathetic to a critique that obscenity laws interfered with the intellectual and social needs of modern adults. He recognized that human interests in sexual matters, especially understanding something as important as contraception, were legitimate interests, not just for the medical readers for whom he thought the book was intended but also for ordinary people whose suffering required sympathy. Nowhere did he see any risk of harm to readers who might be "depraved and corrupted."

Although not as important as an expansive precedent as the *Dennett* case, Ernst and Lindey's defenses of *Married Love* and *Contraception* were important. They applied the new Tariff Act provisions and persuaded the federal courts to expand the logic of the *Dennett* decision to restrict Customs' censorship authority.[121] They also chalked up two more federal court decisions on behalf of serious works of sexology and considerably furthered women's claims to sexual and contraceptive knowledge. Not incidentally, they also found their dream judge in John M. Woolsey, whom they would return to in the *Ulysses* case.

As important, Ernst and Lindey saw that their incremental legal strategy was paying off. Congress was not going to transform obscenity laws, so they set about fashioning a body of cases and expanding case law to advance their anti-censorship cause one strategic step at a time. They did not push the courts to radical rethinking of existing doctrine; rather, they asked the courts to hear challenges to obscenity law statutes and administrative practices that were not meeting the needs of the public or of medical experts.

These two unheralded wins in the federal courts also reveal Ernst's deep understanding of the vast and elusive power of the Comstock laws and their insinuation into various parts of the federal code. Ernst described the act's tenacity and reach.

> The Comstock Act seems to have the prodigious vitality of the Serpent in the fairy tales, which, when the hero hacked it into pieces, came rushing at him with multiplied ferocity, each truncated portion doing quite well without the others, and living a furious life of its own. The Statute was cut up quite early in its history, and now appears in several different portions of the Federal Code. In order to win freedom from its narrow restriction, the proponents of birth control have had to challenge and overcome each section separately.[122]

The *Married Love* and *Contraception* cases helped do that. They were more than just battles against the "furious life" of the Comstock Act and its manifestations in the federal code, sixty years after its passage. They were also cases about freedom of speech and of the press, and Ernst and Lindey effectively framed them as such, in tandem with other censorship matters they were working on, including censorship of literary works. They were part of a larger free speech project, built in increments.

The big case that Ernst and Lindey worked on between Dennett's *Sex Side of Life* and Stopes's *Married Love*, the defense of Radclyffe Hall's lesbian-themed novel *The Well of Loneliness* (the subject of the next chapter), took up those virtues of reading that Judge Woolsey evoked: gaining empathy and having pity, recognizing human suffering, and using information as an antidote to ignorance. Ernst would pursue this course in defense of a book that dared address a taboo topic, homosexuality. This was a category so troubling that New York State legislators had banned its very expression from New York's stages in the late 1920s, making any theatrical treatment subject to criminal penalties. John Sumner and his allies wanted to make homosexuality virtually undiscussable in literature as well. In another series of cases dealing with the importation of an English writer's works, Ernst and his colleagues took up the defense of Radclyffe Hall's *The Well of Loneliness*, aiming to open that topic for rational and empathetic discussion. It would not be easy.[123]

CHAPTER 4

THE TABOO OF INVERSION

Radclyffe Hall and Literary Censorship

AT ITS CORE the modern commercial culture that boomed in the 1920s sold sex to sell its products, amplifying the prospect of unleashed female sexuality. Cultural forms that flaunted moral conventions and transgressed boundaries were bound to meet the censor's ire. The era's censorship battles raised fundamental questions about gatekeeping: Would the commercial vendors, with their appeals to titillation, exploitation, and lowbrow tastes, triumph? Would the cultural modernists, with their excursions into oedipal drives and repressed desires, win out over novels of moral uplift? Or could the moral guardians hold these forces at bay through continued control over the production, distribution, licensing, display, and performance of artistic and expressive artifacts?

In this chapter I look at those questions by examining a transatlantic battle over Radclyffe Hall's 1928 novel, *The Well of Loneliness*. Long regarded as *the* most important English-language lesbian novel of the early to mid-twentieth century, *The Well of Loneliness* brought particular anxieties to the fore because of its subject matter. Lesbianism, or "inversion," as Hall referred to it, was essentially a taboo subject and had been officially banned from New York's theatrical stages by the New York State legislature when it passed the Wales Act in 1927. The law was premised on fears of "homosexual recruitment," especially fear that young female audiences were susceptible to the "contagion" of lesbianism.[1] Passage of the Wales Law unquestionably frames the legal and cultural context of the contest over Hall's book in the United States, which occurred when the publisher, Covici-Friede, decided to publish it, knowing full well that it would produce a showdown with John Sumner.

The Well of Loneliness

The Well of Loneliness focuses on the pains and pleasures of life as "an invert"—the prevailing term in the sexology literature for female homosexuals who presented as masculine and, more generally, those individuals who believed their gender role was opposite to their biological sex.[2] Stephen Gordon, the book's protagonist, is born to wealthy country squire parents who longed for and expected a son but produced a daughter. Despite her sex, they gave her the boy's name they had already chosen. Even at birth Stephen resembles a boy, a "narrow-hipped, wide-shouldered little tadpole of a baby."[3] She remains boyish through her childhood: She hates dressing like a girl, prefers boys' clothes and outdoor roughhousing, wants to be a boy, and at age 7 has her first inklings of inchoate physical desire for a family housemaid named Collins. When Stephen discovers Collins lying with a young man working on the estate, she breaks into a jealous rage. Her father, Sir Phillip, had already discerned his daughter's "difference," and after learning about Stephen's feelings for Collins, he promises he will raise her as though she were a boy, to be strong and courageous. He loves and dotes on her, making her his riding and fox-hunting companion and working to equip her for the world she will encounter. Her mother, Anna, is painfully aware of her feelings of repulsion toward her child and never shows her sustained affection or comes to terms with her daughter's difference.

Hall establishes Stephen's difference from the outset. Other characters know all along that Stephen is somehow "queer" in her refusal of normal girlhood interests, and they comment on it—on her appetite, her tall stature, her apparel, and her habit of riding astride horses as men do. The novel's first 200 pages plot Stephen's gradual realization of her condition as an "invert." Readers learn early on, for instance, that Sir Phillip goes to his study late at night to read the works of early sexologists, including Karl Heinrich Ulrichs and Richard von Krafft-Ebing, to try to understand his daughter.

He intends to explain to her what he has learned but cannot bring himself to do so, even when she asks him if something is wrong with her. In his dying breath, following a tree-pruning accident, he strains unsuccessfully to reveal his discoveries to his wife and daughter.

As Stephen grows into early womanhood, her differences, and the unkindness of others, make her shy and socially awkward. She has none of the typical desires to appeal to and flirt with men, although she admires masculine traits. To everyone's surprise, she becomes a boon companion to Martin Hallam, a visitor from British Columbia, a gentle young man who would have been a fine choice had Stephen been capable of loving him romantically. But when he declares his love for her, she is horrified and runs from his company. He returns home, and she grows lonelier, still not quite understanding herself. At age 21 Stephen falls in love and has her physical passions stirred again, this time with a married woman, Angela Crossby, the flirtatious young American wife of a new neighbor. Stephen is smitten and aroused by Angela and grows jealous when she learns that Angela is also having an affair with a neighboring man whom Stephen loathes as her childhood bully. Stephen writes anguished letters to Angela, but Angela's husband, who refers to Stephen as a freak, discovers them and reveals them to Stephen's mother. Her mother chillingly denounces her "unnatural cravings" and expels Stephen from her beloved home and estate. Stephen fights back against her mother's denunciations, claiming the legitimacy of her love for Angela and how "good, good, good" it feels.

Following the fight with her mother, Stephen repairs to her father's study and unlocks his desk drawer to find that he had been reading the era's most influential studies of sexology and homosexuality. Opening the well-marked book by Krafft-Ebing—presumably his famous *Psychopathia Sexualis*—she finds her name in her father's hand, penned over and over again in the margins of Krafft-Ebing's discussion of sexual inversion. She finally learns what her father knew about her, and now she has a name for it: God made her an invert. Stephen does not reject or run from this self-understanding but feels the loneliness and anguish of other peoples' attitudes toward inverts and recognizes that her God-given "flaw" would always make her an outsider.[4] In a critical scene Stephen stands naked before her mirror and, noting her broad shoulders, small breasts, and long muscular legs, despairs that she cannot have the man's body she desires.

Stephen leaves home and becomes a writer and, like Hall, finds success with her first novel. She moves to London and then to Paris and there discovers and moves through a world of inverts, male and female, gathered around a salon hosted by the seductive Valérie Seymour. During World War I Stephen and others join an ambulance unit, where she falls in love with a younger fellow driver, Mary Llewellyn. Mary—who might or might not be an invert by birth—falls in love as well and eagerly takes Stephen in her arms "and that night they were not divided."[5] Their love is physical, emotional, and erotic, and following the war they live as a couple, happily and amorously, and "at night they would lie in each other's arms."[6] But their happiness crumbles as Stephen becomes more deeply immersed in her writing, and Mary, increasingly lonely and cut off from a social life, descends into the debaucheries of Paris nightlife that Stephen introduced her to. When Stephen's old suitor Martin returns to Stephen's life, he unexpectedly falls in love with Mary. Believing that Mary will find greater happiness with Martin and suffer less from the prejudices of the world, Stephen and Martin conspire to create the impression that Stephen is having an affair with Valérie Seymour, freeing Mary to fall in love with Martin. At the novel's end, Stephen sacrifices her own love for Mary's sake and finds herself in a well of loneliness beseeching God—and the novel's readers—"Acknowledge us, oh God, before the whole world. Give us also the right to our existence!"[7]

Literary Criticism and Public Reception

Although not an autobiographical novel, much of Radclyffe Hall's early life and sense of self can be read into Stephen. Radclyffe Hall's persona as a cross-dressing "mannish lesbian" has always been inseparable from the literary criticism and controversies surrounding her work.[8] As Jane Rule explains about Hall, "She was known to everyone as John. She wore men's jackets and ties, had a short haircut, and in all manners was gallantly masculine."[9] Hall faced and expressed her inversion through her chosen name and manner of appearance, an expression of nature she could not change. Hall described *The Well* as the "first long and very serious novel entirely upon the subject of sexual inversion," and her chief purpose in writing it was to explain inversion as a natural, inborn condition.[10] There was no clearer way to do this other than through a character marked off by her masculine traits but who also becomes fully identified with her "mannish lesbian" self.

Esther Newton writes that Stephen Gordon was created by "an 'out' and tie-wearing lesbian" who put a mannish lesbian at the center of the story because that was a character whose trajectory matched the experiences of generations of readers who would have been eager for Hall's book. As Newton explains, by the turn of the century this cross-dressed figure had become the publicly recognized expression of a new social and sexual category, "lesbian," and Hall, like many other feminists of her era, "embraced, sometimes with ambivalence, the image of the mannish lesbian" because she wanted to embrace the erotic and sexual in her romantic attachments. Moreover, donning masculine clothing was a signal of romantic and sexual availability to other women: "Before they could find one another in the twentieth-century urban landscape, they had to become visible, at least to each other."[11]

The Well of Loneliness created a stir from the time of its publication in July 1928 until deep into the twentieth century and has borne the burden of representation because it has been widely regarded as *the* lesbian novel, as Jane Rule and many others note.[12] It became "a title familiar to most readers of fiction" and for decades was seen as "either a bible or a horror story for any lesbian who reads at all."[13] Although Stephen's embodiment of the mannish lesbian became more problematic for later critics (who came to see it as a "horror story" because of the book's tragic ending and because Stephen reads as a stereotype of lesbianism), Esther Newton writes that the book's strong appeal to generations of readers has always been great "because it confronts the stigma of lesbianism . . . [of having] had to face being called, or at least feeling like, freaks."[14]

Hall drew on the most credible medical and sexological literature available to educate her protagonists and to instruct her readers about inversion. As Rule writes, "Radclyffe Hall had read Krafft-Ebing, as well as the less well-known studies of Karl Heinrich Ulrichs, himself a homosexual trying to prove that inversion was as natural an orientation as left-handedness."[15] Hall also drew on the works of Edward Carpenter, although his name is not mentioned in the novel itself; Carpenter wrote extensively and supportively about "the intermediate sex" (another name for inverts). Hall has one character trumpet Carpenter's ideas, hoping to make Stephen feel better about herself.[16] As Rule explains, Hall was trying to both understand herself and her sexual appetites and give her readers "insight into the experiences of inverts."[17]

When *The Well* appeared in London's bookshops at the end of July 1928, it initially received "largely favorable response[s] by sober reviewers."[18] But those initial positive impressions were almost entirely eclipsed by the controversies that ensued. Hall's English publisher, Jonathan Cape, knew it would likely be scandalous. Indeed, other publishers in England and the United States refused it, including Doubleday, Houghton Mifflin, and Harper's. Blanche and Alfred Knopf had initially agreed to publish a U.S. version but backed out once it became clear that the subject matter would create a publicity stir and likely legal problems as well.[19] Hoping to forestall trouble but also angling to get his imprimatur on the book's treatment of inversion, Hall enlisted Havelock Ellis. She gave him the novel's typescript; she knew that "his endorsement would, among other outcomes, lend the project legitimacy" and declare to potential readers that it was not "simply a 'salacious diversion.'"[20] Ellis agreed and wrote a commentary that functions as the book's foreword, but to avoid legal trouble, Cape bowdlerized Ellis's words, replacing "inversion" with the phrase "one particular aspect of sexual life," a euphemism "so vague as to be practically meaningless."[21]

Nevertheless, Ellis's endorsement worked, and many of the first reviewers noted that they were drawn to the book because his name was attached. Fourteen of England's most prominent newspapers and journals reviewed *The Well of Loneliness* in its first three weeks in print, before the storm hit.[22] The *Nation*, the *Saturday Review*, and the *Times Literary Supplement* all reviewed it, as did influential critics ranging from such modernist gatekeepers as Leonard and Virginia Woolf to "middlebrow hitmakers" like Arnold Bennett.[23] Virginia Woolf famously called *The Well* a "meritorious dull book" that was "paled, tepid, vapid."[24] But other reviewers found that the novel had considerable merit, including Leonard Woolf, who spoke of Hall's "very considerable gifts for novel writing." Although reviewers warned readers that the topic might not suit everyone's taste, they also recommended keeping an open mind, as they knew the book was surely on a dangerous path.[25]

The Well sold well immediately. The original print run of 1,500 copies quickly ran out, and Cape doubled that number for the second printing. Orders poured in after Hall's critics and legal authorities pounced on the book. By the end of its first month in print, 5,000 copies were already in circulation. But the book's legal troubles began within weeks of its release and made the original positive reception by critics recede from memory. The vituperative attacks against it and its subsequent legal travails immediately shifted the conversation from whether it was a good read to whether it was a moral outrage and should be banned. As Doan and Prosser write, the result was that "all future critical discussion of the novel could not but engage with or refer to the controversy" that enveloped the book.[26]

Douglas's Attack and the Resulting Legal Actions in the United Kingdom

Despite his efforts to ward off scandal by using Ellis's bona fides and packaging the book in sober colors with expensive cloth and paper, Jonathan Cape was on his way to court within weeks of publishing The Well of Loneliness. The attacks began in the tabloid press, when James Douglas, a provocative publicity-seeking editor of London's Sunday Express newspaper, warned in banner headlines and in a much promoted review that the book posed moral dangers, was propaganda for perversion, and needed to be immediately suppressed. Douglas's vitriolic campaign against The Well of Loneliness began on Saturday, August 18, 1928, less than three weeks after its publication, with advertising that the next day's paper would expose "A Book That Should Be Suppressed." The preview also offered in bold print a now infamous teaser quote from the editorial, "I would rather give a healthy boy or a healthy girl a phial of prussic acid than this novel. Poison kills the body, but moral poison kills the soul."[27] The next day's Sunday Express continued the attack with three different headlines: "Novel

That Should Be Banned," "Story of Perverted Lives," and "Nauseating," followed by Douglas's editorial, which began by calling the book an "intolerable outrage—the first outrage of this kind in the annals of English fiction."[28] To stave off the publication of any more books like this one and to "prevent the contamination and corruption of English fiction," Douglas described his duty as a critic "to make it impossible for any other novelist to repeat this outrage. I say deliberately that this novel is not fit to be sold by any bookseller or to be borrowed from any library."[29]

Douglas complained that homosexuality had already become "too visible" and demanded immediate suppression so that society could "cleans[e] itself from the leprosy of these lepers." He succeeded, producing prompt legal action against the book by the home secretary, Sir William Joynson-Hicks, who insisted that the director of public prosecutions begin legal proceedings under authority of the Obscene Publications Act of 1857.[30] Because the book might be read by people of all ages, Douglas argued that the theme itself made it impermissible. For Douglas, lesbianism as a subject was obscene, as were the very people about whom Hall had written.

> I am well aware that sexual inversion and perversion are horrors which exist among us today. They flaunt themselves in public places with increasing effrontery and more insolently provocative bravado. The decadent apostles of the most hideous and most loathsome vices no longer conceal their degeneracy and their degradation.[31]

Douglas argued that the "contagion" that "pervades our social life" must be arrested and the book destroyed. Calling homosexuals lepers, moral derelicts, social outliers, perverts, and more, he also warned that the book's literary quality made it even more dangerous: "It is a seductive and insidious piece of special pleading designed to display a perverted decadence as a martyrdom inflected upon these outcasts by a cruel society."[32]

As Douglas hoped, Joynson-Hicks promptly denounced the book as "gravely detrimental to the public interest" and demanded that Cape cease publishing it or face legal action. Cape complied, at least partly. He stopped publishing the book in London but gave the publishing rights to Pegasus

Press in France and sent Pegasus the printing plates he had used for his London imprint. Pegasus promptly used them and mailed copies back to England, to meet the demand stimulated by Douglas's screed. Joynson-Hicks ordered British customs officials to seize all copies shipped from France and began obscenity proceedings against Jonathan Cape.[33]

The British press covered every move of the unfolding scandal, just as Douglas wished. Despite some ambivalence about its literary quality, England's leading literary figures mobilized and roundly denounced the censorial actions of the home secretary. Arnold Dawson, publisher of the *Daily Herald*, enlisted H. G. Wells and George Bernard Shaw to lead the writers' campaign against the prosecution, and Leonard Woolf and E. M. Forster drafted a letter of protest against *The Well*'s suppression. They assembled a list of supporters that included T. S. Eliot, Arnold Bennett, Vera Brittain, Virginia Woolf, and Lytton Strachey.

In preparing to defend the book, Cape's London law firm, Rubinstein-Nash, mailed out more than 160 letters, mostly to writers, seeking witnesses to speak on behalf of the book. By the time of the trial, Cape's barrister, Norman Birkett, had the support of at least forty writers who had agreed to testify. Hall's support among writers wound up having no bearing on the trial itself, because although they showed up in the courtroom, they were not allowed to testify. In fact, the chief magistrate, Sir Chartres Biron, permitted no testimony in the book's defense whatsoever, not even by Hall herself. The publisher, Jonathan Cape, was on trial, not Hall, and when she attempted to defend her novel in court, she was quickly silenced.

The core issue at trial was the topic of female inversion. Hall wanted Birkett to address her book's central argument: that being an invert was inborn and not a matter of choice or failure of will. Hall was a devout Catholic and viewed her orientation as God-given. But her book also aimed to tell the world that the condition was a great burden because of society's rejection. Even though the book was not autobiographical per se, it was certainly a product of Hall's own experiences. She wanted readers—and the court—to know about the genuine love women could have for one another and also about the terrible pain of being outcast and silenced. But Birkett's strategy minimized those issues and focused on the work's literary merit, also arguing that it did not fail the Hicklin test. To Hall's fury, Birkett made no effort to allow her to testify and did not adequately present her book's purposes.[34]

Chief Magistrate Biron held with Douglas's view that the topic of lesbianism itself was obscene and swatted away Birkett's argument about the book's literary value, asserting that its literary merit actually made it more dangerous. Applying the Hicklin test, which was used in courts on both sides of the Atlantic, Biron thought the work would deprave and corrupt potential readers. He added that "a well-written obscene book was even more harmful than a poorly written one."[35] Biron held that the book might have been allowed had it denounced homosexuality and "depicted the 'moral and physical degradation which indulgence in those vices must necessary involve.'" But Hall's refusal to damn her characters made it obscene. Biron ruled that "no reasonable person could say that a plea for the recognition and toleration of inverts was not obscene."[36] He ordered the book destroyed.

On appeal, the enforced silence around the topic was even more pronounced, as the Court of Quarter Sessions not only denied any testimony from defense witnesses but also did not even allow the twelve impaneled magistrates to read and study the book themselves. The court permitted only selected passages read aloud by the attorney general. In December 1928 the Court of Quarter Sessions upheld Magistrate Biron's finding that the book was obscene and ordered all copies seized by police and destroyed.[37]

The decision by the English courts, along with the "intense and sensational publicity" around the trial, sealed the book's place in the history of literary censorship.[38] It also set the stage for Morris Ernst's defense of *The Well of Loneliness* on behalf of its U.S. publishers, a defense plotted as much to wage a censorship fight with John Sumner as to make a commitment to Hall's novel and its goal of producing empathy for inverts.

Covici-Friede and Ernst Team Up

When Knopf withdrew from its commitment to publish Hall's book, it created a chance for Pascal "Pat" Covici and Donald Friede to make a name for their fledgling New York City–based publishing house and perhaps produce big sales.[39] They were willing to publish higher end "erotica," and

FIGURE 7. Radclyffe Hall, British novelist and author of *The Well of Loneliness.*

Friede decided he wanted to publish Hall's novel after he learned about the subject of lesbianism and the scandal around the book at a party at the home of novelist Theodore Dreiser, although Friede presumed the book was more erotic than it was.[40] (Dreiser himself had no shortage of censorship fights over his works, especially *Sister Carrie* and *An American Tragedy*, and was always willing to enter a fray against Sumner.) Friede and Covici immediately took out a loan of $10,000 to buy the copyright from Cape. At that cost, they needed a best seller.[41]

Covici and Friede were not afraid of censorship battles. Both had had run-ins with censors before forming their partnership—Covici in Chicago and in Florida and Friede in Boston. In fact, Covici had already been charged with violating Postal obscenity laws when he worked in Chicago and published a Ben Hecht book with "phallic illustrations." In April 1927 Friede, then employed by Boni & Liveright, had helped set off the Banned in Boston protests by selling a copy of Dreiser's *An American Tragedy* to a police officer. (He was convicted and his case was on appeal when he and Covici bought the rights to *The Well of Loneliness*.)[42] Nor were Covici and Friede interested in displaying the deference to Sumner exhibited by the more established publishing houses, such as the deference Knopf had just shown in backing out of publishing *The Well*. The book was defensible because it was not salacious, but it stood an excellent chance of being attacked by Sumner, which would be good for business.[43]

As early as August 1928, as Douglas was ginning up his attack on the book in London, Covici and Friede began negotiating the U.S. publication rights for Hall's novel with Jonathan Cape and Pegasus Books. (Knopf had withdrawn from its contract with Hall and Cape but had already printed copies before doing so and the *New York Times* had even reported that Knopf would publish the book in the United States.)[44] Seizing their chance, Covici and Friede met with Ernst to plan a strategy for rolling out the book in the United States. The lawyer and his clients knew from the outset that they would have a fight and agreed to take it directly to Sumner. Once they had the rights to the book, they followed Ernst's instructions and notified Sumner that they intended to publish the novel.

Besides provoking Sumner, Ernst wanted to pursue another angle. He believed that publishers needed to incur more of the risk and told Friede he wanted to force Sumner to go after the publishers themselves rather than his usual tactic of arresting "some unsuspecting bookstore clerk."[45] It rankled him that New York's obscenity law made the bookstore clerks (and owners) who sold supposedly obscene works subject to arrests while the book publishers suffered only financially.

Ernst had recently published *To the Pure* (1928) and was making his way into a career built on censorship fights. At the same time he was taking on Covici and Friede as clients, he was engaged in the defense of Mary Ware Dennett's *The Sex Side of Life* and looking for battles with Sumner. As Leslie Taylor notes, Sumner was eager to oblige the publisher's interests in a censorship fight and, when he heard about Covici and Friede's interest in publishing *The Well*, he immediately warned them that it was "literary refuse" and "vicious." He found the novel especially troubling because of Hall's plea that homosexuals be "accepted on the same plane as persons normally constituted."[46] Sumner warned them to reconsider their "intent to publish same here, particularly in view of the fact that the law in England and here and its interpretation is about the same."[47]

Not deterred, Covici-Friede quickly brought out its U.S. edition of *The Well of Loneliness* on December 15, 1928, less than a month after the book was ordered destroyed by Magistrate Biron and despite Sumner's warning letter. In fact, Covici and Friede invited Sumner to personally purchase one of their first copies. Two days after its publication, Ernst accompanied Sumner to Covici-Friede's offices, where Sumner asked Friede perfunctory questions about the book's publication and then bought a copy from him for $5. Sumner turned the copy over to Chief Magistrate McAdoo and obtained a search warrant for the publisher's facilities.[48]

Sumner did not immediately use the warrant, but Ernst and his clients knew a raid was coming. While they waited for the raid, they sent out copies to readers (primarily writers, critics, and public health experts) so they could gather opinions about the novel's literary merits and line up potential expert testimony, hopeful that New York's courts would allow witnesses to speak about the book. Ernst sought information about the book's legal travails in England, beginning an extensive correspondence with Cape's lawyers in London, particularly Harold Rubinstein of the Rubinstein-Nash law firm. Rubinstein provided legal memoranda, trial transcripts, and all the publicity materials surrounding the case, including the petitions and letters of support from British writers that Leonard Woolf had organized. He also gave them a detailed explanation of the English magistrate's bias in the case and even offered to enlist Havelock Ellis's help.[49] These materials chastened Ernst. He admitted in a letter to Rubinstein, "Were it not for the English decision, I think we would surely win."[50]

Ernst and his clients also laid the groundwork with journalists and editors to prepare sympathetic newspaper editorials to be published when Sumner finally struck. He did, on January 12, 1929, just shy of a month after his first visit to the Covici-Friede offices. Sumner returned with warrant in hand, accompanied by two police officers and his usual sidekick in these matters, the Vice Society's Charles Bamberger. Their raid netted 865 copies and garnered some attention from the *New York Times*.[51]

Meanwhile, the notoriety from the British trials and Sumner's raid was auspicious for book sales. As Leslie Taylor reports, Covici-Friede inherited a small number of expensively produced editions from Knopf, which they repackaged and sold as a "prepublication edition" for the price of $10; these immediately sold out. They also sold their own edition at $5 a copy. Covici-Friede sold 20,000 copies of *The Well of Loneliness* within the first month and over 100,000 copies within the first year. Hall's first royalty check from Covici-Friede was more than $60,000 (approximately $900,000 in 2019), getting the publishers "off to a roaring start," as Friede wrote.[52] Whether their luck would hold would depend on their success in the New York courts.

To the Pure Versus the Wales Act

Ernst knew from writing *To the Pure* that a useful body of case law from the early 1920s offered a good chance that New York's courts might hold for the novel. Ernst also appreciated that Sumner was far from invincible in the state's courts and in fact had lost several literary obscenity cases in the

1920s on books dealing with lesbianism or female sexual transgression. Plus, Sumner had far more critics than supporters among New York's journalists, book publishers, writers, and booksellers. Ernst assumed that they would be keen to challenge Sumner's censorship actions against a serious work by a respected English novelist who had won two prestigious book awards.

But other currents were in motion. The theme of lesbianism was already highly contentious in New York State in 1928–1929. In fact, the very topic or representation of lesbianism had been recently banned from New York's stages by the New York State legislature when it passed the Wales Act in 1928. The Wales Act grew out of fears of homosexual recruitment and predation, particularly on susceptible young women. Throughout the 1920s, Sumner, the Vice Society, and the New York Police Department policed "queer" spaces in New York City, including bars, clubs, flophouses, and theaters, making arrests and shutting down business for violating New York State's Public Laws 1141 and 1145 against indecency and obscene performances. The perception that any depiction of homosexuality was indecent and that a sympathetic (and especially an erotically charged) portrayal might lead audience members to unnatural acts could spur police enforcement.

Warnings of homosexual "recruitment" by way of live performance gained particularly attention in New York City in the mid-1920s in response to a play by Edouard Bourdet titled *The Captive*. This play, featuring an older woman keeping a younger woman "captive" in a manipulative relationship turned out to be highly popular among young women in the city, who came singly and in couples to see it performed. The city's moral guardians noticed. As Leslie Taylor and Andrea Friedman both explain, New York officials, at the urging of Sumner and the Vice Society, the Hearst newspapers, churchmen, and women's social hygiene reform groups, mobilized to shut down the play.[53] *The Captive*, first staged in 1926, played for 160 performances before William Randolph Hearst's papers the *New York American* and the *New York Daily Mirror* ran a campaign vilifying it. Sumner and his allies from the Better Public Shows Movement took up the cause, eventually leading to the arrest of the entire cast in February 1927 and the play's closure on obscenity charges.[54]

Soon, a New York State legislative campaign against indecency on stage gained momentum, focusing on sex-themed plays, most dealing with homosexuality, including *The Captive*, *The Virgin Man*, and two Mae West productions, *SEX* and *The Drag*.[55] In 1928 the New York legislature passed the state law known as the Wales Act. This draconian law gave the New York commissioner of licenses broad authority—a so-called padlock law—to shut down any theaters that violated the ban on anything "depicting or dealing with the subject of sex degeneracy, or sex perversion," and to strip the owners of their licenses. It also expanded the reach of the state's obscenity laws into movie theaters. "Padlocking" quickly became a synonym for censorship. The law put enormous pressure on theater owners to keep their stages free of "indecent" productions and was soon used to harass and eventually close down New York City's burlesque theaters as well.[56]

The Wales Act did not define the legal space Ernst and his colleagues could work within in their defense of Hall's *Well of Loneliness* because it did not deal with books.[57] (Public Law 1141 did.) But it potentially made the case more difficult because, among other things, the Wales Act could be construed as a clear expression of legislative intent and current community tastes and mores against any depiction "of sex degeneracy, or sex perversion." It would be difficult for judges to ignore this backdrop.[58] How far might the state's courts go in further prohibiting lesbianism as a topic? Would they essentially extend the logic of the Wales Act and declare the subject matter itself ipso facto obscene and ban it from print, as the legislature had done with theater?

Ernst thought they had New York case law behind them, along with increasingly powerful allies in the press and the publishing world and the momentum of a growing anti-censorship sentiment that had continued to develop in the decade after World War I. Opposition to censorship of literary works, a medium that had more cultural authority than film or burlesque or live theater, was especially strong. New York City, home to many of the nation's most established publishing houses as well as the newer, more adventurous publishers such as Covici-Friede, Boni & Liveright, Viking Press, and Vanguard Press, also meant that the book industry was a formidable and growing economic force in the city. In addition, the city had an important infrastructure of literary journals and newspapers. It was a good place to mobilize readers, writers, editors, academics, booksellers, and others who already reviled Comstockery and Sumner's extension of it into the late 1920s.

Ernst was therefore sure he could garner the support of the city's literary and publishing communities and counted on admiring reviews of Hall's novel. Those, however, were not as forthcoming as he had hoped.

New York City Magistrate Court, Spring 1929

Typically, when Sumner brought an obscene libel action—the legal name for officially charging an object obscene—against a book and its sellers in any of New York City's five boroughs, a magistrate court judge would be the first to offer an opinion on the libeled book's obscenity. If the magistrate thought that there were legitimate grounds for the charge, he would call for a trial in the Court of Special Sessions or could drop the libel if he found the charge unmerited. However, either Sumner or the district attorney's office could challenge that decision and still bring the offending work to the Court of Special Sessions. (Whether Sumner did this usually depended on the depth of his outrage toward a work, or toward the defense counsel.) Those Court of Special Sessions decisions could then be appealed through the state's appellate court system if they were adverse to the defendant.

Ernst assumed Hall's novel would likely be held for trial. As he told Rubinstein, the decisions in the English courts spelled trouble. He was right to worry. Whatever optimism Ernst might have had about the case vanished in the first paragraph of Magistrate Hyman Bushel's February 1929 decision, a remarkable document revealing just how ready he was to condemn "predatory" lesbians.

According to Section 1141 of the New York State Penal Law, "A person who sells . . . or has in his possession with intent to sell . . . any obscene, lewd, lascivious, filthy, indecent or disgusting book . . . is guilty of a misdemeanor." Bushel said that the consideration in the case was to determine whether "as a matter of law" the book was or was not obscene.[59] Like Biron's frequent references to "horrible practices," Magistrate Bushel's opinion repeatedly equated homosexuality with "perversion" and the threat of predation. His ruling drew dichotomies between "normality," "morality," "society," and "the public" and their implicit opposites—"perverts," "perversion," "unnatural tendencies," "queer attraction," and other damning phrases. As Magistrate Bushel explained in his decision, his job was to protect potentially wayward citizen-souls from straying and losing their place in society.[60] He also reported that the court had a duty to uphold "the will of the people," as expressed by the Wales Act. Like Magistrate Biron, he thought literature's power to subvert morality was heightened when it was well written, and so this book's capacity to elicit sympathy and understanding made it more dangerous and subversive. Judge Bushel had no doubt that vulnerable readers would be susceptible to Hall's pleas.

Strikingly, however, Judge Bushel offered up a different vulnerable reader than the usual potential victims. Instead of the young, the female, and the imbecilic, he focused on the book's threat to the cosmopolitan and literary-minded. They were vulnerable not only because they might already have a predisposition toward homosexuality but also because their literary or aesthetic cultivations made them sensitive and therefore empathetic readers. They might be inclined to try "new sensations" and could be recruited through felicitous expression.[61] Bushel thus had in mind the Hicklin standard and the book's potential to deprave and corrupt those into whose hands it might fall. But he quarreled with the idea of gauging "the mental and moral capacity of the community by that of its dullest-witted and most fallible member." This usual interpretation of the Hicklin standard "overlooks the fact that those who are subject to perverted influences and in whom that abnormality may be called into activity . . . are not limited to the young and immature, the moron, the mentality weak, or the intellectually impoverished."[62]

Judge Bushel also explained that the recently passed Wales Act meant he had to adhere to legislative intent.[63] Passage of the Wales Act was irrefutable evidence that "the community . . . has evinced a public policy . . . hostile to the presentation and circulation of matter treating sexual depravity." Favorably quoting Judge McAvoy's decision in *The Captive* case in New York's appellate division, Bushel too thought any treatment of perversion might "give to some minds a lecherous swing, causing a corruption of the moral tone of the susceptible members' of the community."[64] Hall's novel thus failed the Hicklin test: It had a strong prospect of depraving and corrupting those into whose hands it might fall. Neither its literary quality nor the opinions of literary experts had any bearing on its value, as its potential harm was clear.(Like the British jurists, Judge Bushel would not hear from witnesses, asserting that "it has been held that the opinions of experts are inadmissible.")[65]

Like Biron, Magistrate Bushel discussed the plot and the book's central characters. Instead of reading Hall's novel with a sympathetic eye toward those born to the condition, as Hall had hoped readers would do, Bushel focused on the victims of homosexual recruitment. He saw the novel's central question as being whether, after Stephen seduced the "normal girl" Mary, she would also capture her body and soul, thus jeopardizing Mary as a "helpless subject of . . . perverted influence and passion."[66] Magistrate Bushel concluded his decision by reiterating that the book violated New York Public Law 1141, the spirit and purposes of the Wales Act, and the Hicklin test: "I am convinced that *The Well of Loneliness* tends to debauch public morals, that its subject matter is offensive to public decency, and that it is calculated to deprave and corrupt minds open to its immoral influences and who might come in contact with it." He ordered a complaint to be heard against the defendants in the Court of Special Sessions.[67]

Bushel's decision made it clear to Ernst and his clients that they would be up against more than the strict letter of New York State's obscenity law in the Court of Special Sessions. They were up against serious social fears and prejudices. The language about what was "natural" and "unnatural" was deeply problematic for any defense of the book. Redefining the question within a more scientific framework of whether homosexuality was inborn or chosen would shift the conversation away from moral categories toward medical and psychological ones. Although Ernst and Lindey could not push too far on the inconclusive sexological science surrounding homosexuality, they needed support from the scientific literature that inversion was a congenital condition.

Ernst's Legal Strategy

After their drubbing in the magistrate court, the defense counsel had to deal with the complicated question of harm in preparation for the Court of Special Sessions. Homosexuality, described in the law as being unnatural and feared in the culture as a potential contagion, was a vexing subject matter for a legal defense. The British courts and Magistrate Bushel had summoned two core assumptions about harm: first, that any even slightly sympathetic discussion of homosexuality would be morally harmful; and, second, that because of literature's seductive effects, any well-written book that subverted cultural norms might be harmful to its readers. Ernst and his colleagues had to address these assumptions about the novel's potential harms and also make the case for its possible value to readers and for society at large. But they had to downplay—perhaps elide altogether—any discussion of homosexual desire and passion. Perhaps taking a cue from Biron, they had to accentuate Hall's thesis that Stephen's inversion was a tragic condition—a "well of loneliness"—and not a fate anyone would willingly choose after reading the novel.

Because Ernst had already researched and written about how the courts had treated themes of lesbianism and inversion in his 1928 book *To the Pure*, he could effectively situate Hall's book within a recent body of decisions in New York about literary depictions of transgressive sexuality. However, Ernst and his team were not so well versed in the fields of "sexual hygiene" or "sexology" and the relevant literature about lesbianism and inversion in particular. They needed quick schooling to get their footing and to address the specific question of whether homosexuality was congenital or acquired. Their defense rested on whether the book posed a threat of depravity and corruption to its potential readers. Ernst and his colleagues quickly learned that the "scientific" literature about inversion in the field of sexology was rife with competing arguments. Even the sexology literature that Hall drew on to educate Stephen's father and to instruct Stephen (and her readers) was not straightforward on these questions. One psychiatrist whom Ernst and colleagues contacted warned that trying to define the sexological or medical issues for the court would lead to a morass of competing theories and should be avoided. Ernst reached out to several doctors and psychiatrists and ultimately made use of three key resources: lawyer Huntington Cairns, psychiatrist Frederic Wertham, and bibliophile and expert in the literature on homosexuality Kenneth Sweezy.[68]

Cairns admired *To the Pure* and needed Ernst's advice on an obscenity case he was working on on behalf of the Peabody Bookshop in Baltimore. Because the core question at the heart of obscenity law was whether the hypothetical reader would be adversely affected by the materials in question, both Ernst and Cairns were interested in whether potential readers could become corrupted merely by reading a given text. Cairns had made a study of the rules of evidence and succeeded in answering this question in the courtroom by getting a psychiatric witness admitted to testify, Dr. Frederic Wertham of Johns Hopkins University. Wertham testified, Cairns wrote, that "only a psychiatrist or a psychologist could tell whether a book or a picture would tend to degrade or corrupt the individual into whose hands it might fall." Cairns thought this was "the first time . . . that the testimony of a psychiatrist has ever been admitted for this purpose."[69] Although Wertham had testified on behalf of the Peabody Book Shop, in defense of George Moore's version of *Daphnis and Chloe*, that "none of the books or pictures in the case would have a detrimental, degrading or corrupting effect" on the different "classes of persons—the intelligent well-educated individual, the average normal individual, the young impressionable child or adolescent," there was a caveat: The work in question "might have a detrimental effect upon the abnormal individual, that is the invert or the pervert."[70] This could be tricky terrain, especially because both Ulrichs and Krafft-Ebing also thought that masturbation made people susceptible to inversion.

Cairns put Ernst directly in touch with Dr. Wertham, and just days after Covici-Friede published the book, Ernst sent Wertham a copy. Ernst explained that they anticipated action by Sumner's Vice Society and wanted to enlist Wertham's testimony as "the first step in the introduction of common sense in the determination as to just what literature, if any, is harmful."[71] Explaining that his pending showdown with Sumner was part of a larger action among "publishers, authors and critics [who] are independently organizing in opposition to the censorship," he reported that he would be focusing on the legal question of harm and that the "theory of the prosecution will be that the theme of inversion should be barred from literature." He described this as a "retrograde" position, akin to "the stand taken against the distribution of abolitionist literature 75 years ago, or the stand taken in regard to witchcraft 150 years ago."[72]

Wertham was willing to help. Following Sumner's raid in January 1929, Ernst and his colleagues traveled to Baltimore to meet Wertham in person.[73] Their notes from the meeting show that Wertham had already read the book, and he offered them two key points of advice before their first magistrate court hearing scheduled for a week later. He told them, "Don't use words like 'Lesbian.' This is a story of a woman not fully developed; thwarted in life" and that "if the word 'homosexual' is used, we should get a doctor in order to define it." Wertham followed up by sending Ernst his extensive analysis of the book, a document that would prove to be particularly valuable for Ernst and his team for framing their argument for the Court of Special Sessions in April.[74]

Wertham assessed the book's probable effects on readers, analyzed Stephen Gordon's condition, and offered an opinion on whether the book was obscene. Describing it as a "very well-written novel of considerable artistic merit," he focused primarily on Stephen's psychological and emotional development and the pain she suffered from her inversion. Alluding only briefly to her same-sex attachments, Wertham never mentioned her obvious masculine traits, such as her cross-dressing, her physical bearing, or even her name. Instead, she was "an English woman of the upper classes, intelligent and endowed with a strong tendency to moral ideals," whose "outstanding feature of her life is that despite her strong desire to fit harmoniously into the general consensus . . . she is somehow thwarted in the development of her emotional life." This phrase "thwarted development" explained virtually everything for Wertham. Because of her thwarted development—both emotionally and sexually—she "finds herself isolated from the group of people with happier emotional endowments." Her idealism and moralistic disposition made her even more isolated, and as a result the "life of the heroine is a profound tragedy which moves the reader to an understanding of human nature and human ills." The book, he wrote, "is a plea not so much for tolerance as for understanding."[75]

On the question of whether the book was obscene and would recruit readers, Wertham unequivocally stated, "From the point of view of mental hygiene this book has no corrupting influence on the mind and morals of readers." The "general tone and tendency of the book is a moral one," with no "obscene" scenes or "erotic suggestion," certainly not when compared with the "general run of novels perpetrated and promiscuously distributed among the population at the present time."[76]

Ernst's legal memorandum submitted to the Court of Special Sessions for the April 1929 hearing drew extensively on Wertham's interpretive framework and his psychiatric language. Ernst emphasized repeatedly that *The Well* was a tragic story about being thwarted, trapped, and emotionally isolated. It neither titillates the reader nor invites emulation.[77] Ernst and Lindey used Wertham's phrase "It is a plea not so much for tolerance as for understanding" verbatim in their subsequent legal briefs, and the idea that Stephen was a victim of "thwarted development" proved to be the linchpin of their defense of the novel. Wertham, who would gain considerable notoriety in the 1950s with his study of sadism and fetishism in post–World War II comic books, quickly begged off any association with Ernst's defense of *The Well of Loneliness*. Fearing career jeopardy, he enlisted Cairns's help in asking Ernst to not mention his name in connection with the case. (Wertham was certainly not alone among literary and medical experts who wanted to keep their distance from this case, as Ernst and his partners would learn in trying to enlist literary experts.) Ernst never mentioned Wertham further or identified the source of his analysis in his legal briefs, but he certainly used Wertham's ideas. Wertham probably never knew just how influential he was in helping Ernst construct his argument.[78]

Another figure who volunteered time and expertise was far less certain than Wertham that homosexuality was a tragic fate. Kenneth Sweezy, a self-reported student of sociology and psychology, guided Ernst and his colleagues through the sexology literature. He also provided extensive bibliographic suggestions about other available works of fiction or poetry addressing lesbian themes.[79] A dedicated bibliographer of homophile literature through history, he had studied the works of Edward Carpenter, including *The Intermediate Sex, Love's Coming of Age,* and *Intermediate*

Types Among the Primitive Folk (which he noted had surprisingly been left alone by the Vice Society), and used this knowledge to explain Hall's treatment of "the intermediate type."[80]

Sweezy knew which sources in the literature could bolster Hall's argument that inversion was congenital and paid close attention to the proceedings, offering corrections when the prosecution and the courts misread key authorities, especially Krafft-Ebing and Havelock Ellis. Sweezy was especially useful in explaining that Ellis had considerably modified his understanding of inversion since he first wrote *Sexual Inversion* in 1897. He also recommended that Ernst and colleagues would be much better suited using Ellis as their main source of sexological knowledge, keeping Krafft-Ebing at a distance because of his tendency to see inversion as a pathology and masturbation as its major cause. Ellis, by contrast, was not so inclined to equate homosexuality with "degeneracy" or "deviant behavior." He became the more prominent authority on these issues in the early decades of the twentieth century, and his later career assertions that homosexuality was congenital rather than acquired were far more conducive to Ernst's defense arguments than Krafft-Ebing's. As Taylor explains, "It is obvious why Radclyffe Hall became enamored of Ellis's theories: he explained the causes of inversion, he did not vilify inverts nor argue for cures, and he explained Hall's own desire to wear men's clothes and define herself as 'John.'"[81]

Most scholars studying *The Well of Loneliness* have been compelled to address Hall's expressly instructional use of sexology in the novel for how it functions both as a turning point in the plot and as a powerful moment of revelation and self-knowledge for Stephen. Sexology also served Hall's didactic purposes, in that Hall could explain the condition to her readers using scientific-medical literature that did not use damning language or ascribe moral failure to inverts. Rule notes that Hall "worked hard to provide a background of psychological information, intended to deepen understanding and acceptance for her main character."[82] But these sources were not necessarily in agreement. Karl Heinrich Ulrichs, who was homosexual, felt more keenly that people of the same sex ought to be granted permission to marry because inversion was congenital. Krafft-Ebing, as Sweezy warned Ernst, was more problematic, because although he granted

"that some inversion is congenital," he also insisted "that the cause is pathological rather than physiological." Jane Rule writes that Hall "took a great
deal of information from Krafft-Ebing," but she was more sympathetic to
Ulrich's arguments.[83]

There was simply no straightforward path through the literature that
Hall used. Wertham gave Ernst good advice about steering clear of the
potential morass of definitions, interpretations, and unresolved theories of
inversion and homosexuality generally.[84] Ernst's employment of Wertham's
arguments and advice about evasions proved useful. By finding a strategy
for arguing about the book's tragic narrative, one that clearly echoed Hall's
themes and the novel's sad resolution, he did not have to offer a detailed
sexological treatment of homosexuality. And by ultimately choosing not
to bring in expert witnesses from medicine or sexology or psychiatry, he
probably saved himself a great deal of difficulty trying to define controversial terms that reflected contradictory theories of homosexuality.

Support from the Literary World

As Ernst and Lindey were getting to know the psychiatric and sexological
literature, they were also trying to garner the support of writers and critics. They assumed that they could count on strong reprimands of Sumner
and paeans to Hall's work, and because Hall's case came on the heels of
the Banned in Boston events, the timing seemed fortuitous. They learned
right off, however, that anti-Sumner opinion would be easy to muster,
but support for Hall's book from the literati would be tepid at best. Anti-
Sumner sentiment grew from the period anticipating Sumner's raid, when
they began preparing for action, to the Court of Special Sessions trial over
four months later in April, but reviews of *The Well of Loneliness* did not
become more enthusiastic.

A reply to Ernst's entreaty from Carl van Doren, editor of the Literary
Guild's Book Club, gave Ernst an inkling of what was to come. Ernst actually sent van Doren the page proofs before the book was published, along
with a cover letter hinting that van Doren might benefit from including
the book in the Literary Guild's offerings. Mainly, though, he stressed free
speech ideals: "The Literary Guild could make a real contribution to the

freedom of letters if it would see fit to place its stamp of approval on this book. It is my impression that advance in this country will only be made during the next decade by the acceptance of respectable groups of isolated works such as this."[85] Van Doren replied that he was "sorry not to like it so well as you do. The theme is interesting because it is novel, but I find the treatment sentimental to the point where it is almost maudlin. The copy which I am returning to you looks as if it had been slept with. Well, it has."[86]

Ernst also importuned the journalist Walter Lippmann for a piece in the *New York World*, suggesting that he was offering inside dope on Sumner's impending attack on the book: "Confidentially, I am writing at this time that Sumner has referred the book to the District Attorney and it is now being considered." Touting its literary value, Ernst continued, "To me it is a stirring piece of writing in integrity. I would appreciate it greatly, if, whoever of the *World* reads it, would get in touch with me so that I can get an additional opinion."[87] Lippmann did not weigh in. Ernst tried another approach with the *New York Times*'s Arthur Hays Sulzberger, offering the same scoop but with more hyperbole: "I personally feel that it is one of the most important books written in many years. I am sending the proof in advance because confidentially, there is a real possibility that it may be the subject of a complaint by the Vice Society."[88] To *The Nation*'s Oswald Garrison Villard, Ernst vouched for the novel's "integrity far beyond" *The Captive* or MacKenzie Compton's *Extraordinary Women*, both of which were available for sale.[89]

A *New York Telegraph* editorial titled "Obscene Censors" that was published just after Sumner's January raid gave Ernst the public nod he was looking for, but the writer also expressed doubts about the book's worth and the desire for reticence about homosexuality as a subject, even among supporters of publishing freedom. "Doubtless this vice hunter's charge of obscenity will create a flourishing bootleg sale for an otherwise obscure book. If Sumner were not so entirely lacking in humor he would be suspected as an advertising agent skilled in increasing circulation of such books."[90] The editorial's tone suggested that Ernst and Lindey could not count on mounting a crusade around this book.

After the January 1929 verdict in the magistrate court and in preparation for the April hearing, Ernst and his clients stepped up their efforts to generate support from the city's publishing houses and from many more writers. They received wan support. Partly this had to do with the book, but Leslie Taylor notes that publishers' quiescence also stemmed from Sumner's intimidation campaign and support from powerful magistrates and district attorneys.[91] Sumner's financial and reputational threats were real and generally kept the city's publishers quiet. Two exceptions were George Putnam of Putnam's Sons and the bookseller Lowell Brentano; both offered strong support for the anti-censorship principle but ambivalence at best toward Hall's novel. Brentano wrote, "I would like to add my name to the list of those protesting against the suppression of *The Well of Loneliness*, not because I have any sentiments for or against this particular book . . . but merely because at the moment it is the focal point on which the discussion about book censorship is impinging."[92]

Ernst's inability to raise a chorus of support from publishers illustrates his general frustrations with New York's most established publishing houses. Those houses were unwilling to bear the risks of taking leading roles in anti-censorship fights and remained wary of controversial works. After a month of trying to rally support from publishers, it became clear to the lawyers and Covici-Friede that they could not count on them as part of their strategy. Writing to another fledgling publisher, Albert Boni of Boni & Liveright, Ernst confided, "I am afraid that we had better not make any use of the publishers' position . . . because the absence of the several most prominent firms might act as a boomerang."[93] Perhaps the publishers who functioned as the gatekeepers of literary taste and reputation would have been stronger allies had they not found the book tedious and sentimental, but Ernst's overall frustrations with their unwillingness to take risks suggests otherwise.

Ernst eventually managed to enlist support from writers, journalists, newspaper editors, and public health experts—enough to include in his legal brief excerpts from thirty-five letters and telegrams and a further seventy-five names of supporters. But that support was so hesitant that Ernst gave up on building a roster of potential experts available for courtroom testimony.

Opposition to Sumner was high, but support for Hall's novel simply was not strong enough to put witnesses on the stand. A few of the thirty-five supporting letters and telegrams illustrate the general sentiment about the book and Sumner.[94] Dr. Logan Clendening expressed dismay that such a book would be censored, invoking homosexuality as a tragedy in need of attention: "It is incredible to the scientific mind that an honest and sensitive presentation in literary form of a subject familiar and tragic to every physician should be threatened due to the pornographic imagination of a censor."[95] Another writer similarly professed that homosexuality ought to be studied and understood because it "is one of the world's greatest enigmas. . . . We know neither its why nor its whither."[96]

Joseph Collins, who helped found the New York Neurological Institute (and reviewed James Joyce's *Ulysses* for the *New York Times*), also viewed homosexuality as a mystery, arguing that more information would enhance understanding and that suppression would only contribute to intolerance. He encouraged Ernst in his campaign against "Smug Self-Righteousness."[97] The novelist Sherwood Anderson wrote that the book was harmless and banning it seemed "absurd," especially because readers should know more about "the phase of life on which this book centers." And literary critics Joseph Wood Krutch of *The Nation* and Robert Morss Lovett of the *New Republic* weighed in along the lines offered by Sherwood Anderson, including using euphemisms for homosexuality, inversion, or lesbianism. Krutch agreed that the book was a "serious study of an important subject," adding, "There are no indecent facts."[98]

On the other hand, novelist and playwright Edna Ferber was not atypical; she wanted people to know that she opposed censorship but was no fan of the novel. She told Ernst and company that she was willing to support the fight against the "literary padlockers" as long as her support was not misrepresented as appreciation for the book: "I do not feel that it is sufficiently important as a piece of writing, regarded from the point of view of artistic or technical achievement to warrant any great fuss being made about it. But I am willing to have you use my name . . . in connection with a protest against the censoring of this book as a tangible example of literary padlocking in the United States."[99]

By the time of their hearing before the Court of Special Sessions, Ernst reported to Cairns that he had decided not to use any experts in the court-room. Between the decidedly mixed response to the book's literary value and the unresolved and complicated discourse about homosexuality as a psychological or medical problem, any cross-examination might lead to trouble. "We have decided that we will do better without any experts, which means that in our opinion, most of the experts are not so expert."[100]

Court of Special Sessions Trial

Ernst told Hall's London-based solicitor Harold Rubinstein that they re-ceived a "first class trimming" in the magistrate court. He knew that he needed to get Justices Max Salomon, James J. McInerney, and Ellsworth J. Healy of the Court of Special Sessions to read the book very differently than had Magistrate Bushel.[101] He finally brought the case before them on April 8, 1929, and returned to the court on April 19, when the court handed down its decision.[102]

In his memorandum to the court, Ernst reframed the discussion by presenting homosexuality not as a problem of predation but rather as a complex sociological and psychological issue that Hall treated intelligently and delicately. The book would educate readers, not harm them. More crucially, Ernst's team assured the judges that readers would not become vulnerable by reading a book, primarily because homosexuality was inborn, not chosen—a point Hall made clear in her novel. The brief did not chal-lenge the legitimacy of the obscenity laws but drew a sharp distinction be-tween the pornographic materials those laws were aimed at and legitimate literary works, such as Hall's novel. New York Public Law 1141 did not apply to *The Well of Loneliness*, a distinguished work of literature written by a "prominent British writer" that did not contain any lewd or prurient passages.[103] To underscore "Miss Hall's" respectability (thus evading John Radclyffe Hall's chosen name, style of dress, and manner of presentation), Ernst focused on her status as a prize-winning author. Her novel *Adam's Breed* received both the Femina Vie Heureuse Prize and the James Tait Black Memorial Prize. "Miss Hall's" latest work, they wrote, was also a work of distinction "noteworthy for its social significance, moral fervor, integrity of purpose and distinguished style."[104]

But before plunging into its defense of *The Well* on literary grounds, Ernst's brief went after the problem of censorship and John Sumner's record and tactics, which had been repudiated in the city and state courts. Sumner had lost his effectiveness, and New York's courts had consistently accepted the judgments of New York's book world authorities over Sumner's. His era was at a close. Ernst declared:

> In recent years *there has not been a single instance* where a book, modern or classic, which was first generally accepted by the press, literary critics, the reading public and the community at large, and which was openly dealt with by the publishers and the book trade, was ultimately condemned by the courts, even though criminal prosecution was instigated at the outset by the same complainant as in this case.[105]

Ernst and his team used this argument over and over in subsequent cases: that the literary marketplace, with its built-in filters for taste and quality, should be trusted to determine which works have literary value for the reading public. Not only had New York's courts been consistently ruling against Sumner, Ernst and his team argued, but also they had done so in cases dealing with books that were considerably more sexually provocative than Hall's. Ernst listed a roster of books—*Mademoiselle de Maupin, Madeleine, Satyricon, Jurgen, A Young Girl's Diary, Casanova's Homecoming, Women in Love,* and *Replenishing Jessica*—that had all been successfully defended in the New York City magistrate courts or the New York State courts during the 1920s. New York's courts had sustained an "enlightened" pattern of not banning such works, and like publishing professionals, New York's judges had proved quite capable of making distinctions between literature and trash, a distinction Sumner apparently could not make.

Turning to Public Law 1141, New York's version of the Comstock laws, Ernst's brief showed six different ways in which that law did not apply to Hall's novel: (1) *The Well of Loneliness* was a distinguished work of literature and not obscene according to definitions of obscenity formulated by

New York's courts; (2) read comparatively, and in light of recent cases, the book was not obscene; (3) circumstances surrounding the publication and sale of the book showed that it is not obscene; (4) any book must be judged by the mores of the day; (5) in cases where books have been determined to be obscene, those works contained elements "utterly alien to the book before the Court"; and (6) the book must be read as a whole.[106] Not all these arguments, particularly points 3, 4, and 6, had been regularly accepted by New York's courts by 1929, although Ernst and Lindey confidently asserted them in this and other cases. They especially hammered at the Hicklin standard, which was increasingly vulnerable and not the ironclad rule it had been from the 1870s to the early 1920s. Labeling it "the ancient test of obscenity," Ernst and Lindey argued that the Hicklin standard had been supplanted by far more subtle standards of assessment. For one thing, recent decisions had begun to consider the needs of capable and discerning adult audiences, and vulnerable youth were no longer the only audience whose needs ought to be considered. Adults' susceptibility to depravity and corruption was not a given, but their interests in serious materials ought to be.

The brief quoted extensively from Judge Learned Hand's dicta in the 1913 case *United States v. Kennerley* (209 Fed. 119, 121), which offered the most useful repudiation of the Hicklin standard from a federal jurist. Judge Hand wrote, "I scarcely think that [Congress] would forbid all which might corrupt the most corruptible, *or that society is prepared to accept for its own limitation those which may perhaps be necessary to the weakest of its members*" (emphasis in original). Expressly recognizing that the intellectual and cultural needs of adults could not be met by only accepting materials that might not harm the young, he added, in italics, "Indeed, it seems hardly likely that we are even today so lukewarm in our interest in letters or serious discussion as to be content to reduce our treatment of sex to the standard of a child's library in the supposed interest of a salacious few."[107] Although Judge Hand's framework and language had not yet been adopted in the federal courts, his argument provided a persuasive authoritative statement of the courts' need to account for changing tastes and mores and for the needs of various audiences, including serious adults. Judge Hand also recognized that the definition of obscenity was imprecise and subject to change over time and thus could be ascertained only by the specific considerations of a particular time and place. Hand asked, "Should not the word 'obscene' be allowed to indicate the *present critical point* in the compromise between candor and shame at which the community may have arrived *here and now?*"[108] Ernst would return to Hand's formulation of changing standards and the need for redefinition time and again.

Ernst and Lindey's brief then laid out the decisions in New York's state courts that either shrunk the Hicklin test's broad authority or the state's obscenity statute. A 1909 decision in *St. Hubert Guild v. Quinn* drew the distinction between artistic and literary works and mere pornography.[109] This distinction gained additional force in an important magistrate court decision in 1922, in *People v. Boni & Liveright*, when Magistrate Oberwager distinguished between works of literary merit and the commercial pornography "produced for evil purposes and for gain." This decision was especially useful because Oberwager had also repudiated the Vice Society's overreach in not distinguishing between literary works and "scandalous excesses" in its quest for "austere piety."[110] With these decisions in mind, Ernst urged the judges to ask a series of questions that were the best contemporary test of whether something was actually obscene: "Does the novel tend to excite lustful and lecherous desire? Does it suggest impure and libidinous thoughts?" Was the book's primary purpose "the excitation of lasciviousness"? Or was it "the presentation of an honest criticism of life"? From there the court needed to consider questions of harm: "Will it harm only the impressionable child, the moral weakling, the fatuous and the vicious, and leave the ordinary man unaffected? Or will it corrupt and deprave the average intelligent adult as well?"[111]

The Well of Loneliness did what literature ought to do. It shined a light on an important but underdiscussed social problem and elicited sympathy and understanding as a result. By invoking the marketplace of ideas as an instrument of public enlightenment and describing censorship as antithetical to that same ideal, Ernst and Lindey assured the judges that "social problems can be solved only by the free interchange of ideas, never by the throttling of discussion."[112]

Then to the central issue at trial: Should *The Well of Loneliness* be barred simply because it dared to address the theme of homosexuality? Did that theme make the book obscene? There was, Ernst and Lindey argued, no other evidence of obscenity that the court could possibly point to: "In its 500 pages we find not one filthy word, not a single indecent scene, not a single suggestive episode. . . . On the contrary, the novel is written with extraordinary restraint." They elaborated, shrewdly using criticisms leveled against the book by literary critics: "If Stephen were a man and not a woman, the book would be merely a rather over-sentimental bit of Victorian romanticism. There would be no element in it that could bring a blush of embarrassment even to the cheeks of the complainant. The sole objection is the theme itself."[113] The implications of government agents—or private entities such as the Vice Society—searching out and censoring such themes in literature were deeply troubling. Certainly other works readily circulating among readers addressed issues equally if not more troubling than *The Well*'s "unorthodox emotional complications." Did the circulation of this book have "more disastrous social consequences than the incest of *Oedipus Tyrranos*, the sadism of *Uncle Tom's Cabin*, the abortion of the *American Tragedy*," or the "adulteries of the vast mass of contemporary fiction?"[114]

Following Wertham's framing, in the brief Ernst evaded direct mention of lesbianism or inversion, euphemistically describing the book's core theme as "the problem of emotional maladjustment" but averring that this was "not a new one in contemporary literature" and had not been forbidden as a theme. Works dealing with it were widely available in bookstores and public libraries: "Every intelligent biography of Queen Elizabeth (the present best seller by Lytton Strachey, for example) discusses the well-known inability of the queen to adjust herself emotionally to men" (another euphemism). Moreover, "Any high school girl in the city may go to a book store or a circulating library, and obtain without any difficulty copies of *Dusty Answer* by Rosamond Lehman, *Extraordinary Women* by Compton MacKenzie, *Death in Venice* by Thomas Mann, and even *The Captive* by Edward Bourdet." *The Captive* reference was particularly noteworthy because even though the production of the stage play had been stopped, the book itself was "readily available."[115] The state legislature had not extended censorship of the topic to publishing houses, libraries, and bookstores.

The brief then turned to "two outstanding cases" where books in this same thematic vein had been challenged as obscene in the New York courts. Sumner had been unsuccessful in his prosecutions against both the anonymously written *Madeleine: The Autobiography of a Prostitute* (Madeleine Blaire was later revealed as the author) (in the 1920 case *People v. Brainard*) and Theodor Gautier's *Mademoiselle de Maupin* (in the 1922 case *Halsey v. New York Society*). Moreover, both books compared negatively with *The Well* if measured by their more explicitly sexual prose and far more complicated themes of sexual transgression. The brief offered a particularly elaborate comparison with Gautier's *Mademoiselle de Maupin*. As Leslie Taylor points out, Ernst's fierce antipathy for John Sumner made Gautier's novel a delectable choice. "Ernst chose *Mademoiselle de Maupin* because of its explicit lesbianism and because it represented a particularly painful defeat for the NYSSV [Vice Society]." The case was salt in Sumner's wounds, but it was also, Taylor says, "the perfect companion text for Radclyffe Hall's *The Well of Loneliness* and her protagonist Stephen Gordon. Both novels contained sexual activity between women, both novels placed significant weight on dress and gender, and both novels pondered the place of the 'third sex' and the 'invert' in society."[116] By reading Hall's novel against the far more sensual and erotic *Mademoiselle de Maupin*, Ernst and Lindey could read "the sex, desire, 'perversity' out of it, and . . . tragedy into it."[117]

In the brief Ernst never quarreled with the idea that society has an interest in protecting the weak, the vulnerable, and the corruptible from harm. It does. But *The Well of Loneliness* posed no danger to those readers because they were not the audience for it. Returning to the comparison with the pornography that the law was really aimed at curtailing, Ernst explained that people interested in dirty books wanted quick arousal from "vivid and potent" visual materials, and that was simply not available in Hall's book.[118] Compared with the cheap, surreptitiously distributed materials sold to the "morally weak," Hall's 500-page "work involves protracted reading and assiduous application" by its readers. It simply would not satisfy the prurient curiosities and short attention spans of those in search of a pornography fix. Noting that Sumner's complaint did not even identify an objection-able passage through the novel's first 150 pages, Ernst wrote, "No child, no moral defective, no impressionable seeker after prurient details, would ever get that far."[119]

Other elements of the work's material presence also mattered, including its pricing, places of sale, and channels of distribution and exhibition. These factors also made it possible to draw clear distinctions between the legitimate book industry and the underground market. Postcards and "pornographic pamphlets," "purveyed for a few cents," were far more "likely to reach children and moral weaklings" in underground settings.[120] Compared with the legiti-mate book trade, with its dependable filters of taste and reputability—including known publishers, book reviewers writing in established papers and journals, and established bookstores and sellers—pornographic materials circulated in unsavory spaces and its purveyors survived through anonymity. "Vile post-cards are vended by gutter-peddlers. Booklets full of revolting details are sold in dives. Filthy motion pictures are filmed in secret and constitute back-door midnight entertainment." Copies of *The Well of Loneliness*, by contrast, had been selling in large numbers and at high prices in "practically every reputable book store in New York City, including Brentano's, Macy's, and Doubleday Doran." In fact, the book was even openly sold in Boston, "the scene of so many book massacres."[121]

Ernst and Lindey's brief used the published reviews of the novel in U.S. newspapers and journals. Like their experts' opinions, these reviews evinced greater revulsion to censorship than enthusiasm for the book. But they offered evidence that leading papers had not found the book the least bit obscene and had reviewed it and printed advertisements for it. They quoted the *New York Herald Tribune* review, which describes *The Well* as "much more of a sermon than a story, a passionate plea for the world's understanding and sympathy, as much a novel of problem and purpose as *Uncle Tom's Cabin*, as sentimental and moralistic as the deepest-dyed of the Victorians."[122] *The Nation* declared that the novel's "gravity of purpose" was its strongest suit, adding that it was "well worth-while to call public atten-tion to the badly misunderstood plight of many, many men and women." The topic should not be "undiscussable."[123]

In the brief's final section, Ernst argued that "a work of art, and particularly a book, is to be judged in its entirety, not by isolated fragments." Even though this was not yet widely accepted doctrine in either the New York State courts or in the federal courts, Ernst assured the Court of Special Sessions judges that it had taken hold. In this case, Sumner had "singled out eighty-two pages that have apparently caused him particular mortification," and Ernst added, "Let these pages be scrutinized. They will stand inspection by the most fastidious moralist."[124] And even if those pages might mar the work, they did not necessarily make the work obscene, because only the whole work could be judged obscene (at least according to the argument Ernst was asserting).

As Leslie Taylor points out, Ernst aimed to deflect any attention from those passages that Sumner found offensive. He essentially bowdlerized *The Well* to make it seem as Victorian, buttoned up, and unerotic as he could make it, eliding any discussion of scenes that might express lesbian sexual desire and erotic energy. When Ernst dealt with the eighty-two pages that Sumner felt were objectionable, he offered brief summaries instead of direct quotations. Taylor rightly argues that such a strategy was problematic, because to "disallow explicit desire could have profoundly limiting implications for future texts with lesbian representation."[125] Clearly Ernst's decision to avoid lesbian erotic desire was at odds with Hall's intent. But as a legal strategy, it worked.

Although Ernst treated the problematic issue of lesbianism by evading it, a strategy that infuriated Hall when Norman Birkett used it in the United Kingdom, he was aware of the problems of prejudice and legal jeopardy for those whose sexual practices were codified in the laws as being illegal. As I illustrate in Chapter 8, Ernst thrilled at the prospects of challenging the nation's sex laws following publication of Alfred Kinsey's *Sexual Behavior in the American Male* (1948), which so clearly revealed the inconsistencies between the laws penalizing homosexual activity and the prevalence of that activity in the culture itself. He immediately set about proselytizing the legal implications of Kinsey's findings and the need to change the laws to adjust to homosexual practices.

Decision and Sumner's Revenge

Within a stretch of two days (April 19–20, 1929), Donald Friede's obscenity conviction in Boston for selling Theodore Dreiser's *An American Tragedy* was upheld at the appellate level and *The Well of Loneliness* was cleared of obscenity charges in New York City at the Courts of Special Sessions level.[126] Justice Salomon, the presiding judge, read the unanimous decision in *The Well* case: "The book in question deals with a delicate social problem which in itself cannot be said is in violation of the law unless it is written in such a matter as to make it obscene, lewd, lascivious, filthy or indecent, and tends to deprave and corrupt minds open to immoral influence."[127] The only question before the court was whether the book had violated the obscenity law. Because it was a criminal matter, the prosecution "must establish that the defendants are guilty of a violation of Section 1141 beyond a reasonable doubt."[128] The three-judge panel declared the book not to be in violation of the law and acquitted each of the defendants, while eschewing any judgment of the book's merits.[129]

A minimalist decision to be sure.

The publishers quickly followed the decision with a deluxe artifact: an expensive, limited "Victory Edition." For twenty-five dollars readers could purchase a special two-volume edition printed on handmade paper with Ernst's introductory statement and summary of the trial, the Court of Special Sessions opinion, Hall's autograph, and her own preface. It is not clear from Ernst's records what he finally earned from his share of the royalties, but the book did well, selling over 100,000 copies that first year, and profits from *The Well of Loneliness* "helped keep Covici-Friede in business for nine more years."[130]

However, Ernst and his clients were not quite done with the Sumner, or the courts.

In December 1928, as his work with Covici-Friede was unfolding, Ernst knew he needed to resolve any potential problems with the U.S. Customs Service over importation of the book and to protect the publisher's copyright. As he was initiating his fight with Sumner in the New York City Magistrate Court, he also had sent a copy to Walter Eaton, the assistant solicitor of the

U.S. Customs Service, along with a letter saying he would like to have a conversation once Eaton had read the book. Ernst wrote, "I am particularly anxious to see you so as to convey, with more detail than I can in the letter, my feeling that the book is highly moral in that it repels rather than invites, pathetic, unfortunate lives such as those portrayed in the book."[131]

Ernst's preemptive move at staving off a Customs ban was not successful. He received a reply from the assistant collector of customs just days later, rebuffing his judgment: "The moral atmosphere and its suggestiveness are such as to leave no doubt that the action of the English authorities in suppressing it were fully justified and this office feels compelled to deem its importation prohibited under the provisions of Section 305 of the Tariff Act of 1922."[132] Ernst let this Customs ruling lie until after the Court of Special Sessions decision in April, when he then sought to get the book cleared.

Even after the Court of Special Sessions decision, Customs officials in New York refused to be bound by that ruling and barred the books from being shipped into the United States. The *New York Times* reported in May 1929 that the collector of customs, Philip Elting, held that the book fell under the exclusion provisions of Section 305 of the Tariff Act and that Peter Abeles, a Special United States Attorney, also thought the Customs ruling might extend to postal shipments of the book "from point to point within the United States."[133] This was precisely the kind of unchecked administrative authority that Ernst had been fighting in other cases involving Customs and Postal officials. Here was a case where the book was found not obscene in one jurisdiction but where officials in another jurisdiction could arbitrarily halt its distribution. So Ernst and his colleague Meyer Stern brought a suit in the U.S. Customs Court challenging Elting's ruling. Their case came before Chief Justice Israel F. Fischer and Justice William J. Tilson. Ernst's firm used the same 51-page brief they had used in the Court of Special Sessions and obtained the same positive result. Fischer and Tilson reversed the collector of custom's ruling in July 1929, holding the book permissible for importation.[134]

That matter solved, Ernst still had to contest Sumner's various devices to needle and antagonize his opponents. The problem in this case, and in other cases like it, was that Sumner would dig in his heels and refuse to cooperate, frequently by refusing to return the books he had seized. Magistrate Bushel ordered Sumner to return all the seized copies to the publishers, but Sumner stonewalled instead, setting in motion a months-long battle. Following the Court of Special Sessions ruling, Ernst wrote Sumner reminding him that his law firm had "a receipt signed by your representative Mr. Bamberger for 865 copies" but that Sumner's office had "only returned 815 copies" to his clients. "Will you kindly return to the balance before Tuesday April 30th?"[135] Sumner replied by denying that he had the fifty copies in question and also by challenging the legitimacy of the receipt, even though it was signed by his representative. He suggested that Bamberger, who was his right-hand man on most of his book raids, "was not authorized to sign a receipt," and he tried to put the onus on Ernst for somehow manipulating Bamberger. "He tells me," Sumner added, "that you demanded his signature on a memorandum after I had left the premise of Covici, Friede." This infuriated Ernst, who was incredulous that Sumner would dispute the number on the receipt signed by his own representative. "In all fairness," Ernst asked, "what suggestion do you make?"[136]

Sumner denied all responsibility, blaming another policeman who was with him at the time, declaring that he had returned all the copies his office held, and he told Ernst that there was nothing more to be done in the matter.[137] Ernst asked his clients if they might want to initiate a lawsuit: "Kindly advise me what to do. I hate to see you let him get away with it."[138] The clients did not want Sumner to "get away with it," but they did not want a suit either, so they agreed with Ernst that Sumner ought to either return the fifty missing copies or pay the publishers $250 in lieu of the books. By October Sumner was still stonewalling, refusing to entertain the idea of paying, denying he had the books or that the count had been accurate, and claiming more insistently that Ernst was at fault. So Ernst appealed directly to Chief Magistrate William McAdoo, who had signed the warrant in the first place. (McAdoo signed virtually all of Sumner's warrants.) Ernst wrote, "In view of the rather high-handed attitude of the Vice Society in this matter, and their total disregard of the properties to be exercised under a Warrant, we are compelled to bring to your attention for your own investigation. Surely you will agree that property taken under a warrant is held in the form of a real sacred trust and should be returned." He reiterated that Sumner was liable for the books, or for $250, and suggested that McAdoo "look into what we deem to be entirely illegal operations of the Vice Society in connection with the entire use of the Warrant process."[139]

Ernst reported that Sumner had not only raided Covici-Friede's offices but also had conducted "illegal operations" by raiding other booksellers' stores and seizing stockpiles of *The Well of Loneliness* from them, including R. H. Macy & Co., Doubleday Doran, Brentano's, and possibly others. Ernst insisted that this was illegal, as "under the statute as we read it a Warrant can only be issued against a person against whom a complaint is lodged." "In other words," he continued, "we have a spectacle of raids taking place on book dealers in the city, with no complaint ever being served on them. . . . It seems to me to be highly dangerous for the community to permit a private agency to become the law enforcement agency to the extent evidenced in these cases."[140] McAdoo replied several days later, saying he was having the matter investigated, but in early November he sent Ernst a letter that quoted Sumner at length and took Sumner's side. McAdoo, quoting Sumner, wrote, "It was only after I had left the publisher's office and behind my back that Mr. Ernst by some subterfuge or threat, induced Mr. Bamberger to sign such a receipt." McAdoo, offering no comment about the other raids, or the missing books, or the nonpayment, or Sumner's accusation that Ernst had manipulated Bamberger, concluded his "investigation" by telling Ernst that Sumner's letter seemed "to have closed the correspondence."[141]

Deeply frustrated that McAdoo seemed willing to abide Sumner's flaunting of the law, Ernst wrote the chief magistrate once again, but on December 4, 1929, McAdoo ended the matter, again taking Sumner's side and allowing Bamberger to misrepresent his own sloppy police work (if that's all it was) without consequences. McAdoo wrote, "Mr. Bamberger says he did sign the receipt, but he signed it under a mistake and without properly counting the number of copies." He continued, noting that Sumner and Bamberger "are both perfectly willing to testify . . . and I have no reason to believe that they would perjure themselves for 50 copies of the books. At any rate, I am quite convinced they haven't the books." McAdoo ended the inquiry by telling Ernst that he could try further, but it would be to no avail.[142]

This epilogue to *The Well of Loneliness* matter illustrates how Sumner managed, even in defeat, to exert the powers of his office to frustrate the publishers, booksellers, and lawyers who opposed him. Sumner's tactics essentially meant that Covici-Friede, the "victors" in the courtroom, had to pay the price of the extralegal costs he imposed on them (the loss of books, loss of time, additional lawyers' fees, and having to deal with Sumner's punitive and petulant refusal to cooperate with those he opposed). For Ernst it raised an important question: Under whose authority and under what conditions did Sumner continue to get away with these actions? He and his colleagues would go to battle with Sumner to get answers.

CHAPTER 5

THE VOMIT SCHOOL OF LITERATURE

Fighting Censorship in New York City

IN THE EARLY 1930S the battles over obscenity laws and their enforcement took place in a rapidly changing media environment in which "objectionable" images and works were increasingly widespread. Amid the "eroticization of leisure time," to use Jay Gertzman's phrase, Sumner and his moral reform allies were hard-pressed to protect the "genteel literary code" they and an older generation of established publishers and literary gatekeepers had adhered to.[1] By the end of the 1920s the book publishing industry was regularly making modernist works available to an interested public. Sumner attacked all books that violated this genteel code—books he thought were not morally uplifting or appropriately reticent about discussing the physical body, especially sexual issues. As Gertzman writes, Sumner and his fellow "moral entrepreneurs" believed that "since the life of the human body stood as far from morality as self-centered sensual satisfaction stood from disinterested reason, all texts that focused on sex, whether marriage manuals, birth-control tracts, or steamy novels, spoke aloud what for the sake of spiritual health had to be kept hidden."[2]

Although soft-spoken and reserved compared to his predecessor, Anthony Comstock, Sumner viewed the world in similarly stark black-and-white terms. He spoke of decent folks versus cultural pariahs, clean versus dirty, uplifting versus degrading, moral versus immoral, patriotic versus subversive, high versus low, decent versus indecent, and so on. As Gertzman writes, Sumner "thought it necessary to defend a 'one hundred percent American' moral consensus—an amalgam of sexual reticence, patriotism, and Christian piety—against the immigrant, the Bolshevik, the money-grubbing urbanite, the worldly sophisticate, and the effete intellectual."[3] Fighting against such moral absolutism was an insurgent intellectual movement—modernism—that privileged individual experience, subjected inherited cultural standards to criticism, and inspected sex and sexuality as the governing principles driving human existence.[4] These forces and instincts ought to be examined, discussed, performed, and written about, not repressed and silenced.

Thoughtful censorship, however, was not necessarily anathema to intellectuals, publishers, and other book purveyors. Many still believed that literature, as all art, should play a vital role in cultural uplift and instruction. They thought literature should be defended not just from overzealous censors but also from literary hacks and smut peddlers. Indeed, a widely shared sentiment across class, religious, and cultural lines was that the increasingly pervasive pornography and graphic tabloid fare circulating in New York City offered nothing redeeming and deserved no legal protection. Critics who winced at Sumner's attacks on "legitimate" books still wanted him to destroy the smutty side of New York's underground economy of titillating materials.

The increasing traffic in erotica or pornographic print culture proved especially crucial to the ways in which battles over books were fought in New York's courtrooms and newspapers in the early 1930s. John Sumner's efforts to contain erotically tinged literary works were inextricable from the larger transformation of print culture, with its explosion of inexpensive paperbacks, true crime and true romance magazines, police gazettes, dirty playing cards, lewd photographs, and pornography ranging from expensively bound volumes of imported erotic "classics" to cheap pocket-size one-handed "readers." As Gertzman explains, a ready market for erotica ran across class lines, and "erotica distributors quickly assessed which readers would pay what for their wares."[5] The existence of these markets—expensively packaged goods in high-end bookstores and cheaply produced reprints sold through the mails—kept Sumner and his allies busy. Whatever fears they had about respectable book publishers undermining society's moral foundations through modernist works were hugely exacerbated by the increasingly tainted print culture and the explosion of spaces for selling sex, adventure, violence, and gore.

Ernst and Lindey thought they could draw a reasonably bright line between their clients, whose works might invoke sexual themes, and the real smut mongers, whose works reveled in graphic details.

Positioning for Battle over *Casanova's Homecoming*

Hoping to maintain momentum from victories on behalf of Mary Ware Dennett, Marie Stopes, and Radclyffe Hall, Ernst and his associates were eager to continue brawling with the New York Society for the Suppression of Vice and its leader, who had so irked them when he refused to return all of Covici-Friede's copies of *The Well of Loneliness*. Ernst and Lindey plotted with publishers Dick Simon and Lincoln ("Max") Schuster (of Simon & Schuster) and influential journalists connected to the *New York Herald Tribune* and the *New York Telegram* (both Scripps-Howard newspapers), including publisher Roy Howard, writer Harry Elmer Barnes, and journalist and book critic Lewis Gannett. Through letters and meetings they agreed that they wanted to elicit a legal challenge and produce a dramatic confrontation with Sumner. After some deliberation they decided that *Casanova's Homecoming* by the Viennese novelist and playwright Arthur Schnitzler was just the work to provoke Sumner.[6] As Barnes told Howard, "God is never likely to give you a better book to back in such a case."[7]

Casanova's Homecoming was not just a modern classic by an internationally acclaimed Viennese author; it also had the advantage of already having a legal record in New York's courts. Sumner had previously attacked it in 1922 when the publisher, Thomas Seltzer, first offered it in English in the United States. Back then, Sumner had immediately challenged its publication in the New York magistrate court (as he challenged virtually anything Seltzer published). Sumner lost there, but with typical umbrage he refused to accept that court's decision. He then worked with the district attorney to initiate a grand jury indictment and prosecuted Seltzer in a higher court, the Court of Special Sessions. Intimidated by the prospect of an expensive legal battle and possible criminal penalties, Seltzer agreed to withdraw the book from circulation and to destroy extant copies and the publishing plates. Although Sumner had succeeded in preventing the distribution of *Casanova's Homecoming*, the 1922 magistrate court decision clearing the book was on record. Both sides could claim a usable outcome. From Ernst and Lindey's perspective, Seltzer's later agreement to withdraw the book under Sumner's threat was a financial decision, not a legal one. Sumner saw it otherwise.

The plan was straightforward. Simon & Schuster agreed to publish the work in its New York offices as part of its 1930 summer-fall list and would aggressively promote it. The newspapers would assail Sumner for his irresponsible censorious response when he acted against the book, as they knew he would.[8] And Ernst and Lindey would defend the work in the courts. All of them would flay Sumner in the press. But Sumner nearly bollixed the whole *Casanova's Homecoming* strategy by deploying his weapons against *Pay Day*, a novel by Nathan Asch, and by going after another work by Arthur Schnitzler, a cycle of ten stories titled *Reigen* in its original German and *Hands Around* in its English translation. His show of force in attacking these books made the outcome of the *Casanova's Homecoming* skirmish far more precarious than the "godsend" Barnes had originally predicted.

Pay Day and the "Vomit School of Literature"

In February 1930 a small New York publishing house, Brewer & Warren Inc., published the first novel by Nathan Asch, son of the revered New York–based Yiddish writer Sholem Asch. *Pay Day* tells the story of twenty-four hours in the life of an undereducated, economically and sexually frustrated New York City clerk named Jim. Jim is not a likable character. He is antiheroic at best. He lives with his mother, his sister, and her fiancé, whom he loathes and fantasizes about attacking. Jim is basically a charmless loser with little to redeem him, and the novel offers him no redemptive arc or transcendence of his condition. When Lindey and Ernst defended the publisher, their memorandum to the court described the book as a realistic human story that "portrays with vividness and fidelity the frustrations that wrack a humdrum life." They described Jim as an "obtuse, bewildered, weak-willed, blundering individual," and though he was not contemptible, he was pathetic.[9]

Released with an initial run of 5,000 copies, *Pay Day* garnered plenty of advertisement and reviews. Some reviewers praised its sociological realism and honesty. Others criticized its coarseness. None of the reviewers gave it high praise as literature or art, but no one decried it as smut either. And it sold fairly well, roughly 3,500 copies by the time Sumner got an indictment against it and raided the publisher's warehouse in April 1930.[10]

Typical of his strategies, Sumner had his chief Vice Society assistant, Charles Bamberger, set up a sting at the publisher's offices. Bamberger went to the offices in the guise of a book dealer and purchased a copy of *Pay Day* from a salesman at Brewer & Warren. Several days later, on April 17, Sumner and Bamberger returned with a policeman to serve a summons to the firm. They seized fifty-six copies of *Pay Day* along with several other books.[11] As Gertzman notes, seizing other titles along with those named in the warrant was one of Sumner's usual tactics: "The more books he carted off, the greater the chance of winning the case on the basis of the contents of one or more of them."[12]

Magistrate Louis B. Brodsky, who signed Sumner's warrant for the book seizure and arrest, set a date for a month hence to hear the arguments. He requested memoranda of law from counsel. When Brewer & Warren's regular lawyer approached Ernst about helping with the obscenity charges, neither Ernst nor Lindey had heard of the book. Before agreeing to defend it, they needed to read it. They wanted winnable cases, which meant defending books with literary merit, not "smut." Lindey read *Pay Day* and told Ernst that he did not think it was obscene and that they could "win out in the end." They could use the occasion to promote their anti-Sumner agenda, and because the publishers wanted to defend their investment, they were willing to pay Ernst's firm a high retainer fee, with more money to follow if they won in court.[13] Brewer & Warren also hoped to turn the legal action into good publicity while reassuring booksellers of their reliability. Seeing the potential benefits of winning at trial, they mailed a flier to their booksellers: "If you want to be sure of having stock in your store to meet the demand for the book which the publicity will create, send in your orders now."[14] As for the book's credibility, they protested, "We published *Pay Day* in good faith—believing that it represents an actual phase of New York life. And though it is frankly expressed—it is *actual truth*."[15]

Ernst was ever alert to publicity possibilities as well and immediately enlisted allies on behalf of *Pay Day*. Sending copies of the book to journalists Walter Lippmann and Harry Elmer Barnes, he implored them to make some noise about Sumner's activity, offering an anti-censorship bromide: "If this book is banned, no truthful life as to frustrations of adolescents can ever be printed."[16] Lindey cultivated other editorialists, including the *New York World* columnist Harry Hansen, thanking him for his recent support in his coverage of the *Dennett* case and requesting more of his "generous cooperation."[17] Hansen came through, delivering a scathing editorial that noted the irony that Sumner's attacks would only increase sales of Asch's work: "The attack of the self-appointed custodians of the morals of the people" is "another example of the muddle-headedness of censorship. Now that Sumner has pinned the order of martyrdom on it, it will get a tremendous vogue in the under-the-counter market."[18] Lindey thanked Hansen for his "splendid column" and also acknowledged that "none of us have any illusions about *Pay Day* as a great piece of literature." But, he added, "if Asch has something to say he ought to say it, even if we do not like it and even if his mode of expression and his taste may differ from our own."[19]

Lindey's admission about the book's weak literary value was influenced by the aesthetic ambivalence, if not outright disdain, expressed by the belles lettres crowd. Ernst and Lindey had written Sinclair Lewis, Lewis Gannett, Charles and Mark van Doren, Joseph Wood Krutch, the psychiatrist Frederick Wertham, and other writers they could depend on in hopes that they would offer their support. Some refused to endorse *Pay Day*, and more than a few of their usual allies sensed something vital at stake in the very idea of Literature. They could not support a work belonging to what New York's ex-commissioner of health Louis Harris referred to as "the vomit school of literature," with some refusing to accord Asch's novel the status of literature. The responses reflected a few recurrent themes: that standards and taste matter; that the market-driven proliferation of trash ennobled no one and did not contribute to art or culture; and that, though censorship in general was problematic, not all books deserved the light of day.

The Anti-Emulation Argument

Ernst and Lindey received the requisite denunciations of Sumner from their allies, but they heard so much critical commentary about the book itself that they realized they would not be able to attach the usual appendix of supporting letters to their defense brief, paralleling their experience with Hall's *Well of Loneliness*. Lindey told the publisher, "Some of the so-called 'testimonials' are turning out to be boomerangs." Louis Harris, for instance, had been most helpful in both the *Dennett* and Stopes trials but in this instance stayed away; and both Reverend John Haynes Holmes and Rabbi Goldstein of Congregation B'Nai Jeshurun offered "quite sweeping indictments." "Let us hope," Lindey wrote, "we receive at least a few more letters which are commendatory and not otherwise."[20]

These responses forced Lindey and Ernst into a tactical shift, ignoring the work's value as literature per se and focusing instead on the problems with obscenity law and the central question asked by the Hicklin test: Would this book have a tendency to corrupt its readers? Ironically, Lindey and Ernst decided that the vomit school critique could actually be useful, for Harris had gone on to say that "in his opinion no reader would try to emulate the hero. In fact, the book would have an opposite effect."[21] Lindey and Ernst borrowed this idea, taking the book's unlikable protagonist and his unsavory 24-hour escapades and turning them against the prosecution-friendly "tendency to corrupt" obscenity test. Jim's unlikability made him unlikely to corrupt readers.

With only two weeks to go before the official hearing in the magistrate court, Ernst and Lindey quickly fleshed out their two-pronged argument. First, because Asch's fictional world was ugly and his protagonist Jim was not the least attractive physically or psychologically, the book would likely repel rather than attract the vulnerable reader. Second, ugliness notwithstanding, the book was also an insightful and realistic sociological critique of the lives of young, restless urban men and should be available to readers for its documentary accuracy. Because the Comstock laws assumed that virtually any encounter with unseemly materials would have socially and morally destructive effects on vulnerable readers, the defense had to address the question of the book's possible effects head on. Ernst and Lindey argued that Asch's sociological realism made it an effective cautionary tale, writing in their brief to Magistrate Goodman that Jim's "life is not an invitation, but a warning."[22] They built this anti-emulation defense atop a series of other arguments about New York's obscenity law as it had evolved to 1930, contending that the book did not meet the increasingly strict standards of criminal obscenity demanded by New York's courts in literary obscenity cases.

Lindey and Ernst began their Memorandum of Law Submitted by the Defendants by listing books that Sumner had brought actions against but that were not "finally condemned by the courts."[23] Two strong points stood out: Sumner was often wrong, and there was a clear trend toward more liberal protective standards for literary fare in New York's courts, especially in the magistrate courts. Sumner was still working from an "art for moral uplift" framework, but the modernist-influenced artists and writers had moved on to a more complicated understanding of art and its functions. Clearly, art need not be merely about uplift or beauty. Although the literary experts might still want literature that did not degrade taste or art, they were strongly opposed to Sumner applying his own limited standards and they resented that he ignored or mocked their more learned critiques. To the experts, Sumner had been consistently wrong about literature, art, and contemporary mores, and they neither valued his opinions nor trusted his tactics. They might not like Asch's novel, but they rejected Sumner's aesthetic criteria and especially his broad censorial authority and tactics.

Ernst and Lindey closed their elegant and thorough brief by returning to the value for readers (and the courts) of the evaluative mechanisms in place in the book trade economy. They noted that *Pay Day* had sold "many thousands of copies" and that "practically every reputable bookstore in New York City . . . has carried it in stock and sold it openly." Moreover, it had been widely reviewed. "Newspapers do not review smut," they argued, listing the sixty or so newspapers and other publications that had already reviewed the book. The courts, they added, "have shown due deference toward the reaction of the press and the estimate of critics."[24] Although the court might not accept the implication of their argument that obscenity referred only to something that was obviously pornographic, the book's widespread sales and promotion supported their claim that it circulated within the contemporary book world's mechanisms for conferring legitimacy.[25]

Their argument also depended on the distinction they made here and in other cases: that the "smut" they juxtaposed to *Pay Day* circulated in underground markets, was anonymously published, was furtively bought and sold, and was never reviewed by newspaper and journals. Gertzman explains that "frankly obscene erotica was issued privately because anonymity was essential to avoid arrest." And, as Henry S. Canby, founder and editor of the *Saturday Review of Literature*, pointed out, private printing was "a sign usually of weakness in the book, distrust of the reader, or fear of the hand of authority."[26]

Pay Day: The Magistrate's Decision and Sumner's Counterattack

Magistrate Henry M. R. Goodman ruled in the publisher's favor in late May 1930, accepting most of Ernst and Lindey's arguments, including their critique that the language of obscenity law was vague and imprecise and that New York State's case law history was inconsistent—incoherent even. But he was not willing to suspend the central concerns of obscenity law, expressed by the Hicklin standard, about the potentially corrupting or depraving effects on the most vulnerable audience, or the court's duty to protect that audience. Given this concern, he was quite interested in pursuing the question of the book's effects, hoping to learn from expert opinion what those effects might be. He also adopted the idea that readers might be inoculated against depravity, accepting Ernst and Lindey's antiemulation theory. Magistrate Goodman suggested that if the book were to influence its readers, as books were wont to do, it would be positively, as a deterrent even to the most vulnerable readers.[27]

Ernst and Lindey celebrated by promoting their success. They had an expensive habit of making many copies of their extensive briefs and circulating them widely to journalists, other lawyers, and their growing stable of experts. They did so in this case and received glowing tributes in print and in letters. For example, Mary Ware Dennett thanked Lindey for her copy of the brief: "It's a masterpiece, and I'll add it to my collection of Ernst-Lindey works of genius."[28]

Ernst's celebrity increased, and the case reverberated in New York's legal and literary circles, adding momentum to the anti-censorship cause. But the victory celebration was short-lived. Sumner received the verdict angrily, reportedly storming out of the courtroom, and rumors quickly circulated that he was in a "rather ugly mood." It soon became clear that the rumor was true. As he often did, Sumner used a variety of tactics to obstruct the decision's outcome. In this case he pressured District Attorney Harold Hastings to seek a criminal indictment against the book from a grand jury, so that a higher-level state court could try it. Lindey and Ernst assuaged Brewer & Warren's concerns with reassurance about "Magistrate Goodman's unequivocal opinion." But, knowing Sumner, they cautioned, "One cannot be absolutely certain."[29]

Lindey and Ernst tried to head off Sumner by making their own entreaties to Hastings, trying to convince him of the book's legitimacy by supplying him with the letters of support they had received, along with their *Pay Day* brief and Magistrate Goodman's decision.[30] Ernst also importuned the Vice Society's Board of Trustees to reign in Sumner, repeatedly writing its vice president, William Schieffelin, asking for a meeting, but to no avail.[31] They also tried using public suasion, writing to journalist Harry Elmer Barnes, among others, suggesting their editorial pens could forestall an indictment.[32] Despite all these efforts, Hastings took the book before a grand jury and succeeded in getting an indictment, meaning that the book would be tried in the New York Court of Special Sessions. Ernst and Lindey then tried to convince the judges on that court to dismiss the indictment, submitting a lengthy legal memorandum—essentially replicating the magistrate court brief—supplemented by the magistrate's strong decision, editorials supporting the decision, and letters of support from New York's publishing elite. Noting that the decision had been well received by the public and the press, particularly by many newspapers—which could be regarded

as genuinely reflective of sober and enlightened public opinion—they declared that it would be most helpful if the courts restricted Sumner's use
of the Comstock statute "to smutty postcards, and not to permit it to interfere with the expression of ideas."[33] They hoped to make a categorical
distinction that excluded their client's book from smut and suggested that
Sumner was violating protected freedoms.

Lindey and Ernst's memorandum to the Court of Special Sessions drew
extensively on press opinion to skewer Sumner and convey the frustrations felt by men of letters at Sumner's meddling and his wearying tactics.
Quoting a *New York Herald Tribune* piece, they admitted that "*Pay Day*
is no Sunday school story." But it did not need to be. "A novel is, in its
way, a work of art, not a tract. A painter is permitted to paint a cesspool if
he thinks it worth painting, and an artist in words should be permitted to
paint the dirt he meets in the streets." Here they took a distinctly modernist stance: that artists need not provide positive instruction and that art that
does not elevate the viewer or reader is not necessarily harmful. The artist,
the editorial continued, "is not and should not be required to uplift the
community by his work. Some may like his work better and recommend it
more freely if he does so; but the community has a right to interfere with
his expression only when it can actually be shown that it really endangers
the community health."[34] The editorial then blasted Sumner for intellectual
immaturity and petulance incompatible with New York City's vital role in
the publishing world.[35]

Others who had originally enlisted in the scheme using *Casanova's
Homecoming* also blasted Sumner, and their pieces were also used in the
memorandum to the court. Harry Elmer Barnes chimed in with an editorial in the *New York Evening Telegram* titled "The Unregenerate Sumner,"
remarking, "John S. Sumner . . . who has recently been compared to Elijah,
seems incapable of learning by experience or judicial tutelage."[36] Calling
Sumner "obdurate and vindictive" for taking a "copy of the book under
his arm" and going to the district attorney, despite the magistrate's strong
opinion, Barnes's editorial echoed Ernst and Lindey's claim that Sumner
was "persistently overreaching himself."[37] If Sumner "confine[d] himself
to obscene postcards and the like," they argued in their brief, he would be

FIGURE 8. John S. Sumner (in center with dark topcoat and hat), secretary of the New York Society for the Suppression of Vice, supervises the burning of books at police headquarters, alongside Deputy Police Commissioner Martin H. Meaney (next to Sumner in double-breasted suit).
SOURCE: Getty Images.

far more productive in his pursuit of actual smut and would have support from the world of letters. But his pursuit of legitimate literary works put him "out of step with the entire community" in this and "so many recent prosecutions."[38]

But Ernst and Lindey's efforts to convince the court to drop the grand jury indictment were for naught.[39] Judge Otto Rosalsky of the Court of Special Sessions denied their motion on July 22, 1930, and called for a trial. Once again, Sumner won by battling on.

Rather than risk financial losses and a criminal verdict, Brewer & Warren decided to pull their book from the market. Sumner also initially refused to return the fifty-six copies of *Pay Day* he had seized in the raid (the same number of copies of *The Well of Loneliness* he had refused to return to Covici-Friede). He eventually relinquished them but only after a protracted fight that took months to resolve and only culminated when Lindey and Ernst returned to the magistrate court to ask for a court order requiring the copies be returned.[40]

Sumner's inability to compromise explains why Ernst and Lindey and the city's publishers and booksellers shared such animus toward Sumner. He knew what the courts would let him get away with and played an elaborate cat-and-mouse game with the publishers and their lawyers at their moments of victory. When publicity-fueled demand for the book was high, Sumner would interfere with the publisher's market opportunities, financially punishing them at the same time they owed lawyers' fees. This is exactly how Sumner had "won" with *Casanova's Homecoming* in 1924 and against other books as well.

Schnitzler's *Hands Around*: Two Different Verdicts on the Same Book

Sumner made the job of publishing and defending Schnitzler's *Casanova's Homecoming* difficult by attacking not just that novel but also Schnitzler's entire oeuvre of sexually themed stories. Sumner launched a two-pronged offensive against Schnitzler's *Hands Around*. The book is a collection of ten short stories set in Vienna in the late nineteenth century and involving characters from different social classes, each of whom has sexually preoccupied encounters with two other characters in the cycle of stories. One character from each story continues into the next, where they engage with a character with whom they have had a previous sexual history and where another sexual assignation will or has already taken place. The predominantly furtive sex occurs off the page but enmeshes all the characters and stories. The relationships are not tender, loving, or mutual but instead involve prostitution, marital infidelity, and exertions of social prestige and control. A general ennui and theme of promiscuity suffuse all the stories. The stories have such titles as "The Whore and the Soldier," "The Soldier and the Parlor Maid," and "The Count and the Whore."[41]

Sumner, who had previously gone after *Hands Around* in the early 1920s, was horrified by its presence in New York's bookstores. He initiated two separate actions, one against a bookstore in Staten Island and another in Manhattan. Sumner's efforts against *Hands Around* came to fruition just as Ernst and Lindey were preparing to restart their work on behalf of Simon & Schuster's publication of *Casanova's Homecoming*, complicating Ernst and Lindey's plans.

Employing their usual tactics, Sumner's Vice Society raided two bookstores in October 1929, leading to the arrest and prosecution of the clerks who sold his undercover agent, Charles Bamberger, copies of *Hands Around*. Their trials took place in different jurisdictions. Illustrating the lack of clarity or precision with the obscenity statute, the same book produced different verdicts. In the Manhattan Magistrate Court, Judge Brodsky ruled that the book was not obscene. In the Staten Island Court of Special Sessions, the three-judge panel found the book obscene and the book clerk, Philip Pesky, guilty of criminal possession and intent to sell an obscene book. Pesky appealed the verdict, but the Appellate Division of the New York Supreme Court upheld the lower court verdict. Then, in October 1930, when Ernst and Simon & Schuster launched their *Casanova's Homecoming* plan, the New York Court of Appeals—New York's highest court—ruled that there was no reason to overturn the *Pesky* decision or return it to the lower court for reconsideration.[42] In short, Sumner got significant victories over one Arthur Schnitzler book in three separate courts, including the state's highest, just as Ernst and Lindey were set to wage battle with him over another Schnitzler book. Sumner, of course, would try to make great use of the *Pesky* decisions in the ensuing battle over *Casanova's Homecoming*.

The courts' opinions show that New York judges were sympathetic to Sumner's worries that literary works—even ones by internationally renowned writers—could topple or subvert conventional standards of sexual morality, especially their foundation in marital monogamy. Indeed, judges held significant responsibilities to protect and uphold public mores and believed they had an obligation to proscribe such works. No one—not judges, defense counsel, journalists, or book critics—questioned or challenged this foundational premise of judicial duty. The contrasting verdicts in the *Hands Around* cases also reveal tensions over the knotty legal problems and larger social interests in obscenity cases. Some judges took umbrage at what they perceived as literary flouting of bourgeois moral norms, and their decisions expressed a bristling defensiveness about the values of clean living. They especially took offense at cultural elites derisively labeling conventional morality "puritanical." Other judges were more comfortable with the idea of cultural flux and saw the need to protect the work of artists and writers who were trying to explore social transformations. The tensions were not easy to resolve. Commerce was crucial to New York's lifeblood, but cultural morality mattered too.

Moving Toward "Community Standards" as a Test

In trying to mediate these competing claims, New York's judges began to assess the offensiveness of a work in relation to what they referred to as "contemporary community values" or "contemporary community standards." With respect to Schnitzler's works, they asked whether the representations of human sexual desire (e.g., of marital infidelity) would elevate or lower the human prospect. Would these ideas and representations make humans baser by exposing them to more animalistic urges and by undermining institutions and values that keep humans from their weaknesses? These were fundamentally questions framed by a Christian understanding of sex as a threat to moral laws. Other questions were less grounded in moral concerns about human weakness and were more aesthetic and intellectual. For instance, how might the courts distinguish between realistic and psychologically probing literary or artistic expression versus mere pandering to sexual arousal? Another line of questioning, rooted in free speech arguments about protecting speech that met or advanced the public's intellectual interests or needs, asked, To what extent did the author's work contribute to some insight or collective understanding about the world that ought to be considered, no matter how unsettling or provocative?[43] Expert opinion, the judges increasingly agreed, could help answer these complex issues.

Ernst's firm was not at all involved in the Manhattan defense of *Hands Around* and came late to the action in the Staten Island *Pesky* case, after Pesky's conviction had been upheld by the Appellate Division of the New York Supreme Court. They submitted an amicus—or "friend of the court"—brief to the New York Court of Appeals while they were in the midst of preparing for the *Casanova's Homecoming* trial. Given that their defense of *Casanova's Homecoming* centered on Arthur Schnitzler's literary standing, they felt compelled to try to rescue Schnitzler's reputation from the trashing it took in the Appellate Division's opinion upholding Pesky's conviction.

Their amicus brief to the New York Court of Appeals began with the gambit that *Hands Around* had achieved a distinguished place in the marketplace of literary reputation, garnering "universal" acceptance throughout "the civilized world" as both a book and a play. Ernst and Lindey claimed that serious literary exploration of human sexual desires and arrangements, including unhappy coupling, was wholly different from materials appealing to prurience and lust. Those differences were knowable and identifiable. Other courts in Europe had recognized the book's serious purposes.[44] So had readers. By 1920 more than 100,000 copies had been sold in Europe, and the book had been widely staged as a play as well, despite unsuccessful efforts to enjoin its performance in various European cities. Literary authorities, especially those versed in Germanic literature, all knew its importance. As Lindey explained, "Any inquiry among those acquainted with German literature will indicate that the outstanding figures in the cultural life of contemporary Germany appeared in defense of 'Reigen.'"[45] In fact, Ernst and Lindey asserted, the German courts had made precisely the argument they would make about *The Well of Loneliness*, *Pay Day*, and *Casanova's Homecoming*: that a story about the sad and even ridiculous pursuit of pleasure can also be a morality tale.[46] Ernst and Lindey's local expert in Germanic literature, Columbia University's Otto Schinnerer, explained the work's "melancholy train of thought": "The pictures are not intended to have the effect of sexual excitation, but, on the contrary, they are intended to repel one from the kind of 'love' depicted in the ten pictures."[47]

The brief then shifted to another argument, invoking free speech doctrine. Asserting that the First Amendment tradition was increasingly influencing and therefore transforming obscenity law and was a core principle that must be broadly applied, Ernst and Lindey wrote, "Any censorship of literature is, in the final analysis, an impairment of the basic rights of freedom of the press, and must be reluctantly exercised."[48]

Although Ernst and Lindey did not push this argument too hard, aware that the U.S. Supreme Court regarded literary and cultural speech, especially speech involving sexual content, as lower orders of speech and not nearly as important as political speech in advancing ideas, they did assert the First Amendment's putative protection of "freedom for the thought we hate." Jurists might find the work unappealing, but that was no reason to block its distribution.

Shifting to the local milieu, Ernst and Lindey argued that New York's courts had clearly determined that restrictive nineteenth-century obscenity laws did not comport with modern tastes and sensibilities. Moreover, the city's cultural institutions—its universities, theaters, and bookstores—had long embraced Schnitzler the author and also this work by performing, teaching, writing about, and selling *Hands Around*.[49] Turning then to Sumner's regime (as they always did), Ernst and Lindey assailed Sumner's record as out of sync with modern First Amendment ideals, the informed judgments of New York's literary and print economy leaders, and contemporary community tastes.[50] They showed that New York courts had increasingly accepted sexual license in books far more outré than Schnitzler's *Hands Around*. Using the same litany of titles invoked in defense of Radclyffe Hall's *Well of Loneliness*, they pointed again to decisions upholding *Mademoiselle de Maupin*, *Madeleine*, Boccaccio's classic *Decameron*, *A Young Girl's Diary*, and D. H. Lawrence's *Women in Love*, and they added *The Well of Loneliness*.[51]

Notwithstanding their amicus brief and the fervent journalistic criticisms of Sumner's record and judgment, in November 1930 the New York Court of Appeals upheld the two lower court decisions. The jurists chose not to challenge the judgment of the lower courts, holding that the lower courts' decisions that the book was obscene were "not unreasonable." As Judges Pound and Cardozo wrote, "If those charged with the duty to pass judgment upon the facts might say not unreasonably that the book sold by the defendant was obscene, lewd or indecent beyond a reasonable doubt . . . we are not at liberty to substitute our judgment for theirs." They added that they could not "say as a matter of law that the writing was so innocuous as to forbid the submission of its quality" to the trial court.[52]

Limping to *Casanova's Homecoming*

Sumner's successes against *Hands Around* made Simon & Schuster nervous. Ernst and Lindey too. But because they had the earlier (1922) court decision in favor of *Casanova's Homecoming* on their side, along with evidence of Sumner's tactics in the aftermath of that case, they were somewhat assuaged. Simon & Schuster planned to use this previous battle as part of their publicity materials in 1930, knowing that doing so would raise its profile.[53] Advertising *Casanova's Homecoming* as part of their Inner Sanctum series and one of nine Schnitzler works they planned to publish, Simon & Schuster touted the book's rave reviews when Thomas Seltzer first printed it in 1921, proclaiming that Carl van Doren called it "the most finished piece of writing published in the United States in 1921," that Heywood Broun hailed it as "a glorious piece of work," and that the *New York Evening Post* described it as "unsparing" in its "merciless soul vivisection."[54] These advertisements, widely published in the book sections of the city's newspapers on the eve of the publication of *Casanova's Homecoming* in 1930, blasted Sumner for imposing his own judgment rather than accepting the verdicts of such distinguished critics as Columbia University's van Doren. This time around "civilized" readers would prevail: In 1921 "the book was too much for the guardians of American purity. It is republished in 1930 . . . in the assurance that this literary classic cannot fail to be welcomed by the civilized."[55]

Unlike the underground press, part of Sumner's power with legitimate publishers came from controlling which titles even made it into print. He monitored publishers' lists and advertisements and routinely warned publishers that they would find trouble (including big legal expenses) if they proceeded to print titles he disliked. The decision by Brewer & Warren to withdraw Asch's *Pay Day*, even after a magistrate court verdict in their favor, was a case in point about Sumner's doggedness and the financial and legal power he could leverage.

With *Casanova's Homecoming*, however, the publishers, lawyers, and Sumner's many critics in the press wanted Sumner to take the bait. He did. Immediately upon seeing the advertisement for the book in the *New York Sun*, Sumner sent Simon & Schuster a warning: "On July 18, 1923 [publisher] Thomas Seltzer was indicted by a grand jury in this county . . . and the criminal proceeding was discontinued by the District Attorney only upon the promise of Mr. Seltzer to discontinue publication of said book and to keep it from the market. This may have escaped your notice. Yours very truly."[56] Sumner's truncated legal history ignored the fact that the magistrate court had first cleared the book, and he had sought the grand jury indictment subsequent to that decision.

Ernst and Lindey fed updates of Sumner's threats to their journalist accomplices: Harry Elmer Barnes, Lewis Gannett, and Roy Howard. They also requested patience in attacking Sumner until they had lined everything up: With Barnes at the *Telegram* and Howard at the *New York Herald Tribune* ready to pounce with their editorial assault and Simon & Schuster (financially fortified by its robust sales of their crossword puzzle books) willing to incur the legal costs, Ernst, Lindey, and junior associate Newman Levy prepared for battle.[57] They knew the book's credibility as a literary artifact and its defensibility in court would be enhanced if Simon & Schuster published it with an authoritative introduction by a distinguished literary or scholarly figure.[58] They first asked literary critic Harry Hansen, creator of "The First Reader" column for the *New York World* newspaper, to write an introduction, but Sumner's clout was such that Hansen declined, for fear of losing his job.[59] Eventually they agreed that Columbia University scholar Otto Schinnerer would write the introduction; the fact that he actually taught *Casanova's Homecoming* as one of the great works of Germanic literary culture in his world literature course was certainly a bona fide.

Ernst knew that Sumner would pounce on *Casanova's Homecoming* when the New York Appellate Division announced in July 1930 that it had upheld the Staten Island Court of Special Sessions decision declaring *Hands Around* obscene.[60]

The day the book was published, August 7, 1930, Sumner set the arrest and book seizure in motion. His man Charles Bamberger, again using one of his many aliases, went directly to the publishers and purchased a copy. The next day Sumner and a New York City policeman, armed with a warrant, raided Simon & Schuster's offices and warehouse, seizing over 1,500 copies, thus keeping *Casanova's Homecoming* out of bookstores while the legal process unfolded.[61] Ernst and the journalists also leapt.[62] Lewis Gannett at the *New York Herald Tribune* ran an editorial within days, titled "Mr. Sumner vs. Arthur Schnitzler." Gannett wrote that Sumner opened himself up "to being faintly ridiculous," detailing Sumner's 1922 loss in the magistrate court and averring that at "the time of the Seltzer prosecution literary critics and other experts gave the book a clean bill of health. . . . It is scarcely conceivable that the work should have become increasingly erotic with the passing of time."[63]

Gannett continued to excoriate Sumner's failures to serve the city's nexus of readers, writers, publishers, reviewers, and bookstores, suggesting that he was profoundly out of touch with contemporary tastes and the needs of a major New York City industry.

> It is to be hoped that Simon & Schuster, the present victims of Mr. Sumner's myopic morality, will make a determined stand in favor of their publication, as they have announced they intend to do. It will be at once a service to letters and the book-buying public in general to combat the activities of what has been termed "an extra-legal society which has pitted its opinion against the virtually unanimous edict of critics, scholars, men of letters and civilized readers generally."[64]

As planned, other journalists joined the attack.[65]

Both sides chose facts selectively from the book's case history. In 1922 Sumner charged Thomas Seltzer and Mary Marks with possession and intent to sell three obscene books: *Casanova's Homecoming*, D. H. Lawrence's *Women in Love*, and the anonymously written *A Young Girl's Diary*. New York City magistrate court judge Simpson found all three books not obscene.[66] Sumner then went to the district attorney and requested a grand jury hearing on Schnitzler's book. The grand jury found that the book should be held for trial, and the district attorney brought a criminal indictment against the book's publisher. In 1924 Judge Wagner refused the motion to drop the indictment filed by Seltzer's lawyer Jonah Goldstein. (Goldstein would later become an important magistrate court judge on literary cases.) Instead of going to court, Thomas Seltzer agreed to cease publishing the book and destroy the book plates. Two years later, the district attorney dropped the indictment, for lack of a book to prosecute.

In the 1930 battle Sumner claimed that the most important moments of that earlier history were the grand jury's indictment and Judge Wagner's refusal to grant Goldstein's motion. Ernst and Lindey argued that the only legal decision specifically ruling on the book's obscenity was Magistrate Simpson's 1922 decision; the next most important legal fact was the 1926 agreement to drop the indictment. Perhaps most valuably, Sumner's 1930 attack gave Ernst and Lindey the opportunity to mine Magistrate Simpson's 1922 decision, which offered an erudite anti-censorship rationale and established in the city's magistrate courts a high standard of judicial tolerance for literary and artistic expression and thus a high bar for determining obscenity. Although Simpson's decision had no power as a binding precedent on any higher court, through the 1920s it had nevertheless been an influential one in the city's magistrate courts, where so many obscenity actions were initiated.

Besides the book's specific legal history in New York City, Sumner was also up against the juggernaut of expert and journalistic opinion drummed up to criticize him. Immediately following Sumner's seizure of the 1,500 copies in August, Simon & Schuster released a long statement about the book's literary value and its distinguished reputation among critics and then blasted Sumner: "We shall defend the book and fight the case" to "safeguard a classic of modern fiction against the misguided zeal of an extra-legal society which is pitting its opinion against the virtually unanimous edict of critics, scholars, men of letters, and civilized readers generally."[67]

Ernst and the publishers solicited help from their stable of experts, asking them to clarify the stakes of the battle: "We appeal to you because we realize that the battle against censorship, in this case as in every other case, will be won or lost depending on the measure of informed and intelligent support rallying to the cause of the publication to be suppressed."[68] The onslaught of responses from New York's literary intelligentsia was so substantial that Ernst's firm eventually provided the documents to the presiding judge, Magistrate Gottlieb, in a separate bound volume. Sumner felt it necessary to respond to his press critics with two long editorials defending his actions, but his protestations paled next to the avalanche of opinions defending the work.

The mobilization of public intellectuals against Sumner proved a formidable strategy. Compared with critics' ambivalence about *Pay Day* and the vomit school of literature, their effusive support for *Casanova's Homecoming* was telling and clearly influenced the judge. Indeed, after the trial Sam Schur, of Ernst's firm, reported that Judge Gottlieb "thought our office deserved the highest compliment," declaring "he had never seen as fine a piece of work as our Bound Volume of representative opinion."[69] The contributors included notable critics and public intellectuals, such as H. L. Mencken, Oswald Garrison Villard, Felix Adler, Horace Kallen, Karl Menninger, and Heywood Broun. All drew a distinction that Sumner would not seem to make: Human foibles connected to sexuality warrant attention, nuanced treatment, and are not vulgar or prurient simply because they deal with sex. (Given the novel's subject matter—Casanova's aging and his declining masculine vitality—it might not be surprising that these mostly middle-aged men found the book's topic worthy of literary treatment.)

The novelists, social critics, psychologists, and others were giving Ernst an impressive body of intellectual opinion, and the city's editorialists pummeled Sumner. During a three-week stretch in August, before the trial, the *Evening World*, the *New York World*, the *New York Telegram*, the *New York Evening Post*, the *Brooklyn Eagle*, the *New York Times*, and *The Nation* all criticized Sumner.[70] Between the solicited letters and the editorials, Ernst's team offered the court a rich cache of documents testifying to the novel's intrinsic value as literature. Perhaps even more powerfully, these artifacts offered compelling evidence about contemporary community tastes, at least as measured by a broad cross-section of New York's intellectuals.

The Defense Brief: Casanova's Folly as Object Lesson

Simon & Schuster's lawyers organized their legal argument along four lines: (1) that *Casanova's Homecoming* had been thoroughly accepted by the community; (2) that a legal action against this book had already taken place and been dismissed in 1922; (3) that New York case law was filled with precedents that would exonerate this book; and (4) that it had become an established rule in New York courts that a book must be read as a whole, and if so read, it would be clear that this book was not obscene. The brief drew extensively on Magistrate Simpson's 1922 decision.

In case after case, the judges, lawyers, clients, and the many other recipients of Ernst and Lindey's formal legal memoranda remarked on the persuasive richness of their written work. True to form, Lindey, Levy, and Ernst compiled a document thorough in its case law history, engaging as a work of literary history, and artfully packaged as a product. It was also as much a critique of Sumner as a defense of *Casanova's Homecoming*. Beginning with a forceful denunciation of Sumner and his record, they noted that even the "staid New York *Herald-Tribune* has declared that to attack this volume was 'myopic morality.'"[71] They observed that "the head of the Scripps-Howard organization has indicated that the prosecution should not be directed against this book but against the Vice Society." The book-world economy was, they argued, a reputation economy, and New York's judges understood this and accepted the evaluative criteria of that network of publishers, reviewers, scholars, advertisers, and bookstore owners who openly sold the books.[72]

Turning to the work itself, Ernst and colleagues argued that *Casanova's Homecoming* was not immoral at all but offered a clear cautionary tale to its readers. Describing the book for the court, they made it clear that this story was about Casanova's twilight, well past his prime as a famous lover: "He is penniless . . . he is a decrepit wastrel, no longer attractive to women, no longer a figure of romance and glamour, but a man fast sinking into oblivion and clutching vainly at the straw of the conquests of his youth." There was nothing heroic, grand, or gratifying in Casanova's senescence; rather, they explained, Schnitzler's novel served up "a pitiless vivisection of a dotard, so skillfully done as to result at the same time in a profound psychological study, a moral plea and a first-rate work of art."[73] Indeed, *Casanova's Homecoming* had all the elements of art: a style that is "dignified and restrained" and that did not suffer from "that coarseness, that elaboration of offensive detail, that accentuation of the suggestive, which mark so many of our so-called modern novels."[74]

The central legal question was, Will *Casanova's Homecoming* corrupt and debase its likely readers? Ernst's answer was a resounding no. The "effect upon the reader is one of distinct aversion for Casanova," Ernst argued in the brief. "He is not pictured as a gay hero who derives joy from his exploits. He is an outcast and a starveling; unhappy, tormented by his desires, thwarted by failure, embittered by his fading renown, faced—at the very moment of his return to Venice—with a life of obloquy. . . . Contempt is his measure."[75] Reading the book would lead to one conclusion: that personal rectitude was the only appropriate response. Casanova's folly was an object lesson in things to be avoided.

Déjà Vu: The Court's Opinion and Sumner's Response

In late September 1930 Magistrate Gottlieb ruled that *Casanova's Homecoming* was not obscene. Gottlieb embraced Ernst and Lindey's arguments about the changing cultural norms and the relativity of moral standards over time. "The standard of life today as to plays and books, and the very habits of people, has so changed that what was regarded as obscene and immoral yesterday is today reckoned as being in proper taste."[76] Magistrate Gottlieb also quoted Simpson's 1922 decision extensively in his own 1930 decision. He described Magistrate Simpson as "a colleague for whom I have a high regard as a sound thinker and excellent jurist" who had written "an interesting and learned opinion." Gottlieb remarked as well on the body of evidence Ernst and his team compiled. As a result, he said, he could not "substitute a prudish opinion in place of the liberal ideas advanced by those who have judged this book by the present day standard of living."[77]

It was typical Sumner pique when he lost. As in 1922, the court's verdict did not end the matter. Once again Sumner sought a grand jury indictment to prosecute the book in a higher court. As before, he also refused to return to Simon & Schuster the 1,500-plus books he had confiscated, arguing heatedly with Magistrate Gottlieb about this matter before storming out of the courtroom. Sumner succeeded in convincing Manhattan District Attorney Crain's office to seek a grand jury indictment of the book, which it apparently had been reluctant to do. Newman Levy, Ernst's junior associate, initially reported to Ernst that he had learned directly from the district attorney's office that they would not seek an indictment and had also been pressuring Sumner to return the books. Sumner refused their request, and a week later the district attorney's office announced that they would take the book to the grand jury. This unleashed another flurry of activity in Ernst's office and a fusillade from Sumner's critics in the press.[78]

Sumner's tactics played into his opponent's hands, but his obstinacy also created a great deal of work for Lindey, Levy, and Ernst and considerable expense for the publishers. Dick Simon was livid at Sumner's intransigence and told Ernst, "The general public evidently feels that we ought to sue Sumner."[79] But Ernst thought that sustaining the public opinion barrage against Sumner was a better strategy. He sent copies of *Casanova's Homecoming* to reporters, along with the extensive legal memorandum that he and Lindey had developed, and kept Barnes and Gannett updated at every step.

Ernst's wrote a long editorial in the *New York Telegram* that tooted his own horn but also kept attention focused on the maladroit censor-in-chief, describing in some detail Sumner's history of outrageous tactics in refusing to accept the courts' decisions in a variety of cases. He began with *The Well of Loneliness* and went on.

When the complaint against *The Well of Loneliness* was thrown out by the Court of Special Sessions, Sumner, who had taken the books under a search warrant and still had physical possession of the books, failed to return or satisfactorily account for about fifty copies.

When *Pay Day* was fully exonerated by Magistrate Goodman, Mr. Sumner flatly refused to return any of the copies that had been taken under a search warrant, disclaiming that the books were "in his possession." Inquiries directed to the office of the District Attorney and to the Property Clerk of the Police Department failed to yield any results. Mr. Sumner . . . then admitted that he had had physical custody of the books all the time. . . .

When *Casanova's Homecoming* was completely exonerated by Magistrate Gottlieb, I was mindful of the *Pay Day* incident, and I specifically asked the Court to direct Mr. Sumner, who was present at the time, to return all copies taken under the search warrant. In clear violation of the law and in deliberate contravention of the Court's mandate, Sumner refused . . . and he is still unlawfully holding them.[80]

Ernst called on leading citizens and even members of the Vice Society's Board of Directors to demand changes in Sumner's tactics, hoping at least to get the 1,500 seized copies back.

Sumner fought back, offering two public responses to the editorial attacks against him. In the *Herald Tribune* he suggested that Schnitzler revealed his "licentious" nature in writing *Hands Around* and that whatever else he penned was thus guilty of the same moral failing. Defending himself to his fellow New Yorkers, Sumner promoted his role as a defender of their commonsense moral values against those of "a noisy minority" of literary elites who mistook Schnitzler as a literary master rather than a writer of dirty books.[81]

Simon & Schuster, Ernst, and Scripps-Howard editors kept the controversy simmering with a November 1930 *New York Herald Tribune* "symposium" on the book, offering positive reviews of the work and inviting Sumner's response. He defended his work and attacked Ernst along with Simon & Schuster: "We have no apologies to make for action undertaken against the book in question."[82] Once more Sumner attacked Schnitzler, not *Casanova's Homecoming*, implying that the author was a pornographer. He attacked the publishers and Ernst, the latter for his legal tactics and both for their publicity ruses. "Schuster had no right to complain about a 'costly procedure,'" he argued, because they knew full well that he (Sumner) would go after a book that "many persons objected" to. Mocking their publicity strategies, he added, "No doubt expensive and extensive briefs, supplied to the newspapers and other agencies of publicity, constituted an important item of expense." And as to their concerns about their reputation, Sumner caustically added, "It seems odd that gentlemen so offended in their self-esteem should thus keep before the public the fact that they were hauled into court regarding a questionable book." If they had stuck with their usual fare—publishing crossword puzzle books—the "recent unpleasant incident would not have occurred."[83]

Ultimately the grand jury, convinced by the written testimony of Columbia University professor Schinnerer and by Ernst and Lindey's arguments, refused to indict *Casanova's Homecoming* as obscene. Sumner returned most of the 1,500 books, but not all of them, arguing that the original tally had been inaccurate; he was shy of 1,500 by 46 books—10 fewer than he refused to return to Radclyffe Hall's publishers.

The Spirit of the First Amendment

There was no love lost between Ernst and Sumner. They would continue to wage battle throughout the 1930s, as Sumner maintained his considerable powers to police the city's publishing houses, bookstores, magazine stands, theaters, barber shops, and other places where he smelled moral rot and found smut. He took his losses, but as the materials got tawdrier, he also maintained support from his board of directors, religious leaders, politicians, and city police officials. Sumner's legal powers were still significant in part because the First Amendment was undeveloped with respect to cultural expression, with no established tradition for protecting literary and artistic speech and certainly not expressly sexual speech. The First Amendment could not be used to appeal convictions because obscenity laws, operating with their own standards and purposes (to protect the public against the evils of immorality, lust, lewdness) were upheld as constitutional by the U.S. Supreme Court and were an exception to First Amendment protections of speech and the press. It would be decades before the Supreme Court would hear a challenge to their constitutionality.

For Ernst and Lindey, an important part of their overarching project was to diminish Sumner's authority and to help protect New York's publishers, writers, and bookstore owners from his attacks. But their larger goal was strategic, aimed at tightening the definition of what constituted obscenity, to diminish the reach of federal and state obscenity law enforcement, and to get the courts to expand the circulation of materials dealing with sexuality issues that would have legitimate value to the republic of readers. Defending sexual and literary modernism across fields, Ernst and Lindey aimed to protect the rights of authors, doctors, sexologists, and others to offer an array of necessary materials about fundamental issues of human sexuality. This right of production also depended on the public's right of access to those materials. What became increasingly clear in New York courts in the

1930s was that the book publishing industry needed greater regulatory predictability, greater clarity about what the rules were, and less punitive mechanisms for responding to censors' threats.

One outcome that emerged was the rise of civil libertarianism in conjunction with and reinforced by the needs of commercial media. Ernst and Lindey consistently articulated a "marketplace of ideas" argument, and New York's judges were not inclined to disregard marketplace logic or the interests of capital. Ernst and colleagues' body of arguments included a cluster of ideas that slowly made it more difficult for the Sumners, Postal officials, Customs officers, and ambitious district attorneys to seize and censor materials that others regarded as valuable. But Ernst and Lindey also understood that their real impact in challenging the Comstock laws and restricting the legal and economic authority of their enforcers would be at the federal level, not the local one. Those New York magistrate court decisions had no binding power as precedents, but Ernst and Lindey drew effectively on the decisions by New York's jurists to build a persuasive framework for thinking about obscenity law and its limits and for constructing a narrative of progress in the courts in which judges had increasingly recognized the vagueness of the obscenity statutes and their outdatedness.

But those were local skirmishes. Ernst's signal victories took place in the federal courts, including what was perhaps the twentieth century's most prominent literary trial, the defense of James Joyce's *Ulysses*, the subject of the next chapter.

CHAPTER 6

DEFENDING LITERARY GENIUS

James Joyce's Ulysses *on Trial*

NO WORK OF MODERN LITERATURE more fully embodied the experiments in form intrinsic to modernism than James Joyce's *Ulysses*, which critics agreed was *the* masterpiece of the age, putting Joyce in the company of such greats as Chaucer, Shakespeare, Fielding, Balzac, Rabelais, and Flaubert. Malcolm Cowley, editor of the *New Republic*, wrote, "James Joyce's position in literature is almost as important as that of Einstein in science. Preventing American authors from reading him is about as stupid as it would be to place an embargo on the theory of relativity."[1] And yet *Ulysses* had been legally banned in English-speaking countries since its publication in 1922 and was nearly as reviled as it was revered. Even its most ardent advocates had to admit to its many Rabelaisian moments, reveling in what Edmund Wilson described as "this gross body—the body of humanity."[2] As literary historian Paul Vanderham writes, the obscenity in Joyce's work "is more than a Victorian fantasy."[3]

Alexander Lindey and Morris Ernst were especially keen on freeing *Ulysses* from the clutches of American censors.[4] They knew defending it would be their crowning success. With verdicts in the *Dennett* and *Married Love* cases, they felt well positioned to defend *Ulysses* in the federal courts. Victories against John S. Sumner and the New York Society for the Suppression of Vice in New York's magistrate and appellate courts and useful language from jurists amenable to bringing those nineteenth-century obscenity laws in closer concert with twentieth-century tastes also gave them confidence. And they knew that the writers, critics, editors, scholars, and publishers with whom they had built alliances in other censorship cases would strongly support the liberation of *Ulysses*, the suppression of which was the most notorious symbol of American Comstockery gone awry.

The idea that *Ulysses* would still be censored in 1933, eleven years after its publication in Paris, strikes modern audiences as absurd. It struck many in the early 1930s as absurd as well. But Joyce so insistently transgressed literary and moral categories and *Ulysses* was so profane, scatological, and salacious that its successful defense was not at all guaranteed. The liberation of *Ulysses* is rightly understood as a maturation moment for U.S. laws in relation to modern art and literature. It was also an apex of sorts for Ernst and Lindey's work in steering judges toward solutions to the nineteenth-century obscenity laws' prohibitions on matters lewd, indecent, scurrilous, and all the other synonyms used to define obscenity.

Ulysses: The Little Review Cases and Early Legal Travails

Ulysses was first published in episodic form in the American literary magazine *The Little Review* from 1918 to 1920 and then in its entirety in 1922 under the imprint of Shakespeare & Co., a Paris bookstore owned by the American expat Sylvia Beach. From the earliest episodes in *The Little Review*, Joyce's chief financial supporter, New York lawyer John Quinn, and his foremost literary champion, the poet Ezra Pound, feared that Joyce's defiance of well-understood standards of sexual reticence would bring the censors down on him. They were right. By 1920 the U.S. Postal Service had denied second-class mailing privileges to three separate issues of the magazine carrying episodes of Joyce's work. In 1921 the New York Court of General Sessions found a fourth issue obscene, another victim of Sumner's attacks. Seven years later U.S. Customs officials denied the completed book entry into the United States in the case of *Heymoolen v. United States* (1928), when a U.S. Customs Court judge in Minnesota held *Ulysses* obscene, along with a dozen other works seized in the same shipment.

Joyce's fixation on the sexual produced as much outrage among some readers as it did among censors. One complaint addressed to *Little Review* editors Jane Heap and Margaret Anderson epitomized many readers' reactions.

> I think this is the most damnable slush and filth that ever polluted paper in print. . . . There are no words I know to describe, even vaguely, how disgusted I am; not with the mire of his effusion but with all those whose minds are so putrid that they dare allow such muck and sewage of the human mind to besmirch the world by repeating it—and in print, through which medium it may reach young minds. Oh my God, the horror of it.[5]

Even Pound tried to get Joyce to reign in his bawdy humor and insistent erasure of distinctions between "the erotic and the excretory" by selectively editing his submissions. Joyce intentionally provoked broader cultural and ideological clashes. He "not only rejected but attacked" Victorian moral opposition to discussions of sexuality and its pleasures, erotic desire, and religious institutions.[6] Joyce's work was also formalistically revolutionary and anarchistic. Because the individual episodes were first published during the Bolshevik Revolution, they were perceived as having profound political implications. Contemporary critics also thought they glimpsed the links between Joyce's aesthetic ruptures and Bolshevism.[7]

The Little Review editors, Anderson and Heap, were never shy about their own radicalism and the revolutionary causes they embraced. For instance, through their magazine they opposed the World War I military preparedness campaign, urged the shooting of Utah's governor before he could execute the Industrial Workers of the World's Joe Hill, and avowed revolution through art. As a result, they ran afoul of federal postal and national security authorities before they had ever published Joyce. They encountered the same solicitor of the Postal Service, W. H. Lamar, who had troubled Mary Ware Dennett with his refusal to mail birth control materials when she was a birth control pioneer. During World War I the Postal Service placed the entire magazine on its list of subversive literature as a "Publication of Anarchistic Tendency." This made the portions of Joyce's work in press at The Little Review susceptible to close scrutiny by wartime officials.

When the Postal Service banned the January 1919 issue, it did so be-cause of a Wyndham Lewis short story, "Cantelman's Spring Mate," which they found both subversive and obscene. But Postal officials also noticed Joyce's "Lestrygonians" episode in the same issue. In a letter from the Postal Service's Translation Bureau to the postmaster general, an official wrote, "The creature who writes this *Ulysses* stuff should be put under a glass jar for examination. He'd make a lovely exhibit."[8] As Vanderham notes, this was enough to put officials on notice to look for any further issue carrying Joyce's work. Joyce's transgressive humor was evident in the "Lestrygonians" episode, which included Leopold Bloom's reminiscences of making love with his future wife Molly among the rhododendrons on the Ben of Howth above Dublin and of being interrupted by a defecating goat: "Ravished over her I lay full lips full open kissed her mouth. Yum. Softly she gave me in my mouth the seedcake warm and chewed. . . . Pebbles fell. She lay still. A goat. No-one. High on Ben Howth rhododendrons a nannygoat walk-ing surefooted, dropping currants. Wildly I lay on her, kissed her: eyes, her lips, her stretched neck beating, woman's breasts full in her blouse of nun's veiling, fat nipples upright." This was precisely the kind of erotic-excretory convergence that Joyce reveled in and that troubled Pound and others of his supporters, along with the Postal officials.[9]

The Little Review was next denied mailing privileges in May 1919 for the issue that published the second half of the "Scylla and Charybdis" epi-sode, in which Joyce deals with incest, bestiality, and masturbation. The third time that the magazine lost its mailing privileges for an issue was in January 1920 with the magazine's third installment of the "Cyclops" epi-sode, in which violence and anti-English Irish nationalism suffuse Barney Kiernan's bar and Leopold Bloom is sniggered at for being cuckolded by Blazes Boylan. Then, most famously, the Postal Service suppressed *The Little Review* after the July-August 1920 edition, only this time a New York State criminal indictment against Anderson and Heap followed. This issue included portions of Joyce's "Nausicaa" episode, famous for its scene on the beach in which the young Gerty MacDowell, knowing that Bloom was masturbating to the sight of her, leaned backward to see fireworks and, aroused herself, showed him her fleshy thighs and bloomers.

Although the Postal Service suppressed the July-August 1920 issue, some copies slipped through the mail, eventually ending up in the hands of John Sumner. Anderson and Heap, who were trying to increase subscriptions to their magazine, sent an unsolicited copy of the "Nausicaa" issue to the daughter of a prominent New York lawyer.[10] She complained to her father, who then complained to the Manhattan district attorney, Edward Swann. His note to Swann began, "Surely there must be some way of keeping such 'literature' out of the homes of people who don't want it."[11] Swann assigned the complaint to Assistant District Attorney Joseph Forrester, who asked Sumner for his advice. Sumner found the magazine for sale at a Washington Square bookshop, purchased copies, read the "Nausicaa" episode, and filed an obscenity complaint against the owner of the bookstore. The bookstore owner was dropped from the case, but Anderson and Heap were prosecuted.[12]

Sumner and the Vice Society were explicitly trying to protect young female readers from such sexually provocative materials traveling through the mails. Moreover, Joyce's "Nausicaa" episode clearly burlesqued the whole notion of the "vulnerable" and innocent young female as a figment of Vice Society members' imaginations, because Gerty knows exactly what's going on as Bloom masturbates while watching her.[13] In the "Nausicaa" episode Joyce deliberately parodies the Victorian romance novels that Gerty would have been reading, by making her interior monologue redolent of the florid style available in the Victorian lending libraries.[14]

> She leaned back she caught her knee in her hands so as not to fall back looking up and there was no one to see only him and her when she revealed all her graceful beautifully shaped legs like that, supply soft and delicately rounded, and she seemed to hear the panting of his heart his hoarse breathing, because she knew about the passion of men like that.[15]

Joyce was not just satirizing the kinds of romance fiction Gerty might have read; he was satirizing the very idea of the innocent Victorian lass to be protected by the Hicklin standard.

Sumner and the district attorney brought the matter of *Ulysses* into New York's magistrate courts at the Jefferson Market Courthouse on September 29, 1920, for an initial hearing.[16] Anderson and Heap's lawyer, John Quinn, had already met with Sumner and tried to make a deal: In exchange for dropping the charges, they would not publish any more *Ulysses* episodes in *The Little Review*. But Sumner refused. The crux of Quinn's argument to Magistrate Corrigan lay in the work's obscurity and therefore difficulty of apprehension by readers. But Judge Corrigan quite clearly understood what Bloom was doing while watching Gerty McDowell on the beach, and he declared the book obscene and ordered Anderson and Heap to stand trial in the Court of Special Sessions.[17] The New York Court of Special Sessions also found the episode obscene, convicted Anderson and Heap, fined them $50 each, and enjoined them from publishing any more of *Ulysses*. Quinn did not pursue an appeal, and neither Anderson nor Heap had the money to hire new counsel for an appeal.[18]

After the convictions, as he had predicted, Quinn was unable to interest publishers in the book, until Shakespeare & Co. published it in English. American authorities harassed the book from the outset. As Vanderham notes, "By the end of 1922, the U.S. authorities were regularly confiscating copies of the Paris edition—even those Sylvia Beach had disguised with dust jackets bearing titles like *Shakespeare's Works* and (better yet) *Merry Tales for Little Folks*."[19] The English suffragette Harriet Shaw Weaver's Egoist Press in Paris also published the book in English in October 1922, but the Egoist edition fared no better against Customs authorities or Sumner's hypervigilant policing of booksellers' stalls. Of the 2,000 copies of the Egoist Press 1922 edition, Postal authorities in New York confiscated some 500 and Customs confiscated another 400.[20] Nevertheless, Sylvia Beach continued publishing the book, and travelers to Paris filled suitcases with copies for sale and for friends.

A decade later this black market distribution, including to libraries and college classrooms, made Ernst and Lindey's job easier by having the full text of Joyce's book and a decade's worth of critical appraisal and scholarly exegesis to draw on. The growing body of critical work surrounding the novel contributed to a greater understanding of its complexity and thus to a greater consensus among literary scholars and critics that it was a monument of the age. In addition, the earlier associations with political radicalism had virtually disappeared from the critiques surrounding the book. (The concerns with its sexual anarchism, however, had not.) On the other hand, Ernst and Lindey would have the more difficult task of defending the book's final "Penelope" episode, which included the most shocking chapter of the book—when the reader finally hears from Molly Bloom; her half-awake erotic reveries reveal that Leopold Bloom's cuckolding wife loved sex, thought about sex, and thought about exactly the kinds of sexual activities and pleasures that were legally and morally construed as unnatural and perverse and had no place in respectable literature. Molly, far more than Gerty, was the fully embodied, shamelessly sexualized woman that the obscenity laws had been deployed to silence.

Securing a Publisher

And yet Ernst and Lindey were thrilled by the prospects of defending Joyce's masterpiece. As Lindey told Ernst, "I still feel very keenly that this would be the grandest obscenity case in the history of law and literature, and I am ready to do anything in the world to get it started."[21]

They began in the summer of 1931 by working to find an American publisher for *Ulysses*. Both Ben Huebsch at Viking Press and Bennett Cerf at Random House had their eyes on getting *Ulysses* under contract. Ernst and Lindey met with them, trying to determine who would be the American publisher of *Ulysses* and thus who would bankroll the legal defense. It appears that Cerf initially deferred to Viking to try to work out a deal to publish the book. Ernst and Huebsch then met in mid-October 1931, and Ernst followed their meeting with a detailed explanation of the legal challenge and its potential costs. He offered an optimistic forecast about the legal prospects: "In our opinion the volume can now be tested with the real hope of gaining immunity for it." But he followed with sobering details about the potential costs, information that might have seemed ominous as the Great Depression deepened. Ernst laid out a worst-case scenario: "Such proceedings may entail four separate hearings and may necessitate an appeal even up to the United States Supreme Court." Even if they won there and procured "the stamp of approval of the Federal Court, there still remains the possibility of any one of our forty-eight states, or even the Post Office Department proceeding independently against the volume." The financial arrangements would essentially be a contingency fee plan beginning with a $500 retainer, an additional fee of $500 with each appeal (for a maximum of $2,000), plus all out-of-pocket disbursements (printing costs, stenographers minutes, filing fees, etc.), and once victory was achieved, 4% of all sales.[22] After Huebsch apparently lost interest in trying to publish the book, Cerf and his partner, Donald Klopfer, agreed to a contract with Ernst and Lindey.[23] Cerf explained the plan of action to Robert Kastor, Joyce's American agent.[24]

> The procedure as I understand it, will be to ship a copy of *Ulysses* at once and inform the U.S. Customs that it is coming. The book will undoubtedly be seized, and will be brought up in the lower court. . . . Our counsel thinks there is a very slim chance, however, that any judge of a lower court will dare to pass favorably on a book as famous as *Ulysses*. This means that the case will have to go up to the Circuit Court. . . . Our counsel believes that it is in this court that we stand an excellent chance of winning a complete victory. . . . If, however, we fail in the Circuit Court, we have no other course open but to carry the case to the Supreme Court and in that even a two year delay will be almost inevitable.[25]

Ernst and Lindey, it turns out, were fairly accurate with their predictions, including how long it would take and how the circuit court would rule.

Acquiring Expert Testimonials

As soon as the contract between Random House and the law firm was signed in April 1932, Cerf and Lindey immediately went to work. Based on their earlier book importation battles, Lindey and Ernst wanted to work the legal strategy and the publicity front simultaneously. Getting a licensed edition printed in the United States, so that copyright law might protect financially the ever-impecunious Joyce, had considerable sympathy in the literary world. After several failed attempts to get major public figures involved, Ernst and Lindey agreed that Random House should be the recipient of the copies sent from Paris.

Following their lawyers' instructions, Cerf gave Paul Leon, Joyce's agent in France, guidelines about sending a copy of *Ulysses* on its voyage to New York. It was to include a "circular containing opinions of prominent men or critics," which, if pasted into the book, became "for legal purposes, a part of the book" and could be "introduced as evidence." Cerf continued, "Write on the outside of the package the boat that the book is to come by in very plain letters so that there can be no possible mistake made by the postal service. Then send us a cable as soon as you have shipped the book telling us what boat the book will arrive on."[26]

While they awaited the book's shipment and the anticipated seizure by Customs, Lindey and Cerf began gathering information about its circulation, including designing a survey to send to the nation's librarians. Lindey also directed Cerf to collect testimonials "from prominent critics, librarians, authors, physicians, psychologists, psychoanalysts, welfare workers and the like, who have read the book and who are willing to give a brief statement certifying to its literary, scientific or sociological value." And he requested that Cerf compile "all essays, articles and criticisms of Joyce in general and *Ulysses* in particular," adding, "Statistics to its use by educational institutions will have a considerable effect" by showing that despite the ban, *Ulysses* was already assigned in leading colleges and universities and available in the nation's libraries.[27] Within days of sending out his requests, Cerf began receiving replies from the likes of William Rose Benet, Louis Untermeyer, John Dos Passos, Theodore Dreiser, Malcolm Cowley, John Farrar, and F. Scott Fitzgerald. The writers were resolute in their opposition to censorship and unanimous in their estimation of the book's genius.

Ulysses's fate with the censors provided unequivocal proof to the letter writers that the late Victorian moralists empowered to police the mails, surveille ports of entry, raid bookstores, and monitor publishers' lists were egregiously out of touch with contemporary artistic sensibilities. They mocked the innocuous "Elsie books" they thought expressed the tastes of Sumner and the Customs officers.[28] ("Elsie books" refers to the highly moralistic nineteenth-century children's books written by Martha Finley that featured an 8-year-old girl named Elsie Dinsmore.) Like Schnitzler's defenders, they argued that, compared with the smutty materials one could find at newsstands and elsewhere, Joyce's bulky, complex novel could hardly be thought of as pornographic. Many heaped scorn on Sumner, despite the fact that he was not involved in the *Ulysses* case.

Lindey and Ernst used these letters promiscuously, quoting them in the legal memoranda they submitted to the courts and building their testimonial appendixes around such letters. Moreover, these letters helped them process one of their key arguments. As F. Scott Fitzgerald wrote, the "people who have the patience to read *Ulysses* are not the kind who will slobber over a few little Rabelaisian passages."[29] Whatever reputation the book had for its risqué elements, it was far too serious, complex, and cumbersome to be considered obscene, if what was meant by obscenity was that it would be read for its dirty parts to facilitate masturbation. As Cerf told Lindey after reading these letters, those who might want it for those purposes would "certainly throw down the book in hopeless disgust after trying to wade through the first two chapters."[30]

Trying to understand *Ulysses*'s staggering complexity, Lindey also began studying the scholarship. He needed to explain to judges the book's overall design, its technical elements, its stream of consciousness experiments, its occasional baffling indecipherability, and, importantly, the obstacles to those readers in search of smut. Lindey drew especially on a 1929 review by Edmund Wilson in *The New Republic*, which Lindey recommended to Ernst as "a splendid critical evaluation of Joyce's work."[31] Wilson downplays—indeed barely mentions—the notorious sexual parts that produced all the clamor until deep into his essay, and when he does address them, he quickly asserts that these moments are actually Joyce's best writing in the book. Lindey chose a similar tactic (although he certainly could not go as far as Wilson in suggesting that these parts were the book's best-written moments). Wilson did not avoid criticizing what he saw as the novel's considerable defects, but he offered structural, not moral, critiques. Wilson found no fault in Joyce's exploration of the sexual, as it only made his characters more fully human.[32] Molly Bloom's soliloquy was the apex of Joyce's "investigation into the nature of human consciousness and behavior." According to Wilson,

Joyce "studied the trivial, the base, the dirty elements of our lives with the relentlessness of a modern psychologist." He called Joyce "the great poet of a new phase of human consciousness."[33]

Lindey and Ernst could not go so far in their legal arguments as to rhapsodize as Wilson did about Molly as the great "gross . . . body of humanity," but Wilson's essay offered the backbone to the argument Lindey built. It essentially refused to say that there was something troubling in the book akin to obscenity, with its whole chain of adjectives, such as *lewd, dirty, smutty, profane, pornographic*, and *prurient*. Lindey elided those adjectives from his legal memos about the book, just as Ernst had done in his defense of Radclyffe Hall's *Well of Loneliness* and Arthur Schnitzler's *Casanova's Homecoming*.

Importation and Customs Seizure of *Ulysses*

On May 1, 1932, Paul Leon cabled Cerf informing him that a copy of *Ulysses* had set sail on the US *Bremen* and was due in New York harbor on May 3. Lindey immediately contacted the New York Customs House, apprising them of the book's imminent arrival. He cited the novel's literary significance and provided a brief primer on recent obscenity cases, trying to persuade Customs officials to allow the book entry, potentially making a trial unnecessary. "As you may know, *Ulysses* during the last two decades has been praised by critics as probably the most important contribution to the world literature of the twentieth century. Entirely apart from its profound literary significance, we are convinced that *Ulysses* is not violative of the Tariff Act." Citing recent decisions in the *Dennett* case, Stopes's *Married Love* and *Contraception* cases, and the *Youngs* and *Rendling* cases, Lindey contended that there was "no longer any legal sanction" for the restricted status of *Ulysses* and requested that it "be examined by your office in the light" of those decisions.[34] But he also warned Cerf that he thought there was "scant likelihood" that Customs would reverse itself and lift the ban it had "previously imposed on Joyce's book."[35]

He was right. Ten days later, on May 13, Assistant Collector of Customs H. C. Stewart informed Lindey that *Ulysses* was being detained as an obscene book, in violation of Section 305 of the Tariff Act. He explained that *Ulysses* had previously been seized and ruled obscene, along with a number of other books, in a 1928 Customs Court decision, *A. Heymoolen v. United States*, and that it was still banned under that ruling.[36] The language of the 1928 *Heymoolen* decision drew on Section 305(a) of the Tariff Act of 1922, which held that "books which are offensive to chastity, delicacy, or decency, expressing or presenting to the mind or viewing something that decency, delicacy, and purity forbid to be expressed are obscene" were prohibited from importation into the United States.[37] The statute's sweeping definition of obscenity gave Customs considerable cleansing power. Long passages of Joyce's novel could easily be read in such terms.

Lindey and Ernst's first official legal response was to challenge Customs' application of the 1928 decision to *Ulysses*, arguing that in the *Heymoolen* case "*Ulysses* did not come up for separate consideration" and that the other titles were quite "unlike *Ulysses*," as they were "technical works dealing with unnatural passion." But knowing this challenge would go nowhere and wanting to move into the federal courts, they asked Stewart to immediately forward the book to the U.S. Attorneys in New York to commence action against the book.[38] Within a week—by May 24, 1932—Customs officials transmitted the book to the U.S. Attorney for the Southern District of Manhattan.[39]

A Cooperative Prosecution

In the offices of the U.S. Attorney for the Southern District of New York, Lindey and Ernst cultivated a cooperative relationship with Assistant U.S. Attorney Samuel C. Coleman in particular but also with his immediate boss, U.S. Attorney George Z. Medalie. This was not the first time they had worked with these officials on federal obscenity matters (most recently on Stopes's books). The good will between them was evident from the beginning of the *Ulysses* matter, with significant implications for the entire process, from finding a judge, to stipulations about a jury or judge trial, to submission of formal legal memoranda. The whole team behind Joyce was itching to get going and did not have much patience for the legal process.

The defense hoped that a lengthy legal ordeal could be avoided, and that the U.S. Attorneys might just drop the libel, allowing Random House to move ahead with its publishing plans.

A little over a month after Customs transferred the book to the U.S. Attorneys, Lindey called Coleman to see about the prospects for dismissing the obscenity libel. Coleman reported that he was reading *Ulysses*, it was slow going, and he needed more time to give a "definite word." When Coleman finished reading the book at the end of July, he still was not sure what to do about it, suggesting to Lindey the limited capacity of U.S. obscenity law to accommodate something that was both a significant artistic work and sexually frank. He gave Medalie an informal memorandum on the book and left the final decision to him.[40] Medalie told Coleman he needed at least a few weeks and quite possibly a few months and that it was likely nothing would develop until early September. In the meantime Coleman told Lindey and Ernst that he was going to pass the book around the U.S. Attorney's office. They should "not object," he said, as "that was the only way his staff could get a literary education."[41]

After completing *Ulysses*, Medalie told Ernst it was "a very important book," but he was afraid "he will have to proceed with the case." However, he was "pretty sure we can arrange to have it brought before Judge Woolsey"—who had already made obscenity law rulings in Ernst's favor on Marie Stopes's *Married Love* and *Contraception*—"and dispose of it by motion."[42] Medalie reassured Ernst that he was "not at all worried about the children," the usual vulnerable readers protected by the state as potential readers who might be harmed by the work. Aware that Lindey and Cerf were collecting testimonies, Medalie said his office "wanted to see everything that comes from libraries and particularly from colleges," suggesting that the work's status in institutions mattered to him. Medalie also eagerly read the opinions and testimonies of literary critics and was especially interested in reviews in the likes of the *New York Times*, the *New York Tribune*, and the *Boston Transcript*. Learning this, Ernst told Lindey they ought to get Medalie more pieces "particularly [from] those who can write."[43]

Although their exchanges with the U.S. Attorneys may have bolstered Ernst and Lindey's confidence, the slow process irritated Bennett Cerf, especially because he was hearing rumors from booksellers that another edition of *Ulysses* was to be published by a "notorious pirate" by the name of Joseph Meyers, whose company, Illustrated Editions, published cheap knockoffs of classics. The virtual impossibility of an authorized publisher stopping literary piracy of "obscene" works when he had no effective copyright claims made Cerf anxious about his investment.[44] In addition, all those requests for expert opinion that Cerf and Lindey sent out were raising interest in the book's publication, and Cerf could not say when Random House's version of *Ulysses* would be available.

Finally, Ernst and Medalie reached a formal agreement that *Ulysses* would not be read out loud in court. Doing so would have taken weeks, cost Cerf considerably in trial fees, and highlighted the most salacious parts to the jury. A few months later, in January 1933, Coleman offered another proviso that all knew would work to the defense's advantage: The U.S. Attorney did not think that the case needed to be tried by a full jury, just as he had in Stopes's trial.[45] These defense-friendly stipulations were formalized in May 1933, with both sides agreeing to waive a trial by jury.[46] There were other reasons for Cerf to be patient. Coleman intervened repeatedly to keep the trial off the calendars of Judge Coleman (no relation) and Judge Coxe, as he did not "feel that either of these two would be suitable for our purposes."[47]

Turning *Ulysses* into a Classic

Amid these many delays, Lindey made a brilliant move to challenge the *Heymoolen* ruling by another means. In 1930, Section 305 of the Tariff Act was amended to allow for the individual importation of works deemed "classics"—Ernst had in fact worked closely with Senator Bronson Cutting of New Mexico to insert this provision into the revised Tariff Act, aware that it would aid the anti-censorship cause. Ernst and Lindey were keen to test the new exception and to get *Ulysses* declared a classic ahead of the trial in the U.S. District Court.

Lindey ordered a second copy of *Ulysses* mailed to him by another Paris bookseller, Maison du Livre Francais. Despite informing Customs of its imminent arrival, this second copy got through Customs and made it to Lindey.

Lindey immediately wrote the Customs officers to ask whether it had not been seized because the book's official status had changed or whether they had simply missed it.[48] Custom's Assistant Collector H. C. Stewart assured Lindey that the status had not changed and directed him to surrender the copy to the Customs Service's Law Division.[49] Lindey did so, along with a petition to the secretary of the Treasury Department requesting admission of *Ulysses* under the revised Tariff Act.

This was an excellent rehearsal of arguments Lindey would later polish and expand for the Random House trial, as Lindey's petition made use of the hundreds of testimonies his firm had received. Lindey's attached evidence supported a cluster of propositions: that Joyce had achieved an "undisputed reputation" as a writer "of first-rate importance" and that *Ulysses* had earned "world-wide acclaim . . . as the foremost prose masterpiece of the twentieth century."[50] Pausing to acknowledge the possible hyperbole of these assertions, Lindey averred, "One might be inclined to look askance on such extravagant praise, were it not for the enclosed exhibits which appear to justify the claims made for the book and its author." Lindey appended photostatic copies of the dozens upon dozens of statements his office had received and provided excerpts of published critical reviews, statements by librarians revealing their interests in this work, and an extensive bibliography of scholarly works he described as the "vast critical library" that had grown up around the book. These testimonies composed a "trustworthy mirror of all the literate elements in the community."[51]

Within weeks, in June 1933, Lindey and Ernst got the results they were looking for. *Ulysses* had a new legal status as a *classic*. A letter from Customs explained that because the copy was not being imported for commercial purposes, the New York Customs office was authorized to release it to Mr. Lindey. The book's status as a classic meant it would be available for importation by individual recipients. *Heymoolen* was no longer the latest federal decision on the book.[52]

Ernst and Lindey immediately made this development available to the press, and days later the *New York Times* ran a story that reported on both the impending Random House case and Lindey's successful use of the Tariff Act to import a single copy.[53]

For eleven years, *Ulysses*, by James Joyce, has had wide recognition as a modern classic, but only bootleg sales in English speaking countries, where some of the words and situations in the book have been considered obscene. Now Bennett Cerf, head of Random House and The Modern Library, wants to publish the book here. It was learned yesterday that he [*sic*; it was Lindey] had won a preliminary victory by obtaining the admittance of one copy of the book. This was made possible by an exception in the 1930 Tariff Act, presumably made for the benefit of such collectors as J. P. Morgan and the great libraries.[54]

The *Times* piece ends by pillorying John Sumner for his efforts a decade earlier and for his current, glaring failures in unrelated cases.

These actions almost resulted in Ernst and Lindey bringing their motion before Judge Coleman, "a straight-laced Catholic" who, Assistant U.S. Attorney Nicholas Atlas told Lindey, was "about the worst man on the bench for us."[55] However, Atlas was able to get the hearing postponed until August 22, 1933, "at which time—believe it or not—Woolsey will be sitting."[56] Finally, they would get the matter before the judge they had all hoped to preside over the case.[57] Throughout the late summer and early fall of 1933, as both sides waited for Judge Woolsey to complete his study of the book, Ernst and Lindey bombarded Coleman and Atlas with materials they had accumulated, copies of their trial briefs in recent cases, and the most recent New York Court of Appeals decision on the play *Frankie and Johnnie* (in the case of *People v. Rendling*). These materials, they said, offered "eloquent proof of the present mores of the community," referring both to contemporary community standards and modern judicial temperament.[58]

Still trying to convince the cooperative Coleman and Atlas to drop the matter without having to go to trial, Ernst and Lindey wishfully wrote, "We trust that the enclosures will serve to convince you beyond any doubt that *Ulysses* is a work of genius of the first order, that it has been universally accepted . . . and therefore it cannot be deemed to be obscene." None of the US attorneys accepted that logical leap, and the libel suit carried forward. However, they had helped Ernst and Lindey by skillfully steering the matter to Judge Woolsey's docket, and waited patiently for over a year.[59]

Defending *Ulysses*: Lindey's Legal Brief

In September 1933, almost three months before the scheduled hearing, Lindey and Ernst sent Woolsey their trove of research, testimonials, and Lindey's brilliant Preliminary Memorandum. Lindey also sent Paul Jordan Smith's *The Key to the Ulysses of James Joyce* and Herbert S. Gorman's *James Joyce: His First Forty Years*.[60] Lindey's Preliminary Memorandum was a blueprint for the arguments he would develop at length in the Claimant's Memorandum to Dismiss Libel, the formal brief he submitted a month later, in October 1933. In both documents Lindey crafted for Woolsey a rich synthesis of literary analysis and recent legal history drawing on the cases that he and Ernst had won prior to the *Ulysses* defense, making it clear how they had forged a series of decisions that made it viable for them to bring *Ulysses* to trial. *Ulysses* came "in logical sequence after the *Dennett* case, the *Youngs* case, the *Married Love* case, the *Contraception* case . . . all of which have served to liberalize the law of obscenity."[61] Lindey integrated decisions from all levels of New York's courts into an evolutionary narrative about how changing cultural and legal standards reflect the growing public acceptance of matters sexual and erotic. And he made Judge Woolsey's Stopes decisions central to this story of legal progress.

The Claimant's Memorandum also centered on a particular strain of Joyce criticism, focusing on the work's technical difficulty. This suggested that the Hicklin standard's "vulnerable reader" was hardly germane to any discussion about the book's actual readers. In addition, Lindey's recondite brief drew clear distinctions between Joyce's novel as a cause célèbre attended by hullabaloo, and Joyce's austere life and his seriousness as a literary craftsman. Joyce was a sensitive, remarkably well-educated, ascetic man, born of Roman Catholic parents in Dublin in 1882, whose "early home life was steeped in an atmosphere of ritual and theology." His works, Lindey argued, belonged in a wholly different category from the usual fare considered under obscenity law. Joyce's oeuvre was marked by learnedness, heightened sensitivity, and a decidedly noncommercial approach. His rigorous education built the foundations for a man of letters engaging his art at the highest levels. Educated by Jesuits at Clongowes Wood and then at Belvedere College and the Royal University, Dublin, and later a student of medicine at the University of Paris, Joyce "gave this up" and "devoted himself to Latin, German, Norwegian and the Romance languages, [and] became a linguist and a teacher." Although his works were "few in number," Lindey said, Joyce was nevertheless "the most important figure in world literature today."[62] This was not the profile of a purveyor of cheap, commercial trash. Indeed, *Ulysses* took seven years to complete, during which Joyce "led a monastic existence." Nor had Joyce attempted seriously to profit from his achievement. "He has delivered no lectures, given no interviews, posed for no newsreels . . . issued no manifestos, written no magazine articles which might have yielded him easy harvest." In fact, much to the chagrin of Random House publishers, he would not even make reading his masterpiece easier by attaching "explanatory prefaces to his works." In short, Joyce had eschewed the marketplace, spending his life in a proverbial tower.[63]

Lindey argued that the real protagonist of *Ulysses* is the mind. "The arena is not Dublin, but the human skull."[64] Using a quote from Louis Golding, he argued that Joyce's wanderings into "the red chambers of the flesh" were connected to the novel's experimental technique of stream of consciousness.[65] Every time a character's thoughts move toward the bawdy or the body, the discerning reader knows it is because that is where the character's mind took them. Joyce's technique mattered most, and the authenticity of what emerges in his characters' minds was intrinsic to the personages he let loose in Dublin in June 1904. So Leopold Bloom's masturbation at the sight of Gerty's bloomers was not separable from his inability to consummate his marriage to Molly over the previous ten years; Gerty leaning back for Bloom's view cannot be separated from her reading of romance novels and her fantasies about being rescued by inscrutable foreign men; and Molly's ruminations about her sexual pleasures with her lover are indelibly tied to Leopold's own sexual failures in their marriage. This approach made strategic sense for Lindey, whose job was to persuade the court that whatever *obscene* elements the work might have were far outweighed by the work's literary importance and its internal coherence.

Lindey then developed the defense's specific legal arguments along six points: First, the test of obscenity is a living standard, and *Ulysses* must be judged by the mores of the day. Second, *Ulysses* is not obscene according to the accepted definitions of obscenity laid down by the courts. Third, *Ulysses* is a modern classic; the U.S. government has officially acknowledged it as such, and so it cannot be deemed obscene. Fourth, the intrinsic features of *Ulysses*, as well as certain extrinsic facts, negate any implication of obscenity. Fifth, *Ulysses* has been generally accepted by the community and hence cannot be held to be violative of the statute. And finally, *Ulysses* must be judged as a whole.

To his point that the standards of what is indecent or obscene are relative and evolutionary, Lindey examined changing judicial standards, cultural standards, and social mores. The law, Lindey argued, had come to recognize that there was no fixed definition of obscenity. As in the *Well of Loneliness* case, Lindey once again relied on Judge Learned Hand's language from *United States v. Kennerley* (1913), where Hand acknowledged the absence of a fixed or set definition and thereby tried to offer a pragmatic solution for assessing what constituted obscenity at a given historical moment: "If there be no abstract definition, such as I have suggested, should not the word 'obscene' be allowed to indicate the *present critical point* in the compromise between candor and shame at which the community may have arrived *here and now*?"[66] There would always be some things shocking and appalling to the public, Hand argued, but what those things might be and how shocked the public might be were sure to vary over time. Lindey also paraphrased Justice Holmes to the effect that the law should "correspond with the actual feelings and demands of the community, whether right or wrong." And, citing Justice Cardozo's assurance that "we live in a world of change," he quoted him further to assert that "the forms of [moral or immoral] conduct thus discriminated are not the same at all times or in all places." For Cardozo, as for Lindey and Ernst, the question was, How should "the morality of a community" be ascertained? Cardozo said it could be located in "the principle and practice of the men and women of the community whom the social mind would rank as *intelligent and virtuous*"[67] Ernst and Lindey embraced this idea, suggesting both earlier and later in the brief that the moral sensibility of this society at the *present moment* could and ought to be measured by those "representative men" of letters who had replied to their queries about Joyce's work.[68]

To illustrate changing standards, Lindey pointed to many behaviors and ideas once thought obscene or indecent that had become widely accepted. His and Ernst's favorite, oft-used example was women's bathing suits: "In 1900 any female who appeared on a bathing beach without sleeves and a long skirt would have been jailed. By 1911 bare knees could be legally displayed at the seashore; but legs still had to be covered and girls wore stockings rolled down below their knees. A few years ago the one-piece bathing suit came into its own; and today the so-called sunsuits leave very little of the human form concealed."[69] The same pattern of growing acceptance appeared in the arts as well: "A decade ago *September Morn, Paul and Virginia*, Manet's *Olympia* and similar pictures were deemed pornography; now they hardly elicit a second glance." And in literature many books once roundly criticized had become widely read and highly regarded, including George Eliot's *Adam Bede*, Nathaniel Hawthorne's *Scarlet Letter*, Thomas Hardy's *Tess of the d'Urbervilles* and *Jude the Obscure*, and Walt Whitman's *Leaves of Grass*. All examples pointed to the conclusion that *Ulysses* "must be judged in light of present day mores. The standards of yesterday, the abhorrence of any mention of certain biological functions, the excessive prudery, the sex taboo, are as definitely dead today as the horsedrawn carriage and donkey-engines on the Elevated."[70]

Lindey also hoped to persuade the judge that the presumptive readers of *Ulysses* were the contemporary community's bright, educated adults. He argued that central to the story of the courts' revision of the Hicklin test was the fact that judges had come to recognize that the book world was populated by many different readers and consumers, including sophisticated and cosmopolitan ones, and was not dominated by the dullest witted and most vulnerable. Moreover, *Ulysses* could hardly be shocking, given the materials that could be found everywhere one looked: "Our tabloids carry stories of passion and lust, of crime and perversion, told with a degree of vividness and frankness unheard of a generation ago. Every man, woman and child in the community has easy access to the complete details of torch-murders, of marital infidelities, of boudoir intimacies, kidnappings and abnormalities."[71] Here Lindey makes an additional key argument, not just about audience but about what that variegated audience was being protected from.

Not from information, mere titillation, bad taste, or coarseness. Rather, he suggested that the courts had essentially reduced the question of whether an artifact was obscene to a simple biological matter: Did it produce sexual arousal to the point of lust? Lindey could not state it, but the implicit question was, Did it induce masturbation?

Important recent decisions confirmed that the test of obscenity had been refined or distilled to the issue of whether it induced sexual impurity. Looking to the recent (1932) *Wendling* decision about the New York stage production of *Frankie and Johnnie*, Lindey wrote that the New York Court of Appeals had established that "the essence of the crime is *sexual impurity*, not sex," when it held that "the question is whether the tendency of the play is to excite lustful and lecherous desire."[72] In an older Supreme Court case, *Swearingen v. United States* (1896), the Court had also reduced the matter to the question of sexual impurity. Quoting *Swearingen*, Lindey reported that the Court had held "the words 'obscene,' 'lewd' and 'lascivious,' as used in the statute, to signify that form of immorality which has relation to sexual impurity."[73] Although the New York Court of Appeals had offered clarifying language, Lindey bolstered their argument with a litany of decisions from the New York City magistrate courts. These magistrate court decisions were by far their best sources for evidence about the evolution of thinking about obscenity. Even though none of these magistrate court decisions had binding authority in the U.S. federal courts, they provided extensive, cumulative evidence of the judicial thinking about literature and obscenity that was shaping the tenor and direction of the New York State court system.

Importantly, those decisions arose from the center of the U.S. publishing industry, in a location where community mores and tastes were complex, contested matters. These decisions and their language made up an intellectually compelling framework for asserting that the courts had been taking a smaller role in interfering with the flow of artistic and intellectual ideas and had moved to a position in which intervention against literary texts on moral grounds was rather minimal and in which the standard for finding a work obscene came down to whether the work was pornographic. Using this body of opinion to frame the key question about *Ulysses*—is its "main purpose and construction to depict sexual impurity?"—Lindey and Ernst reiterated that the courts had settled on "the *normal* person who must serve as the criterion" for a work's effects. "This Court"—invoking Judge Woolsey's own decision—"has clearly so intimated in the *Married Love* case."[74]

Lindey's move to change the book's status under the *Heymoolen* decision paid off here, as it allowed him to assert that "the words 'classic' and 'obscenity' represent polar extremes. . . . They are mutually antagonistic and exclusive. That which is obscene, corrupts and depraves." Here Lindey knowingly used the Hicklin test. A classic, by contrast, is "of the highest class and of acknowledged excellence."[75] Because of the either-or dimensions of obscenity law and the absence of any legal protection for something deemed obscene, Lindey and Ernst overstated the great gulf between literature and obscenity. They held that these were incompatible categories, because the legal status of being obscene would render a work of great literary significance unmailable and nonimportable and its publisher or bookseller subject to criminal law. Even though both U.S. Attorneys Samuel Coleman and George Medalie thought *Ulysses* was a masterpiece and was also obscene in parts, Lindey and Ernst knew that, according to the letter of the law, it could not be both. So they treated obscenity as being equivalent to pornography and elided all the other synonyms.

Although *Ulysses* dealt with sexual matters at certain moments, Lindey maintained that it had none of those features "almost invariably present in a work of pornography," such as graphic illustrations, anonymity of authorship, and concealment. For those in search of the pornographic it would be "tedious and bewildering." *Ulysses* was "a prodigious work of 732 closely-printed pages," the sex passages were buried, and it was difficult reading, "even for the mature and the intelligent." Someone reading it simply for its sex scenes "would not get beyond the first dozen pages."[76] Lindey and Ernst insisted that pornographic works must be understandable, easily ascertainable. *Ulysses* was neither. Likewise, the book's "Extrinsic Circumstances"—the literary reputation of the author, the opinions of critics, the attitudes of librarians, its networks of sale and distribution, its acceptance in the community—all negated claims of obscenity. As Vanderham notes, Ernst and Lindey argued that Joyce had a reputation and stature as "a supreme literary artist," making the community acceptance of *Ulysses* "incompatible with the charges of obscenity."[77] They stitched three claims together here: that these "eminent persons" both voiced and embodied community standards, that such people would never be "champions of obscenity," and that those people celebrated the book's achievements.[78]

Lindey and Ernst ended their brief with an argument they had rehearsed elsewhere, one that had become well accepted in the New York City magistrate courts and was gaining momentum in the higher courts: that Joyce's novel had to be judged as a whole. They asserted that obscenity is "a question of entirety" and that this book's questionable sections made up a "negligible" fraction of the work as a whole.[79] The brief's conclusion addressed the question of the book's "occasional episodes of doubtful taste" but did so in a series of short points that reiterated the larger argument about its status and genius. *Ulysses* has a "few Anglo-Saxon words to denote certain human organs and functions. However, this does not render it obscene." Such words had recently appeared in Ernst and Seagle's *To the Pure*, Hemingway's *Death in the Afternoon*, *Lawrence of Arabia*, and other books, "all of which have been accepted by the community." *Ulysses* actually offered relatively little sex: "As a matter of actual content it represents an insignificant fraction of the book." Indeed, they argued, the book was not about the body; rather, it was about the mind.[80]

The Claimant's Memorandum reminded Judge Woolsey that a transformative body of obscenity law pertaining to literary works had developed in the previous decade, and even if some of those decisions were in the lower state courts and were not binding in the federal courts, they had accumulated a kind of authoritative effect. The gap between contemporary interests in sexual and cultural modernism and a federal obscenity statue authored in the mid-nineteenth century required that the judge assess this novel's supposed harms in comparison with its manifest values. The far greater harm, they argued, would be denying the nation's readers access to Joyce's masterpiece.

The Government's Case

Coleman and Atlas essentially allowed the defense to define the history of obscenity law, to discuss recent cases, and to present all the evidence and expert opinion about *Ulysses*. Although Coleman offered a few assertions before the judge during the formal hearing that parts of the book were obscene, the prosecution's internal documents evince no interest whatsoever in demonstrating its obscenity, and in fact the U.S. Attorneys began their formal argument by asserting they were not censors. The richest of the U.S. Attorneys' documents actually reveal Atlas's considered engagement with and fondness for Joyce's work. His memorandum specifies in a subheading that it was "To be included in obscenity record"—but nothing about Atlas's memorandum suggests that it was written to shore up the case for prosecution. Indeed, Atlas's erudite "James Joyce" essay—the only sustained argument about the book that the U.S. Attorney's office produced—reads far more like an admiring literary review than a prosecutor's brief.[81] Atlas celebrates the book's poetry, its experimental techniques, and its status in the literary world. Vanderham writes that "by avoiding mention of the objectionable passages, [Atlas] gives the impression that the government's libel has little or no basis."[82]

Atlas drew on the materials lent to him by Lindey and Ernst and introduced his subject with a familiar comparison: "It is no exaggeration to say that among the men of his profession [Joyce's] name is as well known and his works as much discussed as could be among scientists the names and theories of Freud and Einstein."[83] From start to finish Atlas's essay regards Joyce's work with awe. Atlas gives his readers a quick history of Joyce's oeuvre, focusing on the relationship between *Portrait of the Artist as a Young Man* and *Ulysses*. He explains how Joyce's stream of consciousness technique works: "Without warning, without the handy anchorage of a punctuation mark sometimes, or sometimes only without the conventional punctuation, we are whisked from the contemplation of the external fact like 'Dedalus walking,' into the chamber of Dedalus' mind, where we hear Dedalus thinking and where we learn what goes on about Dedalus by what Dedalus is thinking." Joyce brought this method, Atlas explains, into "full fruition" in *Ulysses*.[84] In one of the few instances when Atlas addresses the issue of obscenity, he essentially argues it away by affirming Joyce's precise observations about the world. The putatively obscene moments and words crop up because they would naturally be found in the world that Joyce, "the master scientist," observes.[85]

As for the legal history of *Ulysses*, Atlas makes a remarkable argument for a prosecuting attorney, essentially saying that the U.S. Attorneys in his office should not be prejudiced by either the book's prior legal history or its notorious reputation. He argues "that it is not incumbent upon the libellant to approach this book with disrespect, because it is claimed to be obscene. On the contrary, we approach the book with great respect," especially for its experiment in literary technique.[86] As Vanderham argues, Atlas's memorandum "implicitly argues that the government's motion to confiscate and destroy the novel should be denied."[87]

When Atlas turns to the narrative, he neither describes nor worries about the possible obscenity. Noting that Bloom "goes to a beach," he says nothing about Gerty McDowell on that same beach and nothing about Bloom's masturbation. He is far more interested in explaining the characters, their histories, their milieu, and their minds, reporting that Stephen Dedalus's father Simon is, for instance, "a souse, a weak, inconsequential, little Irishman with a Greek name, a barroom tenor, a rake without dash."[88] This makes Stephen, like Leopold Bloom, an outsider. And he says very little about Molly and her dalliances or her monologue, only noting that Bloom "has his troubles. He is married to an Irishwoman of whom he has reason to believe—and before the day is done, of whom he is sure—that she commits adultery."[89] When Altas turns to Molly's soliloquy, he explains it primarily as the book's resolution: "And the coming of Dedalus [home with Bloom] creates a difference in the home life of the Blooms, subtly and powerfully illustrated in the lengthy reverie of Mrs. Bloom, who lies beside her husband that night, meditating and speaking with herself, shrinking from her husband, planning her design to possess Dedalus too, and going back to her husband. On this note the book closes."[90] Atlas was primarily interested in celebrating the book's "rare poetry."

A second internal memo written by either Coleman or Atlas, which also was never submitted to Woolsey, contains the only real effort to elaborate the problems with *Ulysses*, besides a list of pages with troubling passages they did submit. In the memo, titled "Analysis of Books Submitted to Us by the Claimant in the *Ulysses* Case for Comparison," the writer suggests that some elements of the book are troublesome and maybe even obscene. But still the writer makes no attempt to flesh out a sustained legal argument about the book's possible obscenity. "In *Ulysses* we have to deal with a book highly serious in its purpose but permeated throughout with expressions, allusions, clichés and situations which even in this day and age could not be mentioned in any society pretending to call itself polite, and certainly not in mixed company, no matter how free that mixed company may be."[91] The most damning evidence the government compiled was the list of offending passages that they had annotated and submitted to Woolsey in the confiscated copy of the novel.[92]

The Hearing Before Judge Woolsey

The oral argument finally took place on November 25, 1933, in a court-room in midtown Manhattan. Newspaper coverage provides some of the flavor of the hearing.

> The scene was the tiny oval courtroom on the sixth floor of the Bar Association Building, 42 West Forty-fourth Street, and behind a bench of justice which is said to be one of the most beautifully de-signed bits of furniture in the United States, sat Judge [John] Munro Woolsey, of the United States District Court, hearing the case with-out a jury and pondering over the exact location of that vague line between "candor and shame."

Although arguing the government's position that *Ulysses* is obscene and should not be sold in the United States, Coleman began his argument by im-ploring "the court not to think of him personally as a 'puritanical censor.'"[93]

According to newspaper reports, Judge Woolsey "talked freely from the bench and from time to time told of his extremely difficult position in being required to pass on a book that for ten years had evoked the most violent

denunciations and praise from all manner of learned men and women."
The courtroom broke into laughter "when the judge admitted that to his
'shocking surprise'" he "'perfectly understood' the passages that had been
described constituting the obscene sections of the manuscript." "Laughing
himself, Woolsey then frowned, 'Parts of it are pretty rough, really, but other
parts are swell. There are passages of moving literary beauty, passages of
worth and power. I tell you,' he continued in a louder tone, 'reading parts
of that book almost drove me frantic. That last part, that soliloquy, it may
represent the moods of a woman of that sort. That is what disturbs me. I
seem to understand it.'"[94] When Woolsey reported that *Ulysses* "left him
'bothered, stirred and troubled,' Ernst replied, 'I think that is exactly the
effect of *Ulysses*. You have not used the adjectives 'shocked' or 'revolted.'
You have used the adjectives 'bothered,' 'troubled.'"[95]

As Coleman and Woolsey discussed the definition of obscenity, the
judge "complained of 'the spectrum of adjectives' which bound him by the
law—'obscene, lewd, disgusting'"—indicating that Woolsey shared Ernst
and Lindey's critique of the imprecision of the statutory language. More
important, Woolsey appears to have accepted Ernst and Lindey's argument
that obscenity could be reduced to and defined by the state of sexual arousal.
"One definition is a thing may be said to be obscene when its primary purpose is to excite sexual feeling," he said. But Coleman argued against this
shrinkage of the definition. According to the *New York Herald Tribune*,
Coleman said, "I liked *Ulysses* but there is obscenity in it." He elaborated,
"I should say a thing is obscene by the ordinary language used and by what
it does to the average reader. It need not necessarily be what the author
intended. On these grounds I think there are ample reasons to consider
Ulysses to be an obscene book."[96] Ernst, in response, insisted that obscenity
ought only to refer to direct incitement of lust, essentially making an argument about the inability to prove a cause-and-effect dynamic between book
and reader. He said that "he had 'yet to find one single instance where it
could be proved that the reading of any book had led to the commission
of a *crime of passion*.'"[97] Although this gesture of defining obscenity on the
basis of criminal behavior was a diversion, it illustrates Ernst's efforts to
redefine obscenity as being beyond the pale of acceptability.

Following the hearing, Ernst and Lindey submitted one more document to Judge Woolsey. This Claimant's Supplementary Memorandum reminded Woolsey that this case was a Customs seizure and that the book was not being tried under the New York State obscenity law, whose definition of obscenity was broader in scope than the Tariff Act. "The words lewd, lascivious, filthy, indecent, disgusting," all of which appear in the New York statute, "do not appear in the Tariff Act." The Tariff Act "merely prohibits the importation of 'any *obscene* book.' . . . Hence in passing on *Ulysses* the Court may properly restrict itself to the sole consideration as to whether the book is obscene."[98] Of course, Lindey and Ernst had worked assiduously to shrink that definition of obscenity to make it synonymous with pornography.

Lindey's memo also addressed two questions about burden of proof and standard of proof, arguing that the burden of proof in this case rested entirely on the government. It should have to prove its case beyond a reasonable doubt, as though meeting the standard of proof required in criminal law.

> *Ulysses* stands before the Court as defendant. Charged with being a menace to public morals, it is fighting for its life. If condemned, it faces destruction . . . no less complete than that of hanging or electrocution. Besides it is no upstart, no scrubby little churl of the republic of letters that thus faces annihilation. It is a noble citizen whose stature has been almost universally conceded. Before it is turned over to the executioner, its guilt should be shown *beyond a reasonable doubt*.[99]

Lindey concluded by reminding Woolsey that this was not a standard proceeding against the kinds of materials usually seized by Customs, like "spoiled food-stuffs." A book was different, an object with greater symbolic importance in the Republic of Letters he invoked.[100]

Judge Woolsey's Decision: Limiting "Obscenity" to "Pornography"

On December 6, 1933, Judge Woolsey ruled that the government could not seize *Ulysses* as obscene. His famous decision did what Lindey and Ernst hoped: restrict the definition of obscenity as "tending to stir the sex impulses or to lead to sexually impure and lustful thoughts."[101] Understanding that his verdict would be scrutinized and would have great implications in obscenity law jurisprudence, Woolsey challenged and reworked some of the core assumptions about obscenity law. He drew on the more progressive, book- and publisher-protective positions that had been evolving in the New York City magistrate courts and state courts in the previous decade and in his own federal court decisions in the two Marie Stopes cases (*Married Love* and *Contraception*). He accepted the guidance of Lindey and Ernst's memoranda on the progressive narrowing of obscenity law and also the increasing imperative that the state offer proof of effects. And he gave an appreciative tutorial on Joyce's work, justifying his decision. Woolsey acknowledged the either-or nature of obscenity law and used the terms *obscenity* and *pornography* interchangeably when he declared early in his decision that "if the conclusion is that the book is pornographic, that is the end of the inquiry and forfeiture must follow." He averred, however, that he did not find pornographic intent, famously writing, "In *Ulysses*, in spite of its unusual frankness, I do not detect anywhere the leer of the sensualist. I hold, therefore, that it is not pornographic."[102]

Rather than worrying about the work's titillating effects on the reader, Woolsey's analysis focused instead on the work's intellectual challenges and richness. The bulk of his decision effuses over Joyce's techniques, method, artistry, integrity of purpose, and erudition. Woolsey reasoned that if Joyce was to truly explore experimental techniques of voice, mind, and stream of consciousness, then he had to follow where his characters' wandering minds would lead him. Woolsey essentially accepted the conceit that the characters—with their distinctive traits, tics, and voices—became the authors of the book, with Joyce as their medium. Failing to follow where his characters took him would have violated the integrity of Joyce's artistically grand experiment: "He takes persons of the lower middle class living in Dublin in 1904 and seeks, not only to describe what they did on a certain day early in June of that year as they went about the city bent on their usual occupations, but also to tell what many of them thought about all the while." This technique was not always successful, Woolsey admitted, and this accounted "for much of the obscurity which meets a reader of

Ulysses." But the work had integrity as a work of art; it was truthful in its pursuit of method, and the characters Joyce wrought were real.[103] Woolsey succeeds reasonably well in distilling Joyce's stream-of-consciousness technique. But more important, he understood how that technique embodied the book's far-reaching goal of exploring the technique's implications for drawing characters. For Woolsey, the integrity of pursing this method mattered artistically, and Joyce's sustained effort brought him latitude from the judge.

As Steven Gillers argues, Woolsey's focus on the sincerity of aims, loyalty to technique, and characters' thoughts as natural outcomes of Joyce's method was more of a critical analysis than a legal analysis per se. But as legal analysis, Woolsey recognized that a work of such seriousness of purpose and precision of technique needed protection from a law that might make unavailable to readers a magisterial work that occasionally violated boundaries of acceptability in pursuit of its vision. The obscenity statute was too inflexible to accommodate this work. By asserting the value of the work's artistic integrity, Woolsey made an astonishing argument: that at least one duty of those applying the law is to understand and protect the development of artistic techniques. The implication of Woolsey's reasoning is that if Joyce had not been honest in revealing the "poignant preoccupation with sex in the thoughts of his characters," the result "would be psychologically misleading" and "artistically inexcusable."[104] Here Woolsey was a demanding editor and literary critic as much as he was a federal judge.

To protect works of artistic genius, Woolsey believed that it was appropriate to assume the existence of a highly competent audience for literature and art. *Ulysses* was a challenging work; the book's readership would have to be likewise serious. But even assuming a sophisticated audience, Woolsey acknowledged that the potential, probable, or actual effects ought to be considered by the courts. He argued that because *Ulysses* was not written "with what is commonly called pornographic intent," the effects therefore were presumably not pornographic either. However, he understood that an author's intention was not wholly adequate for assessing a work's effects. How then to assess effects? Here Woolsey initiated in the federal courts an important shift, gesturing toward the necessity of finding some actual readers and some "objective measure of effects" rather than merely assuming negative effects based on the presumption of harm.

The Normal Person, with Average Sex Instincts

Rather than assuming that he himself was the appropriate subject as the "average" reader who might or might not have his sex instincts aroused and that his biases might not make him as objective as he ought be, Woolsey reported that he ran a small experiment seeking some empirical evidence. He enlisted two anonymous readers (both friends of his) to read the novel and report to him whether or not they had been aroused to lust by their experience. These were, he reported, men of his acquaintance whom he admired and trusted and clearly thought reasonable, "learned in the art" of literature, and also of average sex instincts. He gave each the legal definition of obscenity and asked whether they thought the book met that definition, and he asked them to consider the whole book rather than focusing on isolated passages. Woolsey wrote that they reported that the book "did not tend to excite sexual impulses or lustful thoughts, but that its net effect on them was only that of a somewhat tragic and very powerful commentary on the inner lives of men and women."[105] This test of whether or not the book aroused lust really was the only test Woolsey thought germane. The judge noted in his decision's final paragraph that *Ulysses* could be rough going for readers and was even "disgusting" in some parts, but he nonetheless concluded that it did not have the effects of pornography. In fact, he argued that it had more of an anti-erotic, sickening effect. He concluding his opinion by writing, "I am quite aware that owing to some of its scenes *Ulysses* is a rather strong draught to ask some sensitive, though normal, persons to take. But my considered opinion, after long reflection, is that, whilst in many places the effect of *Ulysses* on the reader undoubtedly is somewhat emetic, nowhere does it tend to be an aphrodisiac."[106]

Gillers makes the good point that "it is at most a small overstatement to say that the decision is useful law for only one book. Other publishers and their lawyers would be hard pressed to explain how its obstacle course of tests might benefit them."[107] But Woolsey's decision was the product of a series of precedents in the magistrate courts and Lindey's arguments in his brief. Ernst and Lindey framed the issues for him in such a way that the decision had to assert itself over a body of law in transition.

The *Ulysses* decision marks a moment of maturity, where the courts caught up with the culture. This is when the decisions and logic of the local New York City magistrate courts make their way into the federal courts. The decision made it tough to put the obscenity genie back in the bottle and continued a process of refining obscenity law to account for greater tensions between literary expression and older conceptions of appropriate literary fare. The distinctions that Woolsey implicitly made (adult readers, taking the book as a whole, the importance of literary reputation, the seriousness of a work, the necessity of trying to discern actual effects, recognizing the needs of adult readership) slowly got worked out in federal courts over the next twenty-plus years.

Judge Woolsey's decision became an immediate classic. However, it was not quite the great breakthrough that Ernst and others proclaimed it to be. It was not a constitutional challenge to obscenity law, just a challenge to its application against "One Book Called *Ulysses*." The decision did nothing to challenge or efface the constitutionality of obscenity law per se. Nor did it eliminate the state's presumed interest in controlling the production and distribution of materials whose purposes were the arousal of sex instincts. It helped make obscenity laws less capacious, but these laws remained intact. However, prosecutors and courts were more circumscribed following Judge Woolsey's decision.

Woolsey's Decision Upheld in the U.S. Court of Appeals

After the ruling was handed down and the celebration quieted, U.S. Attorney Martin Conboy appealed Judge Woolsey's decision, much to Ernst and Lindey's dismay and against the advice of his Assistant U.S. Attorneys Sam Coleman and Nicholas Atlas. Random House had already published an American edition with a foreword by Ernst and with Judge Woolsey's decision included.

Just over eight months after Judge Woolsey rendered his decision, the Court of Appeals for the Second Circuit in New York affirmed it, with

Augustus Hand writing the majority opinion, signed by his cousin Judge Learned Hand, but with Judge Martin Thomas Manton dissenting.[108] The backdrop here is important. Both Martin Conboy and U.S. Attorney Francis Horan of Washington, D.C., were devout Catholics and felt compelled to try to keep *Ulysses* from being published. Judge Manton's dissent is a full-throated articulation of the older moral arguments against modernism and its perceived assault on the virtue of women. The majority decision is interesting for what it accepts: the book as a whole; the issue of its reputation and standing among critics as evidence; the book's high-level execution of its experimental technique; and the fact that it is only obscene in parts. The court writes, "In this field *Ulysses* is rated as a book of considerable power by persons whose opinions are entitled to weight. Indeed it has become a sort of contemporary classic, dealing with a new subject-matter. It attempts to depict the thoughts and lay bare the souls of a number of people, some of them intellectuals and some social outcasts and nothing more, with a literalism that leaves nothing unsaid." For the appeals court jurists, the book's stature mattered, and so did the ways in which the obscene parts were subsumed into a larger whole. "Joyce, in the words of *Paradise Lost*, has dealt with 'things unattempted yet in prose or rime'—with things that very likely might better have remained 'unattempted'—but his book shows originality and is a work of symmetry and excellent craftsmanship of a sort."[109]

When the court turned to the issue of obscenity as a legal question, they never defined it beyond the question of whether the book provoked lust. Instead, they implicitly accepted Woolsey's definition of obscenity as equivalent to stirring the sex impulses. When they used the other synonyms that traditionally defined obscenity, such as *vulgarity*, those did not seem to warrant their concern; only the question of whether *Ulysses* provoked lust was at hand. But instead of saying that "it is more emetic than aphrodisiac," they held that the "net effect is . . . pitiful and tragic, *rather than lustful*."[110] This is a different take on Woolsey's puke test, but pity is still a far cry from sexual arousal.

The circuit court also essentially created a space within obscenity jurisprudence where a book can be partly obscene or pornographic, if it is not pornographic on the whole and if its dominant effect is not the arousal of lust.

By considering the dominant effect of this work, the appeals court suggested that a work had better meet high literary standards to pull off partial obscenity and must take readers to some other deeper understanding beyond stirring sex impulses. The court seems to say that the potentially erotic effect of Molly's soliloquy, for instance, is absorbed by the book's tragedy and sadness.

> The net effect even of portions most open to attack, such as the closing monologue of the wife of Leopold Bloom, is pitiful and tragic, rather than lustful. The book depicts the souls of men and women that are by turns bewildered and keenly apprehensive, sordid and aspiring, ugly and beautiful, hateful and loving. In the end one feels, more than anything else, pity and sorrow for the confusion, misery, and degradation of humanity.[111]

Depression, they suggest, makes the lust go away.

When the appeals decision turned to case law, it expressly referred to the *Dennett* decision and several key decisions from the New York courts that Lindey and Ernst had relied on in their memoranda to warrant this "dominant note of the publication" test. They rephrased this key idea several times—including whether a work has a libidinous effect "taken as a whole." Citing *Dennett* as settled law, they wrote, "We think the same immunity should apply to literature as to science, where the presentation, when viewed objectively, is sincere, and the erotic matter is not introduced to promote lust and does not furnish the dominant note of the publication. *The question in each case is whether a publication taken as a whole has a libidinous effect.*" Elsewhere they reiterated, "We do not think that *Ulysses*, taken as a whole, tends to produce lust."[112]

While concurring with much of Woolsey's original decision, the appeals court dismissed Ernst and Lindey's claim about different readerships being more or less capable. Instead, the majority opinion argued that presumed readership is not a mitigating factor in a book's obscenity.[113] The majority opinion concludes with a final nod to the idea that protecting experimentation in art is a good thing and that the courts ought not to limit how writers advance their field and develop new techniques.[114]

FIGURE 9. Morris Ernst, seen here in his official portrait as founding partner of the Greenbaum, Wolff & Ernst law firm, achieved his greatest fame by defending *Ulysses* from censorship.

SOURCE: Harry Ransom Humanities Research Center, University of Texas, Austin.

A Crack in the Door

The ruling on *Ulysses* did not end the struggle over the question of obscenity's relationship to works of art and the public's need for protection. The hearing before Judge Woolsey occurred at the tail end of 1933, just when the Production Code Authority was cracking down on Hollywood movies, beginning the long run of Joseph Breen's control over the so-called

Hays Office. Ernst and Lindey's victory in the *Ulysses* case was a crack in the door, not a door thrown wide open. It was decades before Dr. Kinsey, before Masters and Johnson, before *Playboy*, and before the explosion in pulp fiction. It was also well before birth control information and materials would cease to be banned because they were ipso facto "obscene." In the ensuing years plenty of other books and materials would confront obscenity laws, including *Life* magazine a few years later. Other books considered classics, such as *Lady Chatterley's Lover*, *Strange Fruit*, and *Howl*, had their own censorship battles.

Yet the *Ulysses* case was a significant development in the long process of transforming and narrowing nineteenth-century obscenity laws in the U.S. courts in the 1920s and 1930s. It was also a signal achievement for Ernst and Lindey, making Ernst a celebrity of sorts, and a crucial part of their overall challenge to censorship based on enforcement of the nation's obscenity laws. It was certainly instrumental to their goals of creating more legal room for distributing information about sexuality and a more robust literary marketplace.

Contraception, another area where obscenity law inhibited innovation, information flows, and even physicians treating their patients—not to mention women having control over their reproductive lives—loomed large as the next battleground. Birth control activists, especially Margaret Sanger and her colleague Dr. Hannah Stone, needed the strategic skills and expertise accumulated by Ernst, Lindey, and their colleague Harriet Pilpel. In the next chapter I show how the Greenbaum, Wolff & Ernst lawyers turned their attentions to birth control laws, producing breakthroughs as significant in that realm as their advances in the fields of sexology, sex education, and modern literature.

CHAPTER 7

BATTLES FOR BIRTH CONTROL

Margaret Sanger and the Moral Authority of Doctors

ON APRIL 15, 1929, New York City police raided Margaret Sanger's Birth Control Clinical Research Bureau on West 15th Street in Manhattan. Officers arrested both of the licensed physicians operating the clinic, Dr. Hannah Stone and Dr. Elizabeth Pissort, along with three registered nurses, Marcella Sideri, Sigrid Brestwell, and Antoinette Field. Sanger founded the Clinical Research Bureau in 1923. Renamed the Birth Control Clinical Research Bureau in 1928, it provided contraceptive medical work to married women, including examinations and instructions on how to use their birth control devices, and maintained social work contact with those patients. Many returned for follow-up visits. Dr. Stone became the medical director in 1925, and under her guidance the bureau also conducted research on different kinds of contraceptive devices and taught physicians from around the country the best contraceptive techniques. By the time of the raid, the bureau had accumulated by far the most extensive body of contraceptive research data available in the United States.

Opening this clinic partly fulfilled Sanger's dream for the birth control movement, one she began envisioning when she visited a birth control clinic in Holland in 1915. Knowing that most American physicians were not going to meet women's contraceptive needs in any comprehensive way, she hoped to establish a nationwide system of inexpensive clinics where women could obtain basic contraceptive care.[1] This clinic was the first with legal standing.[2] Despite the clinic's presumptive legality, it was never without

opposition, especially from Roman Catholic Church leadership. In this instance the police did the Church's bidding by using an undercover police
sergeant, Anna K. McNamara, as bait. According to the *New York Times*
reporter—who must have been tipped off about the impending raid—the
clinic was housed in "an old fashioned brownstone house directly across
from the rear of St. Francis Xavier's school." As patients and their children
in the waiting room were sent out into the street during the raid, people
gathered and the school's students "crowded to the windows to watch the
excitement."[3] Fifteen women were waiting when policewomen Mary Sullivan and McNamara, Lieutenant Frank Woods, and several uniformed officers carried out the raid. With warrants issued by Chief Magistrate McAdoo,
they arrested the doctors and nurses, claiming they violated Section 1142
of the New York State Penal Code, which made it a criminal misdemeanor
"for a person to sell, or give away, or to advertise or offer for sale, any instrument or article, drug or medicine, for the prevention of conception."[4]

None of the physicians or nurses had any inkling that McNamara was
actually an undercover police sergeant when she came to the clinic as a new
patient seeking contraception, presenting herself as a mother who wanted
to avoid the risk of another pregnancy. Usually the clinic's staff were wary,
especially of women seeking to terminate pregnancies—which the clinic
refused to do—knowing that these women might well be plants. But no
one had any reason to doubt McNamara's story about having three small
children, one still an infant, and an underemployed truck driver husband
who drank too much. She visited the clinic three times. Two different physicians examined her and concluded that on health grounds she should not
risk another pregnancy at the time. They gave her a Mizpah pessary, a kind
of diaphragm, and hands-on instruction in fitting it.

The police were aggressive, not only arresting the doctors and nurses and
seizing the clinic's medical instruments but also seizing 150 patients' private
medical records.[5] Their zeal exceeded their medical knowledge, the nurses
reported, as they also took "the curio closet," a collection of birth control
devices brought in by patients and displayed as examples of the public's
lack of knowledge about contraception. The seizure of the private medical
records became a rallying point for Margaret Sanger's many supporters, a

battering ram for her lawyers, and a subject journalists would keep return-ing to during and after the ensuing trial. Religious and public health of-ficials who supported birth control voiced their outrage and showed up at the trial en masse. The raid also helped push leaders of New York's medi-cal community to offer at least a vocal defense of Sanger's clinic, as they were aghast at the police department's violation of doctor-client privilege.

Sanger was not at the clinic at the time of the raid, so she was not ar-rested along with the staff. Notified by a phone call from the clinic, she ar-rived in time to watch the police rifle through and seize confidential patient records. She accompanied the nurses and doctors, and some of the seized materials, to the West 20th Street police station, where her colleagues were booked. She then traveled with them to the Jefferson Market Magistrate Court on 6th Avenue, in Greenwich Village, for the arraignment.[6] On the recommendation of Robert L. Dickinson, Sanger called Morris Ernst to represent the clinic. After leaving the courthouse, Sanger and the others went directly to the Greenbaum, Wolff & Ernst law offices at 235 Madison Avenue, where they met with Ernst, who took up the birth control cause.[7]

The raid was not the first time Ernst and Sanger were pulled into the same orbit—they had, for instance, recently shared the same stage at the 1929 Banned in Boston protests—but it began their lawyer-client relation-ship. As Ernst would later say, he was "in Margaret Sanger's Army in any job she assigns."[8] He enlisted in April 1929 and for decades Greenbaum, Wolff & Ernst lawyers ably guided Sanger, Stone, and their allies through the often-treacherous legal shoals surrounding the ever-controversial sub-ject of birth control.[9]

Birth Control's Fraught Nineteenth-Century History

Birth control has never been uncontroversial in American society. From the colonial period on, the cultural imperatives bolstering family forma-tion and prolific reproduction as part of a national narrative of abundance were strongly reinforced by religious injunctions. Historians explain that, stretching back to America's European origins, women's primary social role was to bear children in the name of spreading the Christian faith.[10] Those expectations were duly reinforced in the nation's churches, legislatures, medical schools, and cultural narratives. Yet these official narratives and cultural aspirations were not always in concert with women's private needs or married couples' ideas for their own lives. As birth control historians have made clear, humans have long sought contraceptive techniques—to separate sex from procreation and to limit family size. Americans were no different, and the fertility of American women actually began a long trend downward from 1800 to the 1940s, even when infant mortality rates were still high. By the turn of the twentieth century, the United States had a lower fertility rate than every European country except France.[11]

This pattern emerged long before post–Civil War industrialization transformed the U.S. economy and drew millions of immigrants, primarily from Europe. Changes in family size occurred in both rural and urban populations. The choice to limit family size was part of a nationwide transition to a modern society that valued education, literacy, and geographic mobility. Americans "were increasingly better educated, read more newspapers and books, participated more in the political process, had more faith in material progress," and had more confidence in their economic futures.[12] Lower fertility rates correlated with higher rates of school attendance and literacy, leading to higher educational and economic aspirations, which led to further reduction in fertility rates in the next generation, and so on. These values also meant that reproduction needed to be actively managed for upwardly aspiring men and women.

The financial and social implications of having large families were considerable, but other factors contributed to efforts to control family size. Pursuing economic opportunities required geographic mobility, and this reduced proximity to family. Kinship ties could not necessarily be counted on for raising children or for finding apprentice training or employment for them. In addition, the "separate spheres" that came to define middle-class and upper-class households also meant that the day-to-day management of children fell primarily on women.

These changing patterns of family formation, along with new ideals of companionate marriage, stimulated a burgeoning "marriage manual" literature that included information about contraception. As James Reed writes, "The desire of socially ambitious Americans to control their fertility provided a market for numerous 'little books'" describing birth control methods.[13] Readers of these books learned about the use of condoms, douching, withdrawal, pessaries, and planning for safe periods and periodic abstinence. Coitus interruptus, spermicidal douches, vaginal diaphragms or pessaries, vulcanized rubber condoms, and periodic abstinence could be and were effective "by nineteenth century standards," which by the end of the century meant limiting the number of offspring to three or four children.[14]

By the late 1860s political, medical, and religious figures concerned by the declining birthrates among middle- and upper-class white women began campaigning against contraception and declining fertility rates. As Reed writes, "the wails of social leaders" that middle-class and upper-class women "were shirking their patriotic duty," committing "race suicide," and "sinning against Nature" paved the way for the prohibitions on contraceptive information built into the 1873 Comstock Act.[15] The suppression of contraceptive materials became part of a "great crusade to make America live up to its sexual ideals" of female virtue and manly restraint.[16] Anti-vice reformers and social purity advocates focused their campaigns especially on the sexual threats to the family—prostitution, alcohol, pornography, and venereal disease. In this anti-vice discourse, contraception (especially condoms) became associated with married men's trysts with prostitutes, attaching a moral opprobrium to contraceptives that it still has not entirely escaped.[17]

The Comstock Act crucially collapsed categorical distinctions, connecting the immoral purposes of erotic materials with anything having to do with contraception. The federal law, echoed in most state laws (including Section 1142 of the New York Public Laws, which was the model for the federal law), included informational materials such as medical texts, instructional pamphlets, marital advice manuals, and actual devices, including condoms, diaphragms and pessaries, medicated sponges, abortifacients, and any information about where abortions might be procured.[18] In explicitly linking materials meant to induce sexual arousal with information about contraception and abortion, the federal and state laws also reinforced the idea that birth control had an immoral purpose and was a crime against the natural order, just as dirty as masturbation and as troubling as abortion.

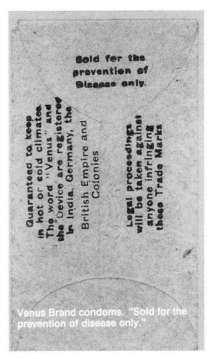

FIGURE 10. Venus Brand Condoms. The packaging suggests why condoms were associated with prostitution.

SOURCE: Marie Stopes Birth Control Collection, University of Santa Barbara Library, Special Collections.

Leading physicians promoted the "race suicide" conceit and reinforced the argument that too much education was leading young women away from family formation. One significant result was that leaders of the medical profession avoided teaching about or doing research on contraception. It was largely left up to radical women, such as Sanger and Emma Goldman, and the rare physicians who challenged the laws and the medical profession's inattention.[19] In addition, instead of using their prestige and authority to treat prostitution and venereal disease as physical rather than moral problems, physicians allowed "purity crusaders" to associate contraceptives with prostitution, thus branding them as instruments of vice and immorality. Because of medical professionals' distance from any positive affiliation with birth control, Sanger's Birth Control Clinical Research Bureau became the most important contraceptive research and training site and a significant provider of birth control devices for the women fortunate enough to have access to the clinic.

One of the ironies here is that by the mid-1920s Sanger recognized that the route to longer-term success for the birth control movement had to run through doctors. In the 1920s and again in the early 1930s she lobbied Congress for a "doctors-only" bill that would make physicians the only legal prescribers of contraceptives, hoping this would enlist doctors' support for birth control and give contraceptives institutional credibility in the eyes of congressmen.[20] Building on that, Ernst's successful arguments, in the 1929 case, and even more so in the 1936 case, firmly attached birth control to doctors' ethical and moral responsibilities to their patients.

Margaret Sanger's Radical History

A nurse by training, Margaret Higgins married architect and socialist William Sanger in 1902, and they had two sons and a daughter. Both Margaret and William were restless and looking for something more vital when they moved to New York City from the suburbs in 1911 after their house burned down. Margaret's father was a freethinker and critic of capitalism; he was also dissolute, and Sanger's family suffered from his inconstant work habits. Her radicalization began when she started attending socialist meetings in Greenwich Village, reading literature about labor struggles, and especially when she and her husband fell into the company of political and cultural radicals, including Alexander Berkman (anarchist editor of *Mother Earth*), "Big Bill" Haywood (leader of the Industrial Workers of the World), socialist journalist John Reed, anarchist and early birth control advocate Emma Goldman, and the radical socialite Mabel Dodge. Margaret became intimate friends with them, and they helped inform her economic and sexual rebellion.[21]

Sanger became a labor activist first but quickly developed an understanding of the relationship between women's pregnancies and their poverty. Her mother, a devout Catholic, had suffered. She was pregnant eighteen times, gave birth to eleven children, buried an infant, suffered from chronic tuberculosis, and died in her 40s. Her mother's fate made Margaret acutely aware of how frequent childbirth deepened the impoverishment and disease conditions of poor working people. As she took up labor radicalism, it did not take her long to recognize that the absence of contraception especially handicapped poor and working-class women—and their children—and kept them in circumstances that were nearly impossible to escape.

Sanger helped organize the famous textile workers' strike in Lawrence, Massachusetts, in 1912 and the silk workers' strike in Paterson, New Jersey, in 1913. Big Bill Haywood picked her to lead the women's committee in charge of evacuating workers' children to foster homes in Philadelphia and New York City during the Lawrence strike, and she saw how malnutrition ravaged the children. Before moving any of them to foster homes, she insisted on giving them medical examinations, and she found an epidemic of enlarged tonsils and rotting teeth. Sanger was called to testify before Congress about the children's conditions, where her clear recitation of facts actually produced action from Lawrence city officials. During the Paterson silk workers' strike, she again witnessed the "misery of the wives and children of the strikers," only this time she aimed her critique at the leaders of the radical labor movement who were blind to the "gnawing fear of pregnancy" that haunted Paterson's women.

Sanger absorbed another critical framework from her radical allies: the foundation of her incipient feminist critique of the bourgeois family and its constraints on women. Sanger was unhappy in her marriage and wanted more freedom. Aware of women's dependence and subordination generally, she saw that middle- and upper-class women suffocated under the "code of female propriety."[22] Life among her bohemian friends in Greenwich Village gave her language for a cultural critique and awareness that sex could be a source of self-fulfillment and pleasure, not just worry, fear, and unwanted children.

Sanger began using the platforms offered by her socialist and Industrial Workers of the World affiliations to promote women's sexual hygiene issues. Her job as a nurse, working in the immigrant tenements of New York's Lower East Side, profoundly deepened her understanding of the feedback loop between immigrant women's grinding poverty, their cycles of pregnancy, and the absence of contraceptive information. She also saw firsthand that doctors would not help their patients by providing contraception. The closer she looked, the more she saw doctors' indifference as a problem. The more she wrote, the better she understood the obstacles posed by the Comstock obscenity laws.

She also saw that too many women dealt with unwanted pregnancies through unsafe, illegal abortions. On Saturdays she would see between fifty and a hundred women lined up outside the office of the $5 abortionist on the Lower East Side, and on the other end of this queue she saw death from botched abortions.[23] Sanger frequently told the story of Sadie Sachs as her revelatory moment. Sadie, she explained, was one of her patients who had died from a self-induced abortion. Sachs already had three children and a husband who was a truck driver—the same story Anna McNamara told—and when Sanger met her, Sachs had nearly died from a self-induced abortion. As Sanger reported, she nursed Sachs back to health for months, and as she was recovering, Sachs asked the visiting doctor how she could prevent another pregnancy. His only advice was that she should tell her husband to sleep on the roof. Several months later, Sanger was called back to Sachs's tenement, this time to find her poor patient in a fatal coma from another self-induced abortion.[24]

Sanger dedicated herself to finding an effective birth control method that depended entirely on women for its use. (Men often refused to use condoms, condoms were often faulty, and withdrawal was a risky technique.) She also wanted more information about the safety and effectiveness of different techniques. Women used a variety of methods, from douching to making spermicidal mixtures, to cervical caps, but no systematic studies had been conducted and dependable information was difficult to obtain, even for well-to-do women.[25]

Sanger began to write articles and pamphlets to provide information to women; she willingly defied the Comstock laws to get that information distributed in the city and out through the mails; and she traveled to Europe in search of better methods and techniques, developing the goal of opening up her own birth control clinic in New York. In 1913 she and her family moved to Europe (her husband wanted to study painting), and she returned "armed with French pessaries, formulas for suppositories and douches, and a new determination to defy the Comstock law."[26] Sanger believed that women's control of their reproductive lives "held the keys to a more abundant life." Through the affairs she had while in Europe, she learned something else that shaped her personal life and her politics: "that the joys of the flesh and the spirit were one."[27]

Writing in 1912–1913 about women's sexual health issues for the socialist daily *The Call*, Sanger provided basic information about women's reproduction, venereal disease prevention, and female hygiene issues. Sanger encountered Comstockery for the first time in February 1913, when the Postal Service pulled an issue as unmailable because it discussed syphilis prevention. This outraged her. Along with brazenly flouting the Comstock laws, she expanded her critique of the medical profession's failures in her writings.

In 1914 Sanger began publishing *The Woman Rebel*, using the old anarchist slogan "No Gods, No Masters!" on the mast. She mostly focused on the theme of women's autonomy through contraception. Five of the seven issues of the *Woman Rebel* were suppressed by Postal authorities, and one in which she discussed assassination made her vulnerable to criminal prosecution. Rather than stand trial, Sanger fled the United States for exile in Europe, leaving her husband and children behind. Before leaving for Europe, she completed a 16-page pamphlet titled *Family Limitation*, her most detailed discussion of available birth control techniques. She had 10,000 copies printed, and when she was safely out of reach of U.S. authorities, she wired her friends to begin distributing the pamphlet. Postal officials and Anthony Comstock's agents eventually solicited a copy from her husband, who was then arrested and brought to trial for distributing an obscene pamphlet while Margaret was in exile.

Sanger's time in exile, beginning in August 1914, was transformative in many ways. Sanger left her husband (he reluctantly agreed to a divorce in 1921) and explored her sexual freedom, having affairs with different famous men, including H. G. Wells and Havelock Ellis. Ellis, the same sexologist whom Radclyffe Hall drew on to promote her book, became Sanger's personal guide to sexual liberation and influenced her framework for thinking about birth control in relation to women's equal right to sexual pleasure.

Perhaps most important, Sanger traveled to Holland to visit the first birth control clinic, established near The Hague. She met with one of the founders, Dr. Johannes Rutgers, attended his classes for midwives trained at the clinic, where she too learned how to fit pessaries for patients, and found a concrete model for how a birth control clinic in New York might operate. She also found a better type of pessary in Holland than the ones available in the United States, but because of the Comstock laws, they could not be imported.[28]

When Sanger returned to New York in October 1915, her husband, Bill, was on trial for distributing *Family Limitation*. The birth control movement's free speech battle with Comstock was in the news, and Comstock's entrapment of Bill had made martyrs of the Sangers.[29] He was convicted and sentenced to thirty days in jail. But the trial drew the support of wealthy women, twenty of whom were arrested for handing out birth control literature at his trial. Tragically, the Sangers' daughter, Peggy, died of pneumonia a mere month after Margaret's return, and U.S. Attorneys dropped the Postal obscenity charges against her for her earlier issues of *The Woman Rebel* rather than giving her even greater sympathetic treatment in the press. Devastated by her daughter's death but unable to set aside her birth control agenda, Sanger left her sons with their father and went on a speaking tour in 1916. She gave 119 speeches across the country, got arrested multiple times, fought Catholic authorities who tried to shut down her speeches, and kept birth control in the headlines wherever she went.

Determined to fight on, in October 1916 Sanger and her sister Ethel Byrne, also a nurse by training, opened the country's first birth control clinic at 46 Amboy Street in the Brownsville section of Brooklyn, modeled after the birth control clinic Sanger had visited in Holland. For a fee of 10 cents, each visitor received Sanger's instructional pamphlet *What Every Girl Should Know*, a short lecture on the female reproductive system, instructions on the use of various contraceptives, and help fitting their devices.[30] The clinic recommended the Mizpah pessary as the most effective pessary available in the United States, and the staff helped fit some of the 488 women who came in the first ten days, before the police raided the clinic and shut it down.

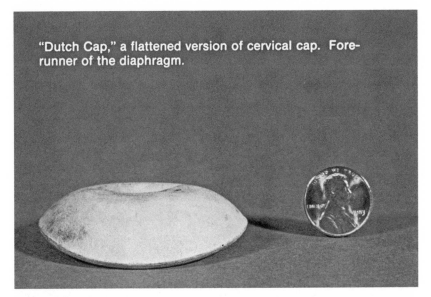

"Dutch Cap," a flattened version of cervical cap. Fore-runner of the diaphragm.

FIGURE 11. Margaret Sanger encountered the "Dutch Cap" in her tour of Dutch birth control clinics, and she and Dr. Hannah Stone imported contraceptive devices for experimental testing in their Clinical Research Bureau.

SOURCE: Marie Stopes Birth Control Collection, University of Santa Barbara Library, Special Collections.

After being arrested, arraigned, and spending a night in jail, Sanger reopened the clinic again a few weeks later. She was then arrested a second time and charged with "maintaining a public nuisance," and police closed the clinic again. Ever persistent, Sanger opened it a third time two days later, "but police forced the landlord to evict Sanger and her staff, and the Clinic closed its doors a final time."[31] They arrested Sanger, her sister Ethel, and Fania Mindell, the clinic's translator, charging them all with violating the New York state statute prohibiting distribution of contraceptive materials (Section 1142 of the New York Penal Code).[32]

People v. Sanger (1918)

The New York appellate court handed down its 1918 decision in *People v. Sanger* nearly two years after the police closed down Sanger's Brownsville clinic in October 1916.[33] Defendants Sanger, Byrne, and Mindell were tried separately. Ethel Byrne went first. Convicted and sentenced to thirty days in Blackwell Island prison, she went on a hunger strike, but the prison guards force-fed her. Word got out, protests ensued, and Sanger and her supporters were able to get New York governor Charles Whitman to pardon Byrne under an agreement that Byrne would not return to birth control work. Fania Mindell was tried, convicted, and fined $50 for disturbing the peace. Sanger was also convicted in early 1917, and state officials offered her a suspended sentence if she promised not to repeat the offense. She refused to make such a promise and also refused to pay a fine instead of going to jail. She spent thirty days in the Queens County Penitentiary, during which time she taught reading to the other inmates and instructed them about birth control.[34]

Sanger appealed her 1917 conviction, arguing that the Brownsville clinic had been legally sanctioned by Section 1145 of the New York Public Law, which provided a "good faith" exception for licensed physicians to prescribe contraception to married patients for health reasons. Used under these circumstances, contraceptives were not illegal *obscene* articles "of indecent or immoral nature or use," as defined and prohibited by Section 1142.[35] In January 1918 the New York Court of Appeals unanimously upheld her conviction, ruling that she had no standing because she was not a licensed physician and thus technically was not directly affected by the law. However, the court also addressed the question raised by Sanger: Did Section 1142 unreasonably prohibit a licensed physician from giving medical advice and help to a *married* patient? In addressing Sanger's arguments, the court confirmed that Section 1145 did provide a physicians' exception from the law's blanket provisions, ruling that contraceptive devices, when prescribed to a married patient for health purposes, were not "an article of indecent or immoral nature or use."[36] The court expressly elaborated this as a "good faith" exception for physicians: "This exception . . . is broad enough to protect the physician who in good faith gives such help or advice to a married person to cure or prevent disease." The court extended that exception to physicians' employees, including nurses.[37]

Judge Crane offered a liberal interpretation of Section 1145 that considered contraception useful for women's health reasons rather than exclusively for the prevention of venereal disease. In effect, the ruling afforded women in New York at least some access to contraception if their physicians, acting under good faith, believed it necessary to prevent pregnancy for the health of women and their children, including for disease prevention, although not for the purpose of contraception without specific health reasons. The decision also offered a broad and flexible definition of disease that might pertain to any pregnancy or childbirth, giving doctors some latitude; poverty would not be a justifiable reason, but a heart, kidney, or lung or mental health condition would be.[38] Ernst would return to *People v. Sanger* time and time again as foundational in holding for the physicians' exception language and for its expanded conception of what constituted "disease."

Under the authority of this 1918 ruling Sanger would have had legal cover to open another clinic under a physician's supervision, but she had to wait five years before she could raise sufficient funds to establish the Clinical Research Bureau. Between 1918 and 1923, Sanger effectively expanded the birth control movement's agenda and even began lobbying Congress (competing with Mary Ware Dennett's organizations, first the National Birth Control League and then the Voluntary Parenthood League). She also began to cultivate support from women of financial means who had shown interest in her cause, especially Mrs. Amos Pinchot and her sister, Juliet Rublee, along with Frances Ackermann. Together they helped finance Sanger's new publication, *The Birth Control Review*. They also helped finance her national organization, the American Birth Control League (ABCL; founded in 1921), which had over 18,000 dues-paying members by 1923, providing an economic foundation to establish the new Clinical Research Bureau.

Sanger kept things up on the publicity front as well. For example, in 1921 Sanger and other ABCL leaders organized the three-day National Birth Control Conference scheduled for Manhattan's Town Hall, which brought thousands of women to New York. On the third day the police shut down the venue for the keynote speech to be given by Harold Cox, a liberal member of the British Parliament and a vocal birth control supporter, under orders from Monsignor Joseph Dineen, secretary to Archbishop Patrick J. Hayes. Sanger was arrested in protest, and her antagonism toward Roman Catholic authorities intensified. The censorship generated considerable publicity, reinforcing the linkage between birth control and civil liberties violations.[39]

When Sanger opened her own clinic on West 15th Street in Manhattan, she hired Dr. Dorothy Bocker as the supervising physician. In that first year the clinic had visits from more than 1,200 individual patients. But Bocker never developed an organized research plan and failed to do follow-up with patients, so it was not clear whether the contraceptives were successful. Sanger wanted research data, and she brought in Dr. Hannah Stone in 1925 as the supervising physician and head of research. Stone amassed extensive data on patients and their results with various contraceptive strategies. In 1928 Stone published a highly regarded article based on results from 1,100 patients, providing strong documentary evidence that a diaphragm with contraceptive jelly was safe and effective.

The clinic also served a vital function that medical schools did not provide by giving instruction and information to physicians who wanted to offer birth control services to their patients. At the 1925 Sixth International Birth Control Conference in New York, for example, more than 1,000 physicians sought admission to the sessions on contraceptive techniques. At this point the American Medical Association still resisted contraceptive research or provision and leading medical schools still did not offer contraceptive training or engage in research. For those who could not make it to New York, Sanger hired Dr. James F. Cooper to lecture on contraceptive techniques to interested physicians. He spoke to hundreds of county medical societies and compiled a list of several thousand physicians willing to help patients. The ABCL, whose offices were in the same building as the clinic, became an information clearinghouse.[40]

The patients who came to the clinic were charged a maximum fee of $5. That funded some of the clinic's work but not enough of it, so Sanger was constantly raising money, including from the John D. Rockefeller Jr. funded Bureau of Social Hygiene in 1924–1925 and again in 1930–1931. The clinic's contribution was considerable, if measured by doctors trained in contraceptive techniques and patient visits. In 1930, a year after the raid, it taught contraceptive techniques to roughly 300 physicians, took in 4,733 new patients and 12,487 returning patients, and continued to accumulate the most comprehensive body of data on contraceptive practice available in the United States.[41]

People v. Sideri et al., 1929

The April 1929 raid and the subsequent trial of nurse Marcella Sideri, the other two nurses, and the clinic's physicians, rallied Sanger's supporters, including leading religious and medical authorities. Ernst and Sanger and their allies berated the city's police officials for their silence about the reasons for the raid and chastised those in the city's leadership (police, judicial, or political) who had signed off on it. The police in particular came in for serious criticism in the city's newspapers, especially because the clinic had been operating legally for six years and because no one on the force would offer a reason for the raid. The *New York World* led the charge, complaining that the police department had been "noticeably silent in the case" and had not answered basic questions. It was "astonishing," the paper wrote, that the police "could not find a better method of obtaining evidence [of possibly illegal activity] than by raiding a long-established and openly conducted clinic as if it were some bit of the underworld."[42]

Ernst and Sanger knew that they could count on a massive turnout by supporters and had arranged for expert medical witnesses of impeccable credentials. On the first day of trial, April 19, 1929, a crowd of 500 filled the Borough of Manhattan Second District courtroom, including clergymen, physicians, public health officials, and the prominent wives of the city's leading industrialists, financiers, and publishers. Members of the League of Women Voters and the Women's City Club also formed a "defense committee of prominent persons," according to the *New York Times*.[43] If the police and anti-birth-control forces had any voluble defenders among clergy, social elites, and the medical community, the press ignored them. The *New York Times* reported that former New York City health commissioner Dr. Louis I. Harris would testify and that he was "one of more than forty physicians . . . who have openly professed sympathy with those in charge of the clinic and resentment at the conduct of the police raid on its premises last Monday." The *Times* also let readers know that this was not the radical Margaret

Sanger from an earlier era but the "leader in the fight for the dissemination of knowledge by physicians concerning birth control."[44]

The first day's overflow crowd did not get the full hearing it came for. When McNamara's superior, Officer Mary Sullivan, failed to show up for the hearing, Magistrate Rosenbluth called it a day after hearing McNamara's forty-five minute testimony.[45] McNamara testified that she did not know who had ordered the raid, only that Mary Sullivan, head of the Women's Division, transmitted the complaint to her.[46] McNamara described her three visits to the clinic and admitted that she had come under false pretenses.[47]

Frustrated by the adjournment, but prepared to argue his case, Ernst explained his position to the gathered journalists. The matter was quite simple: "If the doctor is acting in good faith with the thought that the birth control information will prevent disease, that is all we have to prove. It is the burden of the prosecution to prove the bad faith of the doctor."[48] He also pressed the police on the matter of the missing records, reminding New York's medical community about the violations of seizing and not returning confidential patient records.

Ernst used the gap between the first hearing on April 19 and the second on April 24 to press his case in the papers. Aware of the need for damage control, police officials admitted that the raid had been overzealous, but they blamed lower-level officers and scapegoated Sullivan. Chief City Magistrate McAdoo, who had authorized the warrant for the raid, declared that "policemen who raided the Birth Control Clinical Research Bureau last Monday had gone beyond the authority of their search warrants when they seized physicians' case index cards." He promised that the "case records would be returned upon demand," though they never were.[49]

Attentive newspaper readers noticed that, following the police's internal investigation, the only person who police officials penalized was a woman. Critics lambasted the police leadership, complaining that the commissioner had still failed to acknowledge "anything unusual in the arrest of the clinic personnel."[50] Ernst called the police department's internal inquiry a "star chamber proceeding in which the facts and conclusions are withheld from the public," and Sanger derided it as a "very insignificant reprimand that means nothing compared with the trouble caused for all of us."[51]

When the trial reconvened the second time, the courtroom audience became boisterous, almost circus-like. The crowd cheered when Dr. Foster Kennedy took the stand and testified that "it would be for the mental and nervous good of that patient not to become immediately a mother again."[52] When Ernst followed up with a question about whether "these birth control supplies are very often recommended to prevent or cure disease?" Kennedy replied, "You say very often; I say always." The crowd grew more exuberant during testimony by Dr. Louis Harris, former health commissioner of New York City. When Magistrate Rosenbluth asked Harris whether he thought the clinic should have inquired further into McNamara's actual marital status, Ernst got the audience laughing by asking Harris whether he knew of any case "where a doctor sends out detectives to find out about a patient?" Magistrate Rosenbluth cleared the courtroom.[53]

Hoping to seek readmission, audience members circulated a petition outside the courtroom. Inside, the court heard testimony from three other expert defense witnesses: Bellevue Hospital gynecologist Dr. Frederick C. Holden; gynecologist, chairman of the National Committee on Maternal Health, and the leading medical researcher on birth control Dr. Robert Latou Dickinson; and chief of the Gynecological Bureau at Mount Sinai Hospital, Dr. Max Mayer. All three nurses who were arrested also testified that McNamara received examinations from both doctors. And Dr. Pissort testified that she diagnosed McNamara as having a medical condition indicating that another pregnancy, incurred too early, might result in health difficulties. The prosecution provided no counterevidence to dispute Dr. Pissort's testimony, nor could the district attorneys rebut any of the other expert witnesses Ernst had called to the stand to testify about the clinic's procedures.

Ernst moved for dismissal of the charges, based on the "good faith" exception established in the 1918 *Sanger* decision. "Since the defendants were licensed doctors and nurses who gave the advice in good faith to prevent disease it was the burden of the prosecution to prove lack of good faith," and the prosecution had failed to do that. It would be "disastrous for medicine," he added, if the courts did not assume that physicians acted in good faith.[54] Magistrate Rosenbluth did not immediately dismiss the charges, wanting instead to see the formal legal arguments from both sides.

New York District Attorney Joab H. Banton and Assistant District Attorney John T. Hogan submitted a Memorandum of Facts and Law that depended entirely on McNamara's own testimony. They could not offer counterevidence or countertestimony from their own medical experts because they did not have any. Nor could they offer any evidence to support their charge that the clinic's real purpose was prevention of conception in general or that the pessary the doctors prescribed McNamara was not really warranted from the examinations she received. Because the prosecutors had no medical evidence, their memorandum attacked the idea of legalized birth control in general. They invoked the most controversial implications of birth control, suggesting that women would be treated as prostitutes by their husbands if they used contraception, linked birth control and eugenics, and warned of wanton promiscuity among American women—and widespread "perversion—if contraceptives became socially acceptable. These fear- and morals-based arguments against birth control had all been used in the Comstock era.

Ignoring Judge Crane's 1918 physicians' exception ruling, the prosecutors focused instead on community morality and asserted that the sexual morality of women was the basis of any healthy community. Contraception would necessarily undermine that morality, they contended, because it contributes to female promiscuity, and Section 1142 of New York Public Law expressly articulated the state's interest in prohibiting distribution of what they called "promiscuous devices." "It seems to us that any meddling with the sexual relation to secure facultative sterility degrades the wife to the level of the prostitute," they wrote.[55] They also asserted that birth control would eliminate women's fear of pregnancy, an important moral prophylaxis against sexual immorality. They quoted Judge Cropsey's 1917 ruling in the *Byrne* case for their authority: "While there are other reasons that keep innumerable people from indulging their passions, the fear that pregnancy will result is one of the potent ones. To remove that fear would unquestionably result in an increase in immorality."[56] They again turned to Judge Cropsey when he criticized Byrne for her distribution of Sanger's pamphlet *What Every Girl Should Know*.[57]

None of these issues were germane to the facts in the *Sideri* case, and they ignored the subsequent 1918 ruling. When the district attorneys' memorandum finally turned to the legal question at hand—doctors' protection of women's health—the prosecutors circumvented the role of doctors altogether and instead called on husbands to protect their wives when medical conditions made pregnancy dangerous.

> [Marital continence] is the only ethical course for a man when the life of the woman whom he has promised to love and cherish, the mother of his child, is placed in jeopardy. Of course, this is not easy, but to say that it is impossible is to deny the heroic in every-day life. Paternity demands heroism, the daily struggle to support wife and children demands heroism. . . . What is needed is self-control, not birth control.[58]

The district attorneys contradicted themselves, however, when they made the stunning argument that birth control devices ought to be used in "the tenements," where immigrant men were not so capable of self-restraint. "Birth control likewise must be introduced into the tenements where common sense tells that these [marital continence] methods work poorly in the tenements, showing lesser results with the less intelligent."[59]

Ernst's Defendant's Brief was short, to the point, generally avoided the district attorneys' arguments, and addressed three simple questions: Did the law provide a physicians' exception? Did the clinic's physicians operate in good faith in prescribing a pessary to Sergeant McNamara? And were there medical grounds for this prescription? Drs. Stone and Pissort clearly met the physicians' good faith exemption standard, as testified to by all the medical experts the defense called to the stand. Finally, Ernst argued that the prosecution's lengthy, morality-laden anti-contraception Memorandum of Facts and Law was a legislative matter, stating simply that "the Court need not speculate on the advantages or disadvantages of self-control as against birth control."[60]

For the lawyers and their clients, the public opinion element of this case was clearly important in continuing that process of making contraception more mainstream. To pull doctors in as allies instead of obstacles or unwilling participants, birth control needed a greater aura of acceptability. This case, and particularly outrage at the police, accelerated that process.

FIGURE 12. The defendants posed outside the courthouse following the 1929 police raid on Margaret Sanger's Birth Control Clinical Research Bureau. From left to right: nurses Sigrid Brestwell and A. L. Field, Dr. Elizabeth Pissort, Margaret Sanger (who was not arrested in the raid), Dr. Hanna M. Stone, and nurse Marcella Sideri.
SOURCE: Getty Images.

Magistrate Rosenbluth's Decision

Magistrate Rosenbluth took a full two weeks following the hearing to render his decision. This irritated all parties and increased both public criticism of the police and support for the clinic. The decision, a mere two paragraphs long, accepted the "good faith" argument and upbraided the police and Anna McNamara for not showing the same good faith as the Clinical Research Bureau staff had shown. "Good faith, in these circumstances, is the belief by the physician that the prevention of conception is necessary for the patient's health and physical welfare. Good faith, or the lack thereof, in the prescription, and direction to use the contraceptives, are thus made the basis of guilt or innocence."[61]

Leaders of the birth control movement praised Ernst for his work. Mrs. Penelope B. Huse, executive secretary of the American Birth Control League, wrote, "We all want to congratulate you upon the way you handled the case of Mrs. Sanger's Clinical Research Bureau. It certainly was masterly and you made District Attorney Hogan look like an ape. The poor little creature stuttered around so in his cross examination and showed such a woeful lack of knowledge of anatomy and the sex functions that one might almost have pitied him, unless one realized, as a taxpayer, that he was being paid by all of us."[62]

This was the moment Ernst fully enlisted in Sanger's army. Their alliance surely deepened his understanding of feminist issues and arguments, especially that expanding women's access to contraceptive information and devices would not just contribute to women's health and safety but would also give them greater control over their reproductive lives, greater economic security, and greater marital happiness. Ernst and his colleagues became deeply immersed in the ins and outs of birth control law in the subsequent decades, through their counsel to the organizations led by Margaret Sanger and Hannah Stone.[63]

One clear lesson of the *Sideri* case was that focusing on the role of physicians generally in caring for their patients' health was a winning strategy. The 1918 *Sanger* case and the 1929 *Sideri* decision offered proof that the courts were amenable to doctors' authoritative judgment on birth control as a medical matter. Although those decisions offered no language or recognition of women's choices per se, New York's courts did recognize medical necessity and physicians' duties, assumed that physicians acted in good faith to protect their patients, and acknowledged the many health risks attending pregnancy. Legal and legislative recognition of women as autonomous sexual beings, with claims to private "reproductive rights," would be many decades down the road.

A Landmark Case for Birth Control: *United States v. One Box of Japanese Pessaries* (1936)

By 1930 clinics were finally spreading in the United States—but the U.S. prohibition on the importation of contraceptive devices remained a nuisance. For instance, Sanger hoped to test an experimental pessary that she had seen on a trip to Japan in 1930, but she could not import it. She was also tracking instances of Customs agents seizing contraceptives. By the early 1930s one of her organizations, the National Committee on Federal Legislation for Birth Control, was involved in sixteen separate court actions involving seizures.

In early 1933 Ernst and Lindey proposed a test case, based on the fact that the courts were moving toward recognizing the medical uses of birth control devices. Sanger would order a box of the experimental pessaries from the Japanese birth control clinic and await its inevitable seizure at New York's port of entry. "The Clinic may desire to make this a test case," Lindey told Florence Rose, adding that a successful challenge "would tear the Tariff Act wide open." He thought the case might go all the way to the Supreme Court.[64] Sanger agreed to the fight and soon told Ernst that she had been able "to get the interest of Mrs. Ethel Clyde, who said that if it was necessary to go ahead with litigation, that she would back up the case to go through the Courts."[65] Sanger secured $500 and authorized Lindey and Ernst to proceed.[66] All parties also recognized that a test case would have good publicity value. Mrs. Clyde "figures that we would get more than the value in publicity in the case," Sanger reported, "and I think she is right."[67] Ernst no doubt agreed.

Lindey explained their thinking: "Although the Tariff Act specifically forbids the importation of contraceptive articles, we are of the opinion that if such articles are consigned to a physician, and if the articles are susceptible of a legal as well as an illegal use, they are legal for importation into this country under the Act." If Customs did seize the shipment, he and Ernst were "confident that if the issue were tested out in the courts," the logic of the recent *Youngs* Postal decision "would prevail" and would also apply to Customs law.[68] Lindey and Ernst believed the case was winnable and would be significant in further limiting federal prohibitions on distributing contraceptive devices. The legal status of these items for Customs was clear, however: Importing such devices *was* still forbidden, because Section 305 of the Tariff Act contained a blanket prohibition on importation of contraceptives for any purpose and did not recognize any "legal" uses. Nor was there a physicians' exception in the tariff law.

All parties proceeded, and on February 1, 1933, Ernst and Lindey officially challenged Customs' seizure of the pessaries. They used a 1930 court decision that held that items that may be used for legal as well as illegal purposes must be allowed in the mail and argued that the same logic should apply here. The pessaries should be delivered to the intended recipient, Dr. Hannah Stone, a duly licensed physician who would use them for her legal medical research purposes. The acting assistant collector of customs, Ernest C. Hawkins, replied that his office took literally the "prevention of conception" language of the Customs statute and would not consider the physicians' exception argument from the *Sanger* or *Sideri* cases, as these were from New York state courts based on New York laws and had no authority in a federal jurisdictional matter.[69]

Ernst and Lindey had hoped to get a quick decision from Customs, but it was clear they were in for a fight. Lindey told Florence Rose that the $500 that Sanger had secured would be enough to challenge the Customs ruling in the lower federal court and might be enough to take them through the circuit court of appeals, but things were not going to move as smoothly as they had hoped. He thought the U.S. Attorneys would be more cooperative than the Customs officials and told her he hoped to work with Assistant U.S. Attorney Nicholas Atlas on this matter, as Atlas had been most cooperative in the *Ulysses* case.[70] Moreover, he and Ernst had successfully worked with this same U.S. Attorney's office on other Customs cases, including the Marie Stopes *Contraception* case in 1931.

This time around, though, the U.S. Attorneys did not expedite the process in any way. On the contrary, they essentially sat on it for over two years.

Developing a Legal Strategy: Medical Necessity as Determined by Physicians

By the time Lindey and Ernst began writing formal legal memoranda, organizing expert witnesses, and preparing their case for trial in 1935, they had been working closely with birth control leaders for six years. They had developed a broad legal and sociological framework for understanding the issues surrounding birth control, and because of their detailed knowledge of obscenity law, they were prepared to make a well-honed, precise set of legal arguments about the particulars of *United States v. One Box of Japanese Pessaries.* But they also knew the challenges they faced. Sanger had spun her wheels trying to get Congress to take up legislation to provide a physicians' exception, as had Dennett in trying to legislate broader claims to women's reproductive rights. Congress just would not touch birth control.

Against this legislative stasis, there had been movement in the courts, all built on arguments about medical necessity, physicians' authority, married women's health, and reasonable statutory construction.[71] Lindey and Ernst recognized the expedience of the "medicalization" strategy, with doctors made the only authority on contraceptive decisions. This was certainly a narrower, more restricted strategy than advocates like Dennett had hoped for in their lobbying efforts when they pursued legislation that offered all women the right of access to contraception, without doctors as intermediaries. But Sanger favored getting the conservative American medical establishment to come around, and making doctors responsible for all birth control decisions and prescriptions could be a winning strategy.

As Lindey and Ernst prepared their legal documents for their case, they all but removed the Clinical Research Bureau as the actual claimant. They did not address its history and certainly not its historical significance as the first birth control clinic in Manhattan. Sanger's affiliation was not even noted at trial, nor was Dr. Hannah Stone's long history as the clinic's research director or her status as a defendant in the *Sideri* case following the 1929 raid. Their extensive legal memoranda offered only a brief discussion about the potential value of the imported pessaries for a study. Lindey and Ernst highlighted the role of physicians generally in caring for their patients' health. They drew on the expertise of distinguished New York physicians—all men—who were willing to testify about the circumstances under which they would prescribe or had prescribed contraceptives for their patients. Doctors became the operative moral agents in the trial, with the central "moral" question revolving around doctors' uses of contraception on behalf of their endangered patients whose health would otherwise be adversely affected. This effectively shifted the moral "problem" away from contraception and onto a law that interfered with doctors performing their duties of patient care.

Ernst produced a powerful dramaturgy in the federal courtroom. The core issue at trial was the 1873 statute as a hindrance to effective medical care and how that statute might be interpreted. Here Ernst and Lindey made a compelling claim that statutory prohibitions ought to be read with the understanding that Congress wrote laws with reasonableness in mind. Taken literally, the tariff law was highly unreasonable. Indeed, a literal reading of an inflexible statute could have disastrous real-life implications for women and their families.

Ernst and Lindey carefully cultivated their expert witnesses, enlisting leading doctors who had been involved in maternal health research, some of them pioneers in their fields and some who had served as experts in their other cases, including Robert Latou Dickinson, Louis I. Harris, Foster Kennedy, Frederick C. Holden, Max Mayer, and Ira S. Wile. In bringing their witnesses up to speed on the legal issues before the court, Ernst and Lindey framed the *Pessaries* case for them as the next stage of a series of significant battles against the problem of censorship generally but especially against "illiberalism in matters of sex," a battle in which these men of medicine had "been so long engaged."[72]

The Trial's Dramatic Arc

When the U.S. Attorney's office chose to defend the Customs law and proceed against Sanger and Stone's clinic in 1933, George Medalie had been the U.S. Attorney for the Southern District of New York and Nicholas Atlas the Assistant U.S. Attorney. By the time the matter came to trial at the very end of 1935, a different group of U.S. Attorneys were in charge of the case: Assistant U.S. Attorney Martin Conboy (who had led the appeal of the *Ulysses* decision in the U.S. Court of Appeals), Assistant U.S. Attorney John F. Davidson, and U.S. Attorney Lamar Hardy. Instead of Judge Woolsey, whom Ernst and Lindey hoped to have on the bench, *United States v. One Box of Japanese Pessaries* came before U.S. District Court judge Grover M. Moscowitz in December 1935. Judge Moscowitz had been the original trial judge in the *Dennett* case, the jurist so aware of the delicacy of the masturbation issue that he empaneled three clergy to hear the case with him.

Davidson took the lead for the prosecution and argued that Ernst and Lindey wanted the courts to do what Congress would not and that Congress had made its position clear. This was largely true. Congress had not budged on the total prohibition on importation of contraceptive materials. As Davidson stated when introducing the government's position, "This is a very simple case. There is a statute of the United States called the Tariff Act of 1930, which specifically states that all persons are prohibited from importing into the United States any article whatever for the prevention of contraception." When Judge Moscowitz asked him if this meant that the "government can ban them for any purpose, legitimate or illegitimate," Davidson's reply was quick and unequivocal: "Absolutely."[73] Davidson continued, "The question before the Court here and before the jury is not whether the statute is a good one or a bad one, but whether it has been violated."[74]

Judge Moscowitz questioned Davidson about historical changes between 1873 and 1935 about what is "regarded as unreasonable," adding, "Courts have to advance with the ideas of the times in their attitude." Davidson acknowledged this point generally, but as to the specific law, he repeated that Congress had passed the absolute ban deliberately.[75] To make congressional intent clear, Davidson offered a short history of efforts to amend the law, showing that each time an amendment was introduced, Congress refused it. Clearly, Ernst and Lindey did not have an open-and-shut case. They knew the courts might be reluctant to accept their goal of basically nullifying a law that Congress had had no intention of changing. As Ernst stated in his opening remarks to Judge Moscowitz, "This, very frankly, sir, is a test case. I assume it will go up no matter what the decision is and we do not want any technical victory."[76]

So, Ernst and Lindey essentially ignored the legislative history. They argued their case from three converging angles. First, they put doctors on the stand to testify about their experiences, hoping to show that Congress was uninformed and timid. Second, they leveraged the fact that New York State had a physicians' exception provision for contraceptives that the federal law did not, and, because physicians working in New York imported the seized items, they contended that state law should be operative.[77] And third, both New York State and federal courts had ruled in subject-related

Postal cases that physicians' exceptions ought to be granted. Although the U.S. Attorneys had legislative history on their side, Ernst and Lindey had living, breathing doctors, potentially harmed patients, and key recent federal court decisions.

Ernst also urged that his clients actually had legal history on their side. But unable to completely ignore the long congressional ban, he needed other angles and so aimed his critique of the law on Anthony Comstock. In Ernst's narrative, Comstock and his laws were an aberration in the nation's longer history. He explained, "During the first hundred years in this nation there was no ban on contraceptive material . . . or advice." But "around 1870 Anthony Comstock popped up," and the nation was confronted by its "first censorship laws as to obscenity, birth control material and birth advice." The courts, however, had steadily recognized that doctors and their patients needed remedies from the statutory law. First, with the *Bours* case in 1915, Judge Mack drew a critical "distinction between legal and illegal [purposes] under the wording of the statute." He described the 1918 *Sanger* decision in the New York Court of Appeals as "a philosophical guide" coupled with the *Bours* case. The *Sideri* decision in 1929, "indicate[ed] a trend" in judicial thinking. Two recent decisions by federal court of appeals judges, the *Youngs Rubber* case in the Second Circuit and the *Davis* case in the Sixth Circuit (in Ohio), tempered the strict postal and interstate commerce restrictions. In *Youngs Rubber*, Judge Swan expressly rejected a strictly literal reading of the Comstock Act, writing, "The intention to prevent a proper medical use of drugs or other articles merely because they are capable of illegal uses is not lightly to be ascribed to Congress." In *Davis* the Sixth Circuit Court drew on and bolstered the *Youngs* decision in another Postal case involving contraceptives, reaffirming "the decision that these articles are not illegal *per se*," and adding the useful language that the "statute must be given a reasonable construction."[78] Ernst argued that applying a literal reading of the prohibitory language in the Tariff Act, as Davidson insisted, would certainly not meet this already established "reasonable construction" standard. Using the reasonable construction formulation, Ernst put the burden of proof on the government "to prove that these articles were imported for an illicit use and not for a health use."[79] The U.S. Attorneys denied they had such a burden.

But Ernst and Lindey's case was also stronger than the burden-of-proof argument. The core of their case was that if the government continued to enforce a policy of finding all imported contraceptives illegal, the damage to medicine would be immense, especially to married women and their families. A policy that put doctors "at the mercy [of Customs officials] every time he [*sic*] uses one of these articles" was bad. So was continuing to enforce a strict ban that denied the expertise of physicians who knew the importance of contraceptives for their patients' health. Moreover, doctors should have access to the latest research materials and new techniques that were being developed and effectively used beyond the nation's borders. As Ernst noted, "Possibly somewhere else in the world they have gone further in the art than we have."[80]

After their opening arguments, both sides called on their expert witnesses. Davidson, however, put only one witness on the stand: Dr. Frederick W. Bancroft. Davidson apparently was so intent on asserting literal statutory prohibition that he entirely failed to anticipate defense questions about the legitimate medical purposes of pessaries and contraceptives generally. He showed Dr. Bancroft a box of them and asked what they were for. Bancroft said their purpose was to prevent conception, and Davidson turned the witness over to Ernst. At this point Dr. Bancroft basically become a key witness for the clinic when Ernst asked him whether he had prescribed contraceptives to his patients. Reading the trial transcripts, one can almost hear the tenor of the hearing change as Ernst cross-examines Dr. Bancroft.

ERNST: Doctor, you stated that you have prescribed pessaries or similar articles. Now, I would like you to set forth as fully as you please the medical indications upon which you have found it necessary to make such prescriptions. . . .

BANCROFT: I think there are many medical needs.

ERNST: For example?

BANCROFT: Tuberculosis, threatened tuberculosis, heart disease of the mother—many similar medical conditions.

ERNST: It could be cases of kidney diseases?

BANCROFT: Yes

ERNST: It could be cases of pelvic deformities which make childbirth arduous?

BANCROFT: Not necessarily with a caesarian incision.

ERNST: Not necessarily, but it could happen?

BANCROFT: It might.

ERNST: Diabetes cases?

BANCROFT: Yes . . .

ERNST: Cases where they are suffering from insanity and epilepsy?

BANCROFT: Yes . . .

ERNST: How about the very basic use for the proper spacing of child-birth in relation to the mortality of the off-spring and, with re-gard to the mother, might there not be medical indications for a prescription of some such article to prevent the birth of a child if there had been a child born to the same woman within a few months?

BANCROFT: That is right. . . .

ERNST: . . . to prevent syphilis and gonorrhea through infection at the time of birth or even transmission?

BANCROFT: Yes.[81]

Attorney Davidson, watching his case fall apart, objected to all of Ernst's questions, but Judge Moscowitz overruled him each time and never interfered with Ernst's cross-examination.

Following Bancroft, Davidson introduced into evidence Dr. Hannah Stone's book, *A Marriage Manual*, pointing particularly to that "portion of a chapter on the prevention of conception where it is stated that a pessary or vaginal diaphragm is an article for the prevention of conception and . . . probably the best article for prevention of conception."[82] But following Ernst's cross-examination of Dr. Bancroft, Davidson no doubt knew better than to ask Dr. Stone to the witness stand to ask her to elaborate on why she might prescribe pessaries and why the clinic would want to test their effectiveness. He had no other experts.

That was the sum total of the U.S. government's case. Davidson's case was simple. Ernst exploded it.

Ernst began calling to the stand a roster of prestigious physicians and asked them all the same essential question: Why burden women with pregnancies that might harm them? The implied question was well understood: Why would the U.S. government interfere with doctors preventing potentially harmful or even lethal pregnancies? Ernst began with Dr. Frederick Holden, a specialist in obstetrics and gynecology, a member of the American Medical Association, a member of the New York Academy of Medicine, a fellow of the American College of Surgeons, an emeritus professor at New York University, and an attending physician at ten hospitals in New York City and Jersey City, with forty-three years' experience practicing medicine. Ernst asked Dr. Holden, over Davidson's objection, "From your knowledge and experience can you state whether there are some cases where it is necessary to prescribe some form of contraception for the cure or prevention of disease?" Holden had written about the subject of child spacing as useful for protecting women's health and testified that he also recommended child spacing when poverty conditions affected a mother's or family's ability to take care of existing children, especially when the family already had an unhealthy child who needed scarce family resources and time to recover. The choice to prescribe contraceptives in these circumstances was "very obvious," Holden said.

They then turned to the use of contraceptives to prevent heritable or venereal diseases that might affect the life of the child, slipping into the troubling realm of eugenics.

> ERNST: I have in mind, for example, cases of inheritable diseases.
> HOLDEN: Well, you take the case of the moron for instance. We think in such cases that the mother should not carry on a pregnancy . . .
> ERNST: What about the field of cases of epilepsy and feeblemindedness?
> HOLDEN: I have also come to that category.[83]

Even though definitions of "morons" and "feeblemindedness" or questions about epilepsy and the advisability of reproduction were not pursued any further, all the parties appear to have assented to basic eugenics assumptions about the undesirability of some people reproducing. This was an indication of how widespread eugenics thinking was in the medical community in that era, with few exceptions outside the Catholic Church.[84]

Ernst's next witness was Dr. Foster Kennedy, whose bona fides were as impressive as Dr. Holden's.[85] Kennedy began by saying that he agreed with Dr. Holden on every point. His specialization was different, however, so his testimony addressed pregnancy and mental health issues, including depression, delusions, and psychosis. He described pregnancy as a period of illness for some women, stressing that, because of their mental health conditions, some women should not bear children. Ernst followed this with a question about whether Kennedy's colleagues agreed with him on these issues. Kennedy responded, "The general principle of the need of preventing birth has been accepted by practically all, I believe all—all that I know—all the medical bodies that I know."[86] U.S. Attorney Davidson did not even try to question this testimony.

Having established this line of argument from distinguished physicians in different medical subfields, Ernst then stipulated for the sake of time that the other doctors he was prepared to call would testify similarly with respect to their subfields. Based on their considerable medical knowledge and experience, all would assert that some patients should be prevented from getting pregnant. Ernst entered another dozen experts' names and credentials into the record.[87] Then, in one of the few times that the Clinical Research Bureau came up, Ernst turned to its experimental research work. Noting that the particular box of Japanese pessaries had been imported for experimental purposes, he assured the court that this was a legitimate function of the clinic's scientific and medical activities, that it was duly licensed, and that it was up to the federal government to prove their unlawful uses. Taking the stand, Dr. Hannah Stone testified that a physician from Japan sent the pessaries "for the purpose of trying these out and giving my opinion as to their reliability or usefulness as a contraceptive measure."[88] She also reported that the clinic lawfully used similar contraceptive devices transported through the U.S. mails and distributed through interstate commerce and that imported pessaries ought to be granted the same legal exceptions. After Stone's bona fides were established and all questions of fact addressed, Judge Moscowitz released the jury, asserting that because there were no facts to be disputed, he would address the matters of law. He requested memoranda of law from both sides.

The government's brief, Reply Memorandum for Libellant, attempted to rebut the points raised in the Claimant's Memorandum and the arguments made at trial.[89] But the district attorneys could not move their argument much past the statutory literalism they began with, nor did they challenge the expert witnesses' testimony. They argued that the 1873 statute left "no room for . . . interpretation."[90] The only question of fact was whether the pessaries could be used for contraceptive purposes, and that fact had been "proved beyond any doubt whatsoever."[91]

By contrast, Lindey and Ernst's legal memorandum showed that both New York State and federal courts had conceded the necessity of recognizing medical exceptions to contraceptive bans and had done so with consistency since the *Bours* case in 1915. For Lindey and Ernst, the crux of the matter was clear: Absolute prohibition should apply only when contraceptives were used for illegal purposes. "Any other interpretation would lead to a shocking result," they wrote.[92]

The Federal Courts Respond

Federal court judge Grover Moscowitz ruled in Lindey and Ernst's favor, accepting their argument that a statute must be "given a reasonable construction."[93] He referred specifically to the *Youngs* and *Davis* cases, where the federal courts had read physicians' exceptions into the postal and interstate commerce statutes. Moscowitz held that the medical profession "is in agreement as to the necessity of contraceptives" for health purposes.[94] He thus ruled that the government's strict construction of the statutory prohibitions was unsound, given that in the parallel *Davis* case the Sixth Circuit Court had held that such broad prohibitions did not "prohibit the transportation of contraceptives in interstate commerce unless intended for an illegal use." In the case at bar the government had made no contention, nor had it proved that the pessaries "were intended for illegal use."[95] He quoted *Davis* at length, including the key line "The intention to prevent

a proper medical use of drugs or other articles merely because they are capable of illegal uses is not lightly to be ascribed to Congress."[96] Moscowitz
extended the logic of this argument to include the clinic's purposes as a
research bureau, holding that legitimate experimental research must also
be protected. This was immediately useful to Ernst and Lindey in a subsequent case—the *Himes* case—defending the right of research scientists
to have access to materials related to the history of contraception and to
gather information about different devices and techniques used over time
and across cultures.

On receiving Judge Moscowitz's decision in early January 1936—a
full three years after this matter had begun with Customs' seizure of the
pessaries—the U.S. Attorney's office appealed the ruling to the U.S. Court
of Appeals for the Second Circuit. It took nearly a year for it to hand down
a decision on the appeal, but the circuit court upheld and expanded Moscowitz's ruling with its decision, written by Judge Augustus Hand. The
decision essentially erased any differences between Postal and Customs law,
trying to create a coherent federal policy across administrative units based
on the physicians' exception language and because federal laws regulating
the flow and distribution of so-called obscene goods needed greater consistency. As Judge Hand wrote, "All the statutes we have referred to were
part of a continuous scheme to suppress immoral articles and obscene
literature and should so far as possible be construed together and consistently."[97] This was a more expansive outcome than Ernst, Lindey, Sanger,
and Stone could have hoped for.

This was a landmark decision.[98]

In 1942, five years after the circuit court handed down its landmark
decision, Ernst offered a retrospective view of its implications, writing,
"This decision was a legal triumph for birth control. In a very real sense,
too, it was a medical triumph. Each time the federal courts repeated their
belief in the entire lawfulness of medically authorized contraception, they
emphasized more clearly the important and varied health aspects of the
question." He added, in a nod to the important role physicians had played
in the case as expert witnesses, "Distinguished doctors who [articulated]
their belief in the immense benefits to be won for society by the intelligent

use of contraceptive techniques, contributed materially to the education of judges, which was then reflected in enlightened decisions. Medical opinion has played a vital part in all the more recent birth control cases."[99]

United States v. Nicholas/Himes (1938): A Companion Decision to Japanese Pessaries

The battles over birth control were far from finished after *United States v. One Box of Japanese Pessaries*, as some states still prohibited even married couples from securing contraceptives and prohibited physicians in those states from providing contraceptive information and advice. As might be expected, given the long record of bureaucratic hassles endured by birth control activists and other proponents of sexual liberalism, Postal and Customs officials continued to create obstacles to the flow of contraception information. They insisted that only "privileged" persons of scientific standing were legitimate recipients of these kinds of materials and still routinely seized materials and sent them to the Postal Service's Dead Letter Office. These practices led almost immediately to another case taken up by Ernst and Lindey, mostly handled by Lindey, resulting in what amounts to a companion decision to *Japanese Pessaries* in the matter of *United States v. John P. Nicholas* and *United States v. Norman E. Himes*. The cases were first tried in the federal district court in New York, where Judge Galston dismissed the libels and ordered the books and magazines turned over. The government appealed and the Second Circuit Court heard the appeal, affirming the lower court ruling. However, it did so by splitting the case on the grounds of "privileged status," ruling for Himes but against Nicholas. Because Hines had a doctorate, was the editor of a leading journal, and was doing his research as a social scientist, he had the same "privileged person" status as physicians and licensed clinics in the eyes of the court, so he was able to receive the materials he had ordered. But Nicholas was neither a scientist nor a doctor and was therefore not a "privileged person" and did not receive his book.[100]

Early Victory for Birth Control and a Career Shift

The New York City police raid on the Clinical Research Bureau in April 1929 began a long-term relationship between the Greenbaum, Wolff &

Ernst law firm and the leaders of the birth control movement. Ernst, Lindey, Samuel Schur, and eventually Harriet Pilpel (who became a central legal guide for the birth control movement for decades) worked essentially pro bono for several years, performing extensive administrative work, offering advice and planning, and helping establish Planned Parenthood in 1942. Extensive correspondence in the firm's records show that the bulk of their longer-term counsel was administrative, with many hundreds of unnoticed legal and advisory interventions on behalf of Sanger and the various birth control organizations with which she was involved over time. But Ernst and his colleagues also knew that direct challenges to the obscenity laws were the most effective means to thwart the day-in, day-out censorship actions of Postal and Customs officers.

Postal and Customs obscenity laws established massive administrative hindrances to women hoping to secure safe, affordable, dependable birth control devices and information. These contraceptive materials might provide them with more control over their reproductive lives, make their intercourse less anxious and fraught, and perhaps secure more economic stability. The obscenity laws also established legal obstacles to those physicians who might want to provide greater and better contraceptive care to their patients. With their language of immorality and their total prohibitions on birth control, the laws made doctors uncertain about what they could order through the mails or prescribe to their patients. This in turn made physicians unreliable resources for women needing contraception and undependable supporters of the birth control movement.

Ernst and his colleagues contributed key victories, but they did not claim and should not be mistaken as the birth control movement's pioneers or main agents. They did not go to jail, endure hunger strikes, or sacrifice their families for the birth control movement. Critics also complain that Ernst's legal alliance with Sanger and her focus on physicians as the gatekeepers of women's birth control access contributed to the medicalization of birth control in the United States. Insisting on the rights of a privileged class (licensed physicians) to offer contraceptive devices to another privileged class (married women) left many women out of the protected sphere of recipients of contraception. This critique is accurate, but given the specific historical legal and political constraints that Ernst and the birth control movement's leadership confronted, the strategy of leveraging the 1918 *Sanger* decision to advance the physicians' exception ruling made sense. The *Sideri* case, following the 1929 clinic raid, offered an opportunity to expand that ruling.

In the face of wholesale congressional inaction on any birth control legislation at all from the late 1920s to the mid-1940s, the sweeping prohibitions of the federal Comstock laws, the various states' own extensive prohibitions on contraceptive devices and information, and politically ambitious and religiously committed U.S. Attorneys and state district attorneys insistent on enforcing literal interpretations of those stringent laws, the birth control movement and its lawyers had no clear route for gaining greater legal access to birth control, for either doctors or their patients, except through the courts. Moreover, at the moment when Ernst and his firm joined Sanger's army in 1929, they were also up against intensifying and highly strategic Catholic opposition to birth control, with the increasingly powerful U.S. Catholic Church monitoring legislatures, hospitals, clinics, and other sites where birth control practices or advocates might be found.

The battles over birth control were far from finished following the *Japanese Pessaries* decision. The freedom of individual women to choose birth control devices was still a long way off, especially for unmarried women. The language of women's "reproductive choice" was not really available, and women's access to contraception remained medicalized. But the medical profession was less of an obstacle thanks to this decision.

The great ideological battles of the 1930s through the 1950s interrupted—perhaps even terminated—Morris Ernst's strategic assault on obscenity law and his legal defense of the first sexual revolution. The politics of anti-communism essentially shifted his purposes, alliances, and the civil liberties questions he addressed.[101]

Ernst's shift away from civil liberties commitments began with hotly contested disputes within the ACLU itself over a series of issues, especially whether the ACLU should defend the speech rights of communists and fascists, how the ACLU would defend itself against charges that it was a communist front organization, and whether it should permit communists to serve on its governing bodies. The Nazi-Soviet Pact in August 1939 exploded the always tenuous domestic Popular Front alliances and created a cauldron of suspicion and distrust within and outside the ACLU. ACLU records reveal growing anxiety in the organization about its own vulnerability and its leaders' shift of attention away from industrial union drives, labor defenses, anti-lynching campaigns, and anti-censorship activities and toward the complicated national security matters attendant to war. Neither the ACLU's leaders nor its rank-and-file members could agree on how the organization would define, promote, and defend civil liberties in the cauldron of war or which values—the protection of liberties for all versus the security of the state—would take priority. Winning the long anticipated war against fascism became the foremost goal, and this tied the ACLU's leadership more strongly to Franklin D. Roosevelt's administration.[102] Ernst was firmly in FDR's wartime camp.

As the international crises of the late 1930s deepened, Ernst's focus shifted away from obscenity law issues to international issues and the role of the United States in the world. He never fully refocused on cultural and sexual censorship issues and obscenity law jurisprudence, but his interests were re-engaged by the 1948 publication of Alfred Kinsey's *Sexual Behavior in the Human Male*, which he immediately understood as a breakthrough work that could advance the cause of "sex enlightenment."

CHAPTER 8

THE ALLURE OF THE EROTIC

Alfred Kinsey and Sexual Science, 1947–1957

PROFESSOR ALFRED KINSEY and the Institute for Sex Research at Indiana University quickly became the sensation of the early postwar period with the publication of *Sexual Behavior in the Human Male*, so much so that the book made its way into popular culture's Great American Songbook that same year with Cole Porter's "It's Too Darn Hot."[1] Released in January 1948, Kinsey's study exploded into public consciousness and soon became known simply as the Kinsey Report. The book, based on the findings of detailed sexual histories of 5,300 men conducted over a fifteen-year period asserted that men's sexual orientation ranged across a six-point scale, from strictly heterosexual to exclusively homosexual. It drew attention by reporting that 37% of American men had at least one homosexual experience and that 10% were exclusively homosexual for a three-year period at some point in their lives. Kinsey also refused to use the categories "normal" and "abnormal" and insistently promoted the statistic that 95% of men had broken one or another sex law at some point in their lives. In compiling such extensive data about American men's sexual practices and establishing the gap between expected, legal behaviors and actual ones, the Kinsey Report immediately became a cultural phenomenon and helped accelerate trends already in motion in post–World War II American culture in the realm of sex, particularly by making it permissible to discuss sex more honestly.

The American people's interest in sexuality became more voluble and more acceptable after World War II, but changing attitudes and behaviors outpaced the law's capacity to accommodate them. The Kinsey Reports, both *Sexual Behavior in the Human Male* (1948) and *Sexual Behavior in the Human Female* (1953), made that abundantly clear, providing hard evidence of the considerable gaps between peoples' behaviors and the laws that could be used to punish many of those behaviors.[2] Not surprisingly, straight American men won the most latitude as sexual beings, at least with respect to seeing and reading about their sexual fantasies in print culture. Their wartime experiences weakened the moral justifications for "protecting" them from arousing images and ideas. There simply wasn't much intellectual patience for Comstockery in post–World War II American culture. Obscenity law restrictions on what postwar adult males might get their hands and eyes on yielded, slowly but steadily, as the courts granted more and more exceptions for adult readers. So too, the great postwar insistence on heterosexual mating and exuberant reproduction opened social spaces for addressing women's sexual drives and desires, especially because the emphasis on married sexuality put additional pressures on women to keep their marriages sexually vital and alluring.

This desire for more information and greater freedom of expression, combined with a broader commitment to anti-censorship liberalism, forced courts to be more attentive to arguments about the adult public's rights as readers and viewers and its capacities to confront sexual themes without being "depraved and corrupted," to use the old Hicklin standard phrase. And yet the availability of more expressly pornographic materials heightened anxieties about sexual violence and deviance, sexually maladjusted men, perversion, and the "seduction of innocents," to use the title of one widely selling postwar book by Dr. Frederic Wertham, Ernst's erstwhile expert in the *Well of Loneliness* case. The fear of pornography overlapped with fear of violent popular culture artifacts, especially comic books, energizing anti-pornography campaigns that warned about how boys and men were being trained to fantasize about sexual domination and exploitation. "Sadomasochism" entered the vernacular.

A dramatic increase in inexpensive magazines, pulp novels, stag films, and other mail-order "erotica" produced, according to concerned anti-pornography groups, a "floodtide of filth" that was polluting the culture and was especially affecting young people and their sexual imaginations by directing their attention to the darker, violent, and deviant undercurrents of sexuality. These concerns engendered feverish journalistic and scholarly work and reenergized anti-vice activities through organizations such as Citizens for Decent Literature and the Catholic Church's Legion of Decency. It also led to high-profile congressional investigations of the comic book industry, juvenile delinquency, and the pornography industry. Senators Ernest Gathings and Estes Kefauver and Congresswoman Katherine Granahan all helped keep anxieties about pornography, vulnerable youth, and abnormal sexuality at a high pitch. Literature was one thing; S&M scenarios in graphic comic books were another.[3]

The pressure to keep sexually themed works out of circulation empowered state attorneys general to use obscenity laws to go after recently published works with claims to literary distinction and sexual frankness, including the noted literary critic Edmund Wilson's *Memoirs of Hecate County* (1946), whose publishers were charged with violating New York State's obscenity laws, and Lillian Smith, whose 1944 interracial romance novel *Strange Fruit* was banned in Massachusetts. They also routinely challenged works by Erskine Caldwell, William Faulkner, and James T. Farrell, despite their publication by reputable publishers and favorable critical attention.[4]

The courts groped toward solutions in the 1940s and 1950s. As I have illustrated in previous chapters, by the 1930s the courts had increasingly recognized that different audiences had variable capacities and needs, and decisions such as Judge Woolsey's ruling in the *Ulysses* case offered jurists useful language and a workable framework for advancing the rights of adult readers to have access to serious work. But judges were still driven by a deep belief that society required moral order, and for them the task was figuring out how to draw the line between the obscene and the not quite obscene, the unacceptable and the protected, one book at a time, within that larger cultural flood. The result was legal decisions that could be bafflingly inconsistent from one jurisdiction to the next, or from one decision to the next, even within the same court. The Kinsey Reports epitomized this postwar boom in the marketplace of sexual images and ideas, and they also stimulated it. The studies gave evidence about peoples' sexual appetites and permitted treatment of topics that might even be challenged as obscene if treated in literary works but were scientific facts when discussed by the journalists, critics, and other experts who reported on the details of Kinsey's work or reflected on it as a harbinger of the postwar boom in all matters sexual.

Although Ernst would never again be the chief strategist in the battles against obscenity law that he had been before the war, he did not retire from those issues.[5] At war's end, for instance, he and his colleague Harriet Pilpel eventually became involved in the *Esquire* postal case (*Hannegan v. Esquire, Inc.*), the major wartime obscenity battle in which the postmaster general suspended second-class mailing privileges to *Esquire* magazine because of photos of scantily clad Varga girls and racy articles. The materials were nowhere near pornographic and the postmaster general's action produced howls of protest among magazine publishers and civil libertarians. When the Supreme Court heard the postmaster general's appeal of the Second Circuit Court's unfavorable ruling on his suspension, the Ernst firm joined the action, submitting an amicus brief to the Supreme Court in 1946.

When Ernst got wind of Kinsey's project, his gaze back was pulled back to obscenity law issues. Ernst learned about *Sexual Behavior in the Human Male* in late 1947, just months before its publication, and wanted his firm involved with Kinsey and his institute. He wanted affiliation with the project's voluminous research findings, which provided exactly the kind of credible data about sexual behaviors that Ernst (and the cause of sexual liberalism) had been waiting for. He immediately recognized that Kinsey's work—which he promoted as the "Research Magnificent"—had the potential to transform the nation's sex laws.

Sexuality Meets Social Science

Indiana University professor Alfred Kinsey (1894–1956) trained as a botanist at Harvard and began his career studying gall wasps. His energetic field research took him far and wide, and over time he gathered massive collections (including 5 million gall wasps housed at the Museum of Natural History). Committed to taxonomy as a method and variation within species as a scientific principle, Dr. Kinsey commenced his extensive study of human sexuality when he began teaching Indiana University's undergraduate course on marriage in 1938. Kinsey quickly turned the course into a basic sex education class for the university's senior students and its already engaged or married undergraduate women and men, including offering slide-show-illustrated lessons in biology, anatomy, reproduction, and the mechanics of sex. He found himself giving private advice to students who sought him out to discuss their own sexual problems, and he grew "increasingly irritated by the fact that he was unable to give scientifically valid answers to the simple questions" asked by his students. The entire subject of human sexuality was, he complained, "entangled in a mass of taboos and repressions." Kinsey wanted to separate the biology of sex from the moral tangles and social prohibitions that made it so difficult to study "human sex habits . . . with the same scientific objectivity, and recorded with the same detached precision, as were the sex habits of the lower animals."[6]

Kinsey's various biographers—James Jones and Jonathan Gathorne-Hardy—make clear that Kinsey was deeply irritated by and resented the gulf between his own sexual desires and practices (including his bisexuality, masochistic masturbatory practices, and polyamory) and the religious and cultural conventions that had taught him and most others that these impulses and behaviors were sinful, perverted, and unnatural.[7] When he found evidence of those behaviors in his studies, he insisted that they were not at all unnatural because they were "biological," found in nature, and engaged in by many men and boys who found sexual release in a wide variety of ways beyond marital intercourse. Kinsey and the research team he trained expressly rejected categories such as normal or abnormal, natural or unnatural. Many of the study's participants had violated the laws and the dominant moral codes in finding their sexual "outlets," as the report referred to them, but Kinsey insisted that those laws were grounded in theology, not biology.

Beginning in the 1940s, with the imprimatur of his university, especially its president, Herman B. Wells, and with sustained financial support from the National Research Council and the Rockefeller Foundation's Medical Sciences Division (led by Alan Gregg), Kinsey was able to train a team of researchers (his fellow interviewers), primarily Clyde Martin and Wardell Pomeroy and later Paul Gebhard, along with a small staff of secretaries and librarians. Kinsey and his team gathered their data about sexuality by conducting detailed interviews—they called them sexual histories—with thousands of willing subjects. By 1948 they had interviewed 12,000 men, women, and some children, and by the time of the second report on female sexual behavior in 1953, Kinsey's group had taken 18,000 individual sexual histories. *Sexual Behavior in the Human Male* based its results on 5,300 histories.

Kinsey, like Ernst, was a publicity machine and had assiduously promoted his team's findings to journalists, scholars, and foundation officers before the first book's January 1948 release. He also gave preliminary reports of the findings in lectures, held press conferences, sent out teasers to publications about the institute's research findings, and, most effectively, invited academics and journalists to travel to the institute in Bloomington to see the research operation firsthand and have detailed conversations with him and his fellow researchers. Kinsey convinced many of those visitors to give their own sex histories while there, so they could testify to the method's effectiveness and nonjudgmental approach. These strategies helped shape reporters' and scholars' presentation of the Kinsey Reports' findings and their interpretation of its implications, particularly Kinsey's aim that the reports would lead to reforms in the nation's sex laws, which lagged far behind people's sexual practices.

Kinsey staunchly defended the work, taking on all challengers and closely arguing the details of his team's research techniques, from their interview methods and statistical sampling techniques to their apparently neutral attitude toward all forms of sexual activity. Some critics, then and now, criticized him for his unwillingness to denounce or make moral judgments about sexual behavior that many found abhorrent, including pederasty, bestiality, prostitution, homosexuality, and marital infidelity. His standard response was that they were reporting on sexual behavior, not making moral judgments about it.

Kinsey's promotional strategies led to enthusiastic previews and reviews once the books came out. This is especially evident in journalist and mental health advocate Albert Deutsch's November 1947 piece in *Harper's*, followed months later by the most influential early book on the Kinsey Report, edited by Deutsch, titled *Sex Habits of American Men: A Symposium on the Kinsey Report* (1948). Deutsch's book included essays by sociologists, anthropologists, legal scholars, rabbis and ministers, doctors, psychiatrists, psychologists, penologists, and more, almost all of whom endorsed the book as a whole, despite an occasional quibble.[8]

Intended to be the first of nine volumes, *Sexual Behavior in the American Male* drew on the detailed sexual histories of "bankers and bums, teachers and truck drivers, cowboys and cabbies, the upper crust and the underworld, infants (by special techniques) and nonagenarians, from border to border and coast to coast," Deutsch wrote.[9] Kinsey's team promised complete confidentiality, making informants more willing to sit for interviews that lasted between ninety minutes and three hours, during which time they would answer several hundred rapid-fire questions. Their responses were written down in a special code Kinsey developed with his team, so it was virtually impossible for anyone not on the team to either interpret the answers or know the identity of a given interviewee.

Kinsey's team amassed startling statistics about the prevalence of homosexual encounters, ubiquitous masturbation, widespread extramarital affairs, sex with prostitutes, and even frequently occurring sex with animals. They also found that men's basic sexual attitudes and behaviors were formed in adolescence and remained essentially fixed throughout their sexual lives but that those attitudes and behaviors differed considerably across class and educational lines. Three major factors were most important in influencing sexual behaviors: the social, the biological, and the psychological, with social factors being the strongest determinant of an individual's sex habits. These were formed "mainly by his cultural environment—the social group which he moves in or into," Albert Deutsch explained, with "remarkable conformity among most individuals belonging to the same group."[10] The greatest differences in social practices across groups were shaped by economic factors (and educational aspirations). For instance, college-bound men had far less premarital intercourse and engaged in more petting and mutual masturbation than "lower level" males (as the Kinsey Report referred to them, trying to avoid using the language of social class). Men without college educations and those not bound for college engaged more prostitutes, abjured nudity, had intercourse at much earlier ages, and thought French kissing was unnatural.

Kinsey insistently pushed the idea that the nation's sex laws needed reform. They needed to accommodate the findings of science and reflect actual biological and social behaviors rather than being premised on theological foundations, biases, and idealized moral norms. The legal construction of some sexual acts as contrary to nature could be deeply punitive, especially those activities falling under the category of sodomy laws, namely, homosexual oral and anal sex. Yet many men had had sex with other men—more than one-third of their interviewees. Moreover, the Kinsey Report showed considerable variety in the frequency and type of sexual behavior engaged in by average men and boys. Those variations were not easily amenable to being "adjusted" either, because individual's sexual desires and behaviors were formed and fixed early in life.[11] The overwhelming fact, Deutsch wrote, channeling Kinsey, was that "sex acts condemned as immoral and illegal in our law books are so commonly practiced as to make criminals of the vast majority of the American population."[12] Most other early reviewers focused on the gaps between the nation's sex laws and what journalist Waverly Root referred to as a "startling" variety of activities.[13]

The Kinsey Report was too big and provocative for the institute's research methods, data, and conclusions to be immune from scrutiny by reviewers. It did not take long for the racial composition of the interviewees to gain critical attention or for the fact that roughly one-fifth of their subjects were prisoners, which had no doubt skewed their results on the prevalence of homosexual contact.[14] But even then, most of Kinsey's critics still accepted and endorsed Kinsey's goal of changing the laws to accommodate actual practices. Francis Sill Wickware's "Report on Kinsey," published in *Life* magazine in August 1948, captured the controversies surrounding Kinsey's work. His piece began by noting that the Kinsey Report had been both hailed as a "milestone of science" and also attacked as an "assault on the family as the basic unit of society, as a negation of moral law, as a celebration of licentiousness and as a bad influence generally."[15]

However, Wickware was less inclined to say that the results were startling or revolutionary. Based on his conversations with experts in adjacent medical or social science fields, he asserted that "with few exceptions, Kinsey's findings came as no great surprise . . . on the contrary, the *Report* generally documented and confirmed long-held theories, suppositions, and beliefs."[16]

Wickware pointed to other criticisms by social scientists, psychiatrists, and statisticians that were gaining force, including what he described as the misleading title, *Sexual Behavior in the Human Male*. Kinsey's sample was virtually confined to white U.S. males, and even within that population those surveyed were "far from representative of the U.S. male population." Only 15% of the general population had college educations, but 56% of Kinsey's sample were men in college. The sample not only skewed young and white but also did not adequately represent Catholics or farmers; for instance, "male prostitutes, psychoanalysts, [and] institution inmates" were oversampled. As Wickware and other critics complained, such samples likely skewed toward men who were "psychologically unrepresentative" because of their willingness to reveal private details, men perhaps "motivated by exhibitionism or some unconscious drive to tell all."[17] Kinsey's defenders would acknowledge that they had not adequately figured out a method to account for self-reporting that may have been filled with exaggerations; but they also added that it was unlikely people would boast about sexual behaviors typically thought shameful.

Wickware continued with his litany of critiques: "The most provocative criticisms of the Report are those concerned with what has been called Kinsey's 'atomization of sex'—that is, his exclusive preoccupation with the 'outlet' [the orgasm] as the whole of sexuality and his seeming determination to reduce a highly complicated psychological and emotional phenomenon to a mere biological reaction with as little significance as sneezing."[18] Wickware did endorse Kinsey's position of being morally neutral or nonjudgmental about peoples' sexual expressions and what Kinsey called their outlets, but he pointed out that being nonjudgmental should not be confused with being policy-neutral. Kinsey had a clear public policy agenda: to change the laws governing sex offenders. Wickware was sympathetic to this goal, and in fact his article gave Kinsey the last word to advance that

FIGURE 13. Professor Alfred Kinsey (center, with bowtie) and his staff at the Institute for Sex Research at Indiana University, 1953.

SOURCE: Alamy.

cause: "Asked once about the 'message' of the first *Report*, Kinsey reluctantly answered, 'If I had any ulterior motive in making this study, it was the hope that it might make people more tolerant.'"[19]

Scholars weighed in, too. A *Saturday Review of Literature* "symposium" on the book in 1949 supported Kinsey's goals of legitimizing the science of sexuality, gathering data about sexual behaviors, and transforming the laws, but its contributors expressed concern over his methods, his focus on "outlets" as the sole measure of sexual encounters, and the demographic limitations of his study. Dr. Abraham Stone (the husband of Margaret Sanger's colleague, Dr. Hannah Stone), New York psychiatrist S. Bernard Wortis, anthropologist Ruth Benedict, and Ernst offered brief assessments in the *Saturday Review* symposium.[20] They generally agreed that the data were useful but also cautioned readers that the statistical prevalence of a behavior did not necessarily correlate with its "normality" and that numbers were not substitutes for understanding the psychology of sex. However, all agreed that the laws around sex needed reform. Ernst immediately embraced and trumpeted the Kinsey Report for the purposes of legal reform and public discussion about its results.[21]

Catching Ernst's Attention

As noted earlier, Ernst returned to obscenity law issues when he learned of Kinsey's work in late 1947, and he did so in his efforts to become a public intellectual of sorts, using his reputation for legal expertise to write about a broad range of matters in the public interest. He wrote articles for mainstream magazines, including defending J. Edgar Hoover and the FBI in *Reader's Digest* and *The Nation*, penned book reviews for the *Saturday Review of Literature*, served as a member of President Truman's Civil Rights Commission, and churned out a series of quickly written books on topics ranging from divorce laws to public opinion to chatty autobiographical accounts of his sailing and legal life.[22] He thought about the Kinsey volume through this voice: as public intellectual and general commentator and as an authority on the nation's sex laws.

Ernst also knew that Kinsey was bound to run into troubles with various obscenity laws, and he knew that literary pirates lurked.[23] He forged a relationship with Kinsey, and by early 1948 he and Harriet Pilpel began offering legal counsel to Kinsey and his Indiana University research institute, a relationship that would continue well beyond Kinsey's death in 1956.[24] Just months after Kinsey's book came out, Ernst told Kinsey he wanted to write a book promoting Kinsey's research. He assured Kinsey that he could leverage his reputation to help people understand the "impact of your research on the law."[25] He also wanted to help thwart the inevitable controversies that would swirl around *Sexual Behavior in the Human Male*.[26] Kinsey okayed Ernst's plans, telling him, "You are splendid to back us as you have in this research." Of the inevitable attacks, he wrote, "We are tough enough to take any sort of attack," but he added, "I would be happy to have you work on such a critique as you suggest."[27]

Kinsey did not really need the publicity help from Ernst, but he did need lawyers who knew the ins and outs of publishing contracts, literary piracy, and obscenity law, and he also needed to bolster his support from Rockefeller Foundation officers when the controversies around his book drew negative attention to the foundation's funding. Kinsey and his team met with Ernst and his associates over drinks in New York's hotel bars and at dinner parties hosted by Ernst and his wife, Margaret (Maggie), at their West Village brownstone on West 11th Street, with Kinsey as the guest of honor.[28] Ernst would work his local networks on behalf of the institute, inviting prominent friends from law and media to those dinners, and also met with Rockefeller Foundation officers to try to elicit ongoing support and to assure them that Kinsey's work was already influencing legal thought.[29]

Less than three months after getting the green light from Kinsey, Ernst and his co-author, David Loth, produced a short book titled *American Sexual Behavior and the Kinsey Report* (1948), a title that could have easily been mistaken for the original report (and perhaps was, as its sales were considerable).[30] The book was quickly dashed out—one reviewer called it a "thin résumé"—and had none of the depth or influence of Ernst's earlier books on censorship, especially *To the Pure* (1928) and *The Censor Marches On* (1940). Ernst and Loth gave readers a familiar context, describing the Kinsey Report as another victory over the "proven neurotic" Comstock and also against the contemporary moral scolds who "preferred ignorance to the acceptance of the realities of life." They told readers that Kinsey's data would bridge science and the law and would help eliminate "the remaining restraints imposed on the printed word."[31] Claiming Kinsey's work would bring "greater First Amendment protection to sexual speech," they explained that "in all future cases the Kinsey Report will be available to the courts in order to impress into our law in the field of obscenity statutes, the idea that there shall never be a suppression of books dealing with sex unless the state can prove a clear and present danger of real damage and injury to the readers."[32] This last idea, that Kinsey's research would help disprove any clear and present danger to readers, was the finding Ernst most forcefully urged to others.

Selling Kinsey to Judges Bok and Frank

The timing of the Kinsey Report was fortuitous. Just as it was remaking national conversations, Ernst could promote Kinsey's "Research Magnificent" to two judges, Curtis Bok, a Pennsylvania Commonwealth Court judge with whom he shared a passion for sailing, and Jerome Frank, a brilliant federal court judge and former associate in the Ernst law firm. Both judges had obscenity cases on their dockets in 1948, both were aware of serious problems with obscenity jurisprudence, and both came to Ernst seeking his ideas. He established a three-way colloquy of sorts, sending them copies of his books as well as briefs written by his firm and others and exchanging a series of letters with them. He also offered detailed page-by-page commentary on a late draft of Bok's eventual opinion. In virtually all communications he touted the Kinsey Report.

When Frank rendered his opinion in the 1948–1949 case *Roth v. Goldman*,[33] just a month before Bok delivered his *Commonwealth v. Gordon, et al.* decision,[34] he expressly mentioned the Kinsey Report, cited Ernst's book, and advanced arguments about the value of replacing the long-tattered Hicklin test with the clear-and-present-danger test. Bok's decision offered the same core arguments, and he too credited Kinsey with introducing valuable new evidence for legal consideration. Ernst's midwifery explains some of the deep structural and conceptual similarities in the two judges' decisions, both of them influential and rendered within weeks of each other.

In his formal opinion in *Commonwealth v. Gordon*, Judge Bok held that the libeled books under review were not obscene as charged under the Pennsylvania statute, as that statute stipulated that the work under consideration "must be construed as a whole and *that regard shall be had for its place in the arts*."[35] But he aimed at more than just a piecemeal advance of the law. He wanted to get at the definitional problems, the inability to prove cause and effect, and the problem of presuming that sexual arousal harmed readers. He also wanted to address the constitutionality of obscenity law, asking his higher court brethren to consider whether the obscenity laws violated First Amendment protections. As he told Ernst, "I won't stop at what *is* obscene (tough little word, 'is'): it's what it does—& taste & *mores* have a lot to do with that: above all this the calm, Olympian gaze of the Constitution. Boy o boy, am I eating this up! Most interesting case I have ever had—not to decide, but to make out."[36]

Among legal historians, Bok's richly argued 55-page decision has a reputation as an incisive distillation of the faulty logic in obscenity law jurisprudence.[37] Ernst enthusiastically recommended it to Jerome Frank and told Bok he wanted to make at least 100 copies to distribute to judges, lawyers, and other interested readers. When Ernst later learned that the Superior Court in Pennsylvania had let Bok's decision stand in its January 1950 ruling, he wrote Bok, "This is probably the first time that a higher court has entered into an acquaintanceship with the theory that I have been plugging and which you enunciated in your decision. . . . Never before, as far as I know, has a higher court declared that the clear and present danger rule is a rule of law to be applied to the facts in an obscenity case. As a matter of fact, I know of no case where the courts have held that a constitutional issue is involved in an obscenity case."[38] Bok was more circumspect, replying that when the decision came up before the Pennsylvania Supreme Court, that court might not accept the full implications of his decision, predicting that the Pennsylvania court would "dilute the constitutional point. They will undoubtedly pay high tribute to freedom of speech but will not let pass my holding that criminal conduct is required before a test can be made."[39] Bok was entirely correct. The Pennsylvania Supreme Court accepted the verdict on the books but "did not approve the test of clear and present danger as applied to alleged obscene literature."[40] Nor did Bok get the appellate court review he hoped to provoke.[41] Jerome Frank did, albeit not until seven years later.

Judges Frank and Bok were tilling the same field. In February 1949 Frank made the same core arguments in his concurring opinion in *Roth v. Goldman*. The inability to demonstrate harm was a key legal concern. Frank noted that the Kinsey Report provided valuable evidence about the elusive nature of proving harm. All kinds of people were aroused by all kinds of stimuli, with virtually no evidence of public safety being threatened. If there were indeed harms, they ought to be proved and "such proof ought to be at least as extensive and intensive as the Kinsey Report," he wrote.[42] He suggested that obscenity law should focus exclusively on obviously pornographic materials, the only purposes of which are arousing lust—but even then, his logic implied that this would still be inconsistent with any proof of clear and present danger to public safety. However, no judge in 1949 could or would make the argument that pornography per se might also be protected speech.

To the problem of inadequate evidence, Frank turned to another cluster of arguments about the complexity of human sexuality, the difficulty of demonstrating cause and effect, and the fact that what produced sexual arousal was hardly traceable to just an individual work. As to whether such materials actually produced troubling antisocial behavior, he was skeptical: "Perhaps further research will disclose that, for most men, such reading diverts from, rather than stimulates to, anti-social conduct."[43] Frank completed his concurring opinion by claiming he was "unwilling in this case to oppose my views to those of my more experienced colleagues." Officially, he concurred in the court's opinion upholding the postmaster's ruling. But he did so, he wrote, "with bewilderment."[44]

These decisions by Bok and Frank did not have an immediate effect in the courts, but they finally gained traction and helped push the U.S. Supreme Court to address the broad set of problems with obscenity jurisprudence in 1957, at roughly the same time Kinsey's Institute for Sex Research was going to court over Customs seizures of its materials. The institute benefited greatly from the early groundwork Ernst laid with judges Bok and Frank.

Customs Seizures Set a Kinsey Institute Test Case in Motion

In 1947 the Institute for Sexual Research began importing erotica from abroad, accumulating a massive library and database of sexual artifacts and art objects, literary texts, films, photographs, phallic objects, and other items from around the world. By 1956 it had acquired more than 700 sexual calendars and sexual diaries, had built an extensive library of 19,893 bound volumes of medical, psychiatric, sociological, anthropological, legal, and other works, and had amassed a large collection of erotica, from erotic literature to "crude commercial pornography," to paintings and sculpture, photography, drawings by prison inmates, Japanese scrolls, ancient pottery from Peru, graffiti, and so forth. All told, the institute's library contained 20,000 art prints, 60,000 feet of film, and 20,000 photographs, along with the 18,000 sex histories that Kinsey, Martin, Pomeroy, and Gebhard had taken, coded, and stored.[45] The institute built part of its erotica collection in cooperation with prison officials at numerous institutions who were interested in the institute's study of sex offenders and sexual pathologies. They agreed to send the institute the erotica produced by their inmates, even giving inmates materials (pencils, paper, paints, etc.) to create their homemade erotica, with the expectation that it might contribute to studies on criminal sexuality, sexual pathologies, and the "sex adjustments" of inmates.

Kinsey also made informal agreements with Customs officials to obtain materials from abroad, through the offices of Huntington Cairns, who served as the Customs Service's legal adviser on censorship issues. Before this position Cairns had developed an expertise in obscenity law, fighting cases on behalf of Baltimore's Peabody Bookstore, and had worked with Ernst and Lindey, including introducing them to Dr. Frederick Wertham in the *Well of Loneliness* case. Cairns was a man of letters and a progressive on literary and artistic censorship issues. His appointment by FDR's administration as the Customs Service's legal adviser was heralded as a real breakthrough by Ernst, who took this as strong sign that the Roosevelt administration would be open to modern art and literature. (As Cairns once said about his role as the legal adviser to Customs, "Someone had to do it. Most of the customs people didn't know a Vatican mural from a French postcard.")[46] Cairns granted the institute exceptions under Section 305 of the Tariff Act, based on the premise that the materials might provide insight into "the significance of sex in all aspects of human activities" and would be useful to psychologists, penologists, and others with scientific and policy interests in sexual matters.[47]

This agreement with Cairns proved effective until 1950. Trouble began when a career Customs official, Eugene J. Okron, became Collector of Customs Alden Baker's new assistant collector. Okron disliked the informal agreement between Cairns and Kinsey's institute, believing "it wasn't the place of the Indianapolis office to grant an exception to federal law."[48]

Okron formally protested the arrangement and even brought samples of the imported materials to Washington, D.C., where he met with the assistant U.S. commissioner of customs, David Strubinger. When Strubinger saw the materials, he told Kinsey, "All the books you have submitted are grossly obscene. The most liberal interpretation could not bring them within the statutory limitations of the discretionary authority."[49]

Kinsey and Pilpel tried to work things out with officials in the Washington office of the Customs Service and met with Cairns in June 1950 to try to reach an agreement. Pilpel laid out her core position, that the provisions of the Tariff Act "carried an 'implied exception' in cases of qualified persons who made legitimate use of material which would otherwise be banned." She based this on the *United States v. One Package of Japanese Pessaries* (1936) decision that she and Ernst had won on behalf of Margaret Sanger's birth control clinic, providing "conscientious and competent physicians"[50] access to contraceptive devices for clinical study and for use with their married patients. Pilpel asserted that this implied physicians' exception rule had already been extended to other bona fide scientific researchers, for example, Norman Himes, a social scientist at Colgate University whom the Ernst firm defended in his case when he challenged a Customs seizure of materials he was collecting to write his book on the history of contraceptives.[51]

Pilpel was overly optimistic about convincing Customs authorities that there was a direct legal parallel between importing contraceptive devices for study and to prescribe to married women and the quite raw erotic materials sent to the Institute for Sex Research. In September 1950 a Customs official told Kinsey that Customs would not grant "an administrative exception" and that any claims of exception to the Tariff Act would have to be "cleared by the courts."[52] Customs officials thought that judges should resolve the issue, as a judicial ruling would provide guidelines for subsequent cases. This began a seven-year struggle between Kinsey's Institute for Sex Research and Customs officials. Kinsey wanted to challenge the Customs decision, in the courts if necessary, telling Pilpel he was "increasingly convinced that we should push this until we have clearly established our right to import any kind of sexual material."[53] Pilpel and Ernst were inclined to proceed, seeing this as another winnable case in their decades-long battles with Customs, with a good prospect of establishing another landmark decision on behalf of scientific sex research.

Once Customs decided it would more closely scrutinize and challenge the imported materials, Ernst and Pilpel made two moves they thought would be expeditious in setting up a test case. First, they maneuvered to challenge the Customs decision in the New York courts rather than in Indiana. Kinsey directed his foreign suppliers to route the materials through New York Customs. The deputy collector of customs in the New York offices agreed to seize the packages and hand them off to the U.S. Attorneys in New York, who had promised "prompt federal proceedings."[54] Second, and perhaps unwisely, Ernst and Pilpel upped the ante on the explicit nature of the materials Kinsey purchased from abroad. Kinsey told his dealer in Copenhagen he wanted "'the most openly erotic material' available, particularly 'French cards, photographs and drawings of sexual activity, including mouth-genital contact and if possible, homosexual activity.'" The dealer responded by sending, among other things, three small packages including the thirty-one black-and-white photographs named in the title of the eventual federal court action. He described them to Kinsey as "the most openly erotic . . . anyone could imagine—and rather pretty."[55] Kinsey was uneasy about the expenses and the diversion of resources to legal costs, but he wanted to fight Customs and get a test case.[56] He went along with it.

Whatever hope Ernst and Pilpel might have had for eventually working out a successful negotiation with the New York Customs officials and U.S. Attorneys was dashed when the story of the Customs seizures hit the local Indiana newspapers and then the national newspapers in November 1950. A headline in the *Indianapolis Star* proclaimed "'Science' Says Kinsey; 'Dirty Stuff' Says U.S." The story quoted the local collector of customs, Alden Baker, describing the seized materials as "d—— dirty stuff . . . nothing scientific about it." His assistant said the materials were "so obscene that any scientific value is lost."[57] Other Indiana papers and the Associated Press and United Press International wire services picked up the story, "creating an uproar" and putting Indiana governor Henry F. Schricker on the defensive from outraged constituents and Indiana politicians. He furiously called Indiana University president Herman B. Wells seeking an explanation. Wells, an ardent defender of Kinsey and the institute's work, continued to protect Kinsey, taking pressure off the institute. But the larger narrative of the Kinsey's institute as a morally disreputable enterprise gathered force, making a resolution with Customs officials more difficult.

By the end of 1951 the New York Customs office had seized seven different shipments sent to the institute.[58] Pilpel still tried to negotiate with Customs officials, hoping they might get an administrative agreement if "Kinsey stipulated the safeguards taken to prevent public access to institute materials" and submitted an analysis of "why each of the items now detained is important."[59] But Customs officials were no more willing to compromise than was Kinsey. The Customs solicitor sat on the materials and essentially refused to render a legal decision on the status of the materials. Because he did not actually libel them as obscene, he did not need to forward them to the U.S. Attorneys who had promised to promptly initiate proceedings.

Two years into the stalemate, in May 1953, Pilpel appealed directly to the U.S. secretary of the treasury to exercise his discretionary authority under the "implied exemption" ruling. She assured him that the institute could provide testimony about "social and scientific value" of the institute's research from the "physicians, psychiatrists, psychologists . . . who had benefited from Kinsey's work" and assured Treasury officials that the materials would be under lock and key and "available only by an appropriate and qualified officer of the Institute to bona fide scientists and students of the subject matter constituting the Institute's area of research."[60] She also expressed frustration that the government was ignoring case law, arguing that forcing "citizens to litigate over and over again the same body of questions is to ignore *stare decisis* and to subject both the body politic and the private individual to great and unnecessary expense."[61]

Meanwhile, Kinsey and his team published their long-anticipated second study, *Sexual Behavior in the Human Female*, in 1953, bringing public attention and renewed criticism to their work. Within ten days it was in its sixth printing. Women, it turns out, were also biological animals whose sexual behaviors did not comport with cultural expectations. Kinsey's team

FIGURE 14. Harriet Pilpel joined Greenbaum, Wolff & Ernst in 1936 and was the primary counsel for Alfred Kinsey and the Institute for Sex Research in the 1957 Customs case.

SOURCE: Kinsey Institute Archives, Indiana University.

learned that, although women did not masturbate as frequently as men and did not rely much on erotic materials for masturbation, they did masturbate. For the lawyers, these data seemed to validate their claims that it was nearly impossible to distinguish the direct effects of a particular artifact because, even absent erotic materials, women were sexually allured.[62]

There was virtually no movement by Customs on the matter until November 1955, when Pilpel met with Treasury's solicitor, who suggested willingness to compromise by accepting some of the materials, but not the "dirty postcards." Kinsey refused.[63]

In February 1956 the secretary of the treasury finally ruled, denying the implied exception argument and holding that the *Japanese Pessaries* ruling applied only to the practice of medicine. Because Customs officials found the seized materials obscene, they were not admissible under the secretary's "discretionary authority" granted by the Tariff Act of 1930. The dispute would have to be resolved by the federal courts, which would produce "a ruling applicable to future instances."[64] At long last, Customs officials, under direction from the Treasury, turned the seized materials over to the U.S. Attorneys.

Kinsey was furious and wanted to keep fighting, but he was dying of heart disease. When Kinsey died in August 1956 at age 62, leadership of the institute was turned over to Paul Gebhard, who then became responsible for the lawsuit. Pilpel had long before taken the reins of the institute's defense, and she and her colleagues Nancy Weschler and Leo Rosen were thoroughly prepared when the matter went to trial.

The Defense's Case: Erotica as Raw Data

The official title of the case, *United States v. 31 Photographs 4¾″ × 7″ in size and various pictures, books, and other articles* (156 F. Supp. 350, 1957), highlighted in its name a particular body of photographs, but other materials seized in the seven shipments were also deemed obscene by Customs. They included books that had long been on the Customs list of banned titles, such as Pierre Louÿs's *Manuel de civilité pour les petites filles à l'usage des maisons d'éducation*, the Marquis de Sade's *Les 120 journées de sodome*, and an anonymous pornographic novel, *The Lascivious Hypocrite*.

The libeled artifacts included sheets of graffiti taken from London's public bathrooms, six erotic paintings, twelve lithographs, and several cases containing phallic symbols, antique scrolls, engravings, sculptures, and the Japanese erotica seized by the Indianapolis Customs officials. The three packets containing the photographs were presumably the "dirty postcards" the Treasury solicitor would not compromise on. By any conventional understanding of the word, then or now, the photographs were pornographic. They include one man and two women in various combinations and poses, including shots of cunnilingus, fellatio, intercourse, masturbation with and without a dildo, exposed labial shots, and so forth.

As distinct from all their previous obscenity cases, the Ernst firm lawyers did not try to defend the materials themselves, except as raw data. They did not—perhaps could not—argue for artistic genius, as they had with Joyce, or for the health of women who should not get pregnant, as they had in Sanger's clinic's trial, or for the scholarly importance of a history of contraceptives, as they had with Stopes's *Contraception*. They made no effort to defend the aesthetic or medical value of any of the individual artifacts. The artifacts' value lay in the applied medical and scientific research results they might yield, measured by the value of that research to specialists beyond the Institute for Sex Research. The harm was not in potential arousal but in denying those materials to leading researchers engaged in the work of advancing scientific, medical, and criminological understanding of sexuality and its problems.

Pilpel, Weschler, and Rosen built their case almost entirely around the institute's bona fides as a scientific research entity. The usual concern in obscenity law cases dealing with erotic materials was that the objects would induce morally corrosive lust. The lawyers blunted that concern by repeatedly asserting that the researchers were essentially inured to those corrupting effects of sexual arousal. The artifacts were just data to them. The nonresearchers who might be vulnerable to the materials would also not be corrupted, because the institute secured those materials and kept them locked up. Even in the institute's library itself, "the erotic books and manuscripts are segregated in locked cabinets for which only this affiant, Trustees Martin and Pomeroy, and the librarian, Mrs. Hare, have keys," Gebhard said. None of the material in the institute's research library was circulated. In addition, the 18,000 individual sexual histories that the researchers had taken were kept as confidential material, protected in locked fireproof safes and protected by special coding systems that only the research team knew.[65] In short, there were no vulnerable viewers.

The defense also made an academic freedom argument, one forcefully expressed by Herman B. Wells, Indiana University's president, and its Board of Trustees in their amicus brief. Wells also testified through his affidavit that he and the trustees fully supported the institute as a research arm of the university, whose purposes were intrinsic to the research mission of the modern university: "The Institute scientists, like all the other University scientists, must be free to investigate every aspect of life to the end that knowledge, not ignorance, can be expanded and passed on by the University and its fellow educational institutions."[66]

To build their case, Pilpel and her colleagues obtained detailed affidavits from President Wells, from all the key personnel at the institute, and from distinguished medical and scientific authorities in the fields of penology, psychology, psychiatry, endocrinology, and other medical areas where sexuality (normal and "abnormal") were of concern. The dozen affidavits they obtained described in considerable detail the benefits of the institute's work, present and future. All thirteen affidavits (including Pilpel's) asserted that human sexuality in all its complexity needed study and that the institute provided both raw data and much needed analysis for those purposes.[67]

Paul Gebhard described the institute's immense research undertaking over the previous eighteen years and projected its plans for future research. His affidavit began with a delicious irony: "The Institute has to date amassed and studied factual and theoretical material on human sexual behavior . . . which we believe is more extensive than any other collection, with the exception of that of the Vatican Library in Rome."[68] Gebhard explained that the institute's research made the "actual facts of human sexual behavior . . . available for aid in solving the manifold medical, sociological, legal and other problems which involve sexual behavior."[69] Gebhard also plugged the institute's productivity. Along with its two full-scale research studies based on 18,000 interviews, *Sexual Behavior in the Human Male*

(1948) and *Sexual Behavior in the Human Female* (1953), its researchers had published numerous articles and chapters in other books. Most
important, the institute had a handful of larger-scale projects in progress,
including a study of sex offenders that Gebhard eventually completed as
Sex Offenders: An Analysis of Types (1964). It also planned to produce
other books on such topics as "the heterosexual-homosexual balance";
sexual factors in marriage; "institutional sex adjustment," a matter of serious concern to the penologists who supplied the institute with data;
and "the erotic element in art," a project that would draw on the kinds
of materials at issue in the *31 Photographs* case.[70] Referring to these objects, Gebhard said, "Such representations provide highly significant data
on the sexual interests and desires of the artist or writer who produced
them" and also gave researchers "an invaluable guide to the suppressed
interests and desires of the consuming public," offering evidence of the
wide variability in human sexual desire he described as "the plasticity of
human behavior patterns."[71] All these research fields were related. It was
a matter of scientific principle, Gebhard said, "that all aspects of human
sexual behavior must be studied, including both 'normal' and 'abnormal'
manifestations of sexual behavior."[72] Tying the seized artifacts to his particular work on sex offenders and to the institute's patrons' interests in
understanding sexual pathologies, he said it was imperative to "study and
analyze erotica whose production or consumption may relate to anti-social
or criminal behavior."[73]

The federal government's argument was wholly premised on the idea
that these materials were corrupting of anyone who might encounter them
and that they could have no value because they were pornographic. It was a
species of statutory literalism we have seen in earlier cases: Because the artifacts were ipso facto obscene, there could be no "implied exception" under
the Tariff Act's provisions. No one should see this rank stuff, and the human
interest in pornographic materials was deeply troubling. Because there was
no legitimate use of pornography, these "data" could not be defended as
having any kind of legitimate value either. (Both Bok and Frank, the most
progressive jurists in this arena, would also deny them legal protection.)
They were simply "dirt for dirt's sake," to use Judge Woolsey's phrase.

In stark contrast to the defense that Pilpel and her team built, however, the U.S. Attorneys offered no affidavits or other expert testimony about the materials or the vulnerability of the researchers, or from anyone denying that those materials were adequately secured and protected from the public, or even from anyone criticizing the institute's work in general. This did not go unnoticed by Judge Edmund L. Palmieri of the Southern District of New York, who presided over the case and commented in his decision on the stark imbalance between the evidence mustered by the defense and the prosecution.

The Hearing and Decision

Harriet Pilpel and Assistant U.S. Attorney Benjamin T. Richards Jr. offered oral arguments before U.S. District Court judge Palmieri in July 1957, just a few weeks after the U.S. Supreme Court handed down its decision in *Roth/Alberts v. United States* in June. That decision would have bearing on the *31 Photographs* case but was not decisive because the institute's case was a Tariff Act matter, not a First Amendment case challenging the constitutionality of the obscenity statute. Kenneth Stevens describes Pilpel's oral arguments and some of the case law she drew on in his article on the Kinsey's institute's case. Along with asserting the implied exception argument, Pilpel "also maintained that obscenity was not absolute," as the government asserted, but "variable and dependent on use, as set down in *U.S. v. Levine*" (1936).[74] Pilpel assured the judge that the materials in question would not "arouse the lasciviousness of institute researchers," because they had no salacious interests in the materials.[75] She also advanced their academic freedom argument, developed further in the amicus brief filed by the Indiana University Board of Trustees. Pilpel offered a motion for summary judgment, but Judge Palmieri denied it and requested briefs from both sides.

U.S. Attorney Richards contended that the materials were clearly obscene and were not analogous to the physicians' importation of contraceptives in the *Japanese Pessaries* decision, so there was no implied exception for these libeled materials. Absent an implied exception, the tariff statute was clear about prohibiting the importation of obscene materials, and thus "it was the duty of the court" to enforce the tariff statute. Amending the Tariff Act was Congress's duty, not the court's, and should the court "permit itself to be lured into legislative action in the guise of an implied exception," Richards argued, "it would virtually nullify the obscenity provision of the Tariff Act and invite wholesale commercial traffic in foreign pornography imported and distributed by spurious scientific organizations."[76] Richards then invoked the *Roth/Alberts* (1957) decision, explaining that this most recent Supreme Court ruling supported the government's position because it "affirmed the doctrine that obscenity was outside the bounds of constitutional protection. Since the institute materials were admittedly obscene, they could claim no constitutional refuge."[77] Pilpel, who had written an amicus brief to the Supreme Court on behalf of Roth, offered a decidedly different interpretation of how the *Roth/Alberts* decision should be applied to the *31 Photographs* case.

Although it had only partial bearing on the case, a brief explanation of the 1957 *Roth/Alberts* decision is in order. This combined case was the first time in the twentieth century that the U.S. Supreme Court agreed to hear a constitutional challenge to obscenity law. And, for good measure, this case once again featured Samuel Roth as the appellant.[78] Roth had been convicted of mailing books, periodicals, and photographs (and circulars advertising those materials) alleged to be "obscene, lewd, lascivious, filthy and of an indecent character." The main artifact was his magazine, *American Aphrodite*, which featured erotic tales and nude photographs.[79] A lower federal court trial jury found Roth guilty on four counts and not guilty on nineteen, and the trial judge sentenced him to five years' imprisonment and imposed a fine of $5,000. On his appeal to the Court of Appeals for the Second Circuit in 1956, Roth challenged the constitutionality of the obscenity statute, trying to finally force the First Amendment question of whether the federal obscenity statute under which he had been convicted was constitutional.[80]

This was the moment for Judge Frank to take up these issues once again, and he once again used a concurring opinion to challenge his Second Circuit colleagues' reading of obscenity law. He attempted to persuade the Supreme Court that it needed to face the problems with obscenity law, given recent developments in First Amendment law, with the clear and present danger doctrine more firmly in place and with a greater body of social scientific information available about the effects of reading on people's behavior.[81] In many ways Frank was returning to, updating, and forcing reconsideration of positions he raised in his concurring opinion seven years earlier, but now backed by further developments in the law, in the social sciences, and in the culture generally.

Even though Judge Clark wrote the majority decision for the appeals court, upholding Roth's conviction, his opinion is a footnote in the history of obscenity jurisprudence. Judge Frank's concurring opinion in *Roth/ Alberts v. United States* was the one that mattered. He persuasively updated his 1949 opinion, making it even more forceful. About proof of effects, for instance, he laid out his two main objections to the obscenity statutes in the body of his concurrence. First, he addressed the absence of proof of effects, and then he critiqued the presumption that sexual thoughts and feelings, or even actions, could be overtly dangerous or antisocial.

> The troublesome aspect of the federal obscenity statute . . . is that (a) no one can now show that, with any reasonable probability obscene publications tend to have any effects on the behavior of normal, average adults, and (b) that under that statute, as judicially interpreted, punishment is apparently inflicted for provoking, in such adults, undesirable sexual thoughts, feelings, or desires—not overt dangerous or anti-social conduct, either actual or probable.[82]

He also clarified the usefulness of the clear and present danger test, arguing that the *probability* of immediate danger ought to be the only ground on which speech should be punishable: "At any rate, it would seem that (1) the danger or evil must be clear (i.e., identifiable) and substantial, and (2) that, since the statute renders words punishable, it is invalid unless those words tend, with a fairly high degree of probability, to incite to overt conduct which is obviously harmful."[83]

Recognizing the forcefulness of Frank's arguments (which also included a rich paean to Judge Bok's 1949 decision) and the need to finally address the pressing question of whether the obscenity statutes were unconstitutional because they violated the First Amendment, the U.S. Supreme Court agreed to hear Roth's case on appeal and did so in 1957 in the *Roth/Alberts* case.[84] The Court combined Roth's case with that of David Albert's. Alberts ran a mail order business in California; he had been convicted of violating California's obscenity statute for publishing photos of nude women and also appealed his conviction on First Amendment grounds. Their cases were similar enough that the Court heard them together.

The Supreme Court's *Roth/Alberts* decision was complicated and a halfway measure of sorts. Justice Brennan, writing for the majority, wrote that even though sex is "a great and mysterious motive force in human life" and "a subject of absorbing interest to mankind through the ages," obscenity was not "within the area of constitutionality protected speech or press." So, on the one hand, the ruling affirmed the constitutionality of the obscenity statutes, holding that the First Amendment did not protect "obscene" materials. Because both Roth and Alberts were distributing obscene materials, the Court upheld their convictions. On the other hand, the Court also recognized people's abiding interest in sexual matters, stating that "sexual frankness and obscenity are not synonymous."[85] The Court offered a four-pronged test that differentiated truly obscene works from sexually frank materials, creating exceptions to the obscenity test and providing room for the defense of sexually frank artifacts, particularly literary and artistic works. The test of obscenity was thus: "whether to the average person, applying contemporary standards, the dominant theme of the materials taken as a whole appeals to prurient interest."[86] This was essentially both a negative and a positive test, because it was also interpreted as meaning that the Court ruled that a work could be found not obscene if it had the slightest redeeming social importance, did not predominantly appeal to prurient interest, was directed at adults, and was not offensive to local community standards.[87]

Given the complexity of the Supreme Court ruling and its proximity to the *31 Photographs* case, both sides of the *31 Photographs* case claimed it as authoritative. In her Claimant's Brief, Pilpel and her team recognized that, although the Supreme Court had indeed affirmed the constitutionality of the obscenity law, it had also opened up the law by offering exceptions for materials with serious scientific, literary, artistic, or historical significance.[88] In this instance, the imported materials had definite scientific interest. Moreover, there was a critical distinction between the *Roth/Alberts* case and the institute's. The institute was not engaged in the commercial distribution of erotic or pornographic materials, whereas both Roth and Alberts had been. Because the institute's purposes with such materials were not commercial, the *Roth/Alberts* ruling should not control this action, despite what the U.S. Attorneys asserted. Pilpel also pointed out that the Court's *Roth/Alberts* decision recognized specific exceptions, including the "dissemination [of materials] to institutions or individuals having scientific or other special justification for possessing such material."[89]

Pilpel and her team must have read the Supreme Court's 1957 *Roth/Alberts* decision more carefully than the U.S. Attorneys had, because they were able to point out that even the U.S. government's own solicitor general in the *Roth/Alberts* case had invoked the institute's legitimate work to draw a distinction between different kinds of sexual materials, such as those purveyed by Roth and Alberts, and those reported on by scholars, such as Kinsey and his team. Pilpel's brief distilled these implications for Judge Palmieri: The institute could study these materials and also "freely circulate to the general public the conclusions drawn from a study of sexual behavior."[90] Elsewhere in the brief, Pilpel quoted Justice Brennan and asserted that "it is clear from this passage that scholarly exposition on sexual matters was recognized as excluded from the ban of the law."[91]

Pilpel and her team argued that the recently decided academic freedom case *Sweezy v. New Hampshire* (1957) should be the controlling case. It bolstered their academic freedom position that the federal government should not hamper freedom of scientific inquiry at a state university.[92] The libeled materials were intrinsic to the institute's academic purposes, as testified to by the many affiants.[93] She added, "Research into human sexual behavior which ignored the evidence of erotic literature or art would be incomplete."[94]

On the question of Customs' authority to seize obscene materials, Pilpel denied the applicability of Section 305 to materials imported specifically for scientific research purposes. She did not deny the legitimacy of the Tariff Act generally but argued that it had always provided exceptions for scientific and medical uses, including research, and that a "continuous stream" of decisions had recognized such a "conditional privilege," including the *Japanese Pessaries* decision (1936) and the *Nicholas/Himes* ruling (1938).[95] The body of case law that the Greenbaum, Wolff & Ernst firm had helped establish proved useful once again.

Judge Palmieri's Decision

On October 31, 1957, Judge Palmieri ruled in favor of the Institute for Sex Research in *United States v. 31 Photographs*. His decision rested almost entirely on the question of whether or not the imported materials violated the provisions of Section 305(a) of the Tariff Act of 1930. Interestingly, he essentially refused to address the academic freedom argument, stating, "The question of 'academic freedom,' much bruited in the oral argument by claimant, does not arise in this case."[96] Judge Palmieri fully accepted the institute's arguments about the scientific, academic, and medical value of those materials, the protected nature of those materials, and the researchers' immunity. He did not question that the material would be off limits to members of the general public and available only "for the sole use of the Institute staff members or of qualified scholars engaged in bona fide research."[97] Thus its potential harms were negligible. The *Roth/Alberts* decision had clarified this matter for him, because it articulated a variable effects argument, holding that the question of prurient effect in this case was not about its potentially harmful effects on the average person but on the individuals most likely to encounter these carefully controlled and sequestered materials. Neither the average person nor the public at large was in harm's way.[98] This clearly had become the standard test in the federal courts by 1957. Palmieri also made the same argument that other judges in the same era were making: that the courts needed greater evidence of harmful effects. The government needed a "beholder," he suggested, because the test of prurient appeal could not be determined "without reference to any beholder": "It should be obvious that obscenity must be judged by the material's appeal to somebody."[99] Specificity of audience and the particular uses of suspect materials mattered: "For what is obscenity to one person is but a subject of scientific inquiry to another."[100]

Palmieri also rejected the government's claim that these materials were not necessary to the institute's purposes. "The Tariff Act of 1930 provides no warrant for either customs officials or this court to sit in review of the decisions of scholars as to the bypaths of learning upon which they shall tread."[101] But he also made it clear that this decision was specific to this institution and these particular circumstances and that it did not extend to those who sought to import or sell or distribute these materials for the purposes of "pandering" or to those who simply sought them for "private indulgence." He was not denying the fact that the government, on behalf of the public, had a compelling and legitimate interest in controlling obscene materials. He recognized the government's fear of the slippery slope, that "fake" so-called institutes claiming exceptions would crop up. The proof of seriousness demonstrated by Kinsey's institute, he wrote, "will be a threshold inquiry in each case."[102] Henceforth the burden of establishing serious institutional bona fides would be great.

Harm and Value

Neither the Customs Service nor the U.S. Attorneys sought to appeal this decision, so Judge Palmieri's ruling stood. Reflecting several months later on the implications of the decision, Pilpel framed it in broad terms for Gebhard and Pomeroy. Their case, she wrote, "had revolutionized the law by establishing that the concept of obscenity *per se* is a thing of the past—that from now on, nothing can be considered obscene until the circumstances of its project use are known. Good law—and you and we made it."[103]

The Ernst law firm claimed the largest possible implications for this decision. In the firm's leather-bound volume of materials surrounding the case, it appended an analysis of the decision and explained its importance. Accepting the Customs Service's argument that a decision such as this should be made by the federal courts (and not by the Customs solicitor or by U.S. Attorneys), the Ernst firm argued that Judge Palmieri's ruling was determinative and would likely remain the test case on such a matter: "Although the only ruling was that of the District Court, the opinion is considered authoritative."[104] They located this decision in that "continuous stream" of decisions about serious scientific and medical uses they had begun with the *Dennett* case and advanced with Stopes's *Contraception* case, Sanger's *Japanese Pessaries* case, and the *Himes/Nicholas* case. Placing it as well within the trajectory of significant free speech cases, they wrote, "The result has been to establish a clear-cut affirmation of the principle that the subject matter of objective scholarly inquiry is not an object of federal prohibition. This principle has obvious implications for freedom of the mind in many fields."[105]

The upshot for obscenity law jurisprudence was that by 1957 the new test or standard in the federal courts was that materials were not obscene per se but obscene only in relation to their harmful or prurient effects on some particular audience or user. Judge Palmieri's decision also reflects the effective strategy that Ernst and his colleagues had worked out in their decades challenging obscenity law restrictions. By calling into question the state's assumptions of harm and replacing claims of harm with arguments about value and seriousness of purpose, the Ernst firm won another landmark case.

The case continued the Ernst firm's sexual liberalism project. From the moment Ernst tried to connect himself to Kinsey, he recognized the value of the institute's research for what he called the project of "sexual enlightenment." He saw that the research, with its reams of data and applied science prospects, could help the courts think more carefully about sex, with greater nuance about cause and effects, variability, and the legitimacy of people's interest in sexual materials. Most important, Kinsey's institute gave far greater scientific authority to the study of sex and exploded assumptions about how people actually behaved. As Whitney Strub writes, Kinsey's research pointed to the "overwhelming conclusion that Americans preached one sexual doctrine and practiced another. Not only was premarital, extramarital, and autoerotic sexual behavior widespread and statistically 'normal' (a word Kinsey rejected, precisely for its easy slide into enforced norms), but so were same-sex activity."[106] As Ernst and Lindey had long been arguing, the law needed greater precision and better evidence about actual sexual behaviors and the effects of sexually themed materials on those behaviors.

Ernst and his colleagues successfully pushed the courts to recognize that in criminal law the state could not assert harm without demonstrating it—that clients should not be forced to guess themselves into (or out of) jail. In *United States v. 31 Photographs* Judge Palmieri clearly rejected the state's failure to prove harmful effects along with its failure to even assert a specific beholder who would be affected. This is what Ernst, Bok, and Frank had hoped for when they began their colloquy in 1948. Nearly a decade after Ernst and Kinsey first teamed up, Judge Palmieri rendered a verdict that essentially accepted all their arguments.

FROM THE FIRST TO THE SECOND SEXUAL REVOLUTION

HOW SHOULD WE ASSESS or think about the lasting effects or implications of the legal openings secured by Ernst and his colleagues and the
harm versus value framework they used? They defended the expansion of
knowledge, sharpened legal categories, and provided for adult indepen-
dence from laws and cultural mores rooted in patriarchal, paternalistic assumptions about individuals' weaknesses and the need for protection from
their own desires. The second sexual revolution that followed ushered in
the present age of greater sexual understanding and access that Ernst's
team fought for, but we are still faced with patriarchal oppression. Women
endure misogyny, sexual violence and exploitation, and cruel conditions
of poverty, and Comstock's paternalistic heirs' fear of female sexuality and
insistence on controlling women's sexual autonomy and reproductive self-
determination continues to be a driving force in U.S. politics.

Ernst and his colleagues took up their campaign against U.S. obscenity
laws because those laws blocked the advance of human understanding about
sexuality and violated free press ideals. They aimed to protect morality by
halting the flow of materials that might stimulate sexual desires and that
were especially hostile to women's knowledge about and access to birth control, hindering women's (and couples') efforts to manage their reproductive
lives. The laws impeded literary and artistic expression by writers who dared
probe the mysteries of sexuality. They inflicted cautiousness, self-censorship,
and inhibition on writers, publishers, and booksellers and facilitated a black

market in pirated and unlicensed works that denied the original authors' their due. The federal statutes—reinforced by mini–Comstock statutes in all the states but New Mexico—gave U.S. Postal and Customs agents powerful search and seizure weapons. They cut a wide swath, reinforced by local and state police, vice society investigators, theater and film licensing authorities, and others charged with policing the world of "vice" in theaters, photography studios, underground printing shops, barber shops, saloons, dance halls, newsstands, bookstores, publishers' warehouses, and drugstores.

For Ernst and his colleagues, the value of sexual knowledge and the right of public access to serious materials dealing with sexual matters far outweighed the potential harms of sexual arousal resulting from those materials, especially for the adult public. The value of adult (married) women having access to dependable, safe, inexpensive contraceptives far exceeded any harms that might result from this, harms usually articulated through theological and moral frameworks rather than scientific or medical ones. The demonstrable value of these materials, compared to assertions of harm, in combination with the heavy-handed administration of the obscenity laws by anonymous unchecked Postal and Customs bureaucrats at the federal level or by vice society minions at the local level, also gave their work the aspect of an anti-censorship crusade. Their legal campaign—aided by the ACLU, sympathetic journalists, and public intellectuals—gained support and momentum in the court of public opinion because they had useful foils in droves: policeman, churchmen, Postal and Customs officials, and especially New York Vice Society's John Sumner, who did not object to being photographed shoveling books into a hot furnace. But the key enemy was always Anthony Comstock and the anti-intellectual, antimodern, antisexual attitudes compressed into the label Comstockery.

Comstock's legal and administrative legacy gave Comstockery a long life in the nation's laws, undergirding federal and state censorship policies and activities well into the 1950s and beyond, and aspects of Comstockery's patriarchal and restrictive impulses toward women remain powerful in the culture, especially in reproductive politics. Those laws were aimed at controlling the arousal of lust through the written word. More important, they were rooted in the impulse to control women's sexuality and to make sure that women were not in control of their own reproductive capacities or had the freedom to engage in sex for pleasure. Ernst and his colleagues understood the connections between reading about sex, having greater knowledge of it, being able to control reproduction, and taking pleasure in sex. They were up against powerful cultural impulses and legal obstacles.

Those laws' defenders used the language, and threat, of impending moral and cultural harms, emphasizing human weakness and the linkages between sex and sin. They knew that an unregulated marketplace of goods would be filled with tawdry, exploitative materials and suffered no illusions that the marketplace would lead readers and viewers down an enlightened path or advance human progress. They warned that purveyors of sexual frankness would appeal to base instincts and animal desires, undermine morality and self-discipline, threaten the family, and degrade the human prospect. The public needed protection, the market needed regulation, and legal authorities, especially judges, had a duty to cultivate a public sphere that would uplift the public and protect civilization and its norms.

Concerns about a tawdry marketplace were not unfounded. But Ernst and his partners offered persuasive arguments that the capacious obscenity laws lagged far behind dramatic changes in the culture and that the value of the particular works they defended far outweighed the harms asserted by the state. The courts needed to administer laws that accounted for contemporary tastes and practices and distinguished between adult publics and vulnerable youth. They assailed the imprecise language of the statutes, pointing to the essentially subjective definitions of such terms as *lewd, lascivious, dirty,* and other adjectives used to "define" obscenity. Such vagueness was indefensible as the grounding for criminal prosecutions, they argued, and the widely used Hicklin standard that assumed so-called obscene materials would necessarily deprave and corrupt vulnerable audiences required more than mere assertion to meet the standards of criminal law.

Ernst and his colleagues accumulated a core body of arguments that served as the backbone in virtually all their cases, arguments that were steadily accepted by the courts and helped shift the role of the state from one of paternalistic protector of childlike vulnerable citizens to an arbiter of adult marketplaces of knowledge and entertainment.

- Sexual morality had evolved considerably from the mid-nineteenth century when the Comstock laws were conceived, to the 1930s and beyond, and the legal standards for libeling materials as obscene needed to account for change over time.
- The courts had to jettison the Hicklin standard, with its presumption of easily depraved and corrupted (youthful) readers as the only readers or viewers at stake. Courts also needed to consider the average adult reader, who should be perceived as rational, mature, stable, and in control of his or her impulses, emotions, and behavior. Moreover, because books were just one source of ideas and influence in a modern, mass-mediated society, it was impossible to blame any given book for corrupting unspecified readers or viewers.
- Instead of relying solely on judges' and juries' assessment of the harms of libeled material, the courts needed to draw on the expertise of scientific, medical, and literary authorities who could testify to their value.
- The circulation of goods in a respectable marketplace of ideas mattered, and those institutions in the legitimate book-world marketplace could be depended on. The openness of the legitimate marketplace (as opposed to underground nature of pornography) provided clear evidence of a work's seriousness and potential value.
- Instead of being assessed on the basis of mere parts or passages, books should be read as a whole.
- Instead of accepting prosecutorial assertions of likely moral harm to an undefined but presumably vulnerable public, the courts needed to pay more attention to questions and evidence of harm.
- And finally, even though the First Amendment did not protect obscenity per se, obscenity statutes undermined the promise of the Bill of Rights and interfered with the rich marketplace of ideas necessary to navigate the complexities of modern living.

By the time Morris Ernst left the censorship battleground in the late 1950s, even the federal courts had recognized that perhaps there was no necessary harm in adults becoming sexually aroused by materials aimed at producing that arousal. Whatever harms might result from the production and distribution of pornography, its consumption by adults was a private matter. State intrusion into the realm of adult fantasy would be an unacceptable violation of protections offered by the Bill of Rights, particularly the First Amendment.

It is worth recalling, however, that despite the greater latitude that the 1957 *Roth/Alberts* decision gave to predominantly sexually themed materials, the U.S. Supreme Court still held that obscenity statutes did not violate constitutional protections and that the government maintained an abiding interest in prohibiting distribution of materials "utterly without redeeming social importance."[1] This meant that the courts would get bogged down trying to work out obscenity law solutions to explicitly pornographic materials for decades while providing greater room for the kinds of literary works that were challenged on the grounds of obscenity but were ultimately widely available, such as D. H. Lawrence's *Lady Chatterley's Lover*, Henry Miller's *Tropic of Cancer*, and even John Cleland's classic work of erotica, *Fanny Hill*. Those debates and often-contradictory decisions have been well covered by many distinguished scholars and lawyers.[2]

Ernst, Alexander Lindey, Harriet Pilpel, and other lawyers in the Greenbaum, Wolff & Ernst law firm had the foremost role in transforming obscenity jurisprudence until World War II, when battles over obscenity law took a back seat to other kinds of emergency-era censorship. They used the publicity around their courtroom fights to help articulate and promote an inchoate anti-censorship strain in American liberalism and, even without First Amendment backing, put the protection of literary, artistic, and sexual speech at the center of the U.S. free speech tradition. In short, they shrunk the dominion of the nation's obscenity laws, especially over "serious" cultural expression such as Joyce's *Ulysses* and Hall's *Well of Loneliness*, over scientifically and medically credible information about sex, and significantly advanced the birth control movement's aims of securing women greater access to contraceptive devices and knowledge.

Ernst and his colleagues crucially paved the way for women to assert their interest in sexual information and to claim autonomy as sexual beings with vital interests in controlling their reproductive lives. They did not defend pornographic works, although they did defend the right of Kinsey's

Institute for Sex Research to import such works for research purposes. They aimed to protect women's reproductive autonomy and their rights of access to information about contraception as well as the right to publish, sell, and obtain serious works of literature with sexual themes. Those outcomes had clear value in their harm versus value matrix. They did not aim to ensure the growing right of men (primarily) to have access to increasingly graphic sexual images of women—the value of that was not so clear to them nor were those cases likely winnable. But the legal arguments they helped to frame certainly opened the door to the next phase of obscenity jurisprudence, which dealt directly with pornography.

Ernst and his colleagues carefully selected their cases, choosing to fight on behalf of reputable, if controversial, writers and activists whose works had demonstrable value. Their clients' reputations for excellence and the support they could muster for those claims made it far easier to defend them than if they had been anonymous purveyors of tawdry goods. Case by well-chosen case they slowly created both categorical and artifact-specific exceptions to the reach of censorship laws. Because the federal courts would not take up the question of whether the obscenity laws violated First Amendment guarantees (until the *Roth* case in 1957, when Ernst and Pilpel submitted an amicus brief), the only legal route was to show that the particular artifact or object libeled by the censorship authorities was not in fact obscene. Thus Ernst's team fought their cases at the level of definitions, the vagueness of statutory language, and the inapplicability of that damning obscenity libel to the specific, credible artifacts they defended.

This book does tell a story of progress in the civil libertarian tradition, premised on the idea that Americans ought to have the right to know more about their bodies and the complicated world of sexuality. Focusing on First Amendment law and judicial opinion is the usual narrative frame for detailing the growth of the civil libertarian tradition, but like Leigh Ann Wheeler in her monumental study *How Sex Became a Civil Liberty*, in this book I have focused on the development of the civil libertarian tradition in the realm of sex and physical autonomy. Ernst often described his work as the project of "sex enlightenment," and his contemporaries recognized his firm's victories as key civil liberties developments. Ernst and colleagues' anti-censorship campaign achieved free speech advances in the realm of obscenity law, paralleling developments in First Amendment jurisprudence in the same era. Ernst's description of his work as advancing sex enlightenment knowingly anchored his project in the larger free speech, civil liberties history. Indeed, legal historian Roger Newman called Ernst the most important civil libertarian of the first half of the twentieth century.

Whether Ernst, Lindey, Pilpel, and others in their law firm were primarily civil libertarians, primarily eager opponents of Comstockery and censorship, or champions of sexual knowledge and information as their organizing principle doesn't really matter. All those commitments converged: Advancing civil liberties, fighting censorship, making the law compatible with actual public interests and needs, and contributing to public enlightenment about a vital matter of human concern—all came together under the umbrella of free speech principles in the service of public knowledge. They married larger civil libertarian principles to their core argument about sex rationality or sex enlightenment, consistently asserting that the public ought to have access to credible, serious sexual information, lest it suffer from ignorance, superstition, shame, compromised health, economic hardship, and unhappy marriages.

Although Ernst and his colleagues barely hinted at the right to pursue sexual pleasure (and never suggested the right to become aroused) in their legal arguments, the works they defended certainly claimed the right, and value, of sexual pleasure. Mary Ware Dennett, Marie Stopes, Radclyffe Hall, James Joyce, Margaret Sanger, and Alfred Kinsey all expressed and extolled sexual or erotic pleasure as a fundamental human desire and need. Indeed, those writers' affirmation of the value of sexual knowledge, desire, delight, rumination, expression, and especially reproductive control were the very harms that the censors, prosecutors, and their expert witnesses invoked in their efforts to block those works from being published and distributed.

Ernst and his firm gave legal counsel to some of the central agents of the first sexual revolution. Although their clients did not fully articulate the right to sexual pleasure as a *human right*, they came close, and this posed a revolutionary challenge to Victorian ideals and norms about sexual reticence generally (and female virtue specifically) that the paternalistic laws were premised on and meant to reinforce. Ernst's firm defended women who violated those norms, defending the right of women to write and publish about how women might achieve orgasms if their mates paid closer attention to female desire. They championed the right of lesbian authors to write about same-sex love and attraction and promoted that knowledge as valuable against bigotry and ignorance, aiding peoples' understanding of homosexual individuals punished by a social and cultural order that denied them legitimacy as sexual and emotional beings. They argued that women needed contraceptive information and access to birth control devices to control their lives, achieve greater happiness, be healthier, have better marriages, and rear healthier offspring. And they defended modernist literary expression as intellectually equivalent to the greatest scientific achievements of the age. Across these fields, they helped make anti-censorship principles the core precepts of modern American liberalism.

In short, Ernst and colleagues built a corpus of arguments that exposed the conceptual and evidentiary problems with the nation's obscenity laws. In this way, they helped facilitate the next sexual revolution, by making birth control information and devices easier to obtain and thus clearing the way to the birth control pill. They also implicitly advanced the privacy claims that surround legal abortions. By making it more difficult to prosecute legitimate works of literature with sexual themes and incidents and by making it harder for prosecutors to argue and judges to accept claims that materials specifically aimed at sexual arousal were ipso facto harmful, they paved the way in the law for implicit protection of adult sexual arousal. That the presumptive audience for sexual materials aimed at arousal was male went without saying. Later in his career, Ernst bemoaned the corrosive, debasing effects of pornography along with cinematic and television violence.

When Ernst left the obscenity law battles in the late 1950s, he did not anticipate that one of the long-term consequences of his firm's legal work would result in the unleashing of "anything goes" pornography and the limitation of beyond-the-pale obscenity to the sexual exploitation of children and youth. By the 1960s Ernst was, in fact, chagrined that their work had resulted in the profusion of materials that he thought were coarse, degrading, exploitative, sadistic, and shockingly violent. Their goal had been to provide greater space for the flow of works of literary and artistic distinction, works that promoted and deepened human understanding of human sexuality, and they succeeded.

Indeed, the legal foundation Ernst helped to build to protect cultural, literary, and sexual speech and protect access to contraception paved the way for the second sexual revolution. This revolution, which essentially took off with Kinsey's studies, encompassed the popularity of *Playboy* and other soft-core pornography, the development of the birth control pill, the rise of second-wave feminism, and then the explosion of more sexually explicit literature, magazines, film, and photography in combination with the free love ethos of the late 1960s and 1970s and the insistent presence and advancement of a burgeoning gay and lesbian rights movement. The manuals, books, poems, novels, essays, polemics, films, and other artifacts produced in the second sexual revolution met far less censorship and thus were more easily distributed than those artifacts pushing up against the obscenity laws in the first half of the twentieth century. They helped to educate following generations about sexuality, reduced shame, helped to spread birth control, and increased women's autonomy.

The history of Ernst's work defending the first sexual revolution is crucial to the ways in which more sexually honest cultural expression and the rights to sexual knowledge and reproductive control have become ineluctably tied to our sense of ourselves as modern humans. Some of the central issues that Ernst's firm fought for, especially women's reproductive autonomy, remain a perpetual source of political controversy and site of conservative political mobilization, in part because the patriarchal dimensions of Comstockery remain steadfast in the culture, especially concerning control over women's bodies. Enlarging civil liberties made women's greater freedoms possible, but those freedoms were hard won and are still under threat in a political environment in which men (primarily) continue to strive to enforce strict limits on women's reproductive choices. For example, Planned Parenthood, for which both Ernst and Pilpel served as counsel, is constantly under scrutiny; its funding is precarious, and its support for legal abortion means that all the sex information and contraceptive services it provides are tenuous, including sex education for LGBTQ+

youth, prenatal and postnatal health care, provision of safe, dependable, affordable birth control, and provision of legal abortion services. Planned Parenthood is a lightning rod.

Curiously, control over men's sexuality (a matter of considerable concern to Comstock and his successors) is barely discussed in the contemporary political arena; battles over restricting birth control and abortion are far more important litmus tests on the political right than are, for instance, problems of sexual exploitation and violence against women. A quick take might be that men's sexual interests and prerogatives, illustrated by the endless supply of pornographic images of women engaged in or available for sex, has gone largely unchecked by the law in the last seven or so decades. The question about the "harm" of such arousal to male viewers is barely sustained as a question (nor is there a sustained political inquiry into the harms to the flesh-and-blood women being trafficked, degraded, and exploited in the sex industries that serve men's fantasies). The global pornography industry as an inexorable machinery of male fantasies and female debasement is largely unchecked, unregulated, and immensely profitable, but women's access to affordable birth control is consistently challenged and under threat, is not guaranteed, depends on one's employer's insurance policies, and varies by state. The legal right to safe, medically supervised abortions depends even more on state-by-state restrictions and has been continuously under attack politically and legally since 1973, following the Supreme Court's decision in *Roe v. Wade*. The sexual prerogatives of a misogynistic society are laid bare in that basic juxtaposition.

Even so, the first and second sexual revolutions have produced greater human freedom around sexuality. People are freer than ever before as sexual beings—free to love whom they want to love, to marry, and to form families with, or not, without sacrificing intimate relations and sexual pleasure. They are freer to choose their bodies and identities as sexual beings. There is increasing awareness of the ubiquitous problems of and threats of sexual violence, intimidation, and harassment. People know more about and can speak more freely about their desires, fantasies, and pleasures. Despite the continuing challenges and threats, women have greater control over their reproductive lives than ever before, giving them more autonomy about when and whether they will have children. Queer people can enjoy far greater openness and public presence, self-determination, economic and political rights, and increasingly understanding and protection from abuse, shame, and prejudice. The first and second sexual revolutions have produced more human freedom around sexuality.

Where do we place Ernst and his colleagues in this story of greater sexual knowledge and freedom? As a consequence of their work, we live in a society with a history of increasing sexual liberty—greater freedom of inquiry, knowledge, expression, and rights of personhood as sexual beings. The story of freedom runs from greater access to safe, dependable birth control devices, to the development of the birth control pill and the revolutionary economic and individual freedom it has engendered for three full generations of American women, enhancing married and unmarried women's sexual autonomy and self-determination. The story of increased freedom for queer people—from the beginnings of the gay and lesbian rights movement, through ACT UP activism, queer porn, gay marriage and rights of adoption, through increasing attention to trans presence and trans rights—are all buttressed by deeply developed notions in the culture and the law protecting personal sexual privacy, sexual selfhood, reproductive autonomy, self-determination, and the right to not be discriminated against on the basis of sex and sexual identity. As Wheeler makes clear, sex became a civil liberty across many fronts.

However, these rights and freedoms are politically and legally vulnerable in contemporary U.S. political culture. They remain controversial and are continually contested. The steady cultural and legal advance of a society premised on and committed to the protection of sexual freedom divides American society and roils American politics; sex has been the main issue of most of the culture war disputes over the last four or five decades. The nation's courts have remained the site where our deepest political and cultural battles over sex get heard and "resolved." But legal decisions do not solve cultural conflicts, so the core conflicts remain at the center of our political culture and resurface with great regularity (especially at election time, when reactionary forces hope to rile up and mobilize voters, or whenever a Supreme Court seat is filled). Political and legal challenges to people's rights of privacy, rights of sexual selfhood, rights of reproductive autonomy, rights of equal access, the right to reproductive health care, and rights against discrimination based on sexual preference or identity remain battlegrounds, sites of political (and voter) mobilization and sustained political warfare. The tumult over women's right to reproductive control is perpetual. Clearly, women's sexuality, far more than men's sexuality, is a source of anxiety and site of attack, as was the case when Marie Stopes, Radclyffe Hall, Mary Ware Dennett, and Margaret Sanger were active, provoking changes and winning legal battles. As Senator Kamala Harris pointed out when questioning Supreme Court nominee Brett Kavanagh, there is no area of the law where the state attempts to regulate men's bodies. Yet women's bodies are continually objects of possible or actual state regulation, making female sexual autonomy (and female sexuality) a continuous matter of political and cultural dispute. Indeed, women's right to sexual autonomy, moral anxieties about female sexuality, and control of women's reproductive lives are hardly discernible as discrete categories because they are so intimately connected.

In addition, women continue to be attacked for being sexual beings in ways men have never been. Assumptions that women's bodies are the subjects of men's political and personal access, and state control, sit at the heart of patriarchal thinking—as they did in the age of Comstock. Likewise many people still believe that women and their sexual purity embody or represent the moral condition of the body politic and that they are primarily morally responsible for the family and the future of the nation's citizens. In this framework, women's sexuality reflects the nation's moral well-being. Yet issues of violence against women, women's economic inequality and greater rates of poverty, racism combined with sexism, and economic and sexual exploitation do not fit into the conservative patriarchal framework of concerns about women and their bodies. Instead of addressing the real harms that still fall mostly on women—violence and poverty—they remain obsessed with the need to control women's sexuality and their autonomy or to punish queer and trans people for daring to claim a public presence.

I have written about the Ernstian project of sex enlightenment and his aim to secure greater sexual knowledge and women's reproductive autonomy because he and his colleagues so skillfully attacked the cultural and legal obstacles to those freedoms and pleasures in their era. They understood the implicit link between the right to be an informed, educated, free sexual being as fundamental to human freedom—and they especially understood that this was core to women's freedoms. They helped secure greater intellectual and personal autonomy for generations of Americans and set the stage for additional battles over sexual knowledge and bodily autonomy. This book is a story of progress based in intellectual and sexual freedom. Even though it only nods to these issues and battles in the contemporary era, I trust it helps to explain why earlier battles over sexual information, artistic expression, and reproductive autonomy were so fraught historically and why they matter so much today. The issues Ernst and his team took up continue to roil the culture and the courts today.

MORRIS ERNST'S COMPLICATED LEGACY

ERNST, LINDEY, PILPEL, THEIR CLIENTS, and their supporters and experts all chafed against the idea of censorship, arguing that in a society with a free speech tradition censorship was prima facie illegitimate, anti-intellectual, paternalistic, and old-fashioned. They won their battles in part because they effectively mobilized an already available free speech tradition and lexicon; they gave voice to a body of arguments against censorship and on behalf of deeply held ideas about free speech and political liberty that were familiar and amenable to Americans across social classes.

But other latent forces were operating in the culture as well, including the willingness to censor dangerous political ideas and individuals, and those forces came crashing to the surface in the late 1930s. They did not recede for decades. The free speech commitments of even Ernst and his ACLU colleagues proved fragile, tenuous, and historically contingent when confronted with speech and political associations that seemed to them potentially threatening. Indeed, at the very moment that Ernst and his colleagues were achieving their greatest successes in the courts in expanding that free speech tradition in the cultural and sexual spheres, the titanic forces of fascism, communism, war, and national security concerns consumed and contorted even the institution most dedicated to civil liberties, the ACLU. The ideological clashes unleashed in the mid-1930s to the end of that decade produced deep fissures and contretemps in the ACLU that lasted through the cold war. For many of the ACLU's leaders—Roger Baldwin, Norman Thomas, and

Ernst—certain kinds of censorship and certain limits on association seemed not just justifiable but necessary in the cauldron of the late 1930s and during a world war they fully supported once the United States entered it.[1]

The ACLU's own prewar and wartime history makes it clear that the history of the free speech, free association, civil libertarian tradition in the United States is not a linear history but one punctuated by progress and setbacks, tenuous advances, sustained retrenchments, and, we might well surmise, an uncertain future. In the World War I era and the early 1920s, the free speech battles were fought on the grounds of fears about sedition, subversive speech and propaganda, and radical organizations and their capacity to undermine wartime unity and commitment. By the late 1920s those free speech battles shifted to cultural and sexual speech amid a rapidly transforming commercial culture with leisure activities at its core, where fear of changing attitudes about sex did not seem as threatening as the harms produced by censoring the intellectual lifeline of a democratic public. By the late 1930s fears of fascism, communism, domestic subversion, foreign propaganda, public susceptibility, national disunity, and collective insecurity returned with a vengeance. They have never fully abated.

Threats Against the ACLU Eclipse Civil Liberties

Like many of his associates in the ACLU, Ernst became absorbed by working out the organization's policies toward fascist and communist speech activities and, even more important, trying to adjust the ACLU's aims with the nation's once the United States was at war. Those concerns proved to be not really about civil liberties writ large; to wit, the ACLU failed to raise alarms about wartime civil liberties violations such as the incarceration and internment of Japanese Americans, the Smith Act trial of the Socialist Workers Party, and later the Foreign Agent Registration Act trial of thirty-three far-right publicists and agitators in the mass sedition trial. The ACLU's main focus was not on civil liberties and their defense so much as it was on winning the war once it began. In this way Ernst was not an outlier in his shift to wartime concerns or in his lack of concern for the civil liberties of communists, fascists, and others whose speech and association rights were compromised by wartime measures.

Ernst was deeply committed to the ACLU throughout the 1930s and had devoted enormous time and energy to the organization and its leadership. Not only was he a recognized leader as co-general counsel and an executive board member, but the organization also gave him a perch for promoting anti-censorship challenges nationwide and for helping write state and federal legislation that would thwart censorship practices. This gave him something of a national profile (at least among those who paid attention to the ACLU) and provided him with a media profile as someone who could be routinely asked to weigh in on political matters.[2] Ernst was loyal to the ACLU, spoke for it in many public forums, and was intent on protecting it and its good work from those who tried to make political hay of accusing the ACLU of being a communist organization, especially Congressman Martin Dies, first chair of the House Un-American Activities Committee (HUAC). Ernst's inchoate but increasingly focused anticommunism seems to have crystalized from his desire to protect the ACLU from its congressional and journalistic enemies and from his experiences in liberal-progressive-socialist-communist alliances in the Popular Front era.[3]

Also, Ernst's work in the ACLU and on behalf of its clients had led him to deeply distrust communists, many of whom he had worked side by side with in different organizations from the early 1920s through the 1930s. They were not good coalition players, and questions of loyalty to the USSR lingered. Ernst's deep involvement with figures from across the radical-liberal spectrum began in 1923, when he became the treasurer of the Garland Fund, also known as the Fund for the Republic. This fund, dedicated to progressive and radical causes by Charles Garland, scion of a department store chain, was a small treasure. The financial resources Garland provided for left-leaning causes was intended to build durable or permanent institutions (such as newspapers, publishing houses, labor and trade schools, and other instruments for worker education) and support unionization campaigns and even building funds. As the Garland Fund's official treasurer, Ernst saw firsthand how its money was spent and who was good for paying it back and who wasn't. It collapses a complex history to say that Ernst learned that communist organizations, especially the

International Labor Defense (ILD)—the main entity providing legal defense to communist strikers and Southern sharecroppers and most famously, the Scottsboro Boys—had a terrible track record of paying back their loans to the fund. When the Depression hit and the fund's capital shrunk, it became more crucial that outstanding loans were paid back. The shrinking resources meant that promising organizations, especially the NAACP, with which Ernst was closely involved, were starved of resources at a moment when they really needed them. This irked Ernst and raised his suspicions of communist untrustworthiness.[4]

Throughout the 1930s disagreements deepened within the ACLU and in other progressive Popular Front organizations. Many noncommunists, like Ernst, grew convinced that communists were trying to "bore from within" or take over organizations to which they belonged. This was a frequent complaint in this era. Moreover, Ernst was not at all convinced that communists were committed to protecting the speech rights of those with whom they disagreed; the communists' violent disruption of a socialist meeting at Madison Square Garden was a case in point. So Ernst's commitment to protecting communists' speech rights grew wobbly.

Ernst was also a high-profile leader of the National Lawyers Guild (NLG), another Popular Front era organization whose liberal members battled against what they saw as communist manipulation of the guild's agenda. Leadership conflicts in the NLG came to a head over foreign policy issues, when communist members publicly changed the guild's official policy to support the Spanish Republicans in the Spanish Civil War, fomenting an internecine battle. Ernst and others wanted NLG members to actively pledge commitment to the principles of democracy and foreswear support of dictatorships of any kind, including the USSR.[5] When the NLG's executive committee would not support the pledge, Ernst, Judge Ferdinand Pecora, Jerome Frank, and other leaders left the guild, deepening suspicions between liberals and communists.[6]

These contretemps focused on what Ernst and others saw as the apparent willingness of fellow travelers to defend the Soviet Union no matter what the Soviets did. This rankled liberals who moved and worked in Popular Front circles.[7] The perceived allegiance to the Soviets became a huge question about loyalty, one routinely raised by those who were skeptical that the USSR's staunch defenders could also be committed to civil liberties in the United States. Ernst thought they might be mutually exclusive commitments.[8] For Ernst, sworn opposition to dictatorship became a vital litmus test, especially following the Nazi-Soviet pact in August 1939.[9]

Ernst became more of an outlier in the ACLU by the time the United States entered the war and had made it clear that he was deeply suspicious of fellow travelers and was determinedly in the anticommunist camp. This did not abate over time: Ernst's postwar anticommunism and his ongoing relationship with J. Edgar Hoover and his defense of Truman's loyalty oaths and security investigations that carried over into the Eisenhower years made his increasingly truculent anticommunism stand out in ACLU circles. In the postwar era, when the political affiliations and First Amendment rights of left-wing Americans were the main civil liberties and censorship issues, Ernst was not in the ranks of civil libertarians; rather, he defended the state and its security interests, defended Hoover's growing investigatory authority, and was skeptical that free speech ought to extend to communists.

Ernst Turns Toward J. Edgar Hoover

By 1940 Ernst had begun building a relationship with J. Edgar Hoover. He appears to have been the highest profile liberal who publicly championed Hoover and the FBI, forging what he thought was a close professional and personal relationship. From the outset Ernst touted Hoover's professionalism and vociferously defended him, denying the credibility of accusations about Hoover's tactics. He also offered his services to Hoover, consistently trying to protect Hoover and the FBI by offering advice and insider information from the ACLU and by defending Hoover in first-person essays in liberal and mainstream publications. The relationship benefited Hoover far more than Ernst and tarnished Ernst's reputation.[10] Indeed, his reputation was so tattered that blacklisted screenwriter Dalton Trumbo's polemical 1949 essay *The Time of the Toad*, expressly named Ernst and historian and political operative Arthur Schlesinger Jr. as special examples of erstwhile liberals who should have come to the defense of the Hollywood Ten when they were under attack by the HUAC and who should have offered First Amendment defenses against blacklists and federal loyalty oaths but failed to do so.[11]

Trumbo's essay famously excoriated Ernst, Schlesinger, and others for having the "taste of toad meat" on their tongues for their contorted language explaining their retreat from earlier civil liberties commitments and for using the parlance of liberalism to explain the necessity of ideological containment. It is not entirely clear how much Trumbo actually knew about Ernst's late 1930s history of cultivating relationships with leading countersubversives such as Congressman Martin Dies and his lead investigator, Ben Mandel, but Ernst's ACLU colleagues certainly knew that for a brief time in the late 1930s Ernst had tried to make Dies more respectable while also insisting that Dies should be more attentive to due process as the chairman of the HUAC. But Dies had paved the way for his successor, Congressman J. Parnell Thomas, whose postwar HUAC shone the spotlight on Trumbo and his Hollywood Ten screenwriting colleagues in the late 1940s, destroying their careers, sending them to prison for contempt of Congress, and initiating the blacklist era in the film and television industries; and Ernst was busy defending Hoover, not civil liberties. Trumbo may not have known that, when he was taking aim at Ernst, his target was trying to offer a bit of due process polish to the ambitious young Congressman Richard Nixon, who was quickly building his reputation as a red-baiter. (As with Dies, Ernst counseled Nixon to pay more attention to due process, so that his anticommunist purposes would garner less critical opposition on procedural grounds and thus be more legitimate.)

Trumbo surely knew that by the late 1940s Ernst was routinely touting the work of postwar anticommunism's most powerful executor, J. Edgar Hoover, using his reputation as a leading civil libertarian and ACLU executive to vouch for Hoover's professionalism and his procedural integrity. Moreover, by then Ernst did not believe in civil liberties protections for Communist Party members, arguing that they had lost their claims to freedom of speech and association because of their secrecy, their questionable loyalties, and their possible willingness to abet Moscow's purposes. Ernst fully aligned himself with the anticommunist machinery and cause, and in the decade after the war he framed nearly every issue through the cold war lens of the struggle between democracy and dictatorships. He was certainly not alone. New Dealers, other civil libertarians in the ACLU, anticommunist intellectuals, Democratic Party activists in the Congress for Cultural Freedom and Americans for Democratic Action, and other cold war liberals shared a deep distrust of American communists (both former and active members), especially anyone who did not vociferously denounce communism and the USSR.

But Ernst's peculiarly fierce loyalty to Hoover strained his relations with others who saw Ernst deflecting potential ACLU investigations into the FBI while defending Hoover's near total secrecy about the FBI's sources and methods, which included gathering as much information as possible on anyone Hoover and his agents suspected of being disloyal (a category Hoover got to define). How could Morris Ernst—early ACLU leader and defender of Mary Ware Dennett, Marie Stopes, Margaret Sanger, James Joyce, Alfred Kinsey, and many other sexual modernists—make common cause with J. Edgar Hoover? He acted from both personal ambition and political calculation. Ernst's ambition, his hunger for power and desire to be important, his need to be recognized as an insider and talked about as a "smart fixer," a celebrity of sorts, and his abiding distrust of communism led him to overlook Hoover's method of keeping power by collecting dirt on his enemies and his friends.

Ernst also believed that Hoover was in the best position to investigate real threats of communist subversion. Hoover had legitimate investigatory authority, and Ernst believed that the public ought to know as much as possible about those who were engaged in disseminating ideas and trying to shape public opinion. For Ernst, that marketplace of ideas was crucial, and if some individual or group was skewing it with ideas or propaganda that served a foreign power or antidemocratic purposes, he thought those affiliations ought to be disclosed to the public. For another, Hoover had mastered the art of public relations, touting his FBI as a shining example of an organization committed to due process and police professionalism. The FBI certainly compared favorably with the partisan and reckless HUAC chair Martin Dies and the postwar HUAC chair J. Parnell Thomas (who went to jail for corruption) or the young Richard M. Nixon (whom he had tried to groom), and the bureau certainly looked professional compared to the overwrought Senator Joseph McCarthy. Ernst apparently accepted Hoover's self-promotional propaganda and contended that Hoover's FBI was a beacon of professional integrity doing necessary countersubversive work.

Based on the FBI's files on Ernst and the Ernst-Hoover correspondence in Ernst's papers at the University of Texas, Ernst provided Hoover with essentially inconsequential information when he passed things on to Hoover, including letters he received from others that were critical of Hoover or letters that alerted Hoover that critical statements were forthcoming from the ACLU. But the act of passing on materials was a breach of trust, at the very least. Ernst's far more significant work on behalf of Hoover was more public: protecting Hoover's name and reputation, offering to defend Hoover whenever he was criticized, writing articles on behalf of the FBI that were vetted by Hoover and his staff, and essentially serving as Hoover's high-profile flak.[12] He wrote articles in defense of Hoover in *The Nation* and in mainstream publications such as *Life* and the *Saturday Evening Post*, including a piece in *Reader's Digest* in 1950 titled "Why I No Longer Fear the FBI," an essay that was scrutinized ahead of publication, line by line, by Hoover's lieutenants.

Ernst also tried to make Hoover more attentive to civil liberties nuances, regularly offering counsel on positions Hoover should or should not adopt. Ernst imagined that he was effective with Hoover and represented himself this way to the liberal community. He contended that his constant attention to the FBI made it do its job better, forcing greater attention to due process matters. And perhaps he did—Ernst wrote dozens of letters directly to Hoover, reporting that he had heard a complaint about FBI tactics or its impolitic red-baiting language and asked Hoover for an explanation. He invariably received a quick reply from Hoover, or one of his top lieutenants, but never with Hoover acknowledging any legitimacy to the complaint. Ernst would accept the answer from Hoover and then respond to the originating critic by stating the FBI's position almost verbatim. Hoover and his associates understood Ernst's value to them, and they gave him the perception of being useful and in the loop.[13] For a first-rate thinker, Ernst was easily mollified by Hoover's assurances. He seemed seduced by the idea of having the ear of the nation's "top cop," as he called Hoover. In time, Hoover's secrecy and duplicitous techniques would come to symbolize the antidemocratic excesses of both official anticommunism and the national security state, but that was long past Ernst's time. Despite his protestations that he had kept Hoover on the up-and-up, Ernst proved powerless to alter FBI practices and was supine in his acceptance of Hoover's explanations.

The result of this one-sided relationship was not just a diminution of Ernst's reputation within the community of civil libertarians, where he had been a leader.[14] There was an ethical slippage as well, a sacrifice of his own standards of disclosure for the sake of aiding Hoover in the struggle against communism. As a civil libertarian, Ernst defended disclosure as the most democratic tactic for dealing with potentially subversive groups. But he always defended the confidentiality of the FBI's files, never conceding that the FBI should disclose its methods and the information at its disposal. Nor, of course, did he disclose that he passed on information to the FBI and that it vetted his statements on its behalf before their publication.

As a lawyer, Ernst slipped as well. At the same time that he publicly defended Hoover and the FBI, he still sought to defend clients whose lives were subject to FBI investigation. Perhaps the most compromising materials in the Ernst FBI files are letters indicating that when Ethel and Julius Rosenberg's family met with Ernst about providing legal defense for the accused spies, Ernst passed this information on to Hoover.[15] This duplicity was most bafflingly and alarmingly on display in Ernst's decision to offer a public relations defense to the brutal dictator of the Dominican Republic, Rafael Trujillo. Their relationship began in 1957 and culminated in 1958 with a whitewashing report exculpating Trujillo and his henchmen for the kidnapping and murder of his leading U.S.-based critic, Jesus de Galindez. Ernst was paid $200,000. "How could you, Morris?" many appalled colleagues and friends asked. This Galindez episode verified what Trumbo had seen coming nearly a decade earlier—that Ernst was a former civil libertarian. By the end of the 1950s Ernst had become a pariah in progressive circles, regarded skeptically and even with sadness by longtime former allies. When Ernst died in 1974, not a single representative of the ACLU had a role as a featured speaker at his memorial ceremony. He had become a forgotten leader from an earlier era, at best.

American Liberty

Security crises from World War I to the permanent war on terror always have weakened, if not eviscerated, hard-won civil liberties gains. There is no permanent right to free speech and certainly no consensus about an unchallengeable right to freedom of association when security anxieties are most acute. Put differently, a culture of liberty in no way precludes persistent attempts to squelch liberty. The ideological anxieties of the twenty-first century are different from those when Ernst took his rightward shift, but the tendencies to curtail the speech and penalize the political associations of those perceived as dangerous to the body politic have not gone away. As in Ernst's day, the defense and promotion of untrammeled sexual speech and knowledge appears to be a safer and more propitious ground for expanding freedoms compared with defending fraught and potentially dangerous political ideas and movements. The agreed-on value of sexual knowledge and expression is greater than its agreed-on harms, and those exhorting fears about its dangers to the social and moral order are, at least for now, speaking from the cultural and political margins; it is not so clear that this same pattern holds with respect to the political and ideological furies of the twenty-first century, when so much speech is regarded as dangerous and untrustworthy and political violence looms so close to the surface. Seen from this perspective, Morris Ernst's unquestioning defense of sexual liberties and his deep anxieties about political ones might be more understandable.

ACKNOWLEDGMENTS

Now the fun part. I have many people to thank and no one to blame. The sins of inclusion and exclusion are mine. I have done my best to take into consideration the wealth of advice generously offered by friends, colleagues, anonymous readers, and family—and I humbly thank you for helping to make this a better book.

I began this book at Drew University, where I had the good fortune to have supportive colleagues. Perry Leavell and Barbara Oberg housed and fed me when I trekked to Princeton University to comb through the ACLU papers, and Jonathan Rose, who knew that Morris Ernst was important and understudied, encouraged the project early on and eagerly promoted it late in the process as well. The Friends of Princeton Libraries gave me an early financial boost, and archivist Daniel Linke offered useful tips for navigating the voluminous ACLU papers. Historians Samuel Walker and Athan Theoharis did as well, pointing me to Ernst's complicated relationships with the ACLU and the FBI. Mary Ann Hansen, an award-winning librarian at Montana State University, helped me get started with a thorough bibliographic search. Historian Robert W. Rydell, also of Montana State, gave the manuscript a characteristically astute read and invited me to discuss my work with his doctoral students. Bob, my mentor as an undergraduate, remains a trusted and honored teacher. Bruce Kuklick, my dissertation adviser years ago, once again gave generously of his time, keen intelligence, and red ink. I hope this book satisfies his historian's ethos of presenting the past on its own terms.

The book's long gestation occurred during my years in the Department of Media, Culture, and Communication at New York University. I have had the daunting pleasure of being surrounded by a talented, productive group of colleagues and of being aided by a handful of equally talented and meticulous graduate students. Three department chairs, Ted Magder, Marita Sturken, and Rod Benson, helped me find time to research and write and gave financial support to the doctoral students who assisted me with research and editing. Cynthia Conti's remarkable energy and support I will always remember, as well as Nadja Milner's and Hatim El-Hibri's help. As I turned the research into chapter drafts, a series of doctoral students gave my manuscript their editorial attention. Will Lockett, Kate Brideau, and Tim Wood—all brilliant young scholars—made the book more cogent and more graceful. Master's student Yael Lazarus deployed her organizational skills to help me keep track of all the many details, and doctoral student Diana Kamin displayed wizardry in tracking down biographical details and a trove of images. I am grateful for the intelligence they directed my way.

Along with support from departmental chairs, several colleagues took time out from their busy lives to read my manuscript at crucial moments. Lisa Gitelman and Dana Polan were attentive (and remarkably fast) readers, and Marita Sturken was especially generous at various stages in the book's life. Jon Zimmerman read my preliminary ideas and offered good advice and bibliographic tips. Charlton McIlwain and Rod Benson both invited me to present my work to our doctoral students, and both have kept me reasonably sane and well fed over the years. Yemane Demissie of NYU's Tisch School has been a model colleague with whom I've team-taught several times. He sets a high standard in all he does, and it has been a pleasure to work alongside him teaching the bright, creative, open-minded students at New York University. I am lucky to earn my keep teaching NYU students, who invariably keep me optimistic about the future.

It helped greatly to work through ideas about Morris Ernst, obscenity law, and anti-censorship liberalism at annual meetings of the Modern Languages Association, the American Studies Association, the Organization of American Historians, and the American Historical Association. Kelly Cannon, Jeff Pooley, and Sue Curry Jansen of Muhlenberg College invited me to deliver a keynote address for Banned Books Week and to present a chapter at a workshop with their insightful students. A presentation at a censorship conference at the University of Iowa, organized by Loren Glass, was similarly beneficial; that paper was subsequently published as a chapter in the volume *The Limits of Liberalism.*

NYU's Humanities Council and the University Research Challenge Fund provided much-needed grants. The administrative staff in my home department helped manage them, and more. Judi Stevens, Melissa Lucas, and Jamie Schuler kept track of money flows and student payments in the book's early stages, and their successors, Tracy Figueroa, Annette Morales, and Dani Resto, have overseen them as I write. Darrell Carter, gentleman and departmental troubleshooter, astutely facilitates, and Rebecca Brown is the axis around which the department moves. Thank you so much.

Along with research at Princeton, the New York Public Library, the Eisenhower Presidential Library, and the Kinsey Institute Archives at Indiana University, this book's mother lode of archival research materials are housed at the Harry Ransom Humanities Research Center at the University of Texas, Austin, where Morris Ernst's papers are located. The Ransom Center is a glimpse at what heaven will be for humanities researchers. It holds extraordinary archival and manuscript collections and is run by deeply knowledgeable and supportive administrators, research archivists, and reading room staff. Equally important, it offers generous research grants to provide long-term stays in its collections. I had the good fortune of receiving two grants from the Ransom Center, one being the Woodward and Bernstein/Dorot Foundation Research Fellowship. A subsequent invitation to deliver the Stanley Burnshaw Lecture provided another opportunity to commune with the archives and the archivists. The long list of people at the Ransom Center whom I would like to thank begins with Joan Sibley, Kurt Heinzelman, Stephen Mielke, Danielle Sigler, Tara Wenger, Richard Oram, Richard Workman, and especially a group of archivists who were cataloguing Ernst's papers while I was there. Alex Tasinski, Nicole Davis, Elizabeth Garver, and Jennifer (La-Suprema) Hecker were endless sources of help and insight.

Other friends provided spare beds and delicious food and listened to me discuss the project. Alex Lichtenstein and Lara Kriegel housed me while researching at the Kinsey Archives, for which I am grateful, and Alex, as is his wont, gave my project a valuable boost at an important moment, as did David Greenberg, Jonathan Rose, and Marjorie Heins. My old pal Steve Godla brought me to the Smith River country in northern California to give a series of lectures to high school history teachers about censorship in American history. Then he showed me his favorite swimming holes. Our mutual friend, Sheri Simkins, offered a well-lit work table, delicious wines, and solace as we mourned the too early death of her husband and my dear friend Mitch Simkins.

While on the theme of critically useful boosts, my agent Max Sinsheimer gets (almost) his own paragraph. One day as I was walking through Greenwich Village, I ran into the remarkable food and nutrition scholar Marion Nestle, a friend and my wife's colleague. I told Marion I needed to find an agent, and she said, "Oh, contact Max, I think he's wonderful." I did. She was right. From the very outset of our relationship Max understood my project—its strengths and its limits—and he went to work on my behalf, sharpening my pitch and finding a home for it at Stanford University Press, where it has been ushered along with grace and speed by Marcela Cristina Maxfield. Marcela has been the ideal editor in every way, trimming the book where necessary and urging me to clarify my arguments and their stakes. She has shepherded my book with alacrity. Thank you Max, and thank you Marcela. I would also like to thank Sunna Juhn at Stanford University Press for her quick attention to details and Mimi Braverman for her keen copy editor's eye and insistence on precision.

This book has benefited greatly from the anonymous scholars who, in the critical role of external readers, gave my manuscript their close attention. Their knowledge, insight, detailed observations and criticisms, and generous expenditure of their time to insist that this book meet their exacting professional standards are a testament to the serious commitment of academic historians to the work of knowledge production and to maintaining the standards of the historian's guild. I am grateful to them and hope the book's final version demonstrates my respect for their attentive labors.

Friends who read chunks of the book—that's usually what they were at the time—also asked for clarity, while also giving me the patience and encouragement that friends offer up. Three brilliant lawyer friends read much, if not all, of this book at various stages. They kept me from making too many errors about legal matters, schooled me in the legal arts, and assured me that I was doing justice to what lawyers and judges do and that I had an important story to tell. Marjorie Heins was unstinting with her deep knowledge of obscenity law and judicious with her editor's pen. Jim Vogele read every chapter, thought about the chapters' structure and narrative arc, and reminded me to be a storyteller. Scott Wilson asked me questions about the law that I'm still wrestling with (which is what he does with federal appellate court judges too), and I wish I had the legal training to do those questions justice. Thank you, counselors. Your reassurance was, well, reassuring.

Other friends kept me healthy and in motion. I have a great bicycling crew who make my weekends on the bike paths and roads in and out of New York City a true joy. Michael Hoffman, Dan Rocker, Foster Provost, and Kent Kirshenbaum and I have had our share of flat tires, broken spokes, broken collar bones and fingers, asphalt and gravel contusions, belligerent drivers, and one ambulance. And yet we keep rolling, chugging up hills, zipping down them, always looking for that sweet spot where we hit our collective stride. They have put up with my book worries and gripes for more rides and years than ought to be asked of friends. I'm so happy when I'm in their brainy, twisted, witty midst. I hope they read the book they've been hearing about for almost forever. Likewise Stan Schmidt, a.k.a. Zippy Larkin, has been a steady champion of my work, a boon companion, and a loyal friend since we met on our first day of college.

Another dear friend from my graduate school days would be the deus ex machina who intervened to rescue my book from vengeful or neglectful gods if a Greek dramatist were telling the story. This is the second time Nancy Bernhard helped me figure out what my book was really about, with keen intelligence, generosity, nourishing humor, and insistence on getting to the core power dynamics, guided by the maxim that freedom is never the problem. All my thank yous will never get close to how much you helped, Nancy. While Nancy came to the rescue close to the end, Craig McCormick has put up with me and my book and all my worries about it from its earliest stages. Every year on our annual "campfire therapy" biking, hiking, and camping outings in the northern Rockies, he has listened carefully, reassured me I was onto something, and reminded me to tell readers how this book connects with their lives. (He has also read the chunks.) I don't know if I've attained his idea for what the book could or should be, but he knows I've tried.

My sister Marie Gary always gives generously of her joyous self, her wonderful house, and in our parents' last years also provided me with a solid table and big windows where I could do my work and take in northern light. My unfailingly generous in-laws, Joe and Barbara Bentley, for the last few years designated a picnic table under majestic ponderosa pine trees near their lake cabin as the place where I could work, uninterrupted, chapter after chapter. (I interrupted myself, jumping in the lake five or six times a day.) They gladly share the soul-restorative beauties of their cabin with their big loving family and can bear witness to how many hours I put in at that table, trying to wrestle words and ideas into place.

As ought to be clear at this point, I've been working on this book for a long time—since my now young adult children were young children. They have endured Morris Ernst for much of their lives. I hope they noticed that for most of that time I tried to give them far more attention than I gave Morris. They certainly provided me with more laughter and joy. Joey, Annabelle, and Ruby Bentley Gary have been told a thousand times that I love them more than they'll ever know. It's true. Words don't get anywhere close to that truth. They give me purpose and make me proud every day—in fact I'm a braggart about my beautiful, talented kids, and yet even when I am aware of that tendency, I ask myself, "Why wouldn't I brag about them?" I knock on wood every night, as I watch their lives with gratitude, marveling at their soulful, loving selves. I also try to pause daily to be grateful that I have been married to their mother, Amy Bentley, for three decades. No one has been luckier in life than I am in my mate. Loving, smart, kind, funny, generous, talented, hardworking, ethical, organized, grounded, filled with grace, nurturant, confident, soulful, beautiful, healthy—that's just the beginning of the litany. Along with all that, Amy is a first-rate scholar who has lived with this project when it was just a gleam in my eye. She has read it (chunks and polished chapters) well beyond any call of duty, doggedly edited it, made brilliant strategic cuts, and listened to me work through it ad infinitum (or is it ad nauseam?). Despite all that, she kept telling me she is proud of me and promised it would one day come together. And it has, thanks to her. Lucky me.

Finally, I dedicate this book to the memory of my parents, Joseph B. Gary and Margaret R. (Casto) Gary. Peg and Joe, as everyone knew them, didn't live long enough to see me complete this book. I don't know they would have agreed with my libertarian take on matters sexual, but they would have been proud I used my brain, took my craft seriously, and did my best. They made art of their mutual lives. They laughed together for sixty-three years, raised a big brood in a rollicking household, embodied kindness and decency, and had about a million friends. My siblings—Marie, Joan, Brian, Mark—and I could not have been luckier in the parents we had. Long may their spirit course through the generations they nourished with their love.

"And so, amen," to quote the late bard of Portland, Brian Doyle.

New York City
October 1, 2020

NOTES

Chapter 1

1. On the role of young women in these cultural transformations, see Paula Fass, *The Damned and the Beautiful: American Youth in the 1920s* (Oxford, UK: Oxford University Press, 1977); and Christine Stansell, *American Moderns: Bohemian New York and the Creation of a New Century* (Princeton, NJ: Princeton University Press, 2000). On the cultural upheavals of the "machine age," see Ann Douglass, *Terrible Honesty: Mongrel Manhattan in the 1920s* (New York: Farrar, Straus & Giroux, 1996).

2. For a rich treatment of the perception of the necessity of keeping sex and sin at bay, see R. Marie Griffith, *Mortal Combat: How Sex Divided American Christians and Fractured American Politics* (New York: Basic Books, 2017); and Betty A. DeBerg, *Ungodly Women: Gender and the First Wave of American Fundamentalism* (Minneapolis: Fortress Press, 1990). On vulnerability to powerful media forms, see Brett Gary, *The Nervous Liberals: Propaganda Anxieties from World War One to the Cold War* (New York: Columbia University Press, 1999); for a discussion of the bad tendency of speech theory in World War I, see David Rabban, *Free Speech in Its Forgotten Years* (Cambridge, UK: Cambridge University Press, 1997).

3. On women's groups as part of the battle against obscenity and smut, see Leigh Ann Wheeler, *Against Obscenity: Reform and the Politics of Womanhood in America, 1873–1935* (Baltimore: Johns Hopkins University Press, 2007); Alison M. Parker, *Purifying America: Women, Cultural Reform, and Pro-Censorship Activism, 1873–1933* (Urbana: University of Illinois Press, 1997); Griffith, *Mortal Combat*; and Andrea Friedman, *Prurient Interests: Gender, Democracy, and Obscenity in New York City, 1909–1945* (New York: Columbia University Press, 2000). For studies of women organizing against pornography in the 1970s and beyond, see Whitney

Strub, *Perversion for Profit: The Politics of Pornography and the Rise of the New Right* (New York: Columbia University Press, 2013); Janet R. Jakobsen and Ann Pelligrini, *Love the Sin: Sexual Regulation and the Limits of Religious Tolerance* (Boston: Beacon Press, 2006); Lisa Duggan and Nan Hunter, *Sex Wars: Sexual Dissent and Political Culture* (New York: Routledge, 2006); and Carolyn Bronstein, *Battling Pornography: The American Feminist Anti-Pornography Movement, 1976–1986* (New York: Cambridge University Press, 2011).

4. Ernst was prolific and wrote or co-wrote many books, most of them addressing his anti-censorship arguments in conjunction with his anti-oligopoly positions. See Morris L. Ernst and William Seagle, *To the Pure: A Study of Obscenity and the Censor* (New York: Viking Press, 1928; Kaus Reprint Company, 1969); Morris L. Ernst and Alexander Lindey, *The Censor Marches On* (New York: Doubleday Doran, 1940); Morris L. Ernst, *The First Freedom* (New York: Macmillan, 1946); and Morris L. Ernst and Alan U. Schwartz, *Censorship: The Search for the Obscene* (New York: Macmillan, 1964). I have had a difficult time finding biographical information about Alexander Lindey; he graduated from City College and then New York Law School in 1925, joined the Greenbaum, Wolff & Ernst firm, and, after leaving Greenbaum, Wolff & Ernst, concentrated in entertainment law and wrote a book titled *Plagiarism and Originality* (1952). For information on Harriet Pilpel, see the obituary by Joan Cook, "Harriet Pilpel, 79, Lawyer, Dies; An Advocate of Women's Rights," *New York Times* (April 24, 1991), D23. Pilpel graduated second in her class at Columbia University Law School and joined the Ernst firm in 1936, where she stayed until it dissolved in 1982; from 1973 to 1991 she participated in twenty-seven cases before the Supreme Court.

5. The most complete study of Morris Ernst's career is Joel Matthew Silverman, "Pursuing Celebrity, Ensuing Masculinity: Morris Ernst, Obscenity, and the Search for Recognition," PhD diss., University of Texas at Austin, 2006. Silverman astutely frames Ernst's publicity consciousness and his disposition to "exhibitionism"; see especially pp. 1–54.

6. For earlier treatment of Ernst's work, see Brett Gary, "'Guessing Oneself into Jail': Morris Ernst and the Assault on American Obscenity Laws in the 1930s," in *Obscenity and the Limits of Liberalism*, ed. Loren Glass and Charles Francis Williams (Columbus: Ohio State University Press, 2011), 50–68; and Brett Gary, "Morris Ernst's Troubled Legacy," *Reconstruction* 8, no. 1 (2008), http://reconstruction.eserver.org/084/contents084.shtml#8.1 (accessed September 30, 2013).

7. The Comstock Act, discussed in the next section, elaborated the prohibition on contraceptive and abortion information and devices. On the implications of these prohibitions, see Linda Gordon, *The Moral Property of Women: A History of Birth Control Politics in America*, 3rd ed. (Urbana-Champaign: University of

Illinois Press, 2007). Other works include James Reed, *From Private Vice to Public Virtue: The Birth Control Movement and American Society Since 1830* (New York: Basic Books, 1978); Ellen Chesler, *A Woman of Valor: Margaret Sanger and the Birth Control Movement in America* (New York: Doubleday Anchor, 1992); David Kennedy, *Birth Control in America: The Career of Margaret Sanger* (New Haven, CT: Yale University Press, 1971); and Peter C. Engelman, *A History of the Birth Control Movement in America* (Santa Barbara, CA: Praeger, 2011).

8. The first federal obscenity law in the United States, passed in 1842, authorized the U.S. Customs Service to confiscate "obscene or immoral" pictures imported into the country. By the time of the American Civil War (1861–1865), obscenity statutes were on the books in many individual states, and by 1905 in forty-five states. Most of these statutes shared an English common law language that broadly prohibited "whatever outrages decency and is injurious to public morals." See Frederick F. Schauer, *The Law of Obscenity* (Washington, DC: Bureau of National Affairs, 1976).

9. On mailing obscene matter, the full language of the Comstock Act of 1873, as amended in 1876 (Title 18, Section 334 of the United States Code, Section 211 of Penal Code, amended) reads: "Every obscene, lewd, or lascivious, and every filthy book, pamphlet, picture, paper, letter, writing, print, or other publication of an indecent character, and every article or thing designed, adapted, or intended for preventing contraception or producing abortion, or for any indecent or immoral use; and every article, instrument, substance, drug, medicine, or thing which is advertised or described in a manner calculated to lead another to use or apply it for preventing contraception or producing abortion, or for any indecent or immoral purpose; and every written or printed card, letter, circular, book, pamphlet, advertisement, or notice of any kind giving information, directly or indirectly, where, or how, or from whom, or by what means any of the hereinbefore-mentioned matters, articles or things may be obtained or made, or where or by whom any act or operation of any kind for the procuring or producing of abortion will be done or performed, or how or by what means conception may be prevented or abortion produced, whether sealed or unsealed; and every letter, packet, or package, or other mail matter containing any filthy, vile, or indecent thing, device, or substance; and every paper, writing, advertisement, or representation that any article, instrument, substance, drug, medicine, or thing may, or can, be used or applied for preventing conception or producing abortion, or for any indecent or immoral purpose. . . . Whoever shall knowingly deposit, or cause to be deposited, for mailing or delivery, anything declared by this section to be nonmailable, or shall knowingly take, or cause the same to be taken, from the mails for the purpose of circulating or disposing thereof, shall be fined not more than $5000 or imprisoned not more than five years, or both" (Mary Ware Dennett, *Who's Obscene?* [New York: Vanguard Press, 1930], xix–xx).

10. An extensive literature on Comstock describes his interests, energies, and reach. For a recent excellent and rich treatment of Comstock's rise, his career, and his decline, see Amy Werbel, *Lust on Trial: Censorship and the Rise of American Obscenity in the Age of Anthony Comstock* (New York: Columbia University Press, 2018). See also Nicola Beisel, *Imperiled Innocents: Anthony Comstock and Family Reproduction in Victorian America* (Princeton, NJ: Princeton University Press, 1997). Other excellent treatments include Paul S. Boyer, *Purity in Print: Book Censorship in America from the Gilded Age to the Computer Age*, 2nd ed. (Madison: University of Wisconsin Press, 2002); Marjorie Heins, *Not in Front of the Children: "Indecency," Censorship, and the Innocence of Youth* (New York: Hill & Wang, 2001); Helen Lefkowitz Horowitz, *Rereading Sex: Battles over Sexual Knowledge and Suppression in Nineteenth Century America* (New York: Knopf, 2002); Geoffrey R. Stone, *Sex and the Constitution: Sex, Religion, and Law from America's Origins to the Twenty-First Century* (New York: Liveright, 2017); Heywood Broun and Margaret Leech, *Anthony Comstock: Roundsman of the Lord* (New York: Boni, 1927); and Craig LaMay, "America's Censor: Anthony Comstock and Free Speech," *Communications and the Law* 19, no. 3 (September 1997): 1–59.

11. An excellent source on the relationship between Comstock and the YMCA is Werbel, *Lust on Trial*. Horowitz, *Rereading Sex*, addresses the history of the New York state law and the federal law being modeled on the New York law because it provided search warrant power as well. Beisel, *Imperiled Innocents*, is excellent on the economic interests of Comstock's patrons in the YMCA. Boyer, *Purity in Print*, captures Comstock's wide authority and the antagonisms he produced.

12. Werbel uses the self-descriptive phrase several times in *Lust on Trial*, 4, 35, 51, 53, 203. Ernst and Seagle's *To the Pure* addresses Comstock's implications in his contemporary era. The most salient legal critiques were offered by Theodore Schroeder. For the best study of Theodore Schroeder, see Rabban, *Free Speech*; see also David Brudnoy, "Comstock's Nemesis: Theodore Schroeder," *Reason*, October 1975, https://reason.com/1975/10/01/comstocks-nemesis/ (accessed June 5, 2019).

13. On the birth control component of these bans, see Gordon, *Moral Property of Women*; Andrea Tone, *Devices and Desires: A History of Contraceptives in America* (New York: Hill & Wang, 2001); Beisel, *Imperiled Innocents*; and Horowitz, *Rereading Sex*.

14. Morris Ernst and Gwendolyn Pickett, "Birth Control in the Courts: A Resume of Legal Decisions Clarifying and Interpreting Existing Statutes," October 1942, p. 3, Harry Ransom Humanities Research Center (HRC), Morris L. Ernst (MLE) Papers, Box 5, Folder 22.

15. Beisel, *Imperiled Innocents*, is excellent on the changing social and cultural

factors that worried Comstock's patrons; so too is Werbel, *Lust on Trial*. On the growing presence of women's sexuality in urban life, see Kathy Peiss, *Cheap Amusements: Working Women and Leisure in Turn-of-the-Century New York* (Philadelphia: Temple University Press, 1986); and Friedman, *Prurient Interests*. On women's behavior that disturbed the moral guardians, see Carroll Smith-Rosenberg, *Disorderly Conduct: Visions of Gender in Victorian America*, reprint ed. (New York: Oxford University Press, 1987); and Tone, *Devices and Desires*. For the emergence of a more pronounced male gay culture, see George Chauncey, *Gay New York: Gender, Urban Culture, and the Making of the Gay Male World, 1890–1940* (New York: Basic Books, 1995); see also Paul Boyer, *Urban Masses and Moral Order in America, 1820–1920* (Cambridge, MA: Harvard University Press, 1992).

16. Elaborating the prohibition on contraceptive and abortion information and devices, the Comstock Act enumerated those items to be prohibited by federal law: "every article, instrument, substance, drug, medicine, or thing which is advertised or described in a manner calculated to lead another to use or apply it for preventing contraception or producing abortion, or for any indecent or immoral purpose; and every written or printed card, letter, circular, book, pamphlet, advertisement, or notice of any kind giving information, directly or indirectly . . . [as to how or where] any of the . . . matters, articles or things may be obtained or made, or where or by whom any act or operation of any kind for the procuring or producing of abortion will be done or performed, or how or by what means conception may be prevented or abortion produced . . . or for any indecent or immoral purpose" (Dennett, *Who's Obscene*, xix–xx).

17. On Comstock's anti-abortion crusade and his pursuit of Madame Restelle, see Beisel, *Imperiled Innocents*; and Horowitz, *Rereading Sex*.

18. Gordon, *Moral Property of Women*; Tone, *Devices and Desires*; Beisel, *Imperiled Innocents*; Horowitz, *Rereading Sex*.

19. For more on this concern about race suicide and women not performing their roles in the twentieth century, see Griffith, *Moral Combat*; and DeBerg, *Ungodly Women*.

20. Ernst and Pickett, "Birth Control in the Courts," 2.

21. Ernst and Pickett, "Birth Control in the Courts," 6.

22. Ernst and Pickett, "Birth Control in the Courts," 3.

23. Numerous scholars have examined the Hicklin standard and its application in the American courts. For an excellent overview, see Heins, *Not in Front of the Children*. See also Schauer, *Law of Obscenity*; and Boyer, *Purity in Print*.

24. *Regina v. Hicklin*, L.R. 3 Q.B. 360 (1868). In *United States v. Harmon*, 147 US 268 (1893), the Comstock Act was challenged on constitutional grounds, namely, that it interfered with First Amendment rights. But the federal court held

that it was obvious that the First Amendment did not protect that which "outrages the common sense of decency, or endangers public safety." On *Harmon*, see Heins, *Not in Front of the Children*; and Schauer, *Law of Obscenity*.

25. "Obscene libel" was traditionally an English common law offense, inherited by the American states as former British colonies, and there were a number of state prosecutions for obscene libel in the early nineteenth century, strengthened and extended by the Comstock Act. The Hicklin standard was the common law test for obscene libel and thus had influential precedents in the U.S. courts before the Comstock Act. See Donna I. Dennis, "Obscenity Law and Its Consequences in Mid-Nineteenth-Century America," *Columbia Journal of Gender and Law* 16, no. 1 (2007): 43–95; and Robert P. Davidow and Michael O'Boyle, "Obscenity laws in England and the United States: A Comparative Analysis," *Nebraska Law Review* 56 (1977): 249–88.

26. In 1896 in *Swearingen v. United States* the Supreme Court expressly ruled that something was not obscene (or lewd or lascivious) unless it produced "sexual immorality or impurity," using language more euphemistic than direct to describe a state of mind of arousal, at the least, and the possibility of acting on the state of arousal. *Swearingen v. United States*, 161 U.S. 446 (1896).

27. The same assumptions about the power of words and images to induce lust, disrupt moral norms, and lead individuals into some vaguely defined place of immorality would return in a different form in the famous World War I speech cases when the Supreme Court routinely referred to the "bad tendency" of political speech arguments to uphold the constitutionality of wartime Espionage and Sedition Act convictions.

28. On the early sex radicals and their battles with Comstock, see Horowitz, *Rereading Sex*.

29. For the best study of Theodore Schroeder, see Rabban, *Free Speech*. See also Brudnoy, "Comstock's Nemesis."

30. The Supreme Court did not hear a challenge to this position and thus did not reconsider the possible unconstitutionality of the obscenity laws on First Amendment grounds until 1957 in the *Roth/Alberts* case (*Roth v. United States*, 354 U.S. 476, when it upheld the obscenity law's constitutionality but also offered stricter tests, and thus more "speech protective" standards, for assessing whether something was indeed obscene, thus easing the way for the production and distribution of far more sexually explicit materials.

31. On World War I speech catastrophes, see Harry Kalven, *A Worthy Tradition: Freedom of Speech in America* (New York: Harper & Row, 1988); Zechariah Chafee Jr., *Freedom of Speech* (New York: Harcourt, Brace & Jovanovich, 1920); Anthony Lewis, *Make No Law* (New York: Vintage, 1992); Richard Polenberg,

Fighting Faiths: The Abrams Case, the Supreme Court, and Free Speech (New York: Viking Press, 1987); Rabban, *Free Speech*; Fred D. Ragan, "Justice Oliver Wendell Holmes, Jr., Zechariah Chafee, Jr., and the Clear and Present Danger Test for Free Speech: The First Year, 1919," *Journal of American History* 58 (June 1971): 24–45; David Rabban, "Emergence of the Modern First Amendment Doctrine," *University of Chicago Law Review* 50, no. 4 (1983), art. 2; David Rabban, "The Free Speech League, the ACLU, and the Changing Conceptions of Free Speech in American History," *Stanford Law Review* 45 (November 1992): 47–114; and Geoffrey R. Stone, *Perilous Times: Free Speech in Wartime from the Sedition Act of 1798 to the War on Terrorism* (New York: Norton, 2004). Rabban explains how the "bad tendency" of language assumptions that facilitated the Supreme Court's punitive First Amendment decisions in the war era penalized dissenting speech for its probable "bad effects" or "ill tendencies" rather than for any actual effects. The same assumptions about public vulnerability (and the need for moral order) underlay the widespread use of the Hicklin obscenity standard in obscenity law cases.

32. Two especially influential contemporary studies of wartime excesses include *A Report Upon the Illegal Practices of the United States Department of Justice* (Washington, DC: National Popular Government League, 1920); and Chafee, *Freedom of Speech*. Harvard Law professor Zechariah Chafee Jr. helped write the *Report Upon the Illegal Activities*. His *Freedom of Speech* (1920) became central to the burgeoning civil liberties community. (Notably, sexual and literary or cultural speech issues were very much outside Chafee's idea of what constituted valuable speech or free speech violations.)

33. The literature on the ACLU is considerable. The best work on the ACLU and sexuality as a civil liberty is Leigh Ann Wheeler, *How Sex Became a Civil Liberty* (New York: Oxford University Press, 2012). The classic history of the ACLU is Samuel Walker, *In Defense of American Liberty: A History of the ACLU* (New York: Oxford University Press, 1990). Other excellent studies include Judy Kutulas, *The American Civil Liberties Union and the Making of Modern Liberalism, 1930–1960* (Chapel Hill: University of North Carolina Press, 2006); Robert C. Cottrell, *Roger Nash Baldwin and the American Civil Liberties Union* (New York: Columbia University Press, 2000); Donald Johnson, *The Challenge to American Freedom: World War I and the Rise of the American Civil Liberties Union* (Lexington: University Press of Kentucky, 1963); and Alan Reitman, ed., *The Price of Liberty: Perspectives on Civil Liberties by Members of the ACLU* (New York: Norton, 1968).

34. Wheeler, *How Sex Became A Civil Liberty*. Wheeler makes a series of arguments germane to this study, especially that the ACLU played a major role in creating sexual civil liberties, in part by challenging laws against obscenity. She makes an excellent overall case for the argument that ACLU leaders' positions

and strategies on obscenity evolved from defending only noncommercial (and "serious") material produced by their own members and acquaintances to defending less serious, more commercial entertainment produced by strangers, and also that the ACLU went from defending only producers and distributors to defending consumers as well. Ernst, Lindey, and Pilpel's work remained focused on the defense of "serious" works, as they were trying to win test cases in which the value of the works needed to be demonstrated to the courts, but their arguments hinged on the needs of consumers.

35. Sanger led the American Birth Control League and Dennett the Voluntary Parenthood League. As I illustrate in Chapters 2 (on Dennett) and 6 (on Sanger), both women had considerable conflicts with Postal authorities.

36. See Wheeler, *How Sex Became a Civil Liberty*, for the most detailed and authoritative account of the ACLU's long history dedicated to expanding rights of sexual expression and practice and protecting those rights legislatively and in the courts.

37. For studies of battles with John Sumner, see Boyer, *Purity in Print*; Jay A. Gertzman, *Bookleggers and Smuthounds: The Trade in Erotica, 1920–1940* (Philadelphia: University of Pennsylvania Press, 1999); and Jay Gertzman, "John Saxton Sumner of the New York Society for the Suppression of Vice: A Chief Smut Eradicator of the Interwar Period," *Journal of American Culture* 17, no. 2 (June 1994): 41–47. Ernst and Lindey treat Sumner extensively in Ernst and Lindey, *The Censor Marches On*. See also Rochelle Gurstein, *The Repeal of Reticence: America's Cultural and Legal Struggles over Free Speech, Obscenity, Sexual Liberation, and Modern Art* (New York: Hill & Wang, 1996); Edward de Grazia, *Girls Lean Back Everywhere: The Law of Obscenity and the Assault on Genius* (New York: Random House, 1992); and Walter Kendrick, *The Secret Museum: Pornography in Modern Culture* (Berkeley: University of California Press, 1996).

38. For a vivid discussion of the Banned in Boston spectacles and the bans on and battles over modernist works by such towering figures as Eugene O'Neill, Sherwood Anderson, William Faulkner, Ernest Hemingway, John Dos Passos, Upton Sinclair, and H. G. Wells, see Boyer, *Purity in Print*, 167–206; see also Neil Miller, *Banned in Boston: The Watch and Ward Society's Crusade Against Books, Burlesque, and the Social Evil* (Boston: Beacon Press, 2010).

39. Fred Rodell, "Morris Ernst: New York's Unlawyerlike Liberal Lawyer Is the Censor's Enemy, the President's Friend," *Life* (February 21, 1944), 96–107.

40. Rodell, "Morris Ernst," 96.

41. Marquis James, "Scribner's Examines: Morris L. Ernst," *Scribner's Magazine* 104, no. 1 (July 1938):9. More recently, the novelist Michael Chabon described Ernst as an "erudite, polished, and well-connected New York hustler" who "was known, and much sought-after, as a gifted, skilled, and cagey courtroom attorney

with a discerning eye for the kinds of cases that could change the law if you won them" (Michael Chabon, "'Ulysses' on Trial," *New York Review of Books* [September 26, 2019], 1).

42. James, "Scribner's Examines," 9; Rodell, "Morris Ernst," 97. Silverman's "Pursuing Celebrity" develops Ernst's penchant for publicity and exhibitionism in detail.

43. Silverman's dissertation offers a rich sketch of Ernst's family life and background. Ernst's recollections of his background are strewn throughout various documents and family histories in his papers at the University of Texas. Ernst's papers also include various family history documents, including one titled "Unpublished Family History." See "Morris L. Family History (1961)," HRC, MLE Papers, Box 877 (old file system). In an oral interview with Mary Batten, Ernst discusses his father as a "peddler, like all immigrants." See Mary Batten interview with Morris Ernst, September 13, 1973, HRC, MLE Papers, audiofiles.

44. Quotes from Ernst oral interview with Mary Batten, September 13, 1973, HRC, MLE Papers, audiofiles.

45. Ernst's quotes and recollections are found in Silverman, "Pursuing Celebrity," 18, 28.

46. For a rich treatment of the obstacles confronting Jewish lawyers, see Jerold S. Auerbach, "From Rags to Robes: The Legal Profession, Social Mobility, and the American Jewish Experience," *American Jewish Historical Quarterly* 76, no. 2 (December 1976): 249–84. Silverman notes Auerbach's study and explains that this prejudice helped Ernst and his partners hire excellent young lawyers.

47. Silverman, "Pursuing Celebrity," 28.

48. Auerbach, "From Rags to Robes," suggests that Jewish lawyers' successes in the New Deal agencies and wartime agencies finally provided access to top law firms following the war.

49. Silverman makes the point of the fierce competition ("Pursuing Celebrity," 28). Harriet Pilpel became Ernst's primary associate on reproductive rights issues when she joined Greenbaum, Wolff & Ernst in 1936, following her graduation from Columbia Law School. According to the finding aid for the Harriet Pilpel Papers at Smith College, she participated in twenty-seven cases before the U.S. Supreme Court between 1937 and 1991. Pilpel was also counsel to a number of reproductive rights and sexual education organizations or associations, including Planned Parenthood, the Sex Information and Educational Council of the United States, the Association for the Study of Abortion, and the Association for Voluntary Sterilization. In addition, she served on the boards of the National Abortion Rights Action League, the American Civil Liberties Union, and the Alan Guttmacher Institute.

50. See "Greenbaum, Wolff & Ernst: A Brief History of the Firm Prepared for the Occasion of Its 40th Anniversary and a Postscript Thereto Following Its 45 Anniversary on May 15, 1960," 1960, HRC, MLE Papers, Box 846 (old filing system).

51. Ernst was the ACLU's co-general counsel and an executive board member. His junior associate Alexander Lindey was key legal strategist and analyst for the ACLU-affiliated National Committee on Freedom from Censorship (NCFC), and later Harriet Pilpel had a long affiliation with the ACLU, especially in reproductive rights issues.

52. Wheeler, *How Sex Became a Civil Liberty*, 7, 92. For the most detailed and authoritative account of the ACLU's long history dedicated to expanding rights of sexual expression and practice and to protecting those rights legislatively and in the courts, see Wheeler, *How Sex Became a Civil Liberty*. See also Laura Weinrib, "The Sex Side of Civil Liberties: *United States v. Dennett* and the Changing Face of Free Speech," University of Chicago Public Law and Legal Theory Working Paper No. 385 (2012).

53. As Wheeler shows in *How Sex Became a Civil Liberty*, the ACLU initiated several of the cases I explore in this book and Ernst and his partners took on these cases under the aegis of the ACLU. Wheeler's extensive use of the ACLU records makes the ACLU the driving force. My use of Ernst's papers, including correspondence with his clients and interoffice memoranda of Greenbaum, Wolff & Ernst, leads me to a different emphasis on who drove the cases, and I suggest that, although the ACLU offered publicity for the cases, usually after the case was well under way, the organization had virtually no role in shaping the legal strategies, doing the background research, or shaping the legal arguments. Nor did it finance the cases. The Ernst firm took on the financing burden, and, as far as I was able to discern, it was not reimbursed by the ACLU in any of the cases, many of which it took on pro bono. ACLU board records indicate that the board was called on to "support" the cases, primarily to promote it through various publicity mechanisms, but otherwise the Greenbaum, Wolff & Ernst records indicate that the firm kept its affiliation with the ACLU out of the legal memoranda and its discussions with clients and the press. The Ernst firm did not claim ACLU affiliation, purposes, or aims in any of its internal or external discussion of the cases themselves.

54. For a glimpse into Ernst's alliance with Hoover, see Harrison E. Salisbury, "The Strange Correspondence of Morris Ernst and John Edgar Hoover, 1939–1964," *The Nation* (December 1, 1984): 575–89. For my brief treatment, see Gary, "Morris Ernst's Troubled Legacy."

55. See Ernst and Seagle, *To the Pure*; Ernst and Lindey, *The Censor Marches On*; Ernst, *First Freedom*; and Ernst and Schwartz, *Censorship*.

56. James, "Scribner's Examines," 9.

57. Rodell, "Morris Ernst," 9.

58. Rodell, "Morris Ernst," 97.

59. Although federal and state obscenity laws remain on the books, it is clear that the definition of what is considered obscene has changed dramatically since the late 1950s. See Heins, *Not in Front of the Children*; Whitney Strub, *Obscenity Rules: Roth v. United States and the Long Struggle over Sexual Expression* (Lawrence: University of Kansas Press, 2013); and Stone, *Sex and the Constitution*.

60. This disclosure did not require that their speech activities be shut down, but it did mean that their association with foreign entities and interests needed to be clear to the public. The disclosure idea was the basis of congressional Democrats' and the Roosevelt administration's approach to monitoring the publications and activities of a broad movement of far right and left-wing organizations, and it was written into the Foreign Agents Registration Act, which gave the State Department (and later the Justice Department) tools to penalize individuals and groups who failed to register. See Gary, *Nervous Liberals*, especially chaps. 4 and 5.

61. Ernst had many commitments besides his work in obscenity law matters, many of which were directly related to his concerns about the marketplace and its constrictions. These commitments led him, for instance, to become counsel to the American Newspaper Guild, defending the right of journalists for collective bargaining. He was counsel to the Dramatists Guild and the burlesque theater industry, fighting many battles with the commissioner of licenses in New York City over closings of both "legitimate" and burlesque theaters. In a landmark civil rights and labor rights case, he took Mayor Frank Hague of Jersey City to the U.S. Supreme Court to oppose Hague's ban of the CIO and the ACLU from holding public meetings in Jersey City. Ernst helped found the National Lawyers Guild as an organization for progressive lawyers who felt unrepresented by the anti–New Deal rhetoric and segregationist policies of the American Bar Association, served on the national legal advisory board for the NAACP, and was appointed a member of President Truman's Committee on Civil Rights. And throughout his career he was one of the most insistent critics of oligopoly conditions in the mass communications industries, paying special attention to consolidation of the radio and film industries, the decimation of locally owned newspapers by the newspaper chains, and postal rates that unfairly hindered market access to small newspapers and magazines. Ernst's extensive involvement as counsel in the case *Hague v. CIO* is detailed in *Hague v. CIO*, three bound volumes containing all the Greenbaum, Wolff & Ernst records on the case (HRC, MLE Papers, vols. 59–61). An article about the case by Ernst's junior associate and future chief justice of the Massachusetts Supreme Court Benjamin Kaplan is, "The Great Civil Rights Case of *Hague v. CIO*: Notes of a Survivor," *Suffolk University Law Review* 25 (1991): 913–47.

Chapter 2

1. Wilkinson's closing statement (stenographic transcript), *United States v. Dennett*, January 28, 1929, Harry Ransom Humanities Research Center (HRC), Morris L. Ernst (MLE) Papers, Box 287, Folder 287.4. Excerpted in Mary Ware Dennett, *Who's Obscene* (New York: Vanguard Press, 1930), 61.

2. Dudley Nichols, "Sex and the Law," *The Nation* (May 8, 1929), 553.

3. For a detailed biography of Dennett, see Constance Chen, *"The Sex Side of Life": Mary Ware Dennett's Pioneering Battle for Birth Control and Sex Education* (New York: New Press, 1997). For two excellent studies of Dennett's obscenity battles, see John M. Craig, "The Sex Side of Life: The Obscenity Case of Mary Ware Dennett," *Frontiers: A Journal of Women Studies* 15, no. 3 (1995): 146, 147; and Laura Weinrib, "The Sex Side of Civil Liberties: *United States v. Dennett* and the Changing Face of Free Speech," University of Chicago Public Law and Legal Theory Working Paper No. 385 (2012).

4. Craig, "Sex Side of Life," 145. Dennett and her husband, Hartley, separated formally in 1909, after "Mr. Dennett's affection for another woman" led him to abandon the family. Mary maintained custody of the two children, then ages 9 and 5. She obtained a divorce on grounds of desertion in 1913 in a trial that received extensive and rather sensational newspaper coverage.

5. For a history of the rivalry between Dennett and Sanger over leadership in the birth control movement, see Peter C. Engelman, *A History of the Birth Control Movement in America* (Santa Barbara, CA: Praeger, 2011).

6. Craig explains the differences in strategy and goals. Dennett, who has been treated as more "conservative" than Sanger, actually wanted and fought for a total repeal of the birth control bans, whereas Sanger pursued a physicians' exception, or a "doctors only" law that would allow physicians to provide birth control to their patients but would make women dependent on doctors rather than being able to claim access to birth control themselves. As Craig writes, "Dennett advocated a vigorous national campaign to repeal federal and state statutes forbidding the sending of birth control information through the mails, laws that became known as 'open bills.' She remained true to this position throughout her years as a reproductive rights activist. To Dennett, the matter was a civil liberties issue—the VPL sought the passage of 'legislation for the single purpose of removing the barriers to education'" (Craig, "Sex Side of Life," 146).

7. Weinrib writes that Dennett was a "fierce and vocal opponent of the 1873 Comstock Act" because it "gave the postal authorities immense discretion to censor obscene material, and Dennett considered it a formidable obstacle to birth control reform" (Weinrib, "Sex Side of Civil Liberties," 340).

8. Craig, "Sex Side of Life," 146. Weinrib writes, "Whereas Sanger tempered

her demands for birth control reform in the interwar period by advocating medical regulation rather than open access, Dennett called for repeal of all restrictions on contraception" (Weinrib, "Sex Side of Civil Liberties," 340).

9. Weinrib, "Sex Side of Civil Liberties," 340.

10. As Weinrib explains, "Dennett spearheaded a legislative effort to repeal the prohibition on the dissemination of information about birth control, which she unavailingly distinguished from the dissemination of contraception itself." She lobbied diligently "to find sponsors in the Senate and the House" for the Cummins-Vaile Bill, which she drafted and which "would have prohibited postal censorship of birth control materials." And she published a book in 1926, *Birth Control Laws*, "that criticized the Comstock laws and advocated legislative change" (Weinrib, "Sex Side of Civil Liberties," 342).

11. It did get one small "notice" in *Survey* in 1920.

12. Dennett, *Who's Obscene?* (New York: Vanguard Press, 1930), 7.

13. Robinson's Editor's Foreword to *The Sex Side of Life*, reprinted in Dennett, *Who's Obscene*, 141.

14. In 1918, for example, in an exchange with Carl Zigrosser, editor of *The Modern School: A Monthly Magazine*, Dennett says, "I find that the *Medical Review of Reviews* will not get out the little pamphlet for about two weeks yet, and in the mean time I want some more copies for the Modern School. I have given away all you sent to me, and there are people asking for them, so will you kindly send me ten more? I am enclosing a check for them, as I don't want the magazine to become impoverished by promoting my ideas!" (Dennett to Zigrosser, June 28, 1918, HRC, MLE Papers, Box 287, Folder 287.6). Zigrosser replied a few months later, "I am very sorry to say that the edition of the June number has been exhausted and I haven't any copies I could send you. . . . I certainly think the article ought to spread as widely as possible. I have heard nothing but commendation of it from every source" (Zigrosser to Dennett, September 18, 1918, HRC, MLE Papers, Box 287, Folder 287.6).

15. Among the works that Goodwin Watson cites as being widely used and useful are Havelock Ellis's *Little Essays of Love and Virtue*, M. J. Exner's *Principles of Sex Education* and *Rational Sex Life*, L. H. Gulick's *Dynamic of Manhood*, Herbert A. Gray's *Men, Women, and God*, Winfield S. Hall's "From Youth into Manhood" (Watson notes that he disagrees with Hall on treatment of masturbation in this work and in Hall's *Sexual Knowledge*), William Lee Howard's *Confidential Chat with Boys* (a treatment of masturbation that should be supplemented, Watson argues), C. W. Malchow's *Sexual Life* (frank and scientific, for those older than 21), and Menzies's *Auto-Eroticism*; and in this list, Watson notes that Marie Stopes's works are "extraordinarily informative." See Goodwin Watson of Teachers College, to

Ernst, January 29, 1929, HRC, MLE Papers, Box 46, Folder "Letters to Judge Moscowitz."

16. Dennett, *Who's Obscene*, 34.

17. Dennett, *Who's Obscene*, 35–36.

18. Dennett, *Who's Obscene*, xii.

19. Dennett, *Who's Obscene*, 143.

20. Dennett, *Who's Obscene*, 142.

21. Dennett, *Who's Obscene*, 144.

22. Dennett, *Who's Obscene*, 159.

23. Dennett, *Who's Obscene*, 158.

24. Dennett, *Who's Obscene*, 149–50.

25. Dennett, *Who's Obscene*, 157.

26. Dennett, *Who's Obscene*, 157.

27. Weinrib, "Sex Side of Civil Liberties," 344–45.

28. Weinrib, "Sex Side of Civil Liberties," 345.

29. Craig, "Sex Side of Life," 148.

30. Dennett to Ernst, October 20, 1928, HRC, MLE Papers, Box 287, Folder 287.4.

31. Because the U.S. Attorneys never revealed the forgery, the question of whether Mrs. Miles actually existed did not emerge until after the jury trial. Once Ernst's legal team learned of the circumstances of the letter's origins, it should have been de facto grounds for a mistrial. However, because this orchestrated forgery was not determined until after the trial and because Ernst had long before stipulated that Dennett had mailed the pamphlet in question, the legal question at issue was not how the pamphlet was solicited but whether or not the pamphlet was obscene. See Ernst to Judge Burrows, May 27, 1929, HRC, MLE Papers, Box 287, Folder 287.4.

32. Dennett reprints Wilkinson's letter in *Who's Obscene*, 45. She also wisely observed that the language of the indictment was itself damning: "Framing indictments which state the offending language is too bad to quote in the document, seem to be a governmental method of requesting a jury to convict" (Dennett, *Who's Obscene*, 47). And in fact, at the end of the trial, the judge's charge to the jury used virtually the same loaded language, almost demanding a verdict of guilty.

33. Craig, "Sex Side of Life," 149.

34. Weinrib, "Sex Side of Civil Liberties," 353.

35. Weinrib, "Sex Side of Civil Liberties," 354.

36. The clergy were Monsignor John Belford of the Roman Catholic Church of the Nativity, Rabbi Louis D. Gross of Union Temple, and the Reverend G. P. Atwater of Grace Episcopal Church, Brooklyn.

37. Weinrib, "Sex Side of Civil Liberties," 353.

38. For instance, Ernst wrote a letter to John H. Finley of the *New York Times*, passing on a copy of Dennett's pamphlet, giving him a quick background, and then saying that he hopes that the *Times* "will lend its aid in campaigns against the suppression of 'The Well of Loneliness' and this pamphlet" (Ernst to Finley, January 16, 1929, HRC, MLE Papers, Box 287, Folder 287.4).

39. Ernst wrote that if the court convicts Dennett, "the court in effect will have indicted the Union Theological Seminary, the YMCA's and others, who have used this pamphlet for nearly a decade." He used this line regularly, here in a letter to the editor of the *New York Telegram*, thanking them for an excellent editorial titled "Obscene Censors," printed on January 14, 1929. Ernst to *New York Telegram*, January 15, 1929, HRC, MLE Papers, Box 287, Folder 287.4.

40. Assistant Attorney Wilkinson's statement (stenographic transcript), January 28, 1929, p. 4, HRC, MLE Papers, Box 287, Folder 287.5. Dennett quotes from and comments on Wilkinson's statement in *Who's Obscene*, 60–67.

41. Assistant Attorney Wilkinson's statement, 5.

42. Assistant Attorney Wilkinson's statement, 2.

43. Assistant Attorney Wilkinson's statement, 2.

44. Assistant Attorney Wilkinson's statement, 3.

45. Assistant Attorney Wilkinson's statement, 4.

46. Dennett, *Who's Obscene*, 56.

47. Dennett, *Who's Obscene*, 57.

48. Dennett, *Who's Obscene*, 60. For coverage of the motions, see clippings in HRC, MLE Papers, Box 47, Folder 47 (January 28–29, 1929, clippings from the *New York Times*, The *New York World*, and the *New York Herald Tribune*). See also Dudley Nichols, "Sex and Our Children," *The Nation* (February 6, 1929), 154–55.

49. Dudley Nichols especially ridiculed Wilkinson, in his February 6 piece "Sex and Our Children" in *The Nation* and in his follow up article, "Sex and the Law," *The Nation* (May 8, 1929), 554.

50. I found thirty-six letters in a folder marked "Letters to Judge Moscowitz" in Ernst's papers, thirty-three of which supported the pamphlet. There may have been others that did not wind up in Ernst's papers. See HRC, MLE Papers, Box 287, Folder 287.5.

51. See, for example, Straton to Judge Moscowitz, February 2, 1929, reprinted in Dennett, *Who's Obscene*, 102–7; and Chase to Judge Moscowitz, February 8, 1929, reprinted in Dennett, *Who's Obscene*, 108–9.

52. Smith and Wearne to Judge Moscowitz, February 1, 1929, in Dennett, *Who's Obscene*, 109–13.

53. Kelly to Reverend Chase, n.d., in Dennett, *Who's Obscene*, 122–24. Dr. Kelly

went on, echoing Reverend Straton with his particular race suicide fears bursting to the surface: "If such literature as this is allowed to circulate, the moral life of our country will rot out in a single generation and sink to a standard as low as that of Central and South America, and the Latin countries of Europe and the unspeakable debaucheries of the African jungle."

54. Chase to Judge Moscowitz, February 8, 1929.

55. John Sumner, Secretary of the New York Society for the Suppression of Vice, January 29, 1929, reprinted in Dennett, *Who's Obscene*, 125.

56. Chase to Judge Moscowitz, February 8, 1929; see also Dillingham to Moscowitz, February 4, 1929, in Dennett, *Who's Obscene*, 126–27.

57. Chase to Judge Moscowitz, February 8, 1929.

58. Among those writing unsolicited letters wholly endorsing the pamphlet were Carrie E. Buggie, Judson Memorial, Manhattan, January 29, 1929; Willard Beatty, superintendent of the Bronxville Public Schools, January 29, 1929; Reverend Parkes Cadman, Central Congregational Church, Brooklyn; Reverend George P. Atwater, Grace Church, Brooklyn Heights; William W. Biddle, Hessian Hills School; Charles Webber, Union Theological Seminary; Arthur Swift, Union Theological Seminary; C. J. Bushnell, *New York Telegraph*; Nadina Kavinoky, physician, Los Angeles; Gertrude Laws, assistant chief, Bureau of Parental Education, Los Angeles; John Burwald, chair of geology and paleontology, Cal Tech; Irma Burwalda, director, International Association of Police Women and member of the California Commission for Prison for Women; Reverend George Wilson Plummer, New York City; Charles Cooper Packard, attorney, Los Angeles (and 11 others from New York City and California in this folder); Dr. William H. Cary, February 2, 1929; Mrs. Bertha Barron Berthald; Ethel Lee, who wrote, "The truth is always wholesome & this fundamental basis of nature should be understood & not always half veiled," March 12, 1929; and Lucille Lazar, January 27, 1929, social worker, who wrote, "It is my opinion that this pamphlet presents the subject for young people in a manner more honest, more intelligent, and more wholesome than anything else I have ever seen." Benjamin Winchester, executive secretary of the Commission on Christian Education, Federal Council of the Churches in Christ in America, wrote in a January 31, 1929, letter to Ernst that he had carefully studied the pamphlet and did not find it obscene; nor did his wife—"In fact she had never seen a more satisfactory one." Marie Virginia Smith, social worker and resident of Henry Street Settlement, wrote Ernst on March 5, 1929, to say that the pamphlet was a "helpful and necessary article of instruction," "wholesome and inspiring." All these letters can be found in HRC, MLE Papers, Box 46, Folder "Letters to Judge Moscowitz."

59. Besides the letters directed to the judge, Ernst's archives contain hundreds of letters from people who had read about the case and were outraged, or had read

about it and wanted a copy of the pamphlet. The case struck a chord with the public. Also, Ernst wrote to Dennett, telling her that the ACLU planned to form a committee to work on her behalf. He indicated to the ACLU that taking a case to the Supreme Court would run to as much as $3,000 for printing and traveling expenses alone. He suggested that Dennett get in touch with Roger Baldwin or Forest Bailey and discuss the organization of such a committee but added, "I will have nothing to do with the committee whatsoever primarily because I want no one to feel that I am party to raising money in connection with a case in which I am attorney." Following the first trial, the ACLU remitted $252 toward the appeal (which Greenbaum, Wolff & Ernst litigated for free). There is no correspondence between the ACLU leadership and Ernst's office in Ernst's papers, and I would surmise that this lack of correspondence has to do with Ernst wanting to avoid anything that might look like conflict of interest, as he told Dennett. Nor could he be on the ACLU's dime while his firm was doing this work (Ernst to Dennett, February 16, 1929, HRC, MLE Papers, Box 287, Folder 287.4).

60. More than 150 requests for the pamphlet were sent directly to Ernst's office. *The Nation* informed readers that they could request copies through Ernst's office for 35 cents per copy, and the Ernst firm sent out the copies.

61. Mrs. Anne Bronson to Judge Moscowitz, March 1, 1929, HRC, MLE Papers, Box 46, Folder "Letters to Judge Moscowitz."

62. Veteran birth control champions Dr. Robert L. Dickinson, Louise Bryant, and Dennett used their networks to secure potential expert testimony. Dennett wrote to Dickinson, Dr. and Mrs. Shepard Kerch, Mr. E. J. Allen of Seth Low Junior College, Louise Bryant, and Goodwin Watson, telling all of them that they should be among the twelve experts whose testimony Judge Moscowitz has agreed to hear; all letters were sent on January 29, 1929. Other documents in this file show Dickinson and Bryant's extensive involvement in organizing expert witnesses, including letters from Bryant to Ernst (January 31, 1929), from Dickinson to Jelliffe (January 30, 1929), from Dickinson to Worthington (January 30, 1929), and from Dennett to Dickinson (January 29, 1929). All these letters are in HRC, MLE Papers, Box 287, Folder 287.2.

63. "Points to Be Mentioned," n.d., HRC, MLE Papers, Box 287, Folder 287.2.

64. Harrison Elliot (of Union Theological Seminary) to Judge Moscowitz, February 2, 1929; Smith Ely Jelliffe, M.D., letter, February 6, 1929; and Robert Dickinson letter, February 1, 1929; all in HRC, MLE Papers, Box 46, Folder "U.S. v. Dennett, people who were ready to testify."

65. The YMCA and the YWCA were critical to the support of Dennett and were critical to the pamphlets' broad use. Indeed, despite the indictment, in February 1929 the National YMCA ordered an additional 600 copies of the pamphlet for

distribution among boys' clubs, according to a February 7, 1929, letter from Ernst to Judge Joseph N. Ulman of Baltimore. The defense received numerous letters from YMCA officials who had used the pamphlet. For example, William A. Jenny, from the Prospect Park Branch of the YMCA, used it repeatedly with older boys at summer camp and in work with young men, calling it "a straightforward, scientific treatise" (Jenny to Ernst, January 29, 1929). E. Clayton Baldwin reported that he used the pamphlet with young men in his church, Trinity M.E. Church, Richmond Hill, Long Island (letter of January 29, 1929). And W. H. Dewar, executive secretary of the Prospect Park Branch of the YMCA, reported that both he and Mrs. Dewar found the pamphlet very helpful for boys and young men, with no deleterious effects, and that the author was "sincere in motives" (Dewar to Ernst, January 29, 1929). All letters in HRC, MLE Papers, Box 287, Folder 287.4.

66. Dennett, *Who's Obscene*, 132.

67. Dennett, *Who's Obscene*, 135.

68. Ernst's transcript, in Dennett, *Who's Obscene*, 70–71.

69. Dennett, *Who's Obscene*, 162. Ernst's intended witnesses were Mrs. Larkin, National Committee for Mental Hygiene; Myrtle Le Compte, Teacher's College, Columbia University; Mrs. Cecile Pilpel, Child Study Association of America; Mrs. Clara Savage Littledale, managing editor of *Children: The Magazine for Parents*; William A. Jenny, Young Men's Christian Association secretary, Prospect Park, Brooklyn, New York; Bascom Johnson, legal director, American Social Hygiene Association; Dr. Max Emer, Educational Division, American Social Hygiene Association; Abel J. Gregg, National Council of the YMCA; Edward J. Allen, director of Seth Low Junior College of Columbia University, Brooklyn; Dr. Robert Latou Dickinson, secretary of the Committee on Maternal Health; Jess Perlman, director of the Associated Guidance Bureau; W. H. Dewar, executive secretary of the Prospect Park Branch, YMCA; Prof. Harrison Elliott, Union Theological Seminary; and Prof. Goodwin F. Watson, Teachers College, Columbia University.

70. Trial transcript, in Dennett, *Who's Obscene*, 171. This exchange between Ernst and Dennett appears to be the only moment of success during the trial.

71. Trial transcript, in Dennett, *Who's Obscene*, 173. On the issue of including *Representative Opinions* along with the pamphlet in the envelope mailed to "Mrs. Miles," Judge Burrows told the jury, "Now in this envelope in which the pamphlet was enclosed were certain testimonials, if I may so term them, although I do not recall whether that term has been used in connection with them before or not, but you know what I mean. Those testimonials were admitted, gentlemen, as documents which were included in the pamphlet. You are not to judge those testimonials as though you had absolute facts as to the truth of the pamphlet. They are not there for that purpose, because you can readily see that they are simply

some things which purport to be the statements of certain persons."

72. Trial transcript, in Dennett, *Who's Obscene*, 177–78.

73. Trial transcript, in Dennett, *Who's Obscene*, 179.

74. Dudley Nichols describes the jury's decision as follows: "Late in the afternoon the jurors filed out and cast their first ballot eight to four for conviction. The second brought nine votes against Mrs. Dennett. On the third she lost still another vote. Then a court attendant entered the jury room, the story goes, and warned the twelve men that it was after five o'clock and that if no decision was reached soon they would be held over some time for a 'court supper.' The two jurors who held out immediately fell in line and on the fourth ballot voted with the other ten for conviction" (Nichols, "Sex and the Law," 553).

75. Nichols, "Sex and the Law," 553.

76. See Dudley Nichols's two-part series in *The Nation*, "Sex and the Law" (May 8, 1929) and "Sex and Our Children" (February 6, 1929).

77. Pinchot to Ernst, April 1929, HRC, MLE Papers, Box 287, Folder 287.4.

78. Lindey draft article, with Dennett insert, May 1929, HRC, MLE Papers, Box 47 (new Box 2), Folder 47.2.1. The final article was published in *Birth Control Review* (spring/summer 1929).

79. Lindey draft article, May 1929.

80. Quotes in Craig, "Sex Side of Life," 150.

81. Rich coverage of the journalistic treatment of the case can be found in Dolores Flamiano, "'The 'Sex Side of Life' in the News: Mary Ware Dennett's Obscenity Case, 1929–1930," *Journalism History* 25, no. 2 (summer 1999): 64–74.

82. Flamiano, "Sex Side of Life," 68.

83. Wheeler discusses the *Dennett* case in *How Sex Became a Civil Liberty* to argue that this was a turning point for the ACLU in taking up sexual civil liberties cases. Weinrib advances this argument in "Sex Side of Civil Liberties."

84. See Helen Lefkowitz Horowitz, *Rereading Sex: Battles over Sexual Knowledge and Suppression in Nineteenth Century America* (New York: Knopf, 2002); and especially Wheeler, *How Sex Became a Civil Liberty*, in relation to the ACLU.

85. Weinrib, "Sex Side of Civil Liberties," 339.

86. Weinrib, "Sex Side of Civil Liberties," 339.

87. Craig, "Sex Side of Life," 152.

88. Noted by Weinrib, "Sex Side of Civil Liberties."

89. Lindey had a question for Ernst: What happened to all the letters to Judge Moscowitz, and is there any way of getting those letters before the circuit court? (Memo from Lindey to Ernst, re: Final Draft of Brief, September 19, 1929, HRC, MLE Papers, Box 47 [Box 2], Folder 47.2.1).

90. They wanted pamphlets from the New York State public health agencies

for their appeal brief, including *The Problem of Sex Education in the Schools*; *Healthy Manhood*; *Public Health Is Purchasable Within Natural Limitations*; *Syphilis, Gonorrhea, and Chancroid*; *Healthy Mothers and Babies*; and *Manpower*. From the publisher Doubleday Doran they wanted *Sex and Youth*, by Sherwood Eddy. From the American Social Hygiene Association, they requested Paul Strong Achilles's *Effectiveness of Certain Social Hygiene Literature*. From the U.S. Public Health Service, they requested *Today's World Problem in Disease Prevention*, *The Problem of Sex Education in the Schools*, and *Sex Education: Symposium for Educators*.

91. Memo from Lindey to Ernst, re: Final Draft of Brief, September 19, 1929, HRC, MLE Papers, Box 47 (Box 2), Folder 47.2.1.

92. Lindey memo to Ernst, "Guessing Oneself into Jail," n.d., HRC, MLE Papers, Box 47 (Box 2), Folder 47.2.1.

93. Draft of conclusion to Appellate Brief, n.d., HRC, MLE Papers, Box 47, Folder 47.10.

94. Appellate Brief, *United States v. Dennett*, U.S. Court of Appeals, Second Circuit, p. 4, HRC, MLE Papers, vol. 86.

95. Appellate Brief, *United States v. Dennett*, 5. A quick overview of the brief's structure indicates their overall strategy: (1) The pamphlet is not obscene as a matter of law; (2) the trial court erred in excluding testimony as to the use and distribution of the pamphlet; (3) the trial court erred in excluding evidence consisting of similar publications issued by the U.S. Public Health Service and the New York State Department of Health; (4) the trial court erred in excluding evidence as to the defendant's motive; (5) the trial court erred in charging the jury that it was not to give any credence to the enclosure titled *Representative Opinions*; (6) the trial court erred in refusing the defendant's several requests to charge the jury; and (7) the obscenity statute violates the First Amendment to the U.S. Constitution.

96. Appellate Brief, *United States v. Dennett*, 8.

97. Appellate Brief, *United States v. Dennett*, 28. Judge Hand had written, "Nor is it an objection, I think, that such an interpretation gives to the words of the statute a varying meaning from time to time. Such words as these do not embalm the precise morals of an age or place; while they presuppose that some things will always be shocking to public taste, the vague subject-matter is left to the gradual development of general notions about what is decent."

98. Appellate Brief, *United States v. Dennett*, 11.

99. "In effect, the Court ruled out testimony as to distribution, on the purely speculative ground that it might have been accepted by the jury as opinion testimony" (Appellate Brief, *United States v. Dennett*, 21).

100. Appellate Brief, *United States v. Dennett*, 23. "It is for this reason that the higher Courts have eliminated surmises and have predicated their decisions on the mode of distribution."

101. Appellate Brief, *United States v. Dennett*, 29.

102. In short, what is accepted or rejected by a community "is a fact susceptible to proof," and therefore "the jury is entitled to know such a fact in order to enable it to reach the proper conclusion" (Appellate Brief, *United States v. Dennett*, 29). "When representatives of such organizations as the National Committee for Mental Hygiene, Teacher's College of Columbia University, the Child Study Association, the American Social Hygiene Association, the National Council of Young Men's Christian Associations . . . the Union Theological Seminary, the Academy of Medicine, are ready to testify to the use they have made of certain material in connection with their work for social betterment, they should be heard as to such use" (30).

103. As Weinrib explains, "Ernst [and Lindey were] at pains to distinguish the pamphlet from those modes of speech deemed subject to regulation in the past: 'lurid literature and advertisements distributed by quacks to beguile the public into buying worthless nostrums' (that is, the information on birth control that had once been grist for the Comstock Mill); 'violent attack[s] on religion or religious customs'; 'newspaper reports of crime, immorality or fornication'; 'defense[s] of illegitimacy or moral laxity'; and 'forthright pornography.'" By these comparisons, Dennett's work was "indeed a departure from these earlier forms of sexualized literature, some informative, some prurient" (Weinrib, "Sex Side of Civil Liberties," 356–57).

104. *Swearingen v. United States*, 161 U.S. 446 (1896).

105. Appellate Brief, *United States v. Dennett*, 11.

106. Likewise, these publications also addressed the controversial issues of masturbation and venereal diseases, and Dennett's treatment of these subjects was comparable to the federal government's publications, all of which "vividly set forth" the "horrors of sexual diseases and the dangers of promiscuous sexual relations. Prostitution is condemned both as an unconscionable social evil and as a source of disease" (Appellate Brief, *United States v. Dennett*, 5). Titles of those government publications include *Healthy Manhood*, issued by the New York State Department of Health; *Sex Education: Symposium for Educators*, issued by the U.S. Public Health Service; *Today's World Problem in Disease Prevention*, issued by the U.S. Public Health Service; *Syphilis, Gonorrhea and Chancroid*, issued by the New York State Department of Health; *Sex and Youth*, by Sherwood Eddy, published in 1928 by Doubleday Doran; and other works published by the U.S. Public Health Service and the American Social Hygiene Association.

107. The prosecution argued that profit motive was the key distinction between the governments' publications and Dennett's work: "In other words, the government did not contend that there was any difference between the official publications on the one hand, and the defendant's pamphlet on the other. The sole ground of attempted distinction was that in the one case, there was no profit-making motive, while in the other case there was. And yet, paradoxically, the prosecution violently opposed evidence proffered by the defense as to the absence of the profit motive in writing of the pamphlet and as to its distribution by non-profit making organizations" (Appellate Brief, *United States v. Dennett*, 34).

108. That is, the nineteenth-century obscenity statute put far more power in the hands of Postal and Customs officials than the Constitution's framers ever intended. Ernst argued that democratic life depended on the free flow of information through a wide variety of channels of information and that no channel was more important than the postal system, but the obscenity law gave excessive power to the Postal Service, which interfered with the free exchange of ideas. Quoting *United States v. Harmon* (1896), Ernst and Lindey based their argument on the idea that the founder's intent was "the right to the widest latitude of discussion of all subjects of interest to the people. Any thought which may contain the germ of an idea calculated to benefit any human being, when couched in decent language, ought to be disseminated among the people" (Appellate Brief, *United States v. Dennett*, 51). They wrote that "disregarding the minor limitations of the phrase 'decent language'—a mere matter of changing taste—this statement expresses the philosophy and intent of our Constitution" (51). There was, they averred, a clear consensus among the republic's founder to constrain postal power so that it would not become a censor. This argument was rather easily repudiated by the fact that Congress had passed the Comstock Act in 1873, giving the Postal Service and the Customs Service broad censorship authority, and had on several occasions renewed that authority by updating Customs' tariff authority (in 1922, and again soon, in 1930.

109. Weinrib, "Sex Side of Civil Liberties," 357. This free press argument laid claim not just to the letter but to the spirit of the First Amendment. Weinrib considers the implications of Ernst and Lindey's claim. As Weinrib writes, "Ernst was not naïve about his chances [on the constitutionality question]. The Supreme Court had ruled in *Ex parte Jackson* that the freedom of the press did not prevent Congress from excluding pamphlets from the mail, and it had given no indication that it was about to change its mind. Indeed, Ernst conceded that obscenity statutes repeatedly had been deemed constitutional by the federal courts. He nonetheless contended that changing public mores warranted reconsideration of the issue. Most important, he sought to extend the powerful rhetoric of Justices

Holmes's and Brandeis's dissents in the Supreme Court's recent First Amendment cases, which dealt with political speech, to the obscenity context." She adds, "For example, he quoted from Justice Holmes's dissenting opinion in *United States v. Schwimmer*: 'if there is any principle of the Constitution that more imperatively calls for attachment than any other it is the principle of free thought—not free thought for those who agree with us but freedom for the thought that we hate'" (Weinrib, "Sex Side of Civil Liberties," 357).

110. Appellate Brief, *United States v. Dennett*, 58. Here the full sentence is, "Surely the Federal obscenity statute under which the defendant herein has been convicted, and under which an individual may easily guess himself into jail, does not afford the 'unequivocal warning' that a citizen is entitled to."

111. Appellate Brief, *United States v. Dennett*, 60.

112. Appellate Brief, *United States v. Dennett*, 61.

113. Appellate Brief, *United States v. Dennett*, 63.

114. Craig, "Sex Side of Life," 153. As Craig goes on to explain, "Between 1879 and 1913, relatively few challenges to the Comstock laws or the Hicklin rule appeared in the various state or federal courts. In cases that did go to trial, including a series of decisions during the 1880s, judges applied the Hicklin rule without qualification" (153). Learned Hand's dicta in *United States v. Kennerley* (1913) offered the first real challenge to the Hicklin test in the federal courts. As Craig explains, "District Court Judge Learned Hand condemned the Hicklin rule even in upholding a conviction. Though Hand acknowledged that 'the test had been accepted by the lower federal courts until it would be no longer proper for me to disregard it,' he went on to observe that 'the rule as laid down, however consonant it may be with Victorian morals, does not seem to me to answer to the understanding of morality at the present time.' To Hand, a test that protected the 'lowest and least capable seems a fatal policy.' As a lower court federal justice, Hand was inviting the defendant to appeal, which he did. But the Circuit court in New York proceeded to avoid the matter by simply overturning Kennerley's conviction . . . and judged the book in question not obscene by that standard" (Craig, "Sex Side of Life," 153).

115. *United States v. Dennett*, 39 F.2d 564 (1930), at 568.

116. *United States v. Dennett*, 39 F.2d 564 (1930), at 569.

117. *United States v. Dennett*, 39 F.2d 564 (1930), at 569.

118. Weinrib, "Sex Side of Civil Liberties," 358–59.

119. Weinrib, "Sex Side of Civil Liberties," 359.

120. Weinrib, "Sex Side of Civil Liberties," 359.

121. Weinrib adds that such recognition of a public interest in sex laid the groundwork for the Supreme Court's midcentury extension of First Amendment

protection to "sexually explicit speech" (Weinrib, "Sex Side of Civil Liberties," 359).

122. *United States v. Dennett,* 39 F.2d 564 (1930), at 568–69 (emphasis added).

123. *United States v. Dennett,* 39 F.2d 564 (1930), at 569.

124. Flamiano, "Sex Side of Life," 65. Dennett noted "the large mass of newspaper clippings which have come from all over the country . . . opposed to the censorship of her pamphlet" (Flamiano, "Sex Side of Life," 65).

125. Weinrib, "Sex Side of Civil Liberties," 361. Weinrib quotes, among other pieces, "Mrs. Dennett Vindicated," *New York World* (March 6, 1930); Lewis Gannett, "Books and Other Things," *New York Tribune* (March 20, 1930); and "Mrs. Dennett Freed in Sex Booklet Case," *New York Times* (March 4, 1930).

126. Weinrib, Wheeler, and Craig all point to this result.

127. Weinrib, "Sex Side of Civil Liberties," 362.

128. As noted earlier, Ernst wrote to Dennett, telling her that the ACLU planned to form a committee to work on her behalf but that he could have nothing to do with it, to avoid a conflict of interest. Craig explains that the ACLU did raise money for an appeal: "Even before Dennett's trial began, the American Civil Liberties Union pledged its support if she lost in district court. Eyeing the impending appeal as a significant test case, after the negative verdict it formed the Mary Dennett Defense Committee. This group, chaired initially by publisher Roy W. Howard [initially, but John Dewey wound up being the chair], set to work raising money and organizing a rally at New York's Town Hall on May 21. Within a month the committee had raised over $1,000 in the event the case made its way to the Supreme Court (ultimately it collected over $3,000)" (Craig, "Sex Side of Life," 151).

Chapter 3

1. Lindey to Ernst, September 2, 1930, Harry Ransom Humanities Research Center (HRC), Morris L. Ernst (MLE) Papers, Box 359, Folder 359.1.

2. Dennett had hosted Stopes for a packed meeting in Manhattan's Town Hall in 1921, forever endearing Dennett to Stopes but irritating Margaret Sanger, who considered Dennett a rival for leadership of the birth control movement.

3. The title of the action was *United States v. One Obscene Book Entitled "Married Love,"* 48 Fed. (2d) 821, decided April 6, 1931. Originally titled *Married Love: Or, Love in Marriage,* the book was retitled *Married Love: A New Contribution to the Solution of Sex Difficulties* by the time Ernst and Lindey defended it.

4. Ernst to Stopes, June 29, 1931, HRC, MLE Papers, Box 359, Folder 359.1.

5. For background details, see June Rose, *Marie Stopes and the Sexual Revolution* (London: Faber & Faber, 1992).

6. Rose, *Marie Stopes,* 1.

7. Rose, *Marie Stopes*, 29.

8. Stopes was soon invited to prepare a catalogue for the Natural History section of the British Museum's Geology Department, to deliver a lecture at the Scientific Congress in Vienna, and to join a research lab in the Austrian Tyrol; she took an excursion to the Arctic Circle with a Norwegian scholar and friend; and soon received funding from the Royal Society in 1907 to study fossilized coal in Japan, where she was housed at the Imperial University in Tokyo, staying for 18 months (partly pursuing a possible relationship with a divorced Japanese scientist, but this never came to fruition and she returned home to England in 1909, disappointed in love but making her mark in paleontology).

9. Rose, *Marie Stopes*, 73.

10. Rose, *Marie Stopes*, 76.

11. Rose, *Marie Stopes*, 77.

12. Rose, *Marie Stopes*, 82.

13. Rose, *Marie Stopes*, 82.

14. Rose, *Marie Stopes*, 94.

15. Rose, *Marie Stopes*, 95.

16. Rose, *Marie Stopes*, 101.

17. For a rich discussion of how ideals of female purity informed the culture in the Victorian era and reinforced opposition to contraception, see Nicole Beisel, *Imperiled Innocents: Anthony Comstock and Family Reproduction in Victorian America* (Princeton, NJ: Princeton University Press, 1997), esp. 25–48. Helen Lefkowitz Horowitz also discusses the cultural expectations of women and the crackdown on contraception in Helen Lefkowitz Horowitz, *Rereading Sex: Battles over Sexual Knowledge* (New York: Knopf, 2002), 70–85, 194–209.

18. Rose, *Marie Stopes*, 112.

19. Rose, *Marie Stopes*, 111–12. Rose goes on to explain that "a state of moral panic gripped the nation as the scale of venereal disease, highlighted by the reports in the press and propaganda films, became known. By the end of the war, over 400,000 cases had been treated in the British Army. . . . This made good marital relations seem even more desirable, and Marie's book helped to point the way" (112).

20. Rose, *Marie Stopes*, 111.

21. Rose, *Marie Stopes*, 112.

22. Rose, *Marie Stopes*, 112.

23. Alexander C. T. Geppert, "Divine Sex, Happy Marriage, Regenerated Nation: Marie Stopes's Marital Manual *Married Love* and the Making of a Best-Seller, 1918–1955," *Journal of the History of Sexuality* 8, no. 3 (January 1998): 408.

24. Rose, *Marie Stopes*, 114.

25. Rose, *Marie Stopes*, 114.

26. Rose, *Marie Stopes*, 118.

27. Rose, *Marie Stopes*, 119.

28. Rose, *Marie Stopes*, 118.

29. Rose, *Marie Stopes*, 139.

30. Jessamyn Neuhaus, "The Importance of Being Orgasmic: Sexuality, Gender, and Marital Sex Manuals in the United States, 1920–1963," *Journal of the History of Sexuality* 9, no. 4 (October 2000): 447–73.

31. Neuhaus, "Importance of Being Orgasmic," 461.

32. Neuhaus, "Importance of Being Orgasmic," 456.

33. Neuhaus, "Importance of Being Orgasmic," 456.

34. Stopes to Ernst, January 9, 1930, HRC, MLE Papers, Box 359, Folder 359.1.

35. Apparently this deletion produced a rift with Margaret Sanger, because she had taken a copy of Stopes's *Married Love* to Robinson, of the Critic and Guide Co., who agreed to publish it, but he made the edits without consulting Stopes. According to Rose, Robinson's version was the one that had been declared obscene by the New York Court of Special Sessions in 1921 (see Rose, *Marie Stopes*, 162); this detail about the book's history never showed up in the Ernst records at all, but Ernst and Lindey also did not pursue the ownership and copyright trail for very long.

36. Lindey, file memorandum, January 22, 1930, HRC, MLE Papers, Box 359, Folder 359.1.

37. In his October 7, 1929, decision on *Enduring Passion*, Judge Fischer quoted Justice Phillips in *United States v. Harmon*: "After Adam and Eve ate of the fruit of the tree of knowledge they passed the condition of perfectibility which some people nowadays aspire to, and their eyes being opened, they discerned that there was both good and evil. . . . From that day to this civilized man has carried with him a sense of shame—the feeling that there were some things on which the eye—the mind—should not look: and where men and women become so depraved by the use, or so insensate from perverted education, that they will not veil their eyes, nor hold their tongues, the government should perform the office for them" (Treasury Decision 43606, in *Treasury Decisions Under Customs and Other Laws*, vol. 56 [Washington, DC: U.S. Department of Treasury, 1929], 274–78).

38. Like other birth control activists, Stopes had little good to say about the Catholic Church, privately and publicly, and she had fought numerous battles in the 1920s with her Catholic critics, including one libel suit she filed against a critic that made its way through three different courts, finally being resolved by the House of Lords.

39. "In answer to your question about legal actions against the book *Married Love*, let me say categorically to my knowledge there have been *no* legal actions in any country whatsoever except America, where there was that Robinson and

Putnam's action of which you have in Putnam's hands a full report. I am not able to provide that for you. Then quite recently, last year, when the Irish Free State made all the discussion of Contraception a criminal offence, it automatically banned my books from its shores, but there has been no explicit legal action so far as I am aware. I think here and there in the Colonies the book gets off and on the list of permitted imports as Roman Catholic officials get in and out of office. But again there has been no explicit legal action so far as I am aware" (Stopes to Ernst, October 22, 1930, HRC, MLE Papers, Box 360, Folder 360.1).

40. *United States v. Dennett*, 39 F.2d 564 (1930), at 569.

41. Under the older Section 305 of the 1922 Tariff Act, a Customs officer's decision to withhold materials could be challenged only before a Customs Court judge, with no right of appeal to any other federal court; under this older system, a ruling such as Judge Fischer's on *Enduring Passion* was the final word.

42. Greenbaum, Wolff & Ernst/Lindey to G. P. Putnam's Sons, New York City, July 22, 1930, HRC, MLE Papers, Box 359, Folder 359.1.

43. Ernst to Stopes, March 4, 1930, HRC, MLE Papers, Box 359, Folder 359.1.

44. Stopes wrote, "I have just got a long letter from [Mr. Bedborough] and hope that he has correctly understood you and I have correctly understood him that you are so very kind as to suggest testing out *Married Love* for American publication and arrange publication, fighting for the right of publication without me expecting to spend money on this, but that you will have a percentage of my profits when the books *Married Love* and *Enduring Passion* are put on the market with your kind assistance in America" (Stopes to Ernst, March 31, 1930, HRC, MLE Papers, Box 359, Folder 359.1). Stopes sent a telegram the same day, telling Ernst that she agreed to his general plan—no cash outlay, that he would get a percentage of the American profits, and that the book was sailing on the *Homeric* (Stopes telegram to Ernst, March 31, 1930, HRC, MLE Papers, Box 359, Folder 359.1).

45. Because of the uncertainty about who owned publishing rights, the law firm had early on contacted Vanguard Press about publishing it, but Ernst was "fearful that Putnam might have some possible legal claims which they might inject into the situation in case we can ever legalize the volumes." Because he assumed that Putnam's did not have title, he wanted to move ahead with Vanguard, and therefore he needed to see any copies of contracts and correspondence with Putnam's that Stopes could provide, especially "relative to cancellation of such contracts." This issue would go back and forth for several months. Ernst to Stopes, April 10, 1930, HRC, MLE Papers, Box 359, Folder 359.1.

46. Stopes added in her long discussion of her libel trial that she thought it would be better "in handling *Married Love*, to leave out all such points bearing on the technicalities of contraception, because they are nothing to do with *Married*

Love, not being in that book at all but in my book *Wise Parenthood* which is not at present under consideration" (Stopes to Ernst, October 22, 1930, HRC, MLE Papers, Box 360, Folder 360.1).

47. Ernst to Stopes, April 10, 1930, HRC, MLE Papers, Box 359, Folder 359.1.

48. Stopes to Ernst, May 14, 1930, HRC, MLE Papers, Box 359, Folder 359.1.

49. Wary of the U.S. legal system, Stopes suggested to Putnam's that perhaps getting royalties from one of the U.S. pirated editions might be preferable to incurring the legal costs resulting from a battle with Customs: "This, of course, frightens me a little as I have heard terrible stories of American legal costs," she wrote Putnam's, adding "I do think there should be a reasonable limit to Mr. Ernst's expenditure, etc., as my hearsay about the American courts is terrifying" (Stopes to Putnam's, July 7, 1930, HRC, MLE Papers, Box 359, Folder 359.1).

50. Stopes to Putnam's, July 7, 1930.

51. Ernst to Customs, April 5, 1930, HRC, MLE Papers, Box 359, Folder 359.1.

52. Eaton to Ernst, April 5, 1930, HRC, MLE Papers, Box 359, Folder 359.1. "You will note that the opinion is very strongly against the admission of Mrs. Stopes' book."

53. Ernst to Eaton, April 7, 1930, HRC, MLE Papers, Box 359, Folder 359.1.

54. "Am I to understand that they were admitted or just happened to pass through?" (Ernst to Eaton, April 14, 1930, MLE Papers, Box 359, Folder 359.1). See also Eaton to Ernst, April 15, 1930, HRC, MLE Papers, Box 359, Folder 359.1.

55. Ernst to Eaton, September 3, 1930, HRC, MLE Papers, Box 359, Folder 359.1.

56. Ernst to Eaton, October 15, 1930, HRC, MLE Papers, Box 359, Folder 359.2.

57. Ernst to Balch, October 29, 1930, HRC, MLE Papers, Box 359, Folder 359.2. As Ernst recounted to Earle Balch in Putnam's New York office, the Customs lawyers had told Ernst that "they could not see how they could allow it in because they would not want their women folk to ever read such trash." Balch wrote back, "I can't help pitying the women folk of Mr. Nevius and Mr. Stevens" (Balch to Ernst, October 30, 1930, HRC, MLE Papers, Box 359, Folder 359.2).

58. Greenbaum, Wolff & Ernst to Nevius, October 29, 1930, HRC, MLE Papers, Box 359, Folder 359.2.

59. Ernst's warnings about increased piracy and bootlegging arose out of his immediate concerns, as uncertainty over the American copyright claims to *Married Love* came back at them anew, with an additional actor claiming right of ownership. Joseph Lewis, of Eugenics Publications, claimed to have bought the rights to the book from Dr. Robinson and had an edition of *Married Love*, which he edited, circulating in the United States (Greenbaum, Wolff & Ernst to Nevius, November 1, 1930, HRC, MLE Papers, Box 359, Folder 359.2). Copies of the

Eugenics Press version of *Married Love* are still available from online booksellers, as I bought a 1931 edition.

60. Greenbaum, Wolff & Ernst to Nevius, November 1, 1930.

61. Memo to Ernst, Re: Marie Stopes—"Married Love," October 31, 1930, HRC, MLE Papers, Box 359, Folder 359.2.

62. F. X. A. Eberle, Commissioner of Customs, to Greenbaum, Wolff & Ernst, November 12, 1930, HRC, MLE Papers, Box 359, Folder 359.2.

63. Greenbaum, Wolff & Ernst to Eberle, November 13, 1930, HRC, MLE Papers, Box 359, Folder 359.2. Eberle replied: Eberle to Ernst, November 22, 1930, HRC, MLE Papers, Box 359, Folder 359.2.

64. Stopes tried yet again to clarify the history of the book's copyright but explained that her legal records were both voluminous and incomplete:

> In response to your request for the papers, correspondence, agreements, etc. dealing with the Robinson business, I may tell you that they are perfectly mountainous! A great many of them I have not got as the matter has been partly in the hands of the Society of Authors many years ago, and was taken out of their hands, and in various efforts of my friends, etc., to get the matter straightened up have left an incorrigible tangle of dud papers, some of which I have, some of which I have not got. These copies I sent to you, spread over various years, seem to me to mark the salient point and to show (A) that Robinson never really possessed any legal rights in the book at all because he pirated it from the first in defiance of the agreement I offered him in January 1918, in which Clause IV explicitly states that the copyright is the property of the author.
>
> After endless illtreatment [*sic*] from him I appealed to the American Society of Authors and made the statement, copy of which is headed "To the American People." Both the English Society of Authors with the American Society of Authors and various personal friends like Mr. Huntington tried to straighten matters out for me, but hopelessly until old Major Putnam himself tackled the job and got definite cancellation from Robinson of all his supposed rights, and then Putnam's made a definite agreement with me for publication in 1923, but in the end funked publishing it because of the legal interference in America. Those 1920 and 1923 agreements and letters between myself and Major Putnam and Robinson should, I think, make your legal position clear as regards my complete ownership and freedom to make fresh arrangements.
>
> Once you overcome the only real bar to publication, which is your American authorities, I shall be extremely glad if the matter at last can be put on a proper footing and I repeat the cable I sent you: Glad appoint you Counsel fighting for my books on contingent terms outlined your letter but my cash

liability must be limited two hundred and fifty dollars. Robinson relinquished all rights 1921. Putnam's soon after. Copyright mine. I shall be happy to hear from you further about details and wish you all success in your gallant venture to secure liberty in free America. (Stopes to Ernst, May 14, 1930, HRC, MLE Papers, Box 359, Folder 359.1)

65. For a full, rich study of this underground economy, see Jay A. Gertzman, *Bookleggers and Smuthounds: The Trade in Erotica, 1920–1940* (Philadelphia: University of Pennsylvania Press, 1999).

66. Dennett to Lindey, October 16, 1930, HRC, MLE Papers, Box 359, Folder 359.2.

67. "Draft of Letter to be sent to persons of prominence by G. P. Putnam's Sons re: Married Love," October 1930, HRC, MLE Papers, Box 359, Folder 359.2. Among those whom Ernst directly sought to enlist for opinions on the book were Mr. Jay Schieffelin, vice-president of the New York Society for the Suppression of Vice. Ernst had been trying to cultivate Schieffelin as a critic of the Vice Society's John Sumner, whose misdirected leadership and clumsy tactics were giving the Vice Society a terrible reputation. Ernst asked Schieffelin to read the book and offer his opinion (Ernst to Schieffelin, October 15, 1930, HRC, MLE Papers, Box 359, Folder 359.2). He also tried to elicit a letter from Senator Bronson Cutting of New Mexico, with whom Ernst had worked to revise Section 305(a) of the Tariff Act of 1930. Whether or not he was being ironic wasn't clear; Ernst also asked Cutting whether he wouldn't mind passing on his copy to Senator Smoot of Utah, with whom Cutting had engaged in a high-profile battle over the Tariff Act. Smoot, known for his vigorous support of sex censorship, would have been an unlikely advocate for Stopes's book (Ernst to Cutting, October 15, 1930, HRC, MLE Papers, Box 359, Folder 359.2). Ernst's papers do not contain a reply from Senator Cutting. Schieffelin offered a favorable opinion of the book, which Ernst and Lindey used to good effect in their memorandum to the court: "In my opinion this book should not be banned from the United States under the Tariff Law," Schieffelin wrote (Schieffelin to Ernst, October 24, 1930; Ernst to Schieffelin, October 25, 1930, HRC, MLE Papers, Box 359, Folder 359.2).

68. Jeliffe to Putnam's, January 6, 1931, HRC, MLE Papers, Box 360, Folder 360.3.

69. Klemmer to Balch, January 13, 1931, HRC, MLE Papers, Box 360, Folder 360.3.

70. Gregg to Balch, January 8, 1931, HRC, MLE Papers, Box 360, Folder 360.3.

71. Dr. E. L. Keyes to Balch, December 3, 1930, HRC, MLE Papers, Box 360, Folder 360.3.

72. Ernst-Lindey brief on Stopes, HRC, MLE Papers, vol. 90, pp. 7–8.

73. Ernst-Lindey brief on Stopes, 7–8.

74. The full testimonial is found in HRC, MLE Papers, Box 360, Folder 360.3. It is signed by Arnold Bennett, Havelock Ellis, W. R. Inge (dean of St. Paul's), Sir W. Arbuthnot Lane, W. J. Locke, A. E. W. Mason, Aylmer Maude, Leonard Merrick, E. Phillips Oppenheim, Eden Phillpotts, Sir G. Archibald Reid, G. Bernard Shaw, May Sinclair, H. G. Wells, and M. Stanley Wrench.

75. Goldstein to Ernst, December 3, 1930, HRC, MLE Papers, Box 360, Folder 360.3.

76. Gregg to Balch, January 8, 1931, HRC, MLE Papers, Box 360, Folder 360.3; Ernst-Lindey brief on Stopes, HRC, MLE Papers, vol. 90.

77. Schieffelin to Ernst, October 25, 1930, HRC, MLE Papers, Box 359, Folder 359.2.

78. Ernst-Lindey brief on Stopes, 12 (emphasis in original).

79. Ernst-Lindey brief on Stopes, 12.

80. Memorandum for the Libellant, by George Z. Medalie, U.S. Attorney, and Morton Baum, Assistant U.S. Attorney, HRC, MLE Papers, vol. 90, 14, 15.

81. Memorandum for the Libellant, 15.

82. Memorandum for the Libellant, 13.

83. Lindey to Ernst on his conversation with Baum, March 16, 1931, HRC, MLE Papers, Box 360, Folder 360.3.

84. Lindey, handwritten note, March 20, 1931, HRC, MLE Papers, Box 360, Folder 360.3.

85. Woolsey to Greenbaum, Wolff & Ernst and Baum, March 30, 1931, HRC, MLE Papers, Box 360, Folder 360.3.

86. Woolsey to Greenbaum, Wolff & Ernst and Baum, March 30, 1931.

87. Lindey to Woolsey, March 31, 1931, HRC, MLE Papers, Box 360, Folder 360.3.

88. *United States v. One Obscene Book Entitled "Married Love,"* 48 F.2d 821. Claim of G. P. Putnam's Sons in the District Court, Southern District of New York, decided April 6, 1931.

89. Woolsey decision in *United States v. One Obscene Book Entitled "Married Love"* 821.

90. Woolsey decision in *United States v. "Married Love."* 823.

91. Turning to the legal precedents for his argument, Woolsey added in this connection, *Gelston v. Hoyt*, 3 Wheat. 246, at 312–16; 4 L. Ed. 381; and Waples on Proceedings in Rem, §§ 87, 110, 111, 112, and cases cited therein.

92. The definitions in the *Oxford English Dictionary* are "Obscene—1. Offensive to the senses, or to taste or refinement; disgusting, repulsive, filthy, foul,

abominable, loathsome. Now somewhat arch. 2. Offensive to modesty or decency; expressing or suggesting unchaste or lustful . . . ideas; impure, indecent, lewd"; and "Immoral—The opposite of moral; not moral. 1. Not consistent with, or not conforming to, moral law or requirement; opposed to or violating morality; morally evil or impure; unprincipled, vicious, dissolute. (Of persons, things, actions, etc.) 2. Not having a moral nature or character; non-moral."

93. Woolsey decision in *United States v. "Married Love."* 824.

94. Woolsey decision in *United States v. "Married Love."* 824.

95. "Publisher's Foreword," in Marie C. Stopes, *Married Love* (New York: Putnam's Sons, 1931), x–xi.

96. Ernst to Stopes, June 29, 1931, HRC, MLE Papers, Box 359, Folder 359.4.

97. For treatment of Stopes's eugenicist side, see Robert A. Peel, ed., *Marie Stopes, Eugenics, and the English Birth Control Movement* (London: Galton Institute, 1997).

98. Stopes's cover letter to President Wilson included an astonishingly brash argument about protecting the cause of the "white race" through birth control: "I pray that you, Sir, may be instrumental not only in rescuing Mrs. Sanger, a tender and sensitive mother from injustice, but also that you will hasten the establishment of a new era for the white race, when it may escape the sapping of strength and disease that are the results of too frequent child-birth by overworn or horror-stricken mothers" (Rose, *Marie Stopes*, 91–92).

99. Rose, *Marie Stopes*, 123. It would take the Lambeth Conference of bishops in England another forty years to make such a proclamation, and the Roman Catholic Church has never made such a proclamation, and indeed in 1930 the pope reiterated the inviolability of marital intercourse in his encyclical calling anything that interfered with the prospect of procreation "inherently vicious."

100. Rose, *Marie Stopes*, 134.

101. See Richard Soloway, "The Galton Lecture: Marie Stopes, Eugenics, and the Birth Control Movement," in *Marie Stopes, Eugenics, and the English Birth Control Movement*, ed. Robert A Peel (London: Galton Institute, 1997), 49–76; and more generally, Richard Soloway, "Eugenics and the Birth Control Movement, 1918–1930," in *Demography and Degeneration: Eugenics and the Declining Birthrate in Twentieth-Century Britain*, by Richard Soloway (Chapel Hill: University of North Carolina Press, 1990), 163–92; Clare Debenham, *Marie Stopes' Sexual Revolution and the Birth Control Movement* (London: Palgrave/Macmillan, 2018); and Jane Carey, "The Racial Imperatives of Sex: Birth Control and Eugenics in Britain, the United States, and Australia in the Interwar Years," *Women's History Review* 21, no. 5 (2012): 733–52.

102. Rose, *Marie Stopes*, 125.

103. Rose, *Marie Stopes*, 125.

104. Rose, *Marie Stopes*, 135.

105. Deborah Cohen, "Marie Stopes and the Mothers' Clinics," in *Marie Stopes, Eugenics, and the English Birth Control Movement*, ed. Robert A. Peel (London: Galton Institute, 1997), 77–94; Lesley Hall, "Marie Stopes and Her Correspondents: Personalizing Population Decline in an Era of Demographic Change," in *Marie Stopes, Eugenics, and the English Birth Control Movement*, ed. Robert A. Peel (London: Galton Institute, 1997), 27–48.

106. Geppert, "Divine Sex," 400.

107. In an effort to drum up support for the birth control movement in Britain and to build alliances with American birth controllers, Stopes took up Mary Ware Dennett's invitation to come to New York to speak before Dennett's Voluntary Parenthood League, addressing an audience of more than 1,000 people at Town Hall in October 1921. She thus earned the wrath of Sanger, who refused to come and hear her speak because she spoke before Dennett's rival organization instead of her own American Birth Control League.

108. Geppert, "Divine Sex," 412.

109. In 1931, an enlarged third edition was again taken over by G. P. Putnam's Sons, and they published eight editions by 1952.

110. See Geppert, "Divine Sex," 416. *Contraception* also sold very well in India, Australia, and New Zealand, according to Geppert.

111. Geppert, "Divine Sex," 420.

112. Motion to Dismiss the Libel in the case of *United States v. "Contraception,"* HRC, MLE Papers, vol. 94, p. 5.

113. Motion to Dismiss the Libel, 5.

114. Motion to Dismiss the Libel, 6.

115. *United States v. One Book, Entitled "Contraception," by Marie Stopes*, 51 F.2d 525 (S.D.N.Y. 1931).

116. *United States v. One Book, Entitled "Contraception," by Marie Stopes*, 51 F.2d 525, at 529. Woolsey refers to his previous case, *United States v. One Obscene Book Entitled "Married Love,"* 48 F.2d 821, at 824.

117. *United States v. "Contraception,"* 528.

118. Although I saw no correspondence or other form of communication indicating an agreement to adjudicate Stopes's books out of the limelight, it seems plausible, given the controversies that her opponents could have brought to these materials. The absence of any newspaper coverage of the matter, except for one *New York Times* piece the day before the hearing and one on Judge Woolsey's ruling, would also suggest an effort to not stir up the pot.

119. *United States v. One Book, Entitled "Contraception" by Marie C. Stopes*, District Court, S.D. New York, 51 F.2d 525 (S.D.N.Y. 1931).

120. Ernst memo on *Contraception* case, 1931, HRC, MLE Papers, Box 740, Folder 740.5.

121. In their 1942 report for Planned Parenthood on the state of birth control laws in the United States, Ernst and Planned Parenthood's Gwendolyn Pickett wrote a summary of the *Contraception* case. "The book dealt with the theory, history, and practice of birth control in scientific terms and was intended to instruct the medical profession about contraceptive devices and the proper operation of birth control clinics. It had received high praise in medical and sociological circles at the time of its publication. It was decided to contest the government's action and to make this a test case to determine the 'effect' of section 305." Ernst and Pickett noted that Judge Woolsey's decision echoed the Pennsylvania decision by Judge Kirkpatrick: "Judge Woolsey, of the Federal District Court, dismissed the libel. . . . In the course of his opinion he quoted from the remarks of Federal District Judge Kirkpatrick in an earlier Pennsylvania decision involving three other books by Dr. Stopes which discussed contraception. Judge Kirkpatrick had said: '. . . so far as birth control matter goes, the act prohibits only the importation of drugs, medicine or other articles for the prevention of conception or causing unlawful abortions. These books are, of course, not drugs, medicine or other articles for that purpose, and therefore the only question remaining is whether the books are obscene.'" Judge Woolsey "found himself in complete accord with this interpretation of the statute. He went on to consider whether the book 'Contraception' was obscene. He found it a serious work intended for the medical profession written with great decency, and so not falling within the test of obscenity or immorality laid down in the cases" (Morris L. Ernst and Gwendolyn Pickett, "Birth Control in the Courts: A Resume of Legal Decisions Clarifying and Interpreting Existing Statutes," October 1942, pp. 25–26, HRC, MLE Papers, Box 5.22).

122. Ernst and Pickett, "Birth Control in the Courts," 24.

123. After all that, and to the point of what an obstructive force Customs could be, New York Customs officials were still going after Stopes's books two years later, and Ernst and Lindey were still having to go to battle with them, revealing once more how intent Customs officials were on obstructing the flow of sexual materials into the United States and how important it was to have access to the federal courts outside the Customs Court. After Woolsey had given a clean bill of health to *Contraception*, in 1932 Sanger ordered copies of two of Stopes's other (related) books, *The Practice of Contraception* and *Enduring Passion*. Customs seized the books shipped to her from England in early 1932. Ernst worked on behalf of both Sanger and Putnam's offices. Not surprisingly, there were disagreements between the U.S. Attorneys (who, following the *Contraception* decision, refused to take up an obscene libel proceeding against Stopes's book, *The Practice of Contraception*)

and the collector of customs, who refused to accept the U.S. Attorney's decision that the book was not obscene and insisted that the Customs office would not release the book to Sanger. Ernst and Lindey, armed with their victory in the *Contraception* case (and with the goodwill of the U.S. Attorneys for the Southern District of New York), were eventually able to get Customs to release the books, but only after additional trips to Washington, D.C., to make a direct argument to the U.S. commissioner of customs, F. X. A. Eberle.

Chapter 4

1. Nancy J. Knauer treats the history of this fear of contagion and its expression in the courts in Nancy J. Knauer, "Homosexuality as Contagion: From the *Well of Loneliness* to the Boy Scouts," *Hofstra Law Review* 29 (winter 2000): 401–99.

2. The literature on inversion in the field of sexology is extensive and was used by Radclyffe Hall. See Leslie Taylor, "'I Made Up My Mind to Get It': The American Trial of *The Well of Loneliness*, New York City, 1928–1929," *Journal of the History of Sexuality* 10, no. 2 (April 2001): 250–86. I have relied primarily on the collection of essays in Laura Doan and Jay Prosser, eds., *Palatable Poison: Critical Perspectives on* The Well of Loneliness (New York: Columbia University Press, 2001), which reprints some of the most influential essays about the book and the evolution of its interpretation, especially by LGBQT+ literary scholars. See also George Chauncey Jr., "From Sexual Inversion to Homosexuality: The Changing Medical Conceptualization of Female 'Deviance,'" in *Passion and Power: Sexuality in History*, ed. Kathy Peiss and Christina Simmons (Philadelphia: Temple University Press, 1989), 87–117; and Sonja Ruehl, "Inverts and Experts: Radclyffe Hall and Lesbian Identity," in *Feminism, Culture, and Politics*, ed. Rosalind Brunt and Caroline Rowan (London: Lawrence & Wishart, 1982), 15–33.

3. Radclyffe Hall, *The Well of Loneliness* (New York: Sun Dial Press, 1928), 14.

4. Hall, *Well of Loneliness*, 204.

5. Hall, *Well of Loneliness*, 313.

6. Hall, *Well of Loneliness*, 325.

7. Hall, *Well of Loneliness*, 506.

8. See Taylor, "I Made Up My Mind." For an excellent historiographic essay on how Hall's "mannish lesbian" character and her fate has been written about by three generations of critics, see the following chapters from Doan and Prosser's *Palatable Poison*: Laura Doan and Jay Prosser, "Introduction: Critical Perspective Past and Present," 1–34; Jane Rule, "Radclyffe Hall," 78–88; Esther Newton, "The Mythic Mannish Lesbian: Radclyffe Hall and the New Woman," 89–108; and Judith Halberstam, "'A Writer of Misfits': 'John' Radclyffe Hall and the Discourse of Inversion," 145–61.

9. Rule, "Radclyffe Hall," 80.

10. Hall, quoted in Doan and Prosser, "Introduction," 1.

11. Newton, "Mythic Mannish Lesbian," 95.

12. Some of the key works on Hall and the book's travails include Vera Hall, *Radclyffe Hall: A Case of Obscenity?* (New York: Barnes, 1968); Diana Souhami, *The Trials of Radclyffe Hall* (London: Weidenfeld & Nicolson, 1998); and Michael Baker, *Our Three Selves: The Life of Radclyffe Hall* (New York: William Morrow, 1985).

13. Rule, "Radclyffe Hall," 78.

14. Newton, "Mythic Mannish Lesbian," 90.

15. Rule, "Radclyffe Hall," 78.

16. For a discussion of Hall's use of Carpenter, see Laura Doan, "'The Outcast of One Age Is the Hero of Another': Radclyffe Hall, Edward Carpenter, and the Intermediate Sex," in *Palatable Poison: Critical Perspectives on* The Well of Loneliness, ed. Laura Doan and Jay Prosser (New York: Columbia University Press, 2001), 162–78.

17. Rule, "Radclyffe Hall," 78. Rule writes, "Scientific books were not at that time generally available. Krafft-Ebing's famous *Psychopathia Sexualis* was directed at the medical profession, and details of case studies, like the title, were written in Latin lest the book fall into the wrong hands and corrupt the naïve reader. Hall had read Krafft-Ebing, as well as the less well-known studies of Karl Heinrich Ulrichs, himself a homosexual trying to prove that inversion was as natural an orientation as left-handedness. She obviously read not only with a scholar's interest but with a desire to understand herself, a congenital invert in her own eyes whose sexual appetites were satisfied exclusively by women" (78).

18. Doan and Prosser, "Introduction," 1.

19. Leslie Taylor explains, "Although A. A. Knopf had originally contracted with Hall to publish the book, and despite their public commitment to it, the maelstrom in England changed their position. Fearing the costs of legal prosecution and that *The Well* would be viewed as pornography, Knopf broke their contract with Hall even before the official verdict in England was handed down in November" (Taylor, "I Made Up My Mind," 254–55).

20. Doan and Prosser, "Introduction," 2.

21. Doan and Prosser, "Introduction," 3.

22. Doan and Prosser reprint the first fourteen reviews in Laura Doan and Jay Prosser, "A Selection of Early Reviews," in *Palatable Poison: Critical Perspectives on* The Well of Loneliness, ed. Laura Doan and Jay Prosser (New York: Columbia University Press, 2001), 50–76. Doan and Prosser explain that Cape tried to tread lightly to protect his investment, advertising it without being straightforward about its actual theme and promoting it by calling attention to Hall's previous

book awards. He also published it and priced it in such a way that its "physical appearance and high price worked in tandem to establish the project's credentials as serious and significant" (Doan and Prosser, "Introduction," 4).

23. Doan and Prosser note that usually these writers were contained by "distinctly separate, if not hostile literary and interpretive communities," but reviewers across this domain took note of the book "and this explains the mixed responses it received" (Doan and Prosser, "Introduction," 4).

24. The fact that *The Well of Loneliness* was reviewed for audiences across a spectrum of literary tastes helps explain its mixed reviews as a work of art. Rule explains, for instance, that although the Bloomsbury group (Virginia and Leonard Woolf, E. M. Forster, Vita Sackville-West, Lytton Strachey) publicly supported the novel when it was on trial, some were critical too. Virginia Woolf said that the Bloomsbury group was "Radclyffe Hall's brave allies . . . but they were not her friends, nor could they have been. She was too outlandish, too earnest, and too little gifted" (Rule, "Radclyffe Hall," 81).

25. Leonard Woolf, quoted in Doan and Prosser, "Introduction," 4.

26. Doan and Prosser, "Introduction," 9.

27. *Daily Express* promotional materials for *Sunday Express* editorial, Saturday August 19, 1928, quoted by Doan and Prosser, "Introduction," 1, 10.

28. Headlines quoted in Doan and Prosser, "Introduction," 10. See also James Douglas, "A Book That Must Be Suppressed," in *Palatable Poison: Critical Perspectives on* The Well of Loneliness, ed. Laura Doan and Jay Prosser (New York: Columbia University Press, 2001), 36. Douglas's essay was originally published as an editorial in the *Sunday Express* on August 19, 1928.

29. Douglas, "Book That Must Be Suppressed," 36.

30. Douglas, "Book That Must Be Suppressed," 37; details in Doan and Prosser, "Introduction," 10–13.

31. Douglas, "Book That Must Be Suppressed," 37.

32. Douglas, "Book That Must Be Suppressed," 38.

33. Joynson-Hicks, quoted in Souhami, *Trials of Radclyffe Hall*, 168; for the campaign to ban the book, see Souhami, *Trials of Radclyffe Hall*, 168–72, 175–84.

34. For details of the lawyers' preparation and the trial, see Souhami, *Trials of Radclyffe Hall*, 190–99, 204–12.

35. Sir Chartres Biron, "Judgment," in *Palatable Poison: Critical Perspectives on* The Well of Loneliness, ed. Laura Doan and Jay Prosser (New York: Columbia University Press, 2001), 39. Sir Chartres's judgment was originally handed down in the Bow Street Police Court on November 16, 1928.

36. Sir Chartres Biron, "Judgment," 39.

37. Souhami, *Trials of Radclyffe Hall*, 212–18.

38. Doan and Prosser, "Introduction," 1.

39. Knopf had planned to publish Hall's novel but dropped their plans because of the book's notoriety; they knew it would invite trouble from the censors. See Taylor, "I Made Up My Mind," 254–56.

40. See Taylor, "I Made Up My Mind," 254–57.

41. Leslie Taylor and I draw on many of the same archival materials in the Harry Ransom Humanities Research Center (HRC), Morris L. Ernst (MLE) Papers, University of Texas, Austin; and from her research, she produced her excellent article, "I Made Up My Mind." Taylor discusses Knopf's withdrawal and Friede and Covici's decision to purchase the rights to the novel on pp. 254–57 of that article.

42. See Taylor, "I Made Up My Mind," 257–58.

43. Both Covici and Friede also had an eye for authors who pushed boundaries and who would go on to great successes. For instance, Covici edited such luminaries as John Steinbeck, Saul Bellow, Arthur Miller, and Lionel Trilling, primarily at Viking Press after the Covici-Friede firm went bankrupt in 1937. Friede—a renegade throughout his career, who got himself kicked out of Yale, Harvard, and Princeton and who had left several publishing houses before beginning his partnership with Covici—published or represented Ben Hecht, Theodore Dreiser, Ernest Hemingway, and Ludwig Bemelmans in his career. They ran toward, not away, from a confrontation with Sumner, actually hoping that the publicity value of a fracas with him would be worth the potential costs.

44. "To Print Banned Book Here," *New York Times* (August 30, 1928).

45. Paul Boyer discusses this case and Ernst's frustrations; see Paul Boyer, *Purity in Print: Book Censorship in America from the Gilded Age to the Computer Age*, 2nd ed. (Madison: University of Wisconsin Press, 2002), 128–29. On the different strategies of suing bookstore clerks and publishers, see Morris L. Ernst and William Seagle, *To the Pure: A Study of Obscenity and the Censor* (New York: Viking Press, 1928; Kaus Reprint, 1969), 232–33.

46. John Sumner to Covici-Friede, December 1, 1928, HRC, MLE Papers, Box 383, File "*People v. Covici-Friede.*" Taylor also discusses this letter; see Taylor, "I Made Up My Mind," 260–61.

47. Sumner to Covici-Friede, December 1, 1928; Taylor, "I Made Up My Mind," 261.

48. Chief Magistrate McAdoo appears in various cases, always willing to supply the warrant, and invariably defended Sumner when he failed to return the seized books, birth control clinic records, or other documents seized during raids. Ernst was continually exchanging letters and accusations with McAdoo in the city's newspaper.

49. HRC, MLE Papers, Box 383, Folder 383.2, holds the correspondence with

the Rubinstein-Nash law firm in London, which defended *The Well of Loneliness* in England. Rubinstein was generous with background materials and sent Ernst a long letter explaining the bias of the English magistrate Biron (Rubinstein to Ernst, January 8, 1929, HRC, MLE Papers, Box 383, Folder 383.2). Rubenstein continued to pay attention to the case in the United States, as he remained Hall's counsel, and after Ernst lost in the New York City magistrate court, Rubinstein sent him a letter on March 4, 1929, telling Ernst that he hope Ernst's appeal would be more successful than theirs had been and also telling him that the more recent edition of Havelock Ellis's work reflected views about inversion that were considerably modified from the edition that Ernst quoted from in his first brief. He added, "If you think it would be of assistance for the purpose of your appeal, I could obtain a sworn statement from [Ellis] on the point. As you may imagine, his sympathies are altogether with the author of the book" (Rubinstein to Ernst, March 4, 1929, HRC, MLE Papers, Box 383, Folder 383.2).

50. Ernst to Rubinstein, January 21, 1929, HRC, MLE Papers, Box 383, Folder 383.2.

51. "Police Seize Novel by Radclyffe Hall," *New York Times* (January 12, 1929).

52. Taylor, "I Made Up My Mind," 261–62.

53. Leslie Taylor discusses the Wales Act and its background in Taylor, "I Made Up My Mind," 250, 259. See also Andrea Friedman, "In The Clutch of Lesbians," in *Prurient Interests: Gender, Democracy, and Obscenity in New York, 1909–1945*, by Andrea Friedman (New York: Columbia University Press, 1999), 95–122. *The Captive* was not the first such play to be closed down. It followed by several years the suppression of Sholem Asch's play *The God of Vengeance* from New York's theaters, when police raided the theater and arrested all those involved in its staging. *The God of Vengeance*, first penned in 1907 and performed in a variety of European cities until the early 1920s, had played on New York's stages for two years, primarily in Yiddish theaters downtown, but once it moved uptown to the Apollo Theater on Broadway in 1923, its entire cast, the producers, director, and the theater owners were arrested and charged with obscenity. Both plays had depicted older, more worldly women seducing younger women.

54. That same night New York's police also raided and arrested the members of Mae West's cast in her play *SEX*.

55. See Friedman, "In the Clutch of Lesbians," 106–14. On Mae West's plays being raided, see Marybeth Hamilton, "Goodness Had Nothing to Do with It," in *Movie Censorship in American Culture*, ed. Francis Couvares (Washington, DC: Smithsonian Institution Press, 1999), 187–210.

56. For an excellent discussion of the various uses of the Wales Act, see Friedman, "In the Clutches of Lesbians"; and for a discussion of the pressures on

burlesque theaters, see Andrea Friedman, "The Habits of Sex-Crazed Perverts," in *Prurient Interests: Gender, Democracy, and Obscenity in New York, 1909–1945*, by Andrea Friedman (New York: Columbia University Press, 1999), 61–94. Ernst would take up the defense of several of those burlesque theaters, but defending the "lower brow" fare of burlesque, with its stripteases, near nudity, and rowdy male audiences, would prove more difficult than the defense of books.

57. When Ernst compared *The Well of Loneliness* to the stage production of *The Captive*, he focused on the difference of the medium itself: the stage versus the novel. Although *The Captive* dealt with similar themes as *The Well*, the medium of its performance, the stage, made it more vulnerable to claims of audience susceptibility, whereas the novel required a different kind of audience engagement.

58. Strategically, Ernst would have to delineate important distinctions between the medium of theater and the book as a medium, between the peopled stage and the solitary act of reading, the proximity and live spectacle of theater and the more contemplative nature of print as a medium. Ernst also drew distinctions between audiences, arguing that the novel's adult readers could not be assumed to be affected in the same way that the young female viewers of the recently banned plays might have been affected by the actors' proximity and liveliness. Moreover, the New York legislature's theatrical ban on lesbian productions was never intended to include a ban on books aimed at and read by adult audiences.

59. Magistrate's Opinion, *People of the State of New York v. Donald Friede and Covici-Friede, Inc.*, February 1929, Magistrate Court, City of New York, Seventh District, Borough of Manhattan, in HRC, MLE Papers, vol. 90, p. 2.

60. Magistrate's Opinion, 2.

61. Magistrate's Opinion, 7. Bushel drew on previous court decisions to support his concern that sophisticated readers could be vulnerable readers and thus needed protection. Other courts had acknowledged that literature's very quality can become a lure, an element of recruitment: "As Mr. Justice Wagner said . . . in disposing of a similar situation: 'Charm of language, subtlety of thought, faultless style, even distinction of authorship, may all have their lure for the literary critic. . . . Frequently those attractive literary qualities are the very vehicles by which the destination of illegality is reached'" (quoting Judge McAvoy from *Liveright v. Waldorf Theatres Corporation*, 220 App. Div. 182).

62. Magistrate's Opinion, 7.

63. "The public policy so declared was reaffirmed by the Legislature by its recent amendment to the Penal Law, making it a misdemeanor to prepare, advertise or present any drama, play, etc. dealing (Laws of New York, 1927, Chap. 690)" (Magistrate's Opinion, 5).

64. Magistrate's Opinion, 6.

65. Bushel cited *People v. Muller* and *People v. Seltzer* for authority. See Magistrate's Opinion, 2.

66. Magistrate's Opinion, 2.

67. Magistrate's Opinion, 7.

68. In the mid-1930s President Franklin D. Roosevelt appointed Cairns to the Treasury Department to help settle censorship cases. This post was a significant legal and administrative triumph for Ernst, Cairns, and other anti-censorship lawyers and activists and evidence, for Ernst at least, that Roosevelt's New Deal government could be a progressive ally on censorship issues.

69. Cairns directed Ernst to volume 3 of Wigmore's *Evidence* (2nd ed. 1923), par. 1477, p. 211: "This is the ancient rusty weapon that has always been drawn to oppose any reform in the rules of Evidence, viz., the argument of danger of abuse." He added, however, that the Supreme Court had held that "the Court does not, however, under the decision in *People v. Muller*, have to bear the class in mind in considering the effect of books or pictures" (Cairns to Ernst, December 14, 1928, HRC, MLE Papers, Box 383, Folder 383.2). Bushel had cited *People v. Muller* as authority for not admitting expert testimony.

70. Cairns, quoting Wertham, in Cairns to Ernst, December 14, 1928. Cairns also told Ernst, "Your book *To The Pure* was a great help to me in preparation of the trial," adding that "Havelock Ellis reviews it with high praise in a recent number of the English *Saturday Review*. I am myself planning to review it for the next issue *The Modern Quarterly*."

71. Ernst to Wertham, December 17, 1928, HRC, MLE Papers, Box 383, Folder 383.2. Ernst contacted other psychiatrists as well, including Dr. George H. Kirby, professor of psychiatry at Cornell, and Dr. R. S. Lyman of the University of Rochester Medical School, asking both for their assessment of the book's capacity to arouse readers.

72. Ernst to Lyman, January 15, 1929, HRC, MLE Papers, Box 383, Folder 383.2. The same letter was sent on the same day to Kirby at Cornell.

73. Ernst's records indicate a meeting with Wertham. See "Facts in regard to conference with Dr. Wertham in Baltimore, January 17, 1929," HRC, MLE Papers, Box 383, Folder 383.4.

74. Letter and report from F. I. Wertham to Ernst, January 18, 1929, HRC, MLE Papers, Box 383, Folder 383.1. Wertham attached a cover note to his report on the book: "Concerning our conversation I should like to add that I may have sounded somewhat more dogmatic than I intended to be or am, and that what I said has of course to be taken only as suggestions."

75. Report from F. I. Wertham to Ernst, 2.

76. Report from F. I. Wertham to Ernst, 2.

77. Taylor addresses the Wertham discussion briefly in Taylor, "I Made Up My Mind," 264.

78. Cairns to Ernst, March 28, 1929, asking Ernst not to mention Wertham in conjunction with the case, HRC, MLE Papers, Box 381, Folder 381.1.

79. Sweezy's list included *Dusty Answer*, by Rosamund Lehman; *The Crystal Gap*, by Gertrude Atherton; *Regiment of Women*, by Clemence Dane; Emile Zola's *Nana*; *Marie Bonifas*, translated from the French of Jacques de Lacretelle by Winefred Whale (this work nearly won the Bookman Prize in France in 1925); *The Tortoiseshell Cat*, by Naomi Royde Smith (who gave evidence in Hall case); *Extraordinary Women*, by Compton MacKenzie (dirty by 1928 standards, Sweezy added); *Aphrodite*, by Pierre Louys (Shane Leslie's unabridged translation) ("frankly erotic"); *Chansons de Bilitis*, by Pierre Louys (translated by Shane Leslie); *Mademoiselle de Maupin*, Theophile Gautier ("also frank"); *The Captive*, by Bourdet, translated into a play; and various Sappho translations and imitations, especially Swinburne, in *Poems and Ballads*, series 2, "Anactoria" and "Sapphics."

80. Hall had read Carpenter as well, and although she did not directly refer to his works in her novel, she used his ideas, channeled through Stephen's tutor "Puddle"—herself an invert—to explain to Steven the special place occupied by the intermediate type. As Jane Rule writes, Hall "lets Stephen's tutor, a repressed invert herself, say to Stephen, 'You're neither unnatural, nor abominable, nor mad; you're as much a part of what people call nature as anyone else; only you're unexplained as yet—you've not got your niche in creation'" (Rule, "Radclyffe Hall," 83). This was, as other critics have noted, almost verbatim from Carpenter; see Doan, "Outcast of One Age," 168.

81. Taylor, "I Made Up My Mind," 263. Taylor used correspondence between Hall and Havelock Ellis regarding his preface and her reaction to the British scandal as the basis for her argument; see, for example, Radclyffe Hall to Havelock Ellis, April 18, 1928, and August 23, 1928, HRC, MLE Papers, Box 383, Folder "AP v. Herrick."

82. Rule, "Radclyffe Hall," 83.

83. Correspondence from Sweezy, HRC, MLE Papers, Box 383, Folder 383.2; Rule, "Radclyffe Hall," 83.

84. It is outside the purview of this chapter to explore those debates, but several of the many fine pieces of scholarship on the book help explain Hall's terminology, the sexological categories of lesbianism, inversion, intermediate sex, and homosexuality in Hall's era, and the implications of those categories for generations of Hall's readers.

85. Ernst to Carl van Doren, November 30, 1928, HRC, MLE Papers, Box 383, Folder 383.2.

86. Van Doren to Ernst, December 6, 1928, HRC, MLE Papers, Box 383, Folder 383.2.

87. Ernst to Lippmann, December 7, 1928, HRC, MLE Papers, Box 383, Folder 383.2.

88. Ernst to Sulzberger, December 7, 1928, HRC, MLE Papers, Box 383, Folder 383.2.

89. Ernst to Villard, December 7, 1928, HRC, MLE Papers, Box 383, Folder 383.2.

90. "Obscene Censors," *New York Telegraph* (January 14, 1929).

91. Taylor, "I Made Up My Mind," 269.

92. Brentano to Boni, February 11, 1929, HRC, MLE Papers, Box 385, Folder 385.5.

93. Ernst to Boni, February 4, 1929, HRC, MLE Papers, Box 385, Folder 385.5.

94. Ernst's papers hold thirty-five letters and telegrams that the firm obtained between the time they planned for the publication and Sumner's raid, and the April trial. Virtually all asserted a strong anti-censorship stance, but beyond that positions varied. Quite a few wrote that homosexuality was an important albeit "unfortunate" matter that needed greater understanding and that Hall's book was an honest effort toward that end. Others wrote that censorship of *The Well of Loneliness*, whether a great book or not, was offensive to the modern spirit of scientific inquiry and freedom of expression. A few, not unlike Wertham, feared that their professional reputations might be jeopardized by any connection with the book. Only one, a psychiatrist, expressed opposition to the idea that homosexuality might be portrayed sympathetically. But all in all, the best Ernst and colleagues could do in their formal brief to the court was build in a section with selective quotes from published reviews and their letters.

95. Clendening telegram to Covici-Friede, January 18, 1929, HRC, MLE Papers, Box 383, Folder 383.5.

96. See "Statement from Doctors, Authors & Critics," n.d., HRC, MLE Papers, Box 383, Folder 383.5. The author of the "greatest enigma" quote (p. 1) is not clear in the original document.

97. Joseph Collins, in "Statement from Doctors, Authors & Critics," 2.

98. Sherwood Anderson, Joseph Wood Krutch, and Robert Morss Lovett, all quoted in "Statement from Doctors, Authors & Critics," 3, 2, 5.

99. Edna Ferber, in "Statements from Doctors, Authors & Critics," 5.

100. Ernst to Cairns, April 4, 1929, HRC, MLE Papers, Box 383, Folder 383.1.

101. Ernst to Rubinstein, February 21, 1929, HRC, MLE Papers, Box 383, Folder 383.2.

102. Following Magistrate Bushel's ruling, the defendants then went before

the New York Court of Special Sessions on the charge of selling an obscene book. On April 8, 1929, Ernst tried the case before Justices Salomon, McInerney, and Healy. On April 19, the court handed down its decision absolving the book of charges of obscenity. Ernst subsequently brought the book before the U.S. Customs Court, with Justices Fischer and Tilson hearing the arguments; the U.S. Customs Court also ruled that the book was not obscene and could be legally admitted into the United States.

103. Defendant's Brief, *People of State of New York v. Donald Friede and Covici-Friede*, submitted April 19, 1929, Court of Special Sessions, City of New York, HRC, MLE Papers, vol. 90.

104. Defendant's Brief, 3.

105. Defendant's Brief, 3 (emphasis in original).

106. Defendant's Brief, 4–5.

107. Quoting from *United States v. Kennerly* (209 Fed. 119, 121 [1913]), in Defendant's Brief, 7. Judge Hand continued in this vein, making it clear that the weaker members of society were not the only ones whose interests needed consideration. "I hope it is not improper for me to say that the rule laid down (i.e. in *Regina v Hicklin*, supra), however consonant it may be with mid-Victorian morals, does not seem to me to answer to the understanding and morality of the present time."

108. Quoting from *United States v. Kennerly*, in Defendant's Brief, 7 (emphasis in original).

109. "It is no part of the duty of courts to exercise a censorship over literary production," quoting *St. Hubert Guild v. Quinn*, 64 Misc. 336 [1909], in Defendant's Brief, 7.

110. Quoting *People v. Boni & Liveright* [1922], in Defendant's Brief, 8.

111. Defendant's Brief, 8.

112. Defendant's Brief, 9.

113. Defendant's Brief, 10.

114. Defendant's Brief, 11.

115. Defendant's Brief, 11.

116. Taylor, "I Made Up My Mind," 273.

117. Taylor, "I Made Up My Mind," 272.

118. Defendant's Brief, 26. Ernst elaborates, writing that "the visual impression—for the average and more especially the sub-average individual—is much more vivid and potent than the mental impression which is to be derived from reading the text."

119. Defendant's Brief, 25.

120. Defendant's Brief, 23.

121. Defendant's Brief, 24.

122. Defendant's Brief, 30.

123. Defendant's Brief, 31.

124. Defendant's Brief, 43.

125. Taylor, "I Made Up My Mind," 276.

126. Taylor discusses the Court of Special Sessions decision and its aftermath for Covici-Friede; see Taylor, "I Made Up My Mind," 282–86. Albert de Grazia, in *Girls Lean Back Everywhere: The Law of Obscenity and the Assault on Genius* (New York: Vintage Books, 1993), discusses the *Well of Loneliness* cases in England and the United States (164–208) and the U.S. decisions in particular (197–203), noting Friede's reflections on the irony (201). Morris Ernst discusses the case retrospectively in two different books: Morris L. Ernst and Alexander Lindey, *The Censor Marches On: Recent Milestones in the Administration of Obscenity Law in the United States* (New York: Doubleday Doran, 1940), 7, 233–34; and Morris L. Ernst and Alan C. Schwartz, *Censorship: The Search for the Obscene* (New York: Macmillan, 1964), 71–79.

127. Opinion of the Court of Special Sessions, City of New York, Part VI, New York County, *The People of the State of New York Against Donald Friede and Covici Friede, Inc., Defendants*, April 19, 1929, p. 1.

128. Opinion of the Court of Special Sessions, 1.

129. The court added, "We are not called upon, nor is it within our province, to recommend or advise against the reading of any book. Nor is it without our province to pass an opinion as to the merits or demerits thereof" (Opinion of the Court of Special Sessions, 1).

130. Taylor provides the figure of 100,000 copies in 1929; see Taylor, "I Made Up My Mind," 261; she also reports on the nine-year run (283).

131. Ernst to Eaton, December 10, 1928, HRC, MLE Papers, Box 383, Folder 383.2.

132. Stevenson to Ernst, December 13, 1928, HRC, MLE Papers, Box 383, Folder 383.2.

133. "Customs Seeks to Bar 'Well of Loneliness': M. L. Ernst Files Federal Suit over Novel Held not Obscene by Special Sessions," *New York Times* (May 16, 1938), 18.

134. "Well of Loneliness Held not Offensive," *New York Times* (July 27, 1929), 6. Taylor notes that the August 10, 1929, issue of *Publisher's Weekly* reported, "'The Well of Loneliness' Has Been Pronounced Respectable by the United States Customs Court" (Taylor, "I Made Up My Mind," 284). It actually took until December 1929, however, for the matter with Customs to be entirely closed. That's when the U.S. commissioner of customs, F. X. A. Eberle, declined to appeal the Customs

Court decision. Eberle said he had read the book and agreed with the Customs Court that "it was not offensive to clean minded persons."

135. Ernst to Sumner, April 25, 1929, HRC, MLE Papers, Box 383, Folder 383.12.

136. Ernst to Sumner, May 2, 1929, HRC, MLE Papers, Box 383, Folder 383.12.

137. Summer to Ernst, May 6, 1929, HRC, MLE Papers, Box 383, Folder 383.12.

138. Ernst to Covici-Friede, May 7, 1929, HRC, MLE Papers, Box 383, Folder 383.12.

139. Ernst to McAdoo, October 22, 1929, HRC, MLE Papers, Box 383, Folder 383.12.

140. Ernst to McAdoo, October 22, 1929.

141. McAdoo to Ernst, October 24, 1929, HRC, MLE Papers, Box 383, Folder 383.12.

142. McAdoo to Ernst, December 4, 1929, HRC, MLE Papers, Box 383, Folder 383.12.

Chapter 5

1. Jay Gertzman, *Bookleggers and Smuthounds: The Trade in Erotica, 1920–1940* (Philadelphia: University of Pennsylvania Press, 1999), 50.

2. Gertzman, *Bookleggers and Smuthounds*, 10.

3. Gertzman, *Bookleggers and Smuthounds*, 12.

4. Andrea Friedman uses the phrase "moral absolutism," explaining that the disputes in this era about how to control what New Yorkers could see and read were contests about who would have moral authority and who would speak for the public. She pits two forces with different claims to speaking for and on behalf of the public against one another: the moral absolutists versus what she calls democratic moral authority. See Andrea Friedman, *Prurient Interests: Gender, Democracy, and Obscenity in New York City, 1909–1945* (New York: Columbia University Press, 1999), 1–17.

5. Gertzman, *Bookleggers and Smuthounds*, 10. For an excellent treatment of Sumner and his Vice Society's influence, see Paul Boyer, *Purity in Print: Book Censorship in America from the Gilded Age to the Computer Age*, 2nd ed. (Madison: University of Wisconsin Press, 2002), esp. chaps. 3–7.

6. They thought that N. P. Nezeloff's *Josephine* would be a good play, as it had been targeted by Sumner, but the young publisher, Horace Liveright, had agreed to withdraw it from publication, under Sumner's threat.

7. Barnes to Howard, June 4, 1930, Harry Ransom Humanities Research Center (HRC), Morris L. Ernst (MLE) Papers, Box 386, Folder 386.8.

8. Gertzman notes that Sumner paid close attention to details. Not only did he recall the outcomes of the books he had challenged, but he also "kept careful

track of all books seized by Customs agents, interdicted in the courts, or declared unmailable by the Post Office" (Gertzman, *Bookleggers and Smuthounds*, 108).

9. Memorandum of Law Submitted by Defendants in Support of Motion to Inspect the Grand Jury Minutes and to Dismiss the Indictment), *People of New York v. Brewer & Warren, Inc., and Fred Russey*, May 15, 1930, HRC, MLE Papers, Box 740, Folder 740.5.

10. Sumner got an indictment from Magistrate Brodsky on April 17, 1930, and conducted a raid with police officer William R. Wittenberg, taking fifty-six copies of the book. For details of the case, see HRC, MLE Papers, Box 740, Folder 740.5.

11. Other books seized in the raid included *Seductio ad Absurdum*; *Winds of Gobi* (two copies); *The Diary of Tolstoi's Wife*, vol. II; *The Author's Annual*; and *Devil Drums*. See Summary of Case and Opinion of Magistrate Henry M. R. Goodman, *People of New York v. Brewer & Warren, Inc., and Fred Russey*, HRC, MLE Papers, vol. 90.

12. Gertzman, *Bookleggers and Smuthounds*, 108.

13. In a letter to Ernst, Lindey reviews the fee schedule discussion he had with Brewer & Warren's usual counsel, agreeing that Greenbaum, Wolff & Ernst would get a net retainer of $1,000 and another $2,500 if or when they won. Lindey to Ernst, April 19, 1930, HRC, MLE Papers, Box 385, Folder 385.7.

14. Brewer & Warren flier, April 23, 1930, HRC, MLE Papers, Box 385, Folder 385.7.

15. Brewer & Warren flier, April 23, 1930.

16. Ernst to Barnes, April 23, 1930, HRC, MLE Papers, Box 385, Folder 385.7. Ernst sent the same letter and two copies to journalist Walter Lippmann, fully aware that *Pay Day* had limited virtue as high-minded literature but was not without social documentary value. The salient issues, he reminded Lippmann, were Sumner's tactics and book censorship in general.

17. Lindey to Hansen, April 26, 1930, HRC, MLE Papers, Box 385, Folder 385.7.

18. Hansen, *New York World* editorial, quoted in Memorandum of Law Submitted by Defendants, 8.

19. Lindey to Hansen, May 1, 1930, HRC, MLE Papers, Box 385, Folder 385.7.

20. Lindey to Brewer, May 1, 1930, HRC, MLE Papers, Box 385, Folder 385.7.

21. Lindey to Gregory, May 2, 1930, HRC, MLE Papers, Box 385, Folder 385.7.

22. Memorandum of Law Submitted by Defendants, 6.

23. The list included Gautier's *Mademoiselle de Maupin*; the anonymous *Madeleine*; Petronius's *Satyricon*; Cabell's *Jurgen*; the anonymous *Young Girl's Diary*; Schnitzler's *Casanova's Homecoming* (the 1922 decision); Bodenheim's *Replenishing Jessica*; Hall's *Well of Loneliness*; and Dennett's *Sex Side of Life*. It is worth noting that by invoking the *Hall* and *Dennett* cases, Ernst and Lindey

imputed failure to Sumner where it did not belong, as Sumner was not a party to nor responsible for those prosecutions.

24. Memorandum of Law Submitted by Defendants, 12.

25. This was an argument that Ernst and Lindey continued to press in other cases, with the effect of continuing to shrink the definition of obscenity to the idea that it only meant pornographic materials and of shrinking the "corruption and depravity" test to the specific question of whether it produced lust and "shameful acts."

26. Gertzman, *Bookleggers and Smuthounds*, 66; Canby quoted on the same page.

27. "The Court is therefore constrained to believe that the reading of the book would impress the most immature mind . . . and in that respect the book would have a great tendency, and could be calculated better to benefit the immature, young, inexperienced and uninformed by deterring them from emulating the life deeds of 'Jim' in *Pay Day*, and for that reason the complaint herein is dismissed and the defendants are discharged" (Summary of Case and Opinion of Magistrate Henry M. R. Goodman, *People of New York v. Brewer & Warren, Inc., and Fred Russey*, May 15, 1930, HRC, MLE Papers, vol. 90, p. 11)

28. Dennett to Lindey, May 15, 1930, HRC, MLE Papers, vol. 90. Another example of congratulatory journalism is an editorial in the *New Evening Telegram*, May 17, 1930 (quoted in a subsequent brief written before Brewer and Warren decided to pull the book: Memorandum of Law Submitted by Defendants, 26 [Judge Rosalsky denied their motion on July 22, 1930]). Reverend John Haynes Holmes congratulated them for turning a sow's ear into a silk purse (Holmes to Ernst, May 15, 1930, HRC, MLE Papers, vol. 90). The *New York Times* reviewed the book following the verdict, on May 11, 1930.

29. Lindey to Dun and Taylor [booksellers], May 19, 1930, HRC, MLE Papers, vol. 90.

30. Lindey to Hastings, May 27, 1930; and Newsome Levy to Hastings, June 6, 1930, both in HRC, MLE Papers, vol. 90.

31. See Ernst to Schieffelin, Vice President of Vice Society, April 23, 1930, and a follow-up letter from Ernst to Schieffelin, May 16, 1930; Schieffelin wrote Ernst back on May 20, 1930: "I have spoken several times at the Directors' Meetings, suggesting that you be given a hearing, but I find the other members are very much averse to this." All three letters are in HRC, MLE Papers, vol. 90.

32. Ernst to Barnes, June 4, 1930, HRC, MLE Papers, vol. 90.

33. Memorandum of Law Submitted by Defendants, 14.

34. *New York Herald Tribune* editorial, May 16, 1930, quoted in Memorandum of Law Submitted by Defendants, 26.

35. "New York has, in the last year, seen a series of remarkable judicial decisions dismissing complaints foolishly brought against what to mature minds

were obviously decent books. Magistrate Goodman's decision ranks on the same mature level. Let us hope that the directors of the Society for the Suppression of Vice will now see to it that the society's agents also grow up" (*New York Herald Tribune* editorial, May 16, 1930, quoted in Memorandum of Law Submitted by Defendants, 27). Ernst and Lindey's use of the *Herald Tribune* editorial in their legal memorandum illustrates the collaboration they had envisioned from their initial decision to put up *Casanova's Homecoming*.

36. *New York Evening Telegram*, June 28, 1930, quoted in Memorandum of Law Submitted by Defendants, 27.

37. Memorandum of Law Submitted by Defendants, 27.

38. Memorandum of Law Submitted by Defendants, 28.

39. Lindey to Edward Warren, June 20, 1930; and editorials and clippings from the *New York Evening Post*, June 9, 1930, and the *New York World*, June 10, 1930, all in HRC, MLE Papers, vol. 90.

40. According to documents in Ernst's papers, Ernst also believed that Sumner had instructed the original police officer seizing the books to lie to the lawyers who were trying to track down the books (HRC, MLE Papers, Box 740, Folder 740.5).

41. The other chapters are "The Parlor Maid and the Young Gentleman," "The Young Gentleman and the Young Wife," "The Young Wife and the Husband," "The Husband and the Little Miss," "The Little Miss and the Poet," "The Poet and the Actress," and "The Actress and the Count."

42. Dismissed by Magistrate Brodsky in *People v. Gottschalk* (Brodsky Opinion, Magistrate Court, November 27, 1929). In a subsequent case on Staten Island, *People v. Pesky*, involving the same book, the bookseller Pesky was convicted in the Court of Special Sessions. Both the Appellate Division and the New York Court of Appeals affirmed the judgment of the Court of Special Sessions. Opinion, Appellate Division (*People v. Pesky*); Appellate Division of the Supreme Court, First Dept., July 15, 1930; this decision was upheld by the New York Court of Appeals on a 5 to 2 vote by the New York State Court of Appeals on October 24, 1930 (*People v. Pesky*; 230 A.D. 200; 254 N.Y. 373).

43. The leading free speech proponents at this same time were asking this same question of political speech; for Zechariah Chafee Jr., who was a leading free speech progressive, the question was whether or not the work advanced thought, advanced public debate, and could get itself accepted in the marketplace of political ideas.

44. "Dr. Schnitzler wrote 'Reigen' in 1896–97. It was among the first of his notable series of books that have since won him worldwide acclaim. It was originally published in an edition of about two hundred copies in 1900. The first general edition was published by the firm of B. Harz in Vienna, Austria, in 1903; and more than ten thousand copies were sold. Other editions followed. By 1920 over

one hundred thousand copies of various editions throughout Europe had been distributed. The work was widely discussed. Highly favorable criticism appeared shortly after publication in newspapers . . . widely divergent in attitude. . . . Not only was 'Reigen' thus sanctioned in book form, but its presentation on the stage took place throughout most of Europe" (Ernst Amicus Curiae brief, New York Court of Appeals, *People v. Pesky*, p. 2, HRC, MLE Papers, vol. 90, brief submitted October 1930).

45. Ernst Amicus Curiae brief, 3. Ernst and Lindey's own expert, Professor Otto Schinnerer, echoed this argument as well.

46. "The writer desires to achieve good through his work. This idea is so strikingly apparent to the normal, sensible man that in the present case every non-essential portion of the work that might possibly be regarded as immoral is submerged" (Ernst Amicus Curiae brief, 3).

47. Ernst Amicus Curiae brief, 3–4. The same pattern held in Schnitzler's home city, Vienna, where critics tried to block performance of the play but the courts vindicated it. In addition, the play had been performed throughout Germany and Austria, in Budapest, in Moscow and St. Petersburg (under the tsarist regime), in Holland, in Paris, in Christiana (Denmark), and in Rome—all to the point that this play had been part of European cultural modernism, as a play and a book. And the play had been performed or read in New York theaters since 1923 (on the New York stage in March 1923; in the Green Room Club; and at the Triangle Theater in October 1923).

48. Ernst Amicus Curiae brief, 12.

49. Ernst Amicus Curiae brief, 13.

50. Ernst Amicus Curiae brief, 8.

51. Ernst Amicus Curiae brief, 9.

52. New York Court of Appeals Decision, *People v. Pesky*, 254 N.Y. 373, October 24, 1930. The court ruled in a 5–2 decision to affirm the lower court decision. The *per curium* decision by Judges Pound and Cardozo and colleagues was brief: "This court is a court of review, restricted in cases of this order to a pronouncement of the law, and without power to act as a trier of the facts. If those charged with the duty to pass judgment upon the facts might say not unreasonably that the book sold by the defendant was obscene, lewd or indecent beyond a reasonable doubt . . . we are not at liberty to substitute our judgment for theirs, or to supersede their function as the spokesmen of the thought and sentiment of the community in applying to the book complained of to the standard of propriety established by the statute. A different question would be here if we could say as a matter of law that the writing was so innocuous as to forbid the submission of its quality to the triers of the facts. We cannot say that here" (374).

53. This prior history stemming from Sumner's 1922 action against the book certainly informed the legal history of the 1930 case and framed the journalistic coverage of Sumner's 1930 action. In 1922 Sumner charged Thomas Seltzer and Mary Marks with possession and intent to sell three obscene books. New York City magistrate court judge Simpson found the book not obscene. Not satisfied with that decision, Sumner went to the district attorney and requested a grand jury hearing on the book; the grand jury found that the book should be held for trial, and the district attorney brought an indictment against it. In 1924 Judge Wagner refused the demurrer to stop the indictment, and instead of going to court, Seltzer agreed to cease publication of the book and to destroy the plates; the indictment was dropped in 1926, for lack of prosecution, based on the agreement to cease publication. An internal memorandum in Ernst's office explained this history, drawing from an affidavit by William B. Moore, the deputy assistant district attorney: "There was an agreement between the D.A. and the defendant to cease publishing books, circulation discontinued and plates and types to be destroyed—this was done. On the recommendation of the D.A. the bail was discharged and it was understood that a motion to dismiss the indictment could be made later without opposition on the part of the D.A. by reason of the steps taken by defendant in destroying and discontinuing the circulation, etc." (O'Malley to Shur, August 8, 1930, HRC, MLE Papers, Box 386, Folder 386.7).

54. "Books to be published by the Inner Sanctum of Simon and Schuster," Simon & Schuster flier, fall 1930, HRC, MLE Papers, Box 836, Folder 836.5.

55. "Books to be published by the Inner Sanctum of Simon and Schuster."

56. Sumner to Simon & Schuster, May 27, 1930, HRC, MLE Papers, Box 386, Folder 386.5. A few weeks later, Simon wrote to Ernst, saying, "I saw Sumner the other day; he seemed friendly enough, but didn't commit himself as to whether he would bring up the case even if it wasn't 'brought to his attention'" (Simon to Ernst, June 30, 1930, HRC, MLE Papers, Box 368, Folder 386.5).

57. In a parallel move, Ernst and Barnes agreed to challenge the federal Customs ban on the book, agreeing to have a copy mailed to Ernst from England (see Ernst to Barnes, June 3, 1930, HRC, MLE Papers, Box 386, Folder 386.8). Ernst's firm informs Customs that their client, Harry Elmer Barnes, had received a copy off the S.S. *Bremen* of *Casanova's Homecoming*—and that they would make the package available for customs inspection; Customs replied that they would be glad to submit the volume to their law department for evaluation. Although they kept this possibility open for several months, it seems to have not developed (Greenbaum, Wolff & Ernst to Customs, July 7, 1930, HRC, MLE Papers, Box 386, Folder 386.8).

58. Lindey to Simon & Schuster, June 16, 1930, HRC, MLE Papers, Box 386, Folder 386.8.

59. Simon & Schuster memo on Schinnerer, June 17, 1930, HRC, MLE Papers, Box 386, Folder 386.6. Simon & Schuster initially wanted another Sumner foe, Harry Hansen of *The World*, to write it, but Hansen balked, afraid of getting dragged into the case and jeopardizing his job.

60. Ernst to Simon & Schuster, July 15, 1930, HRC, MLE Papers, Box 386, Folder 386.8. Although he was hopeful that the Court of Appeals would reverse the decision, that decision would be months away. It was not rendered until November 1930, when the Court of Appeals upheld the lower court finding.

61. Handwritten note, August 8, 1930, on Simon & Schuster stationery: "Received from Simon and Schuster Inc 477 copies of Casanova's Homecoming . . . taken for evidence by." And a note is added: "1087 taken from bindery" (HRC, MLE Papers, Box 386, Folder 386.5). Twenty-five of these were turned over to the district attorney's office—and these were the twenty-five copies that were fought over at the end of the trial. Lawrence W. Hoyt, a salesman for Simon & Schuster described the events in his deposition: "On Thursday, August 7, a man came into the office and inquired for a member of the sales staff. He was referred to me. He went into a story of how he sold postcards and novelties to druggists on Long Island, and said that his customers were interested in stocking dollar books. . . . He then stated that one of his customers—a druggist—asked him to obtain a copy of *Casanova's Homecoming*, and inquired as to whether he would be allowed a discount of that copy. We sold him the book for sixty-seven cents. He left the office with the book." The next day, Sumner and police officer William R. Wittenberg, on a warrant issued by Magistrate Gottlieb of the Fourth District Court, seized 477 copies of the book from Simon & Schuster's offices, and the police took another 1,087 from the bindery.

62. Ernst to Schur, August 11, 1930, HRC, MLE Papers, Box 386, Folder 386.7.

63. "Mr. Sumner vs. Arthur Schnitzler" (editorial), *New York Herald Tribune*, August 11, 1930, HRC, MLE Papers, Box 386, Folder 386.4.

64. "Mr. Sumner vs. Arthur Schnitzler."

65. Harry Elmer Barnes, "Irresponsible Sumner" (editorial), *New York Telegram*, August 19, 1930, HRC, MLE Papers, Box 386, Folder 386.4.

66. See internal memorandum in Ernst's office (O'Malley to Shur, August 8, 1930, HRC, MLE Papers, Box 386, Folder 386.7).

67. Statement from Simon & Schuster following Sumner's seizure, re: "Casanova's Homecoming," HRC, MLE Papers, Box 386, Folder 386.5.

68. Draft of letter from Simon and Schuster to its list of readers, August 1930, HRC, MLE Papers, Box 386, Folder 386.7.

69. Shur to Ernst, September 12, 1930, HRC, MLE Papers, Box 386, Folder 386.7.

70. Clippings from the *Evening World*, August 12, 1930; *The Nation*, August 27, 1930; *The World*, August 8, 1930; the *New York Telegram*, August 19, 1930; the *New York Evening Post*, August 9, 1930; the *Brooklyn Eagle*, August 13, 1930; and the *New York Times*, August 9, 1930. Following the trial, the *New York Herald Tribune*, September 26, 1930, described the 1930 trial as a continuation of Sumner's 7-year animus against the book (and Sumner's own letters to the editor suggest the same). See also *New York Herald Tribune* editorial, October 11, 1930; "Schnitzler Book Held not Immoral," *New York Evening Post*, September 5, 1930; and Mr. Sumner's Retort, November 11, 1930. All clippings and editorials found in HRC, MLE Papers, Box 386, Folder 386.4.

71. Defense Memorandum in *Schnitzler* case, p. 2, HRC, MLE Papers, vol. 90.

72. Defense Memorandum in *Schnitzler* case, 2.

73. Defense Memorandum in *Schnitzler* case, 4.

74. Defense Memorandum in *Schnitzler* case, 4.

75. Defense Memorandum in *Schnitzler* case, 4–5.

76. Magistrate Gottlieb's decision, *Sumner v. Simon and Schuster*, re: "Casanova's Homecoming," October 25, 1930, p. 2, HRC, MLE Papers, vol. 90.

77. Magistrate Gottlieb's decision, 3.

78. Sumner argued that the original book, in 1921–1922, had been an expensive $10 and thus was not susceptible to widespread distribution. Ernst rejected the class-bias implications of resolving obscenity questions, and he strongly rejected Sumner's misrepresentation of the book-pricing issues, writing District Attorney Crain, "I sincerely trust that the exploding of the half-truth, if not the actual falsehood which was laid before you in connection with this important price factor, will entirely dispose of this situation" (Ernst to Crain, October 3, 1930, HRC, MLE Papers, Box 386, Folder 386.2).

79. Simon to Ernst, October 3, 1930, HRC, MLE Papers, Box 386, Folder 386.2.

80. Ernst draft of letter to *New York Telegram*, October 1930, HRC, MLE Papers, Box 386, Folder 386.2.

81. Sumner letter to the editor, "Casanova in Court," *New York Herald Tribune*, October 11, 1930, HRC, MLE Papers, Box 386, Folder 386.4.

82. "Mr. Sumner's Retort," *New York Herald Tribune*, November 11, 1930, HRC, MLE Papers, Box 386, Folder 386.4.

83. "Mr. Sumner's Retort."

Chapter 6

1. Cowley to Cerf, May 6, 1932, in Michael Moscato and Leslie LeBlanc, eds., *United States of America v. One Book Entitled Ulysses by James Joyce: Documents and*

Commentary—A 50-Year Retrospective (Frederick, MD: University Publications of America, 1984), 12.

2. Edmund Wilson, "James Joyce," in Moscato and LeBlanc, *United States of America v. One Book Entitled Ulysses*, 93. Wilson's essay was originally published in the *New Republic*, December 18, 1929.

3. Paul Vanderham, *James Joyce and Censorship: The Trials of Ulysses* (New York: New York University Press, 1998), 7–8.

4. In early August 1931, Lindey wrote Ernst the first of many memos about James Joyce's *Ulysses*, revealing that they had already begun planning a defense and were ready to move ahead with the project. Lindey told Ernst he had "stocked in a few copies of the book" for their preparations and asked what he should do next (Lindey memo to Ernst, August 6, 1931, in Moscato and LeBlanc, *United States of America v. One Book Entitled Ulysses*, 77). Ernst, quickly replied, "Tell Mrs. Denis that I want to see her" when he returned to New York City from his vacation house on Nantucket. He confidently noted, "I am sure I can get a good publisher" (Ernst, handwritten note on Lindey memo, in Moscato and LeBlanc, *United States of America v. One Book Entitled Ulysses*, 78).

5. Vanderham, *James Joyce and Censorship*, 1.

6. Vanderham, *James Joyce and Censorship*, 7–8

7. One critic reported that "reading Mr. Joyce is like making an excursion into Bolshevist Russia: all standards go by the board." The critic Shane Leslie also referred to Joyce's "literary Bolshevism" (Vanderham, *James Joyce and Censorship*, 29).

8. Vanderham, *James Joyce and Censorship*, 28. Vanderham avers that "the mere presence of this letter in a file catalogued in the Post Office's 'List of Subversive Literature, WWI' establishes that political motives played their part in the suppression of *Ulysses* in *The Little Review*" (Vanderham, *James Joyce and Censorship*, 29).

9. Vanderham, *James Joyce and Censorship*, 31.

10. Vanderham, *James Joyce and Censorship*, 2.

11. Stephen Gillers, "A Tendency to Deprave and Corrupt: The Transformation of American Obscenity Law from Hicklin to *Ulysses* II," *Washington University Law Review* 85, no. 2 (2007): 252.

12. Gillers, "Tendency to Deprave and Corrupt," 251–52.

13. For discussions of Joyce's intentional provocations and for a brilliant history of the publication history of Joyce's masterpiece, see Kevin Birmingham, *The Most Dangerous Book: The Battle for James Joyce's Ulysses* (New York: Random House, 2014).

14. Vanderham, *James Joyce and Censorship*, 39.

15. Gillers, "Tendency to Deprave and Corrupt," 252–53.

16. Gillers, "Tendency to Deprave and Corrupt," 250.

17. Gillers quotes from Quinn's explanation to Joyce about his strategy, revealing Quinn's condescension toward the judges whom he needed to persuade: "I took the only tack that could be taken with the three stupid judges, and that was that no one could understand what the thing was about. I nearly got away with it. I got two of them to admit that they could not understand it. After the witnesses were examined they said they wanted to read the magazine. So there was an adjournment of a week to February 21st. I knew that two of the judges were more interested in eating and smoking and perhaps drinking and poker-playing probably or church-going, or maybe all. . . . But the third judge was one of these nervous asses. . . . He is an ass without the slightest glimmer of culture, but he knows the meaning of words" (Gillers, "Tendency to Deprave and Corrupt," 260).

18. The preliminary hearing in the Jefferson Market Courthouse before Magistrate Joseph E. Corrigan was, Vanderham writes, "precisely the sort of spectacle that Quinn had hoped to avoid, for he disliked Joyce's writing being associated with Greenwich Village bohemia, and he did not want the connection bandied about in the press" (Vanderham, *James Joyce and Censorship*, 43). Gillers and Vanderham used Quinn's correspondence with Pound, Anderson and Heaps's recollections, and press reports to reconstruct Quinn's initial and subsequent arguments to the court. Both scholars found his legal strategy insufficient, although Kevin Birmingham gave Quinn more benefit of the doubt. Quinn's flippant letters to Pound reveal his disdain for his clients, and the whole West Village bohemian/literati scene: "There was Heep [*sic*] plus Anderson, and plus heaps of other Heeps and Andersons. Some goodlooking and some indifferent. The two rows of them looking as though a fashionable whorehouse had been pinched and all its inmates hauled into court, with Heep in the part of the brazen madam. The stage was filled with police officers in blue uniforms with glaring stars and buttons, women and men by twos and threes awaiting arraignment or sentence, . . . chauffeurs awaiting hearings; pimps, prostitutes, hangers-on and reporters—also whores, on the theory of 'Once a journalist always a whore'" (Vanderham, *James Joyce and Censorship*, 43).

19. Vanderham, *James Joyce and Censorship*, 10.

20. "The second Egoist edition of 500 copies of *Ulysses*, published in January 1923 to replace those destroyed by Customs authorities in the USA, met with a similar fate, this time at the hands of the English Customs authorities, who confiscated 499 copies in Folkestone Harbour. After Miss Weaver declined to contest the forfeiture, the confiscated copies were destroyed. The situation was similar in Canada and Ireland, where Ulysses was confiscated and burned. . . . Thus, by 1923 *Ulysses* was largely banned from the English-speaking world" (Vanderham, *James Joyce and Censorship*, 82–83).

21. Lindey to Ernst, August 6, 1931, in Moscato and LeBlanc, *United States of America v. One Book Entitled Ulysses*, 77.

22. Ernst to Huebsch, October 21, 1931, in Moscato and LeBlanc, *United States of America v. One Book Entitled Ulysses*, 98–100.

23. Regarding the contract Cerf had made with Joyce and the agreement he thinks he's reached with Ernst about the "legal end of this matter," see Cerf to Ernst, March 23, 1932, in Moscato and LeBlanc, *United States of America v. One Book Entitled Ulysses*, 108. Lindey to Cerf, March 24, 1932 (in Moscato and LeBlanc, *United States of America v. One Book Entitled Ulysses*, 109), clarifies the conditions of the contract.

24. As other scholars have noted, Bennett Cerf tended to make himself the hero of this story, essentially erasing other key figures from the process, but it is clear that Ernst and Lindey were the key architects of the entire plan. Cerf's versions are slightly different, according to law professor Steven Gillers: "[As] Cerf described it in a 1934 essay, written shortly after he published *Ulysses*, he was 'summoned' to the brokerage firm of Sartorius & Smith in December 1931 by Robert Kastor, a wealthy businessman, but more importantly, the brother of Helen Joyce, wife of Georgio Joyce, James Joyce's son. Forty-five years later, in his autobiography *At Random*, Cerf would airbrush Kastor out of the story. By then, Cerf was the hero, the person who got the idea to free *Ulysses* in the United States and who wrote to Joyce, care of Sylvia Beach, to elicit his interest. Back in 1934, however, Cerf recalled that Kastor had asked him if Random House was interested in publishing *Ulysses*. After consulting Klopfer, Cerf said yes. By April, Random House had a contract giving it the United States rights to the book. Joyce received a $1,000 advance and would receive an additional $1,500 on publication and royalties on sales of between fifteen and twenty percent. About this time, too, Cerf made what was the most important non-editorial decision on the way to his goal. He called Morris Ernst" (Gillers, "Tendency to Deprave and Corrupt," 275–76). These details offer a corrective to that narrative.

25. Cerf to Kastor, March 22, 1932, in Moscato and LeBlanc, *United States of America v. One Book Entitled Ulysses*, 102–4.

26. Cerf to Leon, April 19, 1932, in Moscato and LeBlanc, *United States of America v. One Book Entitled Ulysses*, 119.

27. Lindey to Cerf, March 29, 1932, in Moscato and LeBlanc, *United States of America v. One Book Entitled Ulysses*, 111–12.

28. The *Elsie Dinsmore* book series by Martha Finley was written between 1867 and 1905. The literary experts whom Lindey and Cerf enlisted used the phrase "Elsie books" repeatedly.

29. Fitzgerald to Cerf, August 29, 1932, in Moscato and LeBlanc, *United States of America v. One Book Entitled Ulysses*, 128.

30. Cerf to Lindey, March 28, 1932, in Moscato and LeBlanc, *United States of America v. One Book Entitled Ulysses*, 110.

31. Lindey to Ernst, March 13, 1931, in Moscato and LeBlanc, *United States of America v. One Book Entitled Ulysses*, 78; Lindey enclosed Wilson's essay, "James Joyce."

32. Wilson, "James Joyce," 90.

33. Wilson, "James Joyce," 91–92.

34. Lindey to Collector of Customs, May 2, 1932, in Moscato and LeBlanc, *United States of America v. One Book Entitled Ulysses*, 133–34. The cases included *United States v. Mary Ware Dennett*, 39 Fed. (2d) 564; *United States v. "Married Love,"* 48 Fed. (2d) 821; *United States v. "Contraception,"* 51 Fed. (2d) 525; *Youngs Rubber Corp v. C.I. Lee & Co.*, 45 Fed. (2d) 103; and *People v. Wendling*, 258 N.Y. 461.

35. Lindey to Cerf, May 7, 1932, in Moscato and LeBlanc, *United States of America v. One Book Entitled Ulysses*, 137.

36. Stewart to Lindey, May 13, 1932, in Moscato and LeBlanc, *United States of America v. One Book Entitled Ulysses*, 142. In *A. Heymoolen v. United States* the collector of customs in Minneapolis had seized forty-three books addressed to A. Heymoolen, a local bookseller. Seven copies of *Ulysses* were seized in the shipment, and the others appeared to be studies of sexual "abnormalities" of one kind or another, disguised as science. Treasury Decision 42907, *A. Heymoolen v. United States*, in Moscato and LeBlanc, *United States of America v. One Book Entitled Ulysses*, 142–43.

37. Treasury Decision 42907, 142–43.

38. Lindey to Stewart, May 17, 1932, in Moscato and LeBlanc, *United States of America v. One Book Entitled Ulysses*, 146.

39. Customs' alacrity was impressive, given Ernst and Lindey's previous experiences. It also belies the story that Cerf told throughout his career about the Customs Service's many failures importing the book, how they lost a copy, and had to reimport the book, and so on. It was a useful story for describing government folly. But in fact, Customs was quite efficient in this matter.

40. Lindey reported his conversation with Coleman about leaving the final decision up to Medalie. See Lindey memo to Ernst, July 30, 1932, in Moscato and LeBlanc, *United States of America v. One Book Entitled Ulysses*, 157.

41. Lindey memo to Ernst, July 30, 1932. This may explain why the original volume was so tattered when it was returned to Bennett Cerf, which he ascribed to mishandling by Customs officials.

42. Lindey memo to Ernst, August 12, 1932, in Moscato and LeBlanc, *United States of America v. One Book Entitled Ulysses*, 158.

43. Ernst memo re: Ulysses, September 27, 1932, in Moscato and LeBlanc, *United States of America v. One Book Entitled Ulysses*, 160.

44. Leon to Cerf, September 27, 1932; Lindey memo on urgency of piracy matter, October 19, 1932; and Cerf to Ernst on Meyers piracy, October 20, 1932, all in Moscato and LeBlanc, *United States of America v. One Book Entitled Ulysses*, 161, 162, 162–63.

45. Lindey to Ernst, January 4, 1933, in Moscato and LeBlanc, *United States of America v. One Book Entitled Ulysses*, 172. Lindey told Ernst that he saw no reason to insist on another procedure because "he [Coleman] will probably get the same results" from the "jury of one" as they got in the earlier *Contraception* case (also heard by Woolsey) when the libel was dropped.

46. Stipulations and Agreements, May 15, 1933, in Moscato and LeBlanc, *United States of America v. One Book Entitled Ulysses*, 179–80.

47. Lindey to Ernst, January 4, 1933, 173.

48. Lindey to Collector of Customs, May 5, 1933, in Moscato and LeBlanc, *United States of America v. One Book Entitled Ulysses*, 177.

49. H. C. Stewart to Lindey, May 10, 1933; and Lindey to Stewart, May 13, 1933, both in Moscato and LeBlanc, *United States of America v. One Book Entitled Ulysses*, 178–79.

50. Lindey, Petition for Release and Admission of Book, in Moscato and LeBlanc, *United States of America v. One Book Entitled Ulysses*, 186–89.

51. Lindey, Petition for Release and Admission of Book," 186–89.

52. Frank Dow, Acting Commissioner of Customs, to New York City Collector of Customs, June 16, 1933, in Moscato and LeBlanc, *United States of America v. One Book Entitled Ulysses*, 203–4. Lindey had heard from the Division of Appeals and Protests in Washington on June 16 that his petition had been favorably passed on, but he was still awaiting official confirmation from Stewart, the collector of customs in New York City, who held the book. Lindey to Collector of Customs, June 22, 1933, in Moscato and LeBlanc, *United States of America v. One Book Entitled Ulysses*, 205.

53. "Ban upon 'Ulysses' to Be Fought Again," *New York Times* (June 24, 1933), reprinted in Moscato and LeBlanc, *United States of America v. One Book Entitled Ulysses*, 205–6.

54. "Ban upon 'Ulysses,'" 206.

55. Lindey to Ernst, June 6, 1933, in Moscato and LeBlanc, *United States of America v. One Book Entitled Ulysses*, 202.

56. Lindey to Ernst July 25, 1933, in Moscato and LeBlanc, *United States of America v. One Book Entitled Ulysses*, 212–13.

57. Lindey to Ernst, July 25, 1933, 212–13.

58. Lindey to Atlas, August 7, 1933, in Moscato and LeBlanc, *United States of America v. One Book Entitled Ulysses*, 214–16. They sent copies of their legal

memoranda from the *Dennett* case and copies of nine books, all of them more risqué than *Ulysses* and all of them exonerated in New York courts. The books were *Madeleine, Mademoiselle de Maupin, Casanova's Homecoming, Eastern Shame Girl, Woman and Puppet* (Pierre Louys), *The Adventures of Hsi Men Ching, God's Little Acre, Female,* and *Flesh.*

59. Shapiro to Ernst and Lindey, August 30, 1933, in Moscato and LeBlanc, *United States of America v. One Book Entitled Ulysses,* 220. Cerf wrote to Leon about the case finally going to Woolsey, and the U.S. Attorney's decision to go ahead with the trial. He told Leon that "the last few postponements . . . were engineered by our own attorneys for the purpose of getting the case before the most liberal-minded judge on the circuit. This is Judge Woolsey, and the case is now in his hands. . . . There was a slight chance for a while that the District Attorney's office would not fight us at all on this case. They informed us finally, however, that they intended to proceed against us because there were too many dirty words in the last section of the book. These are the exact words of the Assistant District Attorney. This is the sort of argument to which there is really no answer. . . . We are only hoping that Judge Woolsey will have a more adult attitude" (Cerf to Leon, August 30, 1933, in Moscato and LeBlanc, *United States of America v. One Book Entitled Ulysses,* 221).

60. As Vanderham describes the scenario, "Shortly after the U.S. Attorney's office had made clear it intended to proceed against Joyce's novel, Woolsey announced that he would hear argument without briefs and that briefs should not be submitted unless he called for them. This arrangement accorded with the wishes of the government, but not with those of Random House and its legal counsel. Cerf was convinced that all material gathered in defense of *Ulysses* should be turned over to Woolsey 'before he has a chance to complete his reading of the book.' Lindey and Ernst were of the same mind. Thus, early in September, Lindey ignored Woolsey's directive, sending him a copy of the 'Claimant's Preliminary Memorandum' (containing the material presented in Lindey's petition) and two critical books on *Ulysses.* Lindey would have sent a third book, but he had learned from Sam Coleman that Woolsey already had a copy of Stuart Gilbert's James Joyce's Ulysses. . . . One month later, Ernst and Lindey would supplement this material with a copy of the 'Claimant's Memorandum.' Due to a number of delays, Woolsey would not hear argument until 25 November 1933. He would have plenty of time to familiarize himself with the material of which Ernst and Lindey hoped he would take 'judicial notice'" (Vanderham, *James Joyce and Censorship,* 93).

61. Claimant's Memorandum to Dismiss Libel, submitted October 14, 1933, in Moscato and LeBlanc, *United States of America v. One Book Entitled Ulysses,* 239.

62. Claimant's Memorandum to Dismiss Libel, 239.

63. Claimant's Memorandum to Dismiss Libel, 239.

64. Claimant's Memorandum to Dismiss Libel, 241.

65. Claimant's Memorandum to Dismiss Libel, 242.

66. Claimant's Memorandum to Dismiss Libel, 244 (emphasis in original).

67. Claimant's Memorandum to Dismiss Libel, 245 (emphasis in original).

68. Claimant's Memorandum to Dismiss Libel, 245.

69. Claimant's Memorandum to Dismiss Libel, 246.

70. Claimant's Memorandum to Dismiss Libel, 246.

71. Claimant's Memorandum to Dismiss Libel, 248.

72. Claimant's Memorandum to Dismiss Libel, 251–52.

73. Claimant's Memorandum to Dismiss Libel, 251. The case Lindey refers to is *Swearingen v. United States*, 161 U.S. 446.

74. Claimant's Memorandum to Dismiss Libel, 256. A decision by Magistrate Greenspan on Erskine Caldwell's *God's Little Acre* had effectively articulated this test and was "peculiarly applicable" to *Ulysses*, because it drew a strong distinction between literary works and materials defined by the promotion or inducement of lustful desire. Greenspan ruled, "The courts have strictly limited the applicability of this statute to works of pornography, and they have consistently declined to apply it to books of genuine literary value" (256).

75. Claimant's Memorandum to Dismiss Libel, 256.

76. Claimant's Memorandum to Dismiss Libel, 257.

77. Vanderham, *James Joyce and Censorship*, 103.

78. Claimant's Memorandum to Dismiss Libel, 264.

79. Claimant's Memorandum to Dismiss Libel, 266. See also Vanderham's treatment of their argument, in Vanderham, *James Joyce and Censorship*, 96–97.

80. Claimant's Memorandum to Dismiss Libel, 266.

81. Paul Vanderham writes that Atlas's memorandum and use of Lindey and Ernst's documents "was motivated by his desire to argue the government's case against *Ulysses* in a manner that would make it clear that the government was not wholehearted in its ostensible desire to censor Joyce's novel" (Vanderham, *James Joyce and Censorship*, 106).

82. Vanderham, *James Joyce and Censorship*, 106.

83. Atlas, "James Joyce," in Moscato and LeBlanc, *United States of America v. One Book Entitled Ulysses*, 293.

84. Atlas, "James Joyce," 294.

85. Atlas, "James Joyce," 294.

86. Atlas, "James Joyce," 295.

87. Vanderham, *James Joyce and Censorship*, 107.

88. Atlas, "James Joyce," 297.

89. Atlas, "James Joyce," 297.

90. Atlas, "James Joyce," 297.

91. Atlas, "James Joyce," 304. Vanderham reports that this memo by Atlas is identical to one that Atlas later published as "James Joyce" in *Scraps*, the newsletter of the U.S. Attorney's office, Southern District of New York. Vanderham explains Atlas's appreciation for the book by noting that he had lived in the bohemian precincts of New York's Greenwich Village in the 1920s. Atlas graduated from Fordham Law School in 1924 and "practiced occasional law," but he also "taught English at City College, and worked as a literary critic at the *Brooklyn Daily Eagle*." He met the abstract realist painter and Greenwich Village denizen De Hirsch Margulies, who on travels to Paris "brought back copies of the Shakespeare & Company edition of *Ulysses*." According to Vanderham, Atlas had "a deep appreciation for the *Ulysses* that had not dimmed when he became involved in the government's case against the book." *Ulysses* had come to him, "as it had come to many of his generation, with the force of a liberating revelation; he could hardly be expected seriously to move the Court to confiscate and destroy it" (Vanderham, *James Joyce and Censorship*, 93).

92. Vanderham reports that Coleman compiled a list of obscene passages that was attached to the confiscated copy of the work. The list contained 260 passages deemed obscene, distributed over 198 pages, roughly 25% of the 1922 Paris edition. Vanderham, *James Joyce and Censorship*, 108.

93. "Ulysses Case Reaches Court After 10 Years: Woolsey Upset Because He Fears He Understands Debatably Lewd Soliloquy," *New York Herald Tribune* (November 26, 1933), reprinted in Moscato and LeBlanc, *United States of America v. One Book Entitled Ulysses*, 284.

94. "Ulysses Case Reaches Court After 10 Years," 286. The core "problem" of the book's possible obscenity was its revelation of female lust, both young Gerty's McDowell's own lack of purity and her knowledge that Leopold Bloom was masturbating while watching her—a doubling of the book's violations of literary cleanliness standards—and the older Molly Bloom's ruminations on her lifetime of robust and eager sexual appetites. Both were serious transgressions against codes of female sexual reticence. And this was indeed the most shocking element of the book: that Leopold Bloom's cuckolding wife loved sex, thought about sex, and thought about exactly the kinds of sexual activities and pleasures that were legally and morally construed as unnatural, perverse, and having no place in literature. Her behavior and ruminations marked her off as an unacceptable woman, beyond her adultery. Her shameless reflections about her lover's penis size and the frequency of their intercourse, of putting penises in her mouth, of anal pleasures, of wiping ejaculate off her buttocks, and more—and she had no "shame"

about any of this. What's more, this was the book's culmination, its final forty pages, and it only sustained giving voice to its female protagonist. This torrent of voluptuously expressed female sexual desire was understood by all to be its most troubling element. Indeed, all the other passages or sections barely earned mention by comparison. Ironically, given the subject matter, the idea of "normal" women readers being aroused by erotic matters was essentially outside the concern of most obscenity discussions, so concerned were they with male lust. Yet the idea of female readers or listeners finding out about and knowing what was inside the pages of *Ulysses* was so troubling that in both the 1921 and the 1933 cases the very presence of women spectators in the courtroom produced its own little spectacle of prurient curiosity and frisson among the journalists.

95. "Ulysses Case Reaches Court After 10 Years," 286.

96. "Ulysses Case Reaches Court After 10 Years," 286.

97. "Ulysses Case Reaches Court After 10 Years," 287 (emphasis added).

98. Lindey, Claimant's Supplementary Memorandum, *United States v. Ulysses*, November 27, 1933, in Moscato and LeBlanc, *United States of America v. One Book Entitled Ulysses*, 289–92.

99. Lindey, Claimant's Supplementary Memorandum, 291.

100. Lindey, Claimant's Supplementary Memorandum, 291.

101. Woolsey decision, *United States v. One Book Called "Ulysses,"* 5 F. Supp. 182, (S.D.N.Y. 1933), December 6, 1933, at 185.

102. Woolsey decision, 183.

103. Woolsey decision, 183.

104. Woolsey decision, 183.

105. Woolsey decision, 185.

106. Woolsey decision, 185. It is useful to think of the aphrodisiac test as the whether-it-induced-masturbation test. The defense, and also Woolsey's ruling, was that the dirty parts were not only a minor part of a much larger work but that they were also obscured, difficult to find, difficult to understand, and not really sustained, and thus although the book might have produced some sexual alertness, some titillation, some frisson, it did not produce lust—it was not a flagitious work. Its predominant effect was not an aphrodisiac: It did not turn its readers into masturbators. Those who would hope to thumb through the pages to find passages that might facilitate their lust or shame were sure to be disappointed. This, then, gave the judges a way out: They could honestly acknowledge that it was dirty in parts, even revoltingly so, that it offended all kinds of sensibilities, but its overall effect was not the production of lust or masturbation or shame, so it could not be "obscene." That is, in the *Ulysses* trial what was clearly at stake but never fully articulated was the deep equivalence between the category of

obscenity and the presumed consequence of masturbation. The equation was never full stated, but it was spoken about, and it was fairly straightforward: obscenity = lust and lust = masturbation. If a work was thought to induce masturbation, it was obscene.

107. Gillers, "Tendency to Deprave and Corrupt," 285, n349.

108. *United States v. One Book Entitled Ulysses*, 72 F.2d 705 (2d Cir. 1934), August 7, 1934.

109. *United States v. One Book Entitled Ulysses*, 706.

110. *United States v. One Book Entitled Ulysses*, 707 (emphasis added).

111. *United States v. One Book Entitled Ulysses*, 707.

112. *United States v. One Book Entitled Ulysses*, 707 (emphasis added).

113. The courts will not make this distinction until the late 1940s, when they begin to gesture toward variable obscenity rulings, based on the idea that different readers have different capacities and that adults have the right to see materials youth should not see.

114. *United States v. One Book Entitled Ulysses*, 707, 708.

Chapter 7

1. For Sanger's background and the history of the birth control movement, see Margaret Sanger, *The Autobiography of Margaret Sanger* (Mineola, NY: Dover, 2004 [1938]); James Reed, *From Private Vice to Public Virtue: The Birth Control Movement and American Society Since 1830* (New York: Basic Books, 1978); Ellen Chesler, *A Woman of Valor: Margaret Sanger and the Birth Control Movement in America* (New York: Doubleday Anchor, 1992); Linda Gordon, *The Moral Property of Women: A History of Birth Control Politics in America*, 3rd ed. (Urbana-Champaign: University of Illinois Press, 2007); David Kennedy, *Birth Control in America: The Career of Margaret Sanger* (New Haven, CT: Yale University Press, 1971); and Peter C. Engelman, *A History of the Birth Control Movement in America* (Santa Barbara, CA: Praeger, 2011).

2. The first clinic Sanger established in 1916 lasted only a few weeks before being permanently shut down.

3. "Raid Sanger Clinic on Birth Control: Police Seize Two Women Doctors and Three Nurses in West 15th Street Bureau," *New York Times* (April 16, 1929), 25. For Sanger's discussion of the raid, see Sanger, *Autobiography*, 400–408. For a rich treatment of the raid and its aftermath, see Joel Matthew Silverman, "Pursuing Celebrity, Ensuing Masculinity: Morris Ernst, Obscenity, and the Search for Recognition," PhD diss., University of Texas at Austin, 2006, 101–35. Silverman's research also draws extensively on documents from the Harry Ransom Humanities Research Center (HRC), Morris L. Ernst (MLE) Papers.

4. Section 1142 of the New York Penal Code also made it illegal "to give information orally, stating when, where or how such an instrument, article or medicine can be purchased or obtained."

5. "Raid Sanger Clinic on Birth Control," 25.

6. "Raid Sanger Clinic on Birth Control," 25. The report begins: "The Birth Control Clinical Research Bureau at 46 West Fifteenth Street, founded by Mrs. Margaret Sanger in 1923 'to test the decision handed down by the New York State Court of Appeals to the effect that "a physician lawfully practicing can give contraceptive advice for the cure or prevention of disease,"' was raided by the police yesterday [Monday]."

7. Although Ernst was already steeped in the history of U.S. obscenity laws from writing his 1928 book *To the Pure*, he had devoted only a few paragraphs to the risks faced by birth control activists when they sent their materials through the mails and did not mention birth control clinics at all. Ernst and his colleagues thus had to make a quick study of the birth control side of the Comstock laws.

8. Ernst to Mrs. Carlos Torres, October 21, 1939, HRC, MLE Papers, Box 267, Folder 267.27.

9. Leigh Ann Wheeler discusses the ACLU's early support of Sanger and the birth control cause, beginning in 1921; when the ACLU staged its protests against censorship in Boston in 1929, Sanger famously took to the stage in Fanueil Hall with her mouth covered by tape as Arthur Schlesinger read her speech. See Leigh Ann Wheeler, *How Sex Became a Civil Liberty* (New York: Oxford University Press, 2012), 22–29, 35–37.

10. Reed, *Private Vice to Public Virtue*, x.

11. In 1800 American women bore an average of 7.04 children; by 1860 the average was 5.21. The fertility rate was 3.56 in 1900, and it continued to fall through the 1930s, when it actually fell below the replacement rate of 2.3. For a discussion of the wide range of strategies people used to control reproduction, despite the laws, see Andrea Tone, *Devices and Desires: A History of Contraceptives in America* (New York: Hill & Wang, 2001), 47–90.

12. Reed, *Private Vice to Public Virtue*, x.

13. Reed, *Private Vice to Public Virtue*, 6.

14. Reed, *Private Vice to Public Virtue*, 6.

15. Reed, *Private Vice to Public Virtue*, 34.

16. Reed, *Private Vice to Public Virtue*, 34. For a discussion of how mid-nineteenth-century medical professionals, clergy, politicians, and anti-vice crusaders rallied behind obscenity legislation to curb women's use of contraceptives, see Nicole Beisel, *Imperiled Innocents: Anthony Comstock and Family Reproduction in Victorian America* (Princeton, NJ: Princeton University

Press, 1997), 25–48. See also Tone, *Devices and Desires*, 3–46. Helen Lefkowitz Horowitz discusses the crackdown on birth control and abortion in Helen Lefkowitz Horowitz, *Rereading Sex: Battles over Sexual Knowledge* (New York: Knopf, 2002), 70–85, 194–209.

17. Section 1145 of the New York code, added in 1881, permitted doctors to prescribe contraceptives for preventive health reasons, widely understood as a way to give men condoms and stave off venereal diseases.

18. There was a large market for "feminine hygiene" products—the code for over-the-counter contraceptive devices. But these products, as Andrea Tone makes clear, were often dangerous to women, generally ineffective, and unregulated. Women ran considerable risks in using such products as Lysol and other harsh astringents as contraceptives. Condoms were available for purchase for "disease" prevention, but they were not under women's control and were also tainted by their association with prostitution. In addition, because they were unregulated, they were often faulty as well. Tone, *Devices and Desires*; see also Andrea Tone, ed., *Controlling Reproduction: An American History* (Wilmington, DE: SR Books, 1997); and Engelman, *History of the Birth Control Movement*.

19. See Engelman, *History of the Birth Control Movement*, 23–73.

20. Despite Sanger's considerable efforts, Congress would not take up the legislation beyond a few committee votes, rejecting her legislation.

21. Sanger describes her radicalization in Sanger, *Autobiography*, 70–105. See also Engelman, *History of the Birth Control Movement*, 23–73.

22. Reed, *Private Vice to Public Virtue*, 76.

23. Reed, *Private Vice to Public Virtue*, 82.

24. Sanger opposed abortion and always kept abortion provision and information about obtaining abortions out of her clinics. She saw abortions as tragedies. She also saw the failure to help women avoid unwanted pregnancies and unwanted children as tragedies. Every child, she argued, should be a wanted child.

25. Reed, *Private Vice to Public Virtue*, 83.

26. Reed, *Private Vice to Public Virtue*, 84.

27. Reed, *Private Vice to Public Virtue*, 85.

28. Once Sanger finally established a legal clinic, she began to work to convince American manufacturers to produce spermicidal jellies and improved versions of pessaries.

29. Engelman describes Bill's legal travails and Sanger's martyrdom in Engelman, *History of the Birth Control Movement*, 23–73.

30. Description from the Margaret Sanger Papers Project, Brownsville Clinic, http://www.nyu.edu/projects/sanger/aboutms/organization_brownsville_clinic.php (accessed May 7, 2015).

31. Description from the Margaret Sanger Papers Project, Brownsville Clinic, http://www.nyu.edu/projects/sanger/aboutms/organization_brownsville_clinic.php (accessed May 7, 2015).

32. According to the decision in *People v. Sanger*, Section 1142 of the New York Penal Code makes it "a misdemeanor for a person to sell, or give away, or to advertise or offer for sale, any instrument or article, drug or medicine, for the prevention of conception; or to give information orally, stating when, where or how such an instrument, article or medicine can be purchased or obtained."

33. Sanger describes the establishment of the Brownsville clinic, the raids, and the ensuing legal fights in Sanger, *Autobiography*, 211–50.

34. Description from the Margaret Sanger Papers Project, Brownsville Clinic, http://www.nyu.edu/projects/sanger/aboutms/organization_brownsville_clinic.php (accessed May 7, 2015).

35. The case was *People v. Sanger*, 222 N.Y. 192 (1918). Because contraceptive devices were legal for the prevention of disease but not the prevention of conception, the 1918 prevention of disease ruling gave legal sanction for clinics to operate; the great unsaid here is that it probably forced licensed medical professionals into all kinds of falsehoods so that their patients could receive the contraceptives they needed and desired. It suggests how birth control restrictions distorted the medical discourse and forced everyone into stratagems of deception. Until women were granted the right to contraception for the purposes of contraception, this stratagem of deception would continue to be necessary. The New York legislature passed Section 1145 in 1881 to modify the blanket prohibitions in Section 1142.

36. *People v. Sanger*, at 194.

37. *People v. Sanger*, at 195. Using *Webster's International Dictionary*, the court defined *disease* rather broadly as "an alteration in the state of the body, or of some of its organs, interrupting or disturbing the performance of the vital functions, and causing or threatening pain and sickness; illness; sickness; disorder" (195).

38. Description from the Margaret Sanger Papers Project, Brownsville Clinic, http://www.nyu.edu/projects/sanger/aboutms/organization_brownsville_clinic.php (accessed May 7, 2015).

39. See Wheeler, *How Sex Became a Civil Liberty*; Engelman, *History of the Birth Control Movement*; and Reed, *Private Vice to Public Virtue*.

40. Reed, *Private Vice to Public Virtue*, 115–16.

41. Reed, *Private Vice to Public Virtue*, 117.

42. *New York World* (April 18, 1929), ACLU Papers, Princeton University, vol. 366.

43. "500 in Court to Aid 5 Seized in Raid," *New York Times* (April 20, 1929), 13. Others whom the *Times* mentioned were Mrs. Fosdick and Mrs. Morgenthau,

Mr. and Mrs. Corliss Lamont, Mrs. Ogden Mills Reid, Mrs. J. Bishop Vandever, Mrs. Charles E. Scribner, Rabbi Sidney E. Goldstein, and thirty people representing New Jersey towns.

44. "500 in Court," 13.

45. "500 in Court," 13.

46. The prosecution's formal memorandum filled in background details from the police perspective, explaining that McNamara went to the clinic for the first time on March 22, 1929, because of a complaint that the clinic's physicians and nurses were "engaged in the unlawful distribution of instruments, articles, etc. for the prevention of contraception." Nurse Brestwell met her first, took basic information about McNamara's reproductive history, and told her to come back and see a doctor. She returned two weeks later, and this time Nurse Field took her history and asked her to again affirm that she did not want to have any more children. Field gave her a Mizpah pessary with instructions about inserting it before "going to bed or having intercourse." McNamara paid $5 for the cap and the doctor's fee and then met with Nurse Sideri and Dr. Pissort, who showed her how to insert it. A week later, she returned again, and this time Dr. Hannah Stone examined her and reminded her again about how to correctly insert the pessary. Memorandum of Facts and Law, *The People of the State of New York v. Marcella Sideri, Sigrid Brestwell, Antoinette Field, Elizabeth Pissort and Hannah M. Stone, Defendants*, submitted by Joab H. Banton, District Attorney, and John T. Hogan, Deputy Assistant District Attorney, May 1929, HRC, MLE Papers, vol. 90.

47. Memorandum of Facts and Law, 2–3.

48. *New York Times* (April 20, 1929), 13.

49. "Clinic File Seizure Held to Be Illegal: McAdoo Officially Finds Police Exceeded Their Authority and Orders Return of Records," *New York Times* (April 21, 1929), 9.

50. "Criticize Whalen in Clinic Move," *New York Times* (May 13, 1929), 19.

51. "Criticize Whalen in Clinic Move," 19.

52. "Uproar Interrupts Clinic Raid Hearing: 200 Are Ejected for Laughing at Magistrate and Cheering Birth Control Defense," *New York Times* (May 25, 1929), 24.

53. "Uproar Interrupts Clinic Raid Hearing," 24.

54. "Uproar Interrupts Clinic Raid Hearing," 24.

55. Memorandum of Facts and Law, 4.

56. Memorandum of Facts and Law, 7.

57. Memorandum of Facts and Law, 7.

58. Memorandum of Facts and Law, 5.

59. Memorandum of Facts and Law, 5.

60. Defendants Brief, *People v. Sideri*, HRC, MLE Papers, vol. 90, p. 8.

61. "The Court's Decision," *People v. Sideri*, HRC, MLE Papers, vol. 90, p. 1.

62. Huse to Ernst, May 20, 1929, quoted in Silverman, "Pursuing Celebrity," 136.

63. Much later in his career, as an elderly man, Ernst would report that he had joined up with Sanger in 1915, but in fact he joined in April 1929, when the Clinical Research Bureau was raided.

64. Lindey to Rose, January 25, 1933, HRC, MLE Papers, vol. 65.

65. Sanger to Ernst, February 15, 1933, HRC, MLE Papers, vol. 65.

66. Rose to Lindey, February 8, 1933, HRC, MLE Papers, vol. 65.

67. Sanger to Ernst, February 15, 1933, HRC, MLE Papers, vol. 65.

68. Lindey to Rose, January 25, 1933, HRC, MLE Papers, vol. 65. Lindey and Ernst's optimism rested in part on the 1930 *Youngs v. Lee* decision, in which New York's Court of Appeals for the Second Circuit held that condoms could be sent through the mail because they could be used for legal purposes as well as illegal ones. They hoped that Customs officials would not take the Tariff Act language literally. The full title of that case is *Youngs Rubber Corporation v. C. I. Lee & Co.*, 45 F.2d 103 (2d Cir., 1930); decided December 15, 1930, before Judges Martin Manton, Thomas Swan, and Augustus Hand; decision written by Swan. Although it was a trademark suit in which Youngs claimed that Lee was illegally distributing condoms across state lines, the Second Circuit Court's argument suggested that the doctor's good-faith use of the condoms was not to be vouchsafed and that the potential illegal use of a device did not mean that all uses were illegal and thus prohibited. Of the federal statute, the court wrote in *Youngs*, "Taken literally, this language would seem to forbid the transportation by mail or common carriage of anything 'adapted,' in the sense of being suitable or fitted, for preventing conception or for any indecent or immoral purpose, even though the article might also be capable of legitimate uses and the sender in good faith supposed that it would be used only legitimately. . . . The intention to prevent a proper medical use of drugs or other articles merely because they are capable of illegal uses is not lightly to be ascribed to Congress" (108). This decision, also drew on the *Sanger* decision from 1918 and strongly asserted physicians' right to prescribe materials for the health of their clients.

69. Hawkins to Greenbaum, Wolff & Ernst, February 8, 1933, HRC, MLE Papers, vol. 65.

70. Lindey to Rose, February 10, 1933, HRC, MLE Papers, vol. 65.

71. The full argument that Lindey and Ernst laid out for the court before the trial can be found in Trial Memorandum for Claimant, *United States v. One Package of Japanese Pessaries*, U.S. District Court for the Southern District of New York, December 10, 1935, HRC, MLE, vol. 65.

72. For an example of the letter sent to physicians, see Lindey to Dr. Wile, November 2, 1935, HRC, MLE Papers, vol. 65.

73. Transcript of Record, U.S. Court of Appeals, Second Circuit, *United States v. One Package of Japanese Pessaries*, HRC, MLE Papers, vol. 69, p. 37.

74. Transcript of Record, 37.

75. Transcript of Record, 37.

76. Transcript of Record, 38.

77. In the same way that Ernst and Lindey evaded legislative history, Davidson rejected any implications that New York State law might protect New York physicians from receiving these articles.

78. *Youngs Rubber Corporation v. C. I. Lee & Co.*, 45 F.2d 103 (2d Cir., 1930); and *Davis v. United States* 62 F.(2) 473 (1933), both cited in Transcript of Record.

79. Transcript of Record, 38.

80. Transcript of Record, 38. Perhaps in a gesture to persuade the Catholics in the U.S. Attorney's office and possible Catholic jury members, Ernst suggested that even the Church was proving more flexible than Customs, having recognized poverty concerns as legitimate criteria for child spacing. Although the Church did not endorse the use of contraceptives, it did accept the rhythm method as a technique for child spacing and recognized that pregnancy prevention had valuable, sometimes necessary health benefits for families. "Books published with the imprimatur of the Catholic Church" indicate and "state frankly that pregnancy should be prevented for not only health reasons arriving out of medical indications but even because of health reasons derived from economic indications." Ernst went on to explain that the dispute was not over the goal of child spacing but rather "the method of preventing conception and birth" and that Catholic authorities recognized "that economic factors, in addition to psychological ones and the burdens of depleted physical energies very often indicate the need for the prevention of birth." The rhythm method was a nontechnological practice, based on avoidance of intercourse during women's periods of highest fertility, just before and just following menstruation (39).

81. Transcript of Record, 40–42. When Ernst brought up reasons of economics and conditions of poverty as another ground for contraception, Dr. Bancroft hedged a bit, saying that this was a matter for other experts—a "state sociological problem that the state should handle"—but he did admit that he recognized the "relation of economics of a family to the number of children."

82. Transcript of Record, 45.

83. Transcript of Record, 49.

84. For a discussion about how widespread acceptance of eugenicist arguments of "undesirables" reproducing was, see R. Marie Griffith, "Crossing the Catholic

Divide: Gender, Sexuality, and Historiography," in *Catholics in the American Century: Recasting Narratives of U.S. History*, ed. R. Scott Appleby and Kathleen Sprows Cummings (Ithaca, NY: Cornell University Press, 2012), 81–107.

85. According to his testimony, Foster Kennedy was a member of the American Medical Association, past president of the Neurological Association of New York, secretary of the New York Academy of Medicine, and fellow of the Royal Academy, Edinburgh; and he was affiliated with four hospitals in New York City, including as a professor of clinical neurology at Cornell, attending physician at New York Hospital, and the director of the Department of Neurology, Bellevue Hospital.

86. Transcript of Record, 55–57.

87. The other witnesses included Dr. Frederick C. Holden, Bellevue Hospital gynecologist; Dr. Robert L. Dickinson, chairman of the Mental Health Committee (and a leading medical authority for the birth control community); Dr. Max Mayer, chief of the Gynecological Bureau at Mount Sinai Hospital; Dr. Elizabeth Pissort; and Dr. Louis Harris, former health commissioner of New York City.

88. Transcript of Record, 58.

89. The state's reply brief, Reply Memorandum for Libellant, in *United States v. One Package Containing 120, More or Less, Rubber Pessaries to Prevent Conception*, Dr. Hannah Stone, Claimant, HRC, MLE Papers, vol. 69. The brief is written and signed by Lamar Hardy, U.S. Attorney, Southern District of New York, Proctor for Libellant; John F. Davidson, Assistant U.S. Attorney; and William P. Young, Special Assistant to the U.S. Attorney.

90. The "Libellant's whole position," they asserted, was that the court should carry out congressional intent "and that it should not attempt to rewrite the statute to carry out any other intent." Citing the "repeated rejection by Congress of attempts to amend the importation statute," they said that the words in the statute remained "clear and unambiguous" (Reply Memorandum for Libellant, 2).

91. Reply Memorandum for Libellant, 10.

92. Trial Memorandum for Claimant, *United States v. One Package of Japanese Pessaries*, 7.

93. Moscowitz's decision, *United States v. One Package of Japanese Pessaries*, 13 F. Supp. 334 (1936), handed down January 6, 1936, at 336.

94. Judge Moscowitz's decision is quoted from Morris L. Ernst and Gwendolyn Pickett, "Birth Control in the Courts: A Résumé of Legal Decisions Clarifying and Interpreting Existing Statutes," October 1942, p. 32, HRC, MLE Papers, Box 5, Folder 5.22.

95. Ernst and Pickett, "Birth Control in the Courts," 85.

96. Ernst and Pickett, "Birth Control in the Courts," 85.

97. Ernst and Pickett, "Birth Control in the Courts," 32. Augustus Hand

wrote the opinion, affirming the decree, in *United States v. One Package of Japanese Pessaries*, 86 F.2d 737 (2d Cir. 1936). The Tariff Act of 1930 (19 U.S.C.A. § 1305(a)), as well Title 18, Section 334, of the U.S. Code (18 U.S.C.A. § 334), and Title 18, Section 396, of the U.S. Code (18 U.S.C.A. § 396) all originated from the Comstock Act of 1873.

98. For a discussion of this decision's legal importance, see Geoffrey Stone, *Sex and the Constitution: Sex, Religion, and Law from America's Origins to the Twenty-First Century* (New York: Liveright, 2017); and David Garrow, *Liberty and Sexuality: The Right to Privacy and the Making of Roe v. Wade* (New York: Macmillan, 1994).

99. Ernst and Pickett, "Birth Control in the Courts," 34.

100. *United States v. John P. Nicholas* and *United States v. Norman E. Himes* (97 Fed. (2) 510), U.S. Court of Appeals for the Second Circuit, Judges L. Hand, Swan, and Chase presiding.

101. The generalized arguments I make here draw on documents in HRC, MLE Papers, and on records of the American Civil Liberties Union (ACLU records, Seeley Mudd Library, Princeton University).

102. For a discussion of the contretemps in the ACLU, see Judy Kutulas, *The American Civil Liberties Union and the Making of Modern Liberalism, 1930–1960* (Chapel Hill: University of North Carolina Press, 2006).

Chapter 8

1. Alfred C. Kinsey, with Wardell B. Pomeroy and Clyde E. Martin, *Sexual Behavior in the Human Male* (Philadelphia: W. B. Saunders, 1948).

2. Alfred C. Kinsey, Wardell B. Pomeroy, Clyde E. Martin, and Paul H. Gebhard, *Sexual Behavior in the Human Female* (Philadelphia: W. B. Saunders, 1953).

3. Numerous scholars treat these larger social trends. The discussion here draws chiefly on frameworks discussed by Andrea Friedman, "Sadists and Sissies: Anti-Pornography Campaigns in Cold War America," *Gender and History* 15, no. 2 (August 2003): 201–27; Whitney Strub, *Perversion for Profit: The Politics of Pornography and the Rise of the New Right* (New York: Columbia University Press, 2010), esp. 11–42; and Paul Boyer, *Purity in Print: Book Censorship in America from the Gilded Age to the Computer Age*, 2nd ed. (Madison: University of Wisconsin Press, 2002), esp. 270–316.

4. Studies that examine the shifting legal treatment of literary works in this era include Marjorie Heins, *Not in Front of the Children: "Indecency," Censorship, and the Innocence of Youth* (New York: Hill & Wang, 2001); Edward de Grazia, *Girls Lean Back Everywhere: The Law of Obscenity and the Assault on Genius*, 2nd ed. (New York: Vintage, 1993); Charles Rembar, *The End of Obscenity: The Trials*

of Lady Chatterley, Tropic of Cancer, and Fanny Hill, 4th ed. (New York: Bantam, 1969); Felice Flannery Lewis, *Literature, Obscenity, and the Law* (Carbondale: Southern Illinois University Press, 1976); Strub, *Perversion for Profit;* Whitney Strub, *Obscenity Rules: Roth v. United States and the Long Struggle over Sexual Expression* (Lawrence: University of Kansas Press, 2013); Boyer, *Purity in Print;* and Geoffrey Stone, *Sex and the Constitution: Sex, Religion, and Law from America's Origins to the Twenty-First Century* (New York: Liveright, 2017).

5. For example, in *United States v. Levine* (83 F.2d 156 (1936)), Ernst was initially Levine's counsel, withdrew, and then was retained again on appeal. The court of appeals decision was a rather complicated argument that essentially reiterated the distinction between vulnerable youth and adult readers but that also reiterated the court's interest in restricting materials whose sole purpose was sexual arousal: "The standard must be the likelihood that the work will so much arouse the salacity of the reader to whom it is sent as to outweigh any literary, scientific or other merits it may have in that reader's hands; of this the jury is the arbiter" (*United States v. Levine,* 158). Ernst was also involved in the *Parmalee* case (1940) but only at the appellate level, writing a brief. And in the *Esquire* case, which began in 1943, the Greenbaum, Wolff & Ernst firm did not get involved until the case went to the Supreme Court in 1946, when they submitted an amicus brief, written by Harriet Pilpel and Alexander Lindey.

6. Albert Deutsch, "The Sex Habits of American Men," *Harpers* (December 1947), 493.

7. Major biographies of Kinsey include James Jones, *Kinsey: A Life* (New York: Norton, 2004); and Jonathan Gathorne-Hardy, *Alfred Kinsey: Sex, the Measure of All Things* (Bloomington: Indiana University Press, 2004). Other studies of Kinsey's influence include Paul A. Robinson, *The Modernization of Sex: Havelock Ellis, Alfred Kinsey, William Masters, and Virginia Johnson* (New York: Harper & Row, 1976); and Donna J. Drucker, *The Classification of Sex: Alfred Kinsey and the Organization of Knowledge* (Pittsburgh: University of Pittsburgh Press, 2014).

8. Albert Deutsch, like other supportive reviewers, focused readers' attention on Kinsey's support from the National Research Council, "the most authoritative scientific body in the land," and from the Rockefeller Foundation's Medical Science Division, led by Alan Gregg, whom Deutsch described as "one of the wisest of medical statesmen." Deutsch quoted Gregg at length to reassure readers of the institute's probity and objective methods and to vouch for its scientific bona fides. See Deutsch, "Sex Habits of American Men," 493–94.

9. Deutsch, "Sex Habits of American Men," 493.

10. Deutsch, "Sex Habits of American Men," 493–94.

11. Deutsch, "Sex Habits of American Men," 495.

12. Kinsey routinely asserted that 95% of all American men had broken a sex law. Among the commonly practiced but illegal acts: 37% had had a homosexual encounter at some point in their lives; nearly 70% of American men by age 35 had had sex with prostitutes; 86% had engaged in premarital intercourse; between 30% and 45% had engaged in extramarital intercourse; and 1 out of every 6 American farm boys had had intercourse with animals. All these practices were punishable under the law.

13. Waverly Root, "Love and Law," *American Mercury* (May 1948), 623. Root also predicted that the Kinsey Report would draw attention to "the problems of lawlessness in America in a way that will make it difficult to ignore" (624). Don Calhoun, found potentially therapeutic effects in the Kinsey Report, hoping it would "enable people to view their own sex life, and the sex life of others, in a somewhat more objective light" (Don Calhoun, "The Kinsey Report," *Politics* [winter 1948], 52–55).

14. Paul A. Gebhard later explained in a legal affidavit taken in 1956 that the institute had done far more than just conduct the 18,000 interviews that he Kinsey, Pomeroy, and Martin had taken, recorded, coded, and stored. He noted in this affidavit that of those 18,000 interviews, 4,000 had been conducted with inmates of penal institutions and a number of others with sex offenders not in prison. See Gebhard Affidavit, p. 10, Kinsey Institute Archives, bound volume (Greenbaum, Wolff & Ernst), *U.S. v. 31 Photographs.*

15. Francis Sill Wickware, "Report on Kinsey," *Life* (August 2, 1948), 87.

16. Wickware, "Report on Kinsey," 88, 89.

17. Wickware, "Report on Kinsey," 88, 89, 94. When Ernst passed on to Kinsey a letter from Isidor Lubin (of the American Statistical Association) about an article by Allen Wallis criticizing Kinsey's statistical methods and their mutual interest in helping him, Kinsey was defensive. Lubin wrote Ernst, "If you can persuade Kinsey to obtain competent statistical help, I am sure that we of the American Statistical Association will do everything we can to see that he gets high type of personnel" (Lubin to Ernst, February 11, 1949, Kinsey Institute Archives, Morris Ernst Folder). Ernst forwarded the letter to Kinsey on March 19, 1949, and Kinsey replied with a detailed letter about the effects of the criticisms on their statistical methods and how little difference it would make. See Kinsey to Ernst, April 2, 1949, Kinsey Institute Archives, Morris Ernst Folder.

18. Wickware, "Report on Kinsey," 94.

19. Wickware, "Report on Kinsey," 98.

20. Abraham Stone, "Eugenics," *Saturday Review of Literature* (March 13, 1949), 17–18; Benjamin Wortis, "The Kinsey Report and Related Fields: Psychiatry," *Saturday Review of Literature* (March 13, 1949), 33; Ruth Benedict, "The Kinsey

Report," *Saturday Review of Literature* (March 13, 1949), 35; Morris Ernst, "Law," *Saturday Review of Literature* (March 13, 1949), 19.

21. At the outset of World War II, the Ernst firm had unsuccessfully tried to challenge Massachusetts's and Connecticut's restrictive state birth control laws in the U.S. Supreme Court in 1943 in the *Tileston* case. Lindey won a surprise victory in successfully defending *Forever Amber* in the Massachusetts Supreme Court in 1944, but Lindey took the lead in that case, not Ernst.

22. Ernst's published writings from the 1940s to 1960s and a long private correspondence between Hoover and him reveal that Ernst became a dependable protector of Hoover and the FBI's reputation and a surreptitious informant as well. For an excellent study of the Ernst FBI files as a preliminary investigation of the Ernst-Hoover relationship, see Harrison Salisbury, "The Strange Correspondence of Morris Ernst and John Edgar Hoover, 1939–1964," *The Nation* (December 1, 1984), 575–89; and Brett Gary, "'Guessing Oneself into Jail': Morris Ernst and the Assault on American Obscenity Laws in the 1930s," in *Obscenity and the Limits of Liberalism*, ed. Loren Glass and Charles Francis Williams (Columbus: Ohio State University Press, 2011). See also Brett Gary, "Morris Ernst's Troubled Legacy," *Reconstruction: Studies in Contemporary Culture* 8, no. 1 (2008), http://reconstruction.eserver.org/084/contents084.shtml#8.1 (accessed September 30, 2013). Some of the other works that Ernst published in this era include Morris L. Ernst and Alexander Lindey, *The Censor Marches On* (New York: Doubleday Doran, 1940); Morris L. Ernst, *Too Big* (Boston: Little, Brown, 1940); Morris L. Ernst, *The First Freedom* (New York: Macmillan, 1946); and Morris L. Ernst and David Loth, *Report on the American Communist* (New York: Holt, 1952).

23. Not surprisingly, one of the plagiarizers Ernst had to deal with almost immediately was Samuel Roth, who had earlier pirated Joyce's *Ulysses* and soon tried to capitalize on Kinsey's research. Under the pen name Norman Lockridge, Roth wrote and published a book titled *The Sexual Conduct of Men and Women: A Minority Report by Norman Lockridge* (New York: Hogarth House, 1948). He also published Gershon Legman's *Minority Report on Prof. Kinsey* (New York: Hogarth House, 1949). Legman had briefly worked with Kinsey's team and tried to assert official affiliation with the project. Ernst and Pilpel directly intervened with Roth about his piracy, essentially their first formal actions on behalf of their new client Kinsey. For a biographical treatment of Samuel Roth, see Jay Gertzman, *Bookleggers and Smuthounds: The Trade in Erotica, 1920–1940* (Philadelphia: University of Pennsylvania Press, 1999), 219–82.

24. Pilpel would eventually become Greenbaum, Wolff & Ernst's key figure on obscenity law issues, especially on reproductive rights matters, serving as Planned Parenthood's counsel in the Supreme Court case *Poe v. Ullmann*; she would write

amicus briefs for the ACLU in the *Griswold v. Connecticut* case and in *Roe v. Wade*. She would eventually argue before or brief the U.S. Supreme Court in twenty-four other cases. Notes from the Finding Aid to Harriet Pilpel's Papers at the Sophia Smith Collection, Smith College, https://findingaids.smith.edu/repositories/2/resources/506 (accessed January 21, 2021). Pilpel was born in New York City in 1911 to Julius and Ethel (Loewy) Fleischl. She graduated from Vassar in 1932 and received a Master's degree in 1933 and a law degree in 1936, both from Columbia University. According to the finding aid, between 1937 and 1991, she participated in twenty-seven cases before the U.S. Supreme Court, and was "a prolific lecturer and author of publications related to copyright, abortion, marriage, birth control, civil liberties, and the law; she was also active in many organizations including the board of directors of Planned Parenthood Federation of America for whom she was legal counsel. Pilpel was also counsel to a number of other associations, including Sex Information and Educational Council of the United States, Association for the Study of Abortion, and Association for Voluntary Sterilization. In addition, she served on the boards of the National Abortion Rights Action League, the American Civil Liberties Union, and The Alan Guttmacher Institute."

25. Ernst to Kinsey, March 2, 1948, Kinsey Institute Archives, Morris Ernst Folder. See also undated memorandum, "Kinsey," ca. February or March 1948; and an outline of the book Ernst sent to Loth with this explanation, March 2, 1948, Harry Ransom Humanities Research Center (HRC), Morris L. Ernst (MLE) Papers, Box 482, Folder 482.2. See also the complete outline in Morris L. Ernst and David Loth, "Outline," February–March 1948, HRC, MLE Papers, Box 482, Folder 482.2.

26. Ernst to Kinsey, March 2, 1948, Kinsey Institute Archives, Morris Ernst Folder.

27. Kinsey to Ernst, March 4, 1948, HRC, MLE Papers, Box 482, Folder 482.2. Kinsey also said that he would send their correspondence to his publisher, W. B. Saunders of Philadelphia, so that they would know about this development. He told Ernst that the attacks had begun and that he had seen one 38-page "attack from one of the psycho-analysts." Kinsey also wrote Ernst's publisher, Fred Drimmer of Greystone Press, that he supported Ernst and Loth's project but was clear to stipulate that Drimmer and Ernst should not "mislead the public into believing that [the project] was a condensation or a supplement to our volume" (Kinsey to Drimmer, March 2, 1948, HRC, MLE Papers, Box 482, Folder 482.2). The title, *American Sexual Behavior and the Kinsey Report*, would certainly suggest it was.

28. Kinsey, Gebhard, and Pomeroy ate dinner at Ernst's house sometime between October 21 and November 7, 1948. In his thank you note Kinsey wrote, "You both have become such strong supporters of the research that it is difficult to tell you how much we appreciate what you are doing. It does contribute definitely,

and we do benefit from it" (Kinsey to Ernst, November 7, 1948, Kinsey Institute Archives, Morris Ernst Folder); another Kinsey visit to the Ernst home took place in November 1949, and they planned to see each other again in New York City in late December 1949.

29. Ernst worked to defend and promote Kinsey with the Rockefeller Foundation directors. In April 1949, Ernst followed up with Alan Gregg of the Rockefeller Foundation—Kinsey's most important funder—in response to a letter Kinsey had sent Ernst worrying about his funding sources. On April 12, 1949, Ernst promoted Kinsey's work by explaining to Gregg how it might change the law, emphasizing that Kinsey's work had already started to show up in legal decisions, writing, "Within a decade you will have been the cause for the making of new judicial history." Ernst could point to the fact that Judge Bok drew on the Kinsey Report, as did Jerome Frank. Ernst's firm sent Kinsey copies of both Bok's and Frank's decisions. See Ernst to Gregg, April 4, 1949; and Ernst to Gregg, April 12, 1949, both in Kinsey Institute Archives, Morris Ernst Folder.

30. Morris Ernst and David Loth, *American Sexual Behavior and the Kinsey Report* (New York: Greystone Press, 1948).

31. Undated memorandum, "Kinsey," ca. February or March 1948, p. 3, HRC, MLE Papers, Box 482, Folder 482.2.

32. Ernst and Loth, "Outline," 1.

33. *Roth v. Goldman*, 172 F.2d 788 (1949), U.S. Court of Appeals, Second Circuit, February 8, 1949.

34. *Commonwealth v. Gordon et al.*, Pennsylvania, Commonwealth Court of Quarter Sessions of the Peace, District and County Reports (March 18, 1949), 101–56.

35. *Commonwealth v. Gordon et al.*, 101 (emphasis in original).

36. Handwritten letter from Bok to Ernst, December 23, 1948, HRC, MLE Papers, Box 56, Folder 3 (emphasis in original). In a letter a few days earlier, Bok wrote, "I am greatly obliged for the briefs you sent for they will be most useful. I have nine books to read with care and that takes time. Writing a full and closely reasoned opinion will also take time. . . . I may chat with you further about the opinion when I get at it. I am particularly interested in knowing just where the line is to be drawn and to draw it with clarity. The constitutional points interest me, too" (Bok to Ernst, December 20, 1948, Indiana University, Lily Library, Morris Ernst Folder). Ernst replied, "I really think that if an opinion is written going back to constitutional principles, the final job of pinpricking out the borderlines of what is dangerous takes on a very different prospective. You reach limits much sooner in statutory than in constitutional terms" (Ernst to Bok, December 22, 1948, Indiana University, Lily Library, Morris Ernst Folder).

37. The case before Judge Bok in *Commonwealth v. Gordon* involved nine literary works. They were not "pornographic materials" written with the sole purpose of "erotic allurement," as Bok would phrase it. He used those words purposefully. Although all nine books were controversial, even slightly notorious, and had been challenged in other quarters too, all of them had serious literary or social commentary purposes. They included James T. Farrell's *Studs Lonigan* trilogy (*Young Lonigan, The Young Manhood of Studs Lonigan, Judgment Day*; Vanguard Press, 1932–1935); William Faulkner's *Sanctuary* (Random House, 1931); and Erskine Caldwell's frequently contested novel, *God's Little Acre* (Random House, 1933). Bok read them all "with thoughtful care," he wrote in his decision, and offered synopses that drew clear lines between these literary works and the pornography he said the obscenity statutes were really aimed at. They were perhaps coarse and vulgar at moments and dealt with tawdry themes and lives, but he reminded the Pennsylvania Supreme Court (his intended audience) that one should not expect modern art to offer uplifting tales or to present the "facile" resolutions insisted on in Hollywood films that "the wages of sin is death, or . . . that the penalty of sinning is suffering" (*Commonwealth v. Gordon et al.*, 110).

38. Ernst to Bok, January 16, 1950, Indiana University, Lily Library, Morris Ernst Folder.

39. Bok to Ernst, January 17, 1950, Indiana University, Lily Library, Morris Ernst Folder.

40. Bok, quoting the decision, in a letter to Ernst, March 30, 1950, Indiana University, Lily Library, Morris Ernst Folder.

41. Bok later wrote Ernst about the Pennsylvania Supreme Court and his decision: "The most I can say for our highest Court is that its order has created a kind of vacuum that has let the law wash a bit farther up the beach. But because it's wholly arguable how far up, the questions stays wide open: at least, a lawyer can put his back up against my decision & argue from there—a bit of a help, I hope" (Bok to Ernst, handwritten letter, April 6, 1950, Indiana University, Lily Library, Morris Ernst Folder).

42. Frank's concurring opinion, *Roth v. Goldman*, 172 F.2d 788 (2d Cir. 1949), at 792. "Interestingly enough," Frank writes, "New Mexico has no obscenity law, and does not seem to feel handicapped by the lack of one. As a footnote to sexual behavior, it would be instructive to discover . . . whether the sexual pattern of the people of New Mexico is substantially different from that of other people who have enjoyed the 'protection' of State censorship of printed materials on grounds of obscenity." He is quoting Ernst and Loth, *American Sexual Behavior*, 129.

43. Frank's concurring opinion, *Roth v. Goldman*, 793. He cites L. M. Alpert's *Harvard Law Review* paper: "Over ten years ago the Bureau of Social Hygiene

of New York City sent questionnaires to ten thousand college and normal school women graduates. Twelve hundred answers were received; and of those seventy-two persons who replied that the source of their sex information came from books, mentioning specific volumes, not one specified a 'dirty' book as the source. . . . The chief source of sex 'education' for the youth of all ages and all religious groups was found to be the youth's contemporaries. These statistical results are not offered as conclusive; but that they do more than cast doubt upon the assertion that 'immoral' books corrupt and deprave must be admitted" (L. M. Alpert, "Judicial Censorship and the Press," *Harvard Law Review* 52 (1938): 40, 72).

44. Frank's concurring opinion, *Roth v. Goldman*, 798.

45. Gebhard described the institute's extensive collection and outlined the extensive, cooperative connections with mental health facilities, prisons, and reform institutions, including the California Institution for Men; the Folsom State Prison Medical Facility, California; San Quentin State Prison; Atascadero State Hospital, California; Metropolitan State Hospital, California; Soledad Prison, California; the Indiana State Farm; Indiana Women's Prison; Westfield State Farm, New York; Ohio Bureau of Juvenile Research; and the Kruse School for Girls, New Jersey. See Gebhard Affidavit, *U.S. v. 31 Photographs*, Kinsey Institute Archives, bound volume "Greenbaum, Wolff & Ernst."

46. Cairns, quoted in his obituary in the *Los Angeles Times*, January 24, 1985, https://www.latimes.com/archives/la-xpm-1985-01-24-mn-11289-story.html (accessed January 3, 2020). Cairns, who took his law degree at the University of Maryland at the age of 20, was no Comstock. Along with his post in the Treasury Department, where his job was to help determine whether materials were artistic or pornographic, he also served at various points as the secretary, treasurer, and general counsel to the National Gallery of Art. He was also a founder of the Center for Hellenistic Studies in Washington, D.C., wrote a book about H. L. Mencken, another highly regarded book titled *The Limits of Art*, and had served as the moderator for a nationally syndicated radio program, "An Invitation to Learning." He died in 1985.

47. Kenneth R. Stevens, *"United States v. 31 Photographs*: Dr. Alfred C. Kinsey and Obscenity Law," *Indiana Magazine of History* 71, no. 4 (December 1975): 300.

48. Stevens, *"United States v. 31 Photographs,"* 300–301; see also Stevens's footnote 7.

49. Stevens, *"United States v. 31 Photographs,"* 301.

50. Stevens, *"United States v. 31 Photographs,"* 302.

51. *United States v. Norman E. Himes*, 97 Fed. (2) 510.

52. Stevens, *"United States v. 31 Photographs,"* 302.

53. Stevens, *"United States v. 31 Photographs,"* 302.

54. Stevens, "*United States v. 31 Photographs*," 302.

55. Stevens, "*United States v. 31 Photographs*," 308.

56. Kinsey was uneasy especially because the materials were worth considerable money to Kinsey and the institute. He complained to Pilpel, "If all of this material is impounded and held up for a couple of years, it will mean considerable . . . interference with the research we are doing" (Stevens, "*United States v. 31 Photographs*," 303).

57. Stevens, "*United States v. 31 Photographs*," 304, 305.

58. Seizures by the U.S. Customs Service at the Port of New York, Collection District No. 10, occurred on March 16, April 19, May 1, May 23, August 2, December 5, and December 8, 1951.

59. According to Stevens, Kinsey "believed firmly in the right of scientific inquiry, and his difficulties with the Customs Bureau simply increased his determination to uphold that right" (Stevens, "*United States v. 31 Photographs*," 309).

60. Pilpel to MacNeill, May 14, 1953, Kinsey Institute Archives, Pilpel Folder 1.

61. Pilpel to MacNeill, May 14, 1953.

62. Pilpel to Kinsey, September 30, 1953, Kinsey Institute Archives, Pilpel Folder 1.

63. Stevens, "*United States v. 31 Photographs*," 309.

64. Treasury to Greenbaum, Wolff & Ernst, February 13, 1956, *U.S. v. 31 Photographs*, Kinsey Institute Archives, bound volume "Greenbaum Wolff & Ernst." Stevens reports that Secretary of Treasury George M. Humphrey ruled against the institute on February 13, 1956; Greenbaum, Wolff & Ernst records indicate that it was Acting Secretary Kimball who wrote the official order to the Justice Department to initiate forfeiture proceedings against the detained materials.

65. Gebhard Affidavit, *U.S. v. 31 Photographs*, pp. 12–14, Kinsey Institute Archives, bound volume "Greenbaum Wolff & Ernst."

66. Wells Affidavit, *U.S. v. 31 Photographs*, Kinsey Institute Archives, bound volume "Greenbaum Wolff & Ernst."

67. The defense team took affidavits from and built their formal legal memorandum around the arguments presented by Paul A. Gebhard (who replaced Kinsey as the institute's director); Wardell B. Pomeroy (one of the main members of Kinsey's longtime research team); Indiana University president Herman B. Wells; and a group of physicians and penologists, including Dr. Walter C. Alverez, Dr. Frank A. Beach, James V. Bennett (director of the U.S. Bureau of Prisons), Dr. Karl M. Bowman, Dr. George W. Corner, Dr. Manfred S. Guttmacher, Reverend Arthur L. Swift Jr., and the institute's secretary and gatekeeper, Eleanor Johnson. (Pilpel and Gebhard also had their affidavits taken.)

68. Gebhard Affidavit, 10. Ernst always liked the irony that the Vatican had the world's largest collection of banned materials.

69. Gebhard Affidavit, 10, 4.

70. Gebhard Affidavit, 10.

71. Gebhard Affidavit, 12–14.

72. Gebhard Affidavit, 10.

73. Gebhard Affidavit, 10. Other affidavits presented these core arguments. Dr. Walter Alvarez, a specialist in endocrinology, testified about the complexity of issues around his study of "sex variants" resulting from hormonal, psychological, and behavioral factors. James V. Bennett, director of the U.S. Bureau of Prisons for twenty years, needed research into the "sexual adjustment" of prison inmates. Dr. Manfred S. Guttmacher, a specialist in psychiatry and the law, found the work highly useful to the field of psychiatry, particularly in the treatment of sex offenders. Not all of the experts studied sexual pathologies or criminal behavior. Arthur L. Swift, an ordained Congregational minister, a faculty member at the Union Theological Seminary, and the editor of *Religion Today*, also testified to the institute's scientific thoroughness and objectivity.

74. In the *Levine* case, which the Ernst firm had joined with an amicus brief, the federal court in Washington, D.C., had ruled that "the standard of obscenity had to weigh the likelihood of material's appeal to the 'salacity of the reader.'" Judge Frank would also invoke the *Levine* case in his concurring opinion in *United States v. Roth* (1956), explaining that, as in the *Levine* case, Roth had targeted adults as his consumers and that the Second Circuit in the case *United States v. Levine* (83 F.2d 156) had long ago made it clear that the "correct test is the effect on the sexual thoughts and desires, not of the 'young' or 'immature,' but of average, normal, adult persons" (Frank, *United States v. Roth*, 11).

75. Stevens, "*United States v. 31 Photographs*," 314, 315.

76. Stevens, "*United States v. 31 Photographs*," 314, 315.

77. Stevens, "*United States v. 31 Photographs*," 315.

78. When in 1956 the Supreme Court finally agreed to hear a challenge to the unconstitutionality of the federal obscenity law (in the landmark case *Roth/Alberts v. United States*, discussed later in the chapter), the Ernst firm had turned down the request to take on Sam Roth as their client. When Roth's wife approached Ernst and Pilpel about defending her husband following his arrest in 1952, Ernst wanted nothing to do with Roth, a booklegger, literary pirate, and smut monger whose notoriety Ernst wanted to avoid. He even suggested to Pilpel that they make their defense too expensive for Roth and his wife to countenance. However, Pilpel wanted in on the case, knowing that their obscenity law project would finally arrive in the Supreme Court. When the Court agreed to hear Roth's case on appeal, the Greenbaum, Wolff & Ernst firm submitted an amicus brief, written primarily by Pilpel and Nancy Weschler, although Ernst's name appears

first on the brief. So Pilpel knew the case inside and out and well understood the implications of the Court's ruling for the Kinsey case. There is correspondence between Ernst and Frank about the 1956 *Roth* case in HRC, MLE Papers, Box 4, Folders 4.5–4.7. Folder 4.7 includes extensive correspondence with Frank and others about the Ernst firm's amicus brief in Roth's appeal to the Supreme Court. For a brief biographical treatment of Samuel Roth, see Jay Gertzman, *Bookleggers and Smuthounds: The Trade in Erotica, 1920–1940* (Philadelphia: University of Pennsylvania Press, 1999), 219–82.

79. Judge Clark said that Roth, the defendant, was an "old hand at publishing and surreptitiously mailing to those induced to order them such lurid pictures and material as he can find profitable" (*United States v. Roth*, 7).

80. Whitney Strub treats these issues in all their subtle complexities in his brilliant book *Obscenity Rules* and in particular offers a close reading of Jerome Frank's concurring opinion. Marjorie Heins gives it close attention as well, as does Paul Boyer. They all show, for instance, how several law review pieces by Lockhart and McLure, a review of obscenity law by the American Law Institute, and Marie Jahoda's bibliographic essay on the social scientific literature on the effects of reading provided Frank with an even stronger body of arguments and evidence than he had in his 1949 opinion. Frank's 1956 opinion makes the same basic argument but with more case law and research to bolster his critique. There is extensive correspondence between Ernst and Frank about the 1956 *Roth* case in HRC, MLE Papers, Box 4, Folders 4.5–4.7, and they reveal that Frank is somewhat dismissive of Ernst's approach to the issues on this point, as Ernst is interested in state versus federal jurisdiction questions and Frank takes the First Amendment issue head on.

81. *United States v. Roth*, 237 F.2d 796, argued June 6, 1956, decided September 18, 1956. Writ of Certiorari granted January 14, 1957. See 77 Sup. Ct. 361.

82. Frank, *United States v. Roth*, 14.

83. Frank, *United States v. Roth*, 15.

84. See *Alberts v. California*, 138 Cal. App. 2nd Supp. 909, 292 P.2d 90. Both Roth's and Alberts's convictions were upheld, as the courts affirmed that obscenity was not protected by the First Amendment. But the courts defined the obscenity test more strictly, so that only materials that "taken as a whole appealed to prurient interest" of the "average person, applying contemporary community standards" could be found obscene. Materials that had other redeeming values—scientific, literary, or historical—could be protected.

85. *Roth v. United States*, 354 U.S. 476 (decided June 24, 1957).

86. Frank, in his concurring lower court opinion, had asserted that the "test is not whether it would arouse sexual desires or sexually impure thoughts in those

comprising a particular segment of the community, the young, the immature or the highly prudish." Rather, he said, "you must determine its impact upon the average person in the community" (*United States v. Roth*, 805n1).

87. The *Roth/Alberts* decision's still vague phrases—"utterly without redeeming social interests," "dominant effect," "community standards," "prurient interests"—continued to befuddle appellants, prosecutors, other judges, and the public for decades. Its main effect was that appellants and their lawyers would successfully draw on these exceptions to find far greater protection for literary works with sexual themes, opening the door for the likes of *Lady Chatterley's Lover*, *Tropic of Cancer*, *Fanny Hill*, and eventually more hard-core pornographic materials. Marjorie Heins argues that American courts for the next sixteen years struggled to apply Brennan's "utterly without redeeming social importance" formula to sexual art and literature.

88. In the *Butler v. Michigan* decision in the same 1957 term, the U.S. Supreme Court essentially eliminated the "presumed harm to minors" test as grounds for keeping works from adults. The Court's decision sought to find a balance between competing needs and suggested a "variable obscenity" test as a compromise, offering greater leeway for adults in soliciting materials of interest to them, but it did not retreat from the goal of protecting youth from obscene materials. That is, it ruled that a general obscenity test could no longer rest entirely on keeping materials away from everyone because of a presumed harm to minors. By recognizing that adults had a right to sexually themed materials, the Court essentially funneled the question into a matter of marketing: To whom were the materials being marketed?

89. Claimant's Brief, *United States v. 31 Photographs*, 45.

90. Claimant's Brief, 45.

91. Claimant's Brief, 43.

92. *Sweezy v. New Hampshire* (No. 175, June 17, 1957). Pilpel wrote, "The instant case is governed by the *Butler* and *Sweezy* cases, both decided by the United States Supreme Court at this term" (Claimant's Brief, 6). As a result of those decisions, Section 305 of the Customs Act did not apply to these materials. See *Roth* decision, June 14, 1957; and *Alberts* decided on the same date; *Sweezy v. New Hampshire* was decided on June 17, 1957.

93. To this point, they cited Judge Frank: "One distinguished judge of this Circuit, Judge Jerome Frank . . . thought that intelligent enforcement of the obscenity laws required a 'Kinsey Report' on the actual effects of obscenity on sexual conduct." Such work, they added, would be "hardly feasible if scientists cannot have access to obscene materials which are said to be the source of the problem" (Claimant's Brief, 28). Pilpel noted as well that the issue of the relationship of obscenity to masturbation (the "effects of erotica") was not yet fully understood and that the findings in *Sexual Behavior in the Human Female* showed "limited

use of erotica as stimuli to masturbation" (and they cited Kinsey, *Sexual Behavior in the Human Female*, 653, 662, 670–71, and noted that the same issues about use of erotica to stimulate masturbation were treated in Kinsey, *Sexual Behavior in the Human Male*, 363, 510).

94. Claimant's Brief, 30.

95. Claimant's Brief, 58.

96. *United States v. 31 Photographs*, 350. Judge Palmieri does not clarify why he did not consider the academic freedom arguments germane; it may be that he did not find federal case law fully enough developed on academic freedom issues.

97. *United States v. 31 Photographs*, 354.

98. *United States v. 31 Photographs*, 354. In *Commonwealth v. Landis*, the court had held that "while scientific and medical publications 'in proper hands for useful purposes' may contain illustrations exhibiting the human form, the court held that such publications would be obscene libels 'if wantonly exposed in the open markets, with a wanton and wicked desire to create a demand for them'" (*Commonwealth v. Landis*, Q.S. 1870, 8 Phila., Pa., 453). Palmieri cited a series of cases to this point that the determination of obscenity depended on the circumstance of use: *United States v. Chesman*, C.C.E.D. Mo. 1881, 19 F. 497; *United States v. Clarke*, D.C.E.D. Mo. 1889, 38 F. 500; and *United States v. Smith*, D.C.E.D. Wis. 1891, 45 F. 476.

99. *United States v. 31 Photographs*, 358.

100. *United States v. 31 Photographs*, 358

101. *United States v. 31 Photographs*, 360.

102. *United States v. 31 Photographs*, 360.

103. Pilpel to Gebhard and Pomeroy, November 21, 1958, Kinsey Institute Archives, Pilpel Folder 3.

104. Summary, *United States v. 31 Photographs*, 5, Kinsey Institute Archives, bound volume "Greenbaum Wolff & Ernst."

105. Summary, *United States v. 31 Photographs*, 5.

106. Strub, *Obscenity Rules*, 88.

Conclusion

1. In *Roth v. United States*, 354 U.S. 476 (1957), Justice Brennan wrote:

The dispositive question is whether obscenity is utterance within the area of protected speech and press. Although this is the first time the question has been squarely presented to this Court, either under the First Amendment or under the Fourteenth Amendment, expressions found in numerous opinions indicate that this Court has always assumed that obscenity is not protected by the freedoms of speech and press. . . . In light of this history, it is apparent that the unconditional phrasing of the First Amendment was not intended to protect every utterance. . . .

At the time of the adoption of the First Amendment, obscenity law was not as fully developed as libel law, but there is sufficiently contemporaneous evidence to show that obscenity, too, was outside the protection intended for speech and press. . . . But implicit in the history of the First Amendment is the rejection of obscenity as utterly without redeeming social importance. This rejection for that reason is mirrored in the universal judgment that obscenity should be restrained, reflected in the international agreement of over 50 nations, in the obscenity laws of all of the 48 States, and in the 20 obscenity laws enacted by the Congress from 1842 to 1956. This is the same judgment expressed by this Court in *Chaplinsky v. New Hampshire*, 315 U.S. 568, 571–572. . . . There are certain well-defined and narrowly limited classes of speech, the prevention and punishment of which have never been thought to raise any Constitutional problem. *These include the lewd and obscene. . . . It has been well observed that such utterances are no essential part of any exposition of ideas, and are of such slight social value as a step to truth that any benefit that may be derived from them is clearly outweighed by the social interest in order and morality. . . .* We hold that obscenity is not within the area of constitutionally protected speech or press. (481, 483–85; emphasis added)

2. The explosion of pornography since the *Roth* case and the complicated terrain of obscenity law jurisprudence since the *Roth* case is a rich, nuanced history that has been well studied by a host of top scholars. I humbly defer to them. See, for example, Whitney Strub, *Perversion for Profit: The Politics of Pornography and the Rise of the New Right* (New York: Columbia University Press, 2010); Whitney Strub, *Obscenity Rules: Roth v. United States and the Long Struggle over Sexual Expression* (Lawrence: University of Kansas Press, 2013); Marjorie Heins, *Not in Front of the Children: "Indecency," Censorship, and the Innocence of Youth* (New York: Hill & Wang, 2001); Carolyn Bronstein, *Battling Pornography: The American Feminist Anti-Pornography Movement, 1976–1986* (New York: Cambridge University Press, 2011); Geoffrey R. Stone, *Sex and the Constitution: Sex, Religion, and Law from America's Origins to the Twenty-First Century* (New York: Liveright, 2017); Paul S. Boyer, *Purity in Print: Book Censorship in America from the Gilded Age to the Computer Age*, 2nd ed. (Madison: University of Wisconsin Press, 2002); Frederick F. Schauer, *The Law of Obscenity* (Washington, DC: Bureau of National Affairs, 1976); Edward de Grazia, *Girls Lean Back Everywhere: The Law of Obscenity and the Assault on Genius* (New York: Random House, 1992); and Richard F. Hixson, *Pornography and the Justices: The Supreme Court and the Intractable Obscenity Problem* (Carbondale: Southern Illinois University Press, 1996).

Epilogue

1. For a rich treatment of how these issues fractured the ACLU and threatened its political respectability, see Judy Kutulas, *The American Civil Liberties Union and the Making of Modern Liberalism, 1930–1960* (Chapel Hill: University of North Carolina Press, 2014). For the larger cultural and political battles on the left over communism, see Judy Kutulas, *The Long War: The Intellectual People's Front and Anti-Stalinism, 1930–1940* (Durham, NC: Duke University Press, 1994). Ellen Schrecker takes up these issues from a different angle, looking at how right-wing mobilization against American communists gained force in 1930s; see Ellen Schrecker, *Many Are the Crimes: McCarthyism in America* (Boston: Little, Brown, 1998).

2. Ernst was a regular guest on New York City radio programs such as "Town Hall of the Air" and in public forums and debates, and he advanced the ACLU's positions forcefully in those settings.

3. At least as early as October 1938, the National Lawyers Guild (NLG) and the ACLU were working together to formulate a response to Dies's HUAC and its accusations about their disloyalty. Ernst and Osmond Fraenkel (and others), who were executive members of both the NLG and the ACLU, attempted to develop a response to the Dies committee to defend both organizations. But Popular Front divisions in both organizations came to the fore in this moment. See, for instance, Ernst to Fisher, October 7, 1938, Harry Ransom Humanities Research Center (HRC), Morris L. Ernst (MLE) Papers, Box 404, Folder 404.5; and Ernst to Riemer, January 3, 1939, HRC, MLE Papers, Box 750, Folder 750.2. The ACLU worked up a detailed study of all six volumes of the Dies committee's hearing records and produced numerous documents in response. See Baldwin affidavit, December 31, 1938; and the materials compiled by ACLU executives Haynes, Huebsch, and Baldwin, along with Ernst memo, "re: Dies Report," January 17, 1939, all in HRC, MLE Papers, Box 750, Folder 750.2. See also the "Recommendations Suggested for the National Lawyers Guild (forming the conclusions of the Report on the Dies Committee)," HRC, MLE Papers, Box 348, Folder 348.5.

4. Ernst's involvement with the Garland Fund was extensive over many years. See Ernst's Garland Fund correspondence and records, in HRC, MLE Papers, Boxes 370, 371, 377, and 378. The $39,250 balance that was in the Garland Fund in 1928 would be worth $650,000 in 2020.

5. Several documents in Ernst's papers reveal the deepening distrust in the NLG. See "Recommendations Suggested for the National Lawyers Guild" and the companion documents "Mr. Ernst's Memo," the "Draft of Report on Dies Committee," and "Comments on Frankel's Analysis" (these documents were produced in January and February 1939), all in HRC, MLE Papers, Box 348, Folder 348.5.

6. This same loyalty test was soon used by the ACLU.

7. Judy Kutulas studies these conflicts in detail in both *The American Civil Liberties Union and the Making of Modern Liberalism, 1930–1960* (Chapel Hill: University of North Carolina Press, 2014) and *The Long War*. Ernst's papers reveal how the internal suspicions and conflicts hardened as ACLU leadership attempted to develop a response to the Dies committee's attack on the ACLU as a communist front organization. The ACLU's Roger Baldwin established a subcommittee of the ACLU to look into the Dies committee, with Raymond Wise as chair and Morris Ernst, Florina Lasker, Roger W. Riis, Arthur Garfield Hays, Abraham Isserman, and Osmond K. Fraenkel as members. This group was divided over whether the ACLU should try to distance itself from the Communist Party and other Popular Front organizations and reveals the deepening divisions between the anticommunist liberals (Wise, Riis, Lasker, and Ernst) and the progressives, especially Fraenkel and Isserman, particularly over the liberal members' increasingly strident anticommunism. See Roger William Riis to R. L. Wise, November 30, 1939, HRC, MLE Papers, Box 403, Folder 403.3.

The "Report of the Special Committee of the Board of Directors of the ACLU on the Special Committee of the House of Representatives on Un-American Activities," filed and submitted on January 8, 1940, shows how these rifts were made more immediate by the Nazi-Soviet Pact in August 1939. These distempers did not abate until U.S. entrance into the war in December 1941, and Ernst never lost those suspicions. See, for instance, Ernst to Baldwin, January 8, 1941; and Ernst's "Memorandum re Dies Report," both in HRC, MLE Papers, Box 403, Folder 403.3.

Somewhat notoriously, amid these contretemps, Ernst, Baldwin, and Arthur Garfield Hays attempted to develop a more cooperative relationship with Dies, throwing a cocktail party for him and presumably offering him a deal: If he would back off his attacks on the ACLU, the ACLU would suspend communists from its executive board. (For a sense of Ernst's tone trying to convince Dies to be more attentive to due process matters, see Ernst to Dies, November 17, 1939; and Ernst to Dies, December 30, 1939, both in HRC, MLE Papers, Box 750, Folder 750.2.) One result was that Dies did "retract" his accusations about the ACLU, and the ACLU's Executive Board voted to purge members of the Communist Party from serving on it. Ernst was active in these efforts, explaining to Roger Baldwin the necessity of forcing communists out of the ACLU's leadership. (See Ernst to Baldwin, February 1, 1940, Seeley Mudd Archives, ACLU Papers, Box 75, Folder 15; Ernst included a draft of expulsion, "Resolution," under the same cover of his February 1, 1940, letter to Baldwin.) For more on the expulsion of Elizabeth Gurley Flynn, see Seeley Mudd Library, Princeton University, American Civil Liberties Union

Records, Boxes 74 and 75, Elizabeth Gurley Flynn Ouster, 1940–1975. Kutulas examines this in close detail in *American Civil Liberties Union*.

It is also clear that during this period Ernst began corresponding directly with Martin Dies's investigators, particularly Ben Mandel, although he used the intelligence he gleaned from those letters to warn his allies in the Justice Department (DoJ) about Dies's plans for attacks on the DoJ. See, for instance, Ben Mandel to Ernst, November 28, 1940, HRC, MLE Papers, Box 750, Folder 750.2, which Ernst followed up by warning Attorney General Robert Jackson that Dies was planning unwarranted attacks on the DoJ and its personnel. See letters from Ernst to Attorney General Robert Jackson on December 3, 1940, December 6, 1940, and December 7, 1940, all in HRC, MLE Papers, Box 750, Folder 750.2. Although he aligned himself with Dies's and Mandel's anticommunist aims, Ernst ultimately kept his distance from Dies and Mandel because of their animosity toward Franklin Roosevelt, to whom Ernst was deeply loyal, and their absence of due process. When Mandel sent Ernst Congressman Dies's plans for anticommunist legislation, Ernst directly rebuked him. See Mandel to Ernst, December 5, 1940; and Ernst to Mandel, December 6, 1940, both in HRC, MLE Papers, Box 750, Folder 750.2. Ellen Schrecker exposes and castigates Ernst's exchanges and collaboration with Dies's investigators and other "counter-subversives"; see Schrecker, *Many Are the Crimes*. She is rightly critical of Ernst and how he undercut his ACLU colleagues. Ernst found Dies and his investigators unreliable, antidemocratic, and crude in their methods, but this did not keep him from moving into the sphere of the professional anticommunists, where he developed a strong allegiance to the more respectable, polished, and professional J. Edgar Hoover, whose "due process" methods he admired.

8. Ernst to Fisher, October 7, 1938, HRC, MLE Papers, Box 404, Folder 404.5.

9. Ernst to Baldwin, February 1, 1940, Seeley Mudd Archives, ACLU Papers, Box 75, Folder 15. For more on the Flynn expulsion, see Seeley Mudd Archives, ACLU Papers, Boxes 74 and 75.

10. The two most complete folders of Ernst-Hoover correspondence are in HRC, MLE Papers, Box 99, Folders 1 and 2: "J. Edgar Hoover & MLE 1/2/47– 6/28/50, misc. corresp., RE: wiretapping, RE: loyalty program, etc." Many other boxes hold some correspondence. In general, I am distilling this correspondence and the materials found in Ernst's FBI files, a nearly 1,000-page file available through the Freedom of Information Act, Privacy Acts Section, FBI File number 94-4-5366. Ernst's published writings from the 1940s to the 1960s and a long private correspondence between him and Hoover reveal that Ernst became a dependable protector of Hoover and the FBI's reputation and a surreptitious informant as well. For an excellent study of the Ernst FBI files as a preliminary investigation of the

Ernst-Hoover relationship, see Harrison Salisbury, "The Strange Correspondence of Morris Ernst and John Edgar Hoover, 1939–1964," *The Nation* (December 1, 1984), 575–89. See also Brett Gary, "'Guessing Oneself Into Jail': Morris Ernst and the Assault on American Obscenity Laws in the 1930s," in *Obscenity and the Limits of Liberalism*, ed. Loren Glass and Charles Francis Williams (Columbus: Ohio State University Press, 2011), 50–68; and Brett Gary, "Morris Ernst's Troubled Legacy," *Reconstruction* 8, no. 1 (2008), http://reconstruction.eserver.org/084/contents084.shtml#8.1 (accessed September 30, 2013).

11. Dalton Trumbo, *The Time of the Toad: A Study of Inquisition in America by One of the Hollywood Ten* (Hollywood, CA: The Hollywood Ten, 1949). For a rich treatment of the Popular Front and anticommunism in the film industry, see Larry Ceplair and Steven England, *The Inquisition in Hollywood: Politics in the Film Community, 1930–1960* (New York: Anchor Press/Doubleday, 1980).

12. For examples of how Ernst defended Hoover, see his correspondence with Frida Kirchwey, for example, Ernst to Frida Kirchwey, August 26, 1943, HRC, MLE Papers, Box 134, "Correspondence 1943," vol. 29, Folder 2, in response to a two-part article published in *The Nation* in 1943: XXX [anonymous], "Washington Gestapo," *The Nation* (July 17, 1943), 64–66; and part II, *The Nation* (July 24, 1943), 92–95. See also Freda Kirchwey, "End the Inquisition," *The Nation* (July 31, 1943), 116–17; and I. F. Stone, "XXX and the FBI," *The Nation* (September 25, 1943), 342–43.

13. Hoover to Ernst, August 8, 1943, HRC, MLE Papers, Box 134, "Correspondence 1943," vol. 29, Folder 2.

14. Joel Silverman thoughtfully and provocatively treats this rightward turn and its effects on Ernst's colleagues and his reputation in Joel Matthew Silverman, "Pursuing Celebrity, Ensuing Masculinity: Morris Ernst, Obscenity, and the Search for Recognition," PhD diss., University of Texas at Austin, 2006, 209–46.

15. Salisbury, "Strange Correspondence." Salisbury does a good job teasing out these implications from the Ernst-Hoover correspondence. Unfortunately, the "Julius Rosenberg" file was missing from Ernst's papers at the University of Texas, making it difficult to find more evidence about the nature of this relationship. But based on the FBI files, it would appear to be a stunning ethical lapse, at the least.

INDEX

Page numbers in *italics* indicate illustrations. Works with known authors will be found under the author's name.

Customs suit over, 82–84; defense memorandum, 90–93; *Dennett* case and, 65–67, 80–82, 84–87, 89, 90, 92–98, 108, 109; expert testimony and testimonials in, 88–90, 91, 94, 348n67; Joyce's *Ulysses* and, 180, 190, 196, 201, 208; judicial ruling on, 96–98; legacy of, 107–10; on masturbation, 90; media coverage, lack of, 351n118; Philadelphia court declaration of nonobscenity of Stopes' works, 86–88, 92, 93, 94, 97; piracy problems in U.S. market, 66–67, 80–81, 346–47n59, 346n49; Post Office ban on mailing of, 81, 83, 84; prosecution memorandum, 93–95; publication in America after nonobscenity verdict, 97–98, 107; sex education and, 73–75, 91, 92, 94; on sexual pleasure, 69, 70, 71–76, 94; sympathetic judge, prosecution and defense seeking, 95–96; "Tabulation of Symptoms of Sexual Excitement in Solitude," 70; tariff laws and, 66, 67, 82, 84, 85–87, 93, 96; U.S. marriage manual market and, 79–80; Goodwin Watson on, 331–32n15

Stopes, Marie, other works: *Enduring Passion*, 82, 85, 98, 344n37, 345n41, 352–53n123; *The First Five Thousand*, 86, 94, 98; *A Letter to Working Mothers . . .*, 101; *The Practice of Contraception*, 352–53n123; *Radiant Motherhood*, 101; *Wise Parenthood*, 78, 86, 94, 100–101

Stowe, Harriet Beecher, *Uncle Tom's Cabin*, 143, 145

Strachey, Lytton, 119, 143, 355n24

Straton, John Roach, 45, 333n51, 334n53

Strong, William, 11

Strub, Whitney, 285, 319–20n, 329n59, 389–90nn3–4, 399n80, 401n106, 402n2

Strubinger, David, 270

Sullivan, Mary, 217, 232

Sullivan, T. DeLeon, 38

Sulzberger, Arthur Hays, 136

Sumner, John: Asch's *Pay Day*, efforts against, 155–64; burning books, *163*, 288; as Comstock's successor at Vice Society, 16, 17; on *Dennett* case, 45; details, attention to, 364–65n8; Ernst's animus against, 16, 17–18, 144, 151, 164, 176–79, 367n40; Hall's *Well of Loneliness* and, 122–25, 127, 131, 132, 135–38, 140, 146–51, 154, 176; Joyce's *Ulysses* and, 181, 184, 185, 188–89, 195; literary censorship efforts of, 152–54; McAdoo and, 149–51, 356n48; publishers, tactics against, 169; on Schnitzler as author, 177; Schnitzler's *Casanova's Homecoming*, efforts against, 154–55, 169–79; Schnitzler's *Hands Around*, efforts against, 164–65, 168; Stopes' *Married Love* and, 81, 84, 348n67

Sunday Express, 117–18

Supreme Court, U.S.: "bad tendency" of language assumptions, 324n27, 325n31; Comstock laws upheld by, 9, 13, 178; on constitutionality of obscenity statutes, 278, 279–82, 291, 398–99n78; on definition of obscene materials, 58, 281; Joyce's *Ulysses* and, 186, 187; on sex speech versus religious or political speech, 14–15, 168; stricter tests for obscenity